Law and Legal Theory

Studies in Moral Philosophy

VOLUME 6

The titles published in this series are listed at brill.com/simp

Law and Legal Theory

Edited by

Thom Brooks

BRILL

LEIDEN · BOSTON
2014

Many of the articles collected in this volume were previously published in Brill's *Journal of Moral Philosophy*.

Library of Congress Cataloging-in-Publication Data

Law and legal theory / edited by Thom Brooks.
pages cm. -- (Studies in moral philosophy)
Includes bibliographical references and index.
ISBN 978-90-04-24774-1 (hardback : alk. paper) -- ISBN 978-90-04-26293-5 (e-book) 1. Law--Philosophy. 2. Law--Moral and ethical aspects. I. Brooks, Thom, editor of compilation.

K231.L39 2014
340'.1--dc23

2013038358

This publication has been typeset in the multilingual "Brill" typeface. With over 5,100 characters covering Latin, IPA, Greek, and Cyrillic, this typeface is especially suitable for use in the humanities. For more information, please see www.brill.com/brill-typeface.

ISSN 2211-2014
ISBN 978-90-04-24774-1 (hardback)
ISBN 978-90-04-26293-5 (e-book)

This book is printed on acid-free paper.

CONTENTS

PART FOUR

LEGAL RIGHTS

PART FIVE

PUNISHMENT

INTRODUCTION

Thom Brooks

Philosophical questions rarely lack clear relevance to practices. Similarly, any examination into the problems and prospects of current practices will often, if not always, include some consideration of significant philosophical issues. This is no different with the area of law and legal theory. What is the relation between law and democracy and how might it be improved? What values should inform the body of laws that govern us all? How should we determine crimes from non-crimes? What justifies state punishment, if anything? This book brings together some of the most important essays in this area written by leading scholars and offering significant contributions to how we understand law and legal theory. Most of the essays originally appeared in the *Journal of Moral Philosophy*, an internationally recognized leading philosophy journal. However, there is also some new content with a never before published chapter and several previously published chapters have been revised subsequently for this new book. This introduction will provide a general survey of the essays included and provide some background.

Part One: Law and Democracy

The first part considers central issues concerning the relation of law and democracy. Samantha Besson (2005) focuses on an important debate between Jeremy Waldron and Joseph Raz concerning legal authority. Waldron claims we should not think about authority as between an official and a subject, but instead take a broader view incorporating officialdom in general and those over whom it ultimately rules. There are a package of relations that we must unpack and legal authority in modern democracies is perhaps more multi-layered and complex than often thought. This critique raises difficulties for Raz's account of authority relating to the public and collective character of democracy and collective law-making procedures. Interestingly, Raz provides a new restatement brilliantly captured by Besson who shows how this account might face Waldron's challenge.

In the second essay, Brian Butler (2004) examines another area of importance concerning law and democracy: free speech and its regulation. What kinds of speech should be protected? Butler argues for a Rorty-inspired approach which rejects the concept of 'truth' and the uncritical allowance of viewpoint-based discrimination into speech protection. The problem with truth/false distinctions in this area, for Butler, is that it is too wide and can be improved through Rorty-inspired antirealism with implications for US Supreme Court jurisprudence.

Andrew March (2011) discusses whether there is any right to polygamy.[1] He considers four different arguments in favour of banning polygamy and argues each suffers from serious problems in a wide-ranging critique. March argues that the liberal state should leave the 'marriage business' altogether and no longer regulate in this area.

Part Two: Legal Norms

There are three chapters that cover a wide-range of issues concerning legal norms. The first is a newly revised contribution that expands and updates Sean Coyle's (2009) article. Coyle discusses Ronald Dworkin's *Justice in Robes* and Nigel Simmonds's *Law as a Moral Idea* as offering two different challenges to legal positivism. For Coyle, Dworkin operates within background assumptions shared with opponents while Simmonds critiques these same assumptions. Coyle's comparative analysis reveals not only new insights into the legal philosophies of two major figures, but new implications for jurisprudence more generally as well.

The next two chapters focus on recent work by Joseph Raz, one of the preeminent philosophers of law working today. Leonard Kahn (2012) considers Joseph Raz's *Between Authority and Interpretation* with a focus on three topics: theories of law, separability and necessity, and law's normativity. Kahn offers a sympathetic, but critical, examination of these issues with some doubts about Raz's legal theory concerning the relationship between law and morality. Hanoch Sheinman (2006) examines *The Practice of Value* by Joseph Raz in an illuminating essay. Sheinman critically engages with Raz's formulation of the social dependence thesis – whereby values depend on social practices subject to specific conditions – raising new problems for it that may be compounded by challenges arising from relativism for his view. Together, Kahn and

[1] See Brooks (2009) on polygamy more generally.

Sheinman sharpen and deepen our understanding of Raz's highly influential contributions.

Part Three: Legal Reasons

Reasons are an integral part of law in providing a crucial foundation for the justification of law and legal decision-making. María Cristina Redondo (2005) considers two different perspectives on legal reasons: universalism and particularlism. Each perspective offers mutually exclusive theories linked to incompatible conceptions of norms, such as the dichotomy between norms understood as strict universal conditions versus norms as defeasible conditionals. Redondo argues that this difference between the universal and particular can be approached alternatively through the perspective of rules and principles. Whether we favour a particularist or universalist character of legal reasons may depend on a deeper view about how we conceive law which this essay helps clarify.

Part Four: Legal Rights

Part Four includes three chapters on the subject of legal rights. The first is a never before published by Thom Brooks. This chapter consider the relation between crimes and wrongs. It is not uncommon for crimes to be understood as some form of immorality, but is this the most compelling way to consider the kinds of wrongs that crimes are? Brooks argues against such natural law-inspired mistaken perspectives to show that they fail to offer an adequate view about law and criminalization.

In the second chapter, Rowan Cruft (2010) argues that our most fundamental rights are often held to have great instrumental value in securing the protection of important human needs and interests. Cruft considers this position, but then discusses a non-instrumental value of rights deriving from their constitutive role in a universal form of community. Cruft argues that a 'mixed' theory is possible and compelling: rights have both instrumental and non-instrumental value for us.

This part concludes with a chapter on group rights by Adina Preda (2012). This chapter is a revision of an article originally published in the *Journal of Moral Philosophy*. Most debates about rights concern the justification of rights holding by individuals between so-called interest theories and will theories. Often several groups are excluded from standard discussions about rights, such as the incapacitated and young children. A third group often excluded is 'the group'. Preda offers a novel theory of group rights and their justification that breaks new ground in the debate.

Part Five: Punishment

Part Five concerns the philosophy of punishment.[2] Christopher Bennett (2006) defends the communicative theory of punishment – the idea that punishment not only gives expression of public denunciation to an offender, but also the expression of remorse 'communicated' from the offender to the community – from charges that it may be contrary to contemporary liberalism. Does the denunciation of crime by the state violate liberal freedoms? Bennett offers a powerful argument for why the communicative theory might avoid this problem.

Richard Lippke (2006) argues that theories about punishment are often incomplete. Theories such as retribution or crime reduction tend to focus on the justification of punishment and its distribution, but rarely – if at all – their imposition. Lippke convincingly argues that any theory of punishment must incorporate some view about the justification of imprisonment and its use.

A second essay by Richard Lippke (2010) considers the adage by William Blackstone it is better to let ten guilty persons go free than mistakenly punish one innocent person. This is a famous claim, but one that lacks any substantive critical scrutiny provided here with real insight and depth. Lippke argues that Blackstone offers us not a principle, but a point about the importance of weighing risks and maintaining balance within the criminal justice system.

Matt Matravers (2006) examines the particular communicative theory of punishment defended by Antony Duff. Duff has argued that the state must possess the moral standing to call offenders to account as an important precondition of criminal liability. The state's moral standing may be undermined by permitted and/or lingering social injustices. Relatedly, Duff also claims that an individual's own behaviour may undermine his standing. Matravers raises serious criticisms of this latter argument which reveal new insights into potential problems for communicative theories of punishment.

In the final essay to this collection, Leo Zaibert (2009) considers a paradox at the heart of forgiveness. Some have argued that forgiveness may

---

2 See Brooks (2012a) for a comprehensive overview of debates about punishment.

lack justification because there is no reason to forgive an unrepentant offender and, should the offender repent, there would no longer be anything left to forgive. Zaibert uncovers new distinctions in how we might understand forgiveness which reveal it may not be paradoxical after all.

Conclusion

Together, these essays reveal new insights and lasting contributions to our understanding of law and legal theory across a range of important topics and issues by some of the leading figures working in the field today.

A final comment should be made about how these essays were selected for publication. Most chapters originally appeared in recent issues of the *Journal of Moral Philosophy*. I founded the journal with Fabian Freyenhagen in 2003 and it launched the following year. The *JMP* has been published quarterly since 2009 and we have started publishing six issues per volume from 2013. All submissions were subjected to rigorous anonymous peer review by our international editorial board and referees. We publish a list of our referees in the final issue of each volume. Our standards are high and acceptance is about 5%. We receive submissions from all over the world with the great majority coming from either the United States or Great Britain. Furthermore, we have endeavoured to ensure high quality review standards with swift turnarounds and we are normally able to review about 90% of all submissions in three months and about 85% in two months or less.

The previously published essays in this volume have satisfied these high standards by appearing in recent issues of the *Journal of Moral Philosophy* ensuring their quality and timeliness. Each was selected for this book because of its genuine contribution to the topic of law and legal theory. Rather than offer a single narrative, the essays instead may be read in any order and present a number of important perspectives and insights on the topic that should help provide further clarifying illumination on central debates and ideas in this field. Readers interested in learning more about what other essays have been published in the *JMP* should consult this book's bibliography towards the end where the full publication details of all articles is listed. Anyone interested in submitting new work for future issues should submit through our online submission system found on our website.[3]

[3] The *Journal of Moral Philosophy* website may be found here: http://www.brill.com/jmp.

This book is part of our new *Studies in Moral Philosophy* book series published by Brill, the publishers of the *JMP*. The book series aspires to fulfil the same high standards and quality of its sister journal. We aim to publish leading work in the areas of moral, political, and legal philosophy. This book is one of a few that bring together *JMP* essays. Others include volumes on *Ethics and Moral Philosophy*, *Global Justice and International Affairs* and *Just War Theory* (Brooks 2011, 2012b, 2013) and other important new work.[4] Prospective authors interested in submitting a proposal for a monograph or edited book for this series should contact me.[5]

I hope that you will enjoy reading the essays in this book as much as I have. Many thanks are due to Suzanne Mekking at Brill for her strong support for this book and the book series. My thanks also to Liesbeth Hugenholz for her assistance, too. I am also most grateful to Fabian Freyenhagen for his assistance over the years, as well as to our advisory committee for this book series. Finally, my most sincere thanks must be reserved for the authors for choosing the *Journal of Moral Philosophy* for their work. The journal's success is primarily not through any particular effort of its editors, but rather a reflection of the high quality of our author's important contributions. We look forward to producing further volumes on other topics in future.

Bibliography

Bennett, Christopher (2006). 'State Denunciation of Crime', *Journal of Moral Philosophy* 3(3): 288–304.

Besson, Samantha (2005). 'Democracy, Law, and Authority', *Journal of Moral Philosophy* 2(1): 89–99.

Brooks, Thom (2009). 'The Problem with Polygamy', *Philosophical Topics* 37(2): 109–22.

Brooks, Thom (ed.) (2011). *Ethics and Moral Philosophy*. Leiden: Brill.

Brooks, Thom (2012a). *Punishment*. London: Routledge.

Brooks, Thom (ed.) (2012b). *Global Justice and International Affairs*. Leiden: Brill.

Brooks, Thom (ed.) (2013). *Just War Theory*. Leiden: Brill.

Butler, Brian E. (2004). 'Rorty, the First Amendment and Antirealism: Is Reliance upon Truth Viewpoint-Based Speech Regulation?' *Journal of Moral Philosophy* 1(1): 69–88.

Coyle, Sean (2009). 'The Ideality of Law', *Journal of Moral Philosophy* 6(4): 521–34.

Cruft, Rowan (2010). 'On the Non-instrumental Value of Basic Rights', *Journal of Moral Philosophy* 7(4): 441–61.

Kahn, Leonard (2012). 'Legal Theory, Law, and Normativity', *Journal of Moral Philosophy* 9(1): 115–26.

[4] Full information about the books published in this series can be found here: http://www.brill.com/simp.

[5] My contact details are available on my personal website: http://thombrooks.info.

Lippke, Richard L. (2006). 'Imprisonable Offences', *Journal of Moral Philosophy* 3(3): 265–87.
Lippke, Richard L. (2010). 'Punishing the Guilty, Not Punishing the Innocent', *Journal of Moral Philosophy* 7(4): 462–88.
March, Andrew F. (2011). 'Is There a Right to Polygamy? Marriage, Equality and Subsidizing Families in Liberal Public Justification', *Journal of Moral Philosophy* 8(2): 246–72.
Matravers, Matt (2006). '"Who's Still Standing?" A Comment on Antony Duff's Preconditions of Criminal Liability', *Journal of Moral Philosophy* 3(3): 320–30.
Preda, Adina (2012). 'Group Rights and Group Agency', *Journal of Moral Philosophy* 9(2): 229–54.
Redondo, Maria Cristina (2005). 'Legal Reasons: Between Universalism and Particularism', *Journal of Moral Philosophy* 2(1): 47–68.
Sheinman, Hanoch (2006). 'Raz on the Social Dependence of Values', *Journal of Moral Philosophy* 3(1): 77–87.
Zaibert, Leo (2009). 'The Paradox of Forgiveness', *Journal of Moral Philosophy* 6(3): 365–93.

PART ONE

LAW AND DEMOCRACY

REVIEW ARTICLE: DEMOCRACY, LAW AND AUTHORITY

Samantha Besson

L.H. Meyer, S.L. Paulson and T.W. Pogge (eds.), *Rights, Culture, and the Law: Themes from the Legal and Political Philosophy of Joseph Raz* (Oxford: Oxford University Press, 2003), 282 pp. ISBN 0199248257 (hbk). £35.00.

Published in the same year and in the same series as another collection of essays dedicated to Joseph Raz's writings on moral philosophy,[1] *Rights, Culture, and the Law* brings together original essays on some of the main issues of his legal and political philosophy. The book comprises thirteen chapters and a final chapter in which Raz comments on and replies to the foregoing essays. The chapters are divided in two parts: one entitled 'Issues in Jurisprudence and Legal Philosophy' with six essays addressing issues as varied as the nature of law, practical reason, authority and gaps in the law; and the other part 'Perspectives on Liberal Society', which gathers seven essays on themes such as equality, incommensurability, group rights and multiculturalism.

The essay format together with the uneven quality of the essays make it difficult for the reviewer to do justice to the rich range of issues addressed. As a choice has to be made, I shall concentrate on a single essay, Jeremy Waldron's 'Authority for Officials' (pp. 45–69) and on Raz's reply (pp. 259–64). Such a focus is justified by virtue of the fact that this chapter pertains to legal authority, and thus to one of Raz's seminal contributions to legal philosophy, and throws light on a growing challenge for Raz's service conception of authority. This challenge is that of democracy and, more generally, of accommodating the importance of law-making procedures and their publicity for legal legitimacy.[2] In conditions of

[1] R.J. Wallace, P. Pettit, S. Scheffler and M. Smith (eds.), *Reason and Value: Themes from the Moral Philosophy of Joseph Raz* (Oxford: Oxford University Press, 2003).

[2] See, e.g., J. Waldron, *Law and Disagreement* (Oxford: Oxford University Press, 1999); S. Hershowitz, 'Legitimacy, Democracy and Razian Authority', *Legal Theory* 9 (2003), pp. 201–20; S. Besson, *The Morality of Conflict. A Study of Reasonable Disagreement in the Law* (Oxford: Hart Publishing, forthcoming [2005]). This resurgence of interest for democratic authority is also due to Waldron's and others' different attempts over the last ten years to promote a coordination-based conception of law, which culminates in the essay presently reviewed. See, e.g., J. Waldron, 'Special Ties and Natural Duties', *Philosophy and Public Affairs* 22 (1993), pp. 3–30; J. Waldron, 'Lex Satis Justa', *Notre Dame Law Review* 75 (2000), pp. 1829–58. See also before him, J. Finnis, *Natural Law and Natural Rights*

reasonable disagreement about matters of common concern, it is in the publicity and the procedural nature of our legal settlements that much of the justification of law's authority lies.[3] In fact, the particular importance of Waldron's essay in the collection is attested by the length of Raz's response, his acknowledgement of the 'illuminating' (p. 261) nature of Waldron's remarks, and his concession of an additional 'condition for the legitimacy of an authority' following his acknowledgement of the force of 'one of Waldron's criticisms' (p. 264). The present review is therefore situated half-way between a critical study of Waldron's essay in *Rights, Culture, and the Law* and an overview of the current debate over the accommodation of democratic law-making procedures in Raz's account of legal authority.

1. *Waldron's Argument*

'In philosophical discussions of authority', says Waldron, 'we usually have in mind a confrontation between an official and a subject' (p. 45). His argument is that there are other questions of authority to consider and in particular *authority as between officials or institutions*. In short, this implies taking a broader look at what is at stake in the relationship between a citizen and an official. As Waldron acknowledges, indeed,

> ...it is usually not possible to understand the relation between one official or institution and another without understanding the relation between officialdom in general and those over whom officialdom ultimately rules (ordinary citizens). The relations come in one package. (p. 45)

Waldron's argument is inspired by the 'principle of institutional settlement' (PIS) as expounded by the Legal Process scholars of the 1950s. According to this principle, 'decisions which are the duly arrived at result

---

(Oxford: Clarendon, 1980); J. Finnis, 'The Authority of Law in the Predicament of Contemporary Social Theory', *Journal of Law, Ethics and Public Policy* 1 (1984), pp. 115–37; J. Finnis, 'Law as Coordination', *Ratio Juris* 2 (1989), pp. 97–103, as well as G. Postema, 'Coordination and Convention at the Foundations of Law', *Journal of Legal Studies* 11 (1982), pp. 165–203; G. Postema, 'Law's Autonomy and Public Practical Reason', in R. George (ed.), *The Autonomy of Law* (Oxford: Clarendon, 1996), p. 79.

3 Public authority and the authority of democratic law are too important a dimension of daily law-making to be analysed as a special case of political and legal authority in general. Of course, this does not necessarily imply that Razian authority should be able to account for political and legal authority without further conditions (p. 263). These are restrictive conditions, however, whereas, as we will see, some instances of public authority cannot even be captured as cases of general practical authority in the Razian account as it is.

of duly established procedures ought to be accepted as binding upon the whole society unless and until they are duly changed'.[4] The principle applies to citizens as much as to institutions and officials. With respect to the latter, 'the principle characteristically commands respect for a given settlement from other bodies whose function it might also be, in certain circumstances, to arrive at binding settlements' (p. 47). Waldron argues by reference to Raz that 'a theory of authority is not just a list of the conditions under which an authority claim is justified: it must also illuminate the *justificandum*' (p. 49). Thus, for PIS to be deemed the basis of a theory of authority, 'a duly arrived at settlement should be respected only if the following *condition* is justified: "Human interdependence generates questions of common concern which have to be settled, one way or another"' (p. 49). Something is a question of common concern, says Waldron, 'if it is better for a single answer to be accepted among [the parties] than for each person to deal with the question on his own, as best he can, as far as it affects or interests him, acting unilaterally on the basis of his own answer' (p. 49). To summarize,

> ...a duly arrived at settlement X should be respected by the members of the group G, only if the following condition is satisfied: X is chosen from a set of answers to a question arising in G such that, for each item in that set of answers, it would be better that that answer be adopted by all the individuals in G than that each individual in G select and act unilaterally on his own answer to the question. (p. 50)

This is not a sufficient explanation of institutional settlement. As Waldron argues, 'we still need to analyse "duly arrived at"' (p. 50). Duly established settlements are settlements reached according to publicly recognized procedures. What is needed is for the salience of one of the options at stake to be revealed, that is: 'for one of the options to be marked for all the members to see as *the one for everyone to follow*' (p. 53). This applies to pure coordination problems as much as to partial conflict coordination problems, that is to say, cases where there are several ways of disposing of a question of common concern but where, respectively, some involve options among which everyone is indifferent, while others may involve options over which people disagree (pp. 50–52). It also applies, however, to cases where there is only one option and everyone converges on it, as we need to know that this question of common concern has been answered

[4] H.M. Hart and A.M. Sacks, in W.N. Eskridge and P.P. Frickey (eds.), *The Legal Process: Basic Problems in the Making and Application of Law* (Westbury, NY: Foundation Press, 1994), p. 4.

officially and that it is now time for this option to be enforced (p. 51). Publicly established settlements like law provide new reasons for us to act upon; the law is such that it can provide signals of salience of the appropriate kind. We share an attitude towards it and a practice 'of looking to it for solutions to problems of this sort, being alert to its dispositions, communicating this alertness to others, and refraining from doing anything to diminish the confidence that others may have in the appropriateness of regarding the outputs of this procedure as salient' (p. 54). Waldron unpacks four elements of the respect one owes to such a publicly established settlement as law:

> First, one must acknowledge that what is at stake is a question of common concern; second, one must recognize the presence of established arrangements for producing answers to such questions; third, one must ascertain whether such arrangements have actually produced a decision that answers the question; and, fourth, if they have, one must play one's part in the social processes that are necessary to sustain and implement such decision as settlement. (p. 56)

This model of the authority of publicly established settlement applies equally to citizens and officials (p. 69). The novelty in Waldron's argument lies, of course, in inter-official and inter-institutional authority. As Waldron argues, like a citizen, 'by holding out for his own, and by choosing unilaterally to run the risk of society's failing to settle on and implement a common answer to the question, [the official] is making light of efforts that have been made already to solve these problems' (p. 57). But this is even more serious on the part of an official, 'when ordinary citizens must take their cues from the behaviour of officials as to when a settlement has been duly enacted'; 'it is important', indeed, 'that these cues be available and reliable so that citizens know when it is appropriate for them to defer to a decision' (p. 57). After all, as Waldron argues, the officials' relationships among themselves are *about* their relationships to citizens as a whole and their authority over them (p. 67). Thus, it is only if they do not disrupt that relationship that they can have legitimate authority over citizens, and this can only be the case if they coordinate over what citizens should coordinate over (pp. 67–69). Waldron concludes therefore that

> [o]nce an official directive has been issued that holds a fair chance of securing coordination among the citizens, other officials ought to be prepared to swallow hard and refrain from issuing contrary directives, even when they are convinced that it would be better for the citizens to coordinate on their directive rather than on the basis of the one that has already been issued. (p. 69)

The remainder of Waldron's essay assesses whether this account of public authority can be accommodated 'within the four walls' of Raz's conception of authority which he deems as 'the richest and most fertile account we have' (p. 69). His argument is that it can be, provided the latter is revised to accommodate the public dimension of law's authority (pp. 59–66). In this review, I would like to separate two lines of argument in Waldron's complex essay: first, the connexion between officials' authority over citizens and authority among officials and, second, the compatibility between Raz's account of authority, on the one hand, and the legitimacy of democratic law or its procedural legitimacy, on the other. It is important to keep both arguments apart, since the latter applies to both authority for citizens and authority for officials and may therefore apply independently however successful the former may be.

2. *From Authority for Citizens to Coherence for Officials*

According to Waldron, authority for officials not only mirrors authority for citizens, but is a direct consequence of it within the package of relations between these different actors. It is important, however, to distinguish more clearly between the nature of the authority for citizens and that for officials and institutions.

Waldron is right to argue that inter-official relationships are *about* their relationships to citizens and their authority over them (p. 67). Accordingly, they give rise to second-order obligations related to the main relationship between citizens and officials and their in-built first-order obligations. Where Waldron gets it wrong, however, is when he argues that this kind of respect or deference among officials is rightly called *authority* (pp. 55–59). It is the outcome or the reflexion of officials' authority over citizens, but it is not authority *per se*. True, one may refer to authority on the part of officials when they are regarded as citizens, but when they are wearing their additional officials' cap, it is another principle of public morality which applies to them. This principle is *coherence,*[5] i.e. consistency in principle.

Coherence requires that officials 'speak with just one voice', to borrow Dworkin's expression.[6] What it implies is that, in conditions of reasonable disagreement where people are to coordinate over conceptions of justice, officials should try to express a unified conception of justice such that it

---

[5] See Besson, *The Morality of Conflict* for a detailed argument for legal coherence.

[6] See R. Dworkin, *Law's Empire* (London: Fontana, 1986), p. 165. See also Waldron, *Law and Disagreement.*

can apply to a single person. Authority over citizens implies the possibility of 'authorship' on the part of citizens and this calls for coherence in the authority's directives. It is central to the law's task of guiding intelligent human action that it enable rational self-directing agents to achieve a degree of coherence, on the one hand, by relating present official directives among themselves and, on the other, by anchoring present official decisions in past decisions of officials.[7] It is only when the law is coherent and applies *as a system* that it is able to provide the unique coordinating guidance that it is expected to give.[8]

The advantage of this account of inter-official and inter-institutional coherence over authority lies in the gap it preserves between principled consistency and absolute conformity. Coherence accommodates other potentially conflicting principles of deference that flow from those institutions' respective *de facto* constitutions, i.e. what they are in fact (p. 262). For instance, inter-institutional authority of the kind proposed by Waldron would require the legislature to defer absolutely to a prior judicial decision over which people coordinate, although this is not what the legislature's constitution requires in terms of authority. Coherence with that decision, by contrast, would ensure the consistency necessary for the coordination of citizens' actions, independently of what institutional constitutions require. Besides, either way, coherence respects the benefits of checks and balances and of inter-institutional cooperation in conditions of reasonable disagreement.[9] Finally, coherence enables officials to respect and accommodate each other's diverse viewpoints and to strike principled compromises among them, instead of deferring absolutely to some of them.[10]

3. *Razian Authority and Democratic Legitimacy*

Even if one reduces its scope to the relationship between citizens and officials, Waldron's argument about the limits of Razian authority does not

[7] G. Postema, 'Law's Melody: Time and the Normativity of Law', *Associations* 7.1 (2003), pp. 227–39 (234–36).

[8] See p. 57: 'To assure himself that his compliance with any number of these directives is not in vain, a citizen C1 must assume that officialdom is operating coherently as a system, so that (for example) C1 is not responding to Supreme Court directives on affirmative action while his fellow citizens C2, C3 etc. are responding to contrary legislative directives.'

[9] See Besson, *The Morality of Conflict*.

[10] See S. Besson, 'Four Arguments Against Compromising Justice Internally', *Oxford Journal of Legal Studies* 23.2 (2003), pp. 211–41.

lose any of its bite. In drawing on this argument and Raz's reply and taking them further, I will sketch a revised account of Raz's conception of authority that can accommodate the public and collective dimensions of legal authority. There are three theses that need to be satisfied before a public authority can be regarded as a justified authority in Raz's account: the pre-emption thesis, the dependence thesis and the normal justification thesis. Note that although I am assuming for reasons of space that Waldron's coordination-based argument for public authority is correct, the following reasoning can be understood independently of the validity of coordination-based arguments.[11] Democracy, and collective law-making procedures, more generally raise difficulties for Raz's account of authority that pertain to their public and collective character.[12]

3.1. *The Pre-Emption Thesis*

According to this first thesis, the subjects of an authority can benefit from its directives 'only if they can establish their existence and content in ways which do not depend on raising the very same issues which the authority is there to settle'.[13] It is only so that these directives can make a *practical difference* to the deliberations of those to which they apply. According to Raz,

> [t]he fact that an authority requires performance of an action is a reason for its performance which is not to be added to all other relevant reasons when assessing what to do, but should exclude and take the place of some of them.[14]

This condition is respected in Waldron's account of public authority, since the point of the legal settlement of a disagreement is precisely a matter of setting aside the substantive reasoning that brought us to this problem in the first place.[15] Legal coordination, and settlements more generally, are only possible if the parties can identify the salient option without having to engage in the reasoning that was necessary to get to that decision and, most importantly, without having to disagree again on what it should be.

---

[11] Raz argues that coordination is not law's only function and understands coordination in the impoverished sense given by Lewis and others of coordination of interests, rather than of common concerns (p. 259). See Besson, *The Morality of Conflict*, for a critique and an account of the nature of coordination-based obligations to obey the law.

[12] See, e.g., Hershowitz, 'Legitimacy, Democracy and Razian Authority'.

[13] J. Raz, *Ethics in the Public Domain* (Oxford: Oxford University Press, 1995), p. 203.

[14] J. Raz, *The Morality of Freedom* (Oxford: Clarendon, 1986), p. 46.

[15] See p. 60. See also Finnis, 'Law as Coordination', p. 101 ff.

The only departure from the pre-emption thesis, however, lies in the *identification of a public authority*. According to Waldron, this identification should result from the awareness of the existence of a question of common concern that needs coordination (pp. 60–61) or a legal settlement, first, and from the awareness of others' participation in a coordinative or legal effort (pp. 49, 59), second. If one follows the pre-emption thesis very strictly, however, the law must, in order to be authoritative, precisely pre-empt the subject's own reasoning in determining when we are actually facing disagreement and a coordination problem and when we need authority.[16] This implies that there is a way of identifying the law's authority without having to engage in the sort of activity that was necessary to produce it and therefore without figuring that we are actually facing a coordination problem.

This discrepancy need not worry us too much, however, and Waldron gives up somewhat too quickly on Razian authority. Even in Raz's account, true respect for and acceptance of a decision as being authoritative, by contrast to mere submission to it (pp. 60–61), cannot arise without first observing that the question is a question of common concern that needs a legal settlement and that there is a legal scheme at work. It is often wrongly assumed that to abide by an exclusionary reason for action implies that one ought not to think about other reasons. All an exclusionary reason does is pre-empt people from *acting* for an excluded reason and *not from thinking* about it or concurrent reasons.[17] One needs to be able to identify an authority and determine whether it has the abilities it claims to be a legitimate authority in certain matters and classes of cases, before the authority can apply and pre-emption can take place.

One may refer to this additional condition to the pre-emption thesis as the *knowability of authority*.[18] In fact, Raz concedes this point in his reply to Waldron and contends that

---

[16] See J. Raz (ed.), 'Introduction', in *Authority* (Oxford: Blackwell, 1990), p. 10; Raz, *The Morality of Freedom*, pp. 203, 209.

[17] See J. Raz, *Practical Reason and Norms*, 2nd edn (Oxford: Oxford University Press, 1999), p. 184.

[18] This process of identification of an authority is clearly evaluative. One may therefore question its compatibility with Raz's practical difference thesis, but more particularly with the sources thesis. True, there remains a gap between identifying an authority in a *general class of cases* and determining the merits of each of its decisions. Besides, Raz might want to reduce the scope of the practical difference and sources theses to cases of *de facto* legal and political authority, for the recognition of which the three theses including the pre-emption thesis and its knowability addendum need not be given. It is not entirely clear, however, how this last move might be of interest to any account of authority whose ultimate claim is bound to be legitimacy.

> [i]t seems plausible to add a condition for the legitimacy of an authority. Something like a requirement that people over whom it has authority should have reason to find out, and should be able to find out whether it has such authority (at a cost not disproportionate to the benefit in tracking the reason its supposed authority can bring). Perhaps it should also be a condition of the authoritative standing of any directive that those subject to it have reason to find out whether it exists and can find out its content. (p. 264)

3.2. *The Dependence Thesis*

What the dependence thesis implies is that there can be no separate set of reasons for authorities to use that would not in principle be appropriate for the subjects of the authorities to use (p. 62). According to Raz, 'all authoritative directives should be based on reasons which already independently apply to the subjects of the directives and are relevant to their action in the circumstances covered by the directives'.[19] In a disagreement, the problem arises from the fact that very different sets of reasons dictate the different participants' conflicting opinions about what should be done. By the time they decide to settle their disagreement, therefore, the set of reasons underlying the salient directives cannot correspond to all the potential reasons underlying each of the individual opinions (p. 61). Besides, the presence or possibility of an authority changes the nature of the choices participants face, thus making it difficult to associate the authoritative set of reasons with each and all of the choices possible, apart from the existence and actions of the authority (p. 62). For instance, the emergence of a coordination problem and the possibility of coordination give rise to reasons to coordinate which people might not have had before. According to Waldron, therefore, Raz's model is appropriate only in cases where a person's choice on the merits roughly identifies with the choice on the merits as options for the entire population, that is to say, in cases where there is no disagreement and hence no need for coordination (p. 62).

Interestingly, Raz concedes this in his reply. His recent re-interpretation of the thesis states that it does not require that the reasons for action authorities provide correspond perfectly to existing individual reasons for action. Arguing the contrary would imply that the existence of a public authority could not enable us to achieve desirable goals which would be unachievable without it. All the dependence thesis requires therefore is that we have the abstract reasons which the public authority gives us new

[19] Raz, *Ethics in the Public Domain*, p. 47.

opportunities to pursue, even though we did not have the opportunity to do so on our own (p. 260). Thus, the dependence relationship can be *indirect* and fit cases where disagreement and the presence of an authority change the nature of the choices people face.

3.3. *The Normal Justification Thesis*

According to the normal justification thesis, we must be able to comply better with our own reasons by abiding by authoritative decisions than on our own, whether or not we believe we do. The normal justification thesis is not based on a subjective assessment of what is in our reasons' best interest, but on an objective truth. According to Raz,

> ...the normal and primary way to establish that a person should be acknowledged to have authority over another person involves showing that the alleged subject is likely better to comply with reasons which apply to him (other than the alleged authoritative directives) if he accepts the directives of the alleged authority as authoritatively binding and tries to follow them rather than if he tries to follow the reasons which apply to him directly.[20]

Like the other two, this third thesis is in need of thorough revision, if it is to accommodate the reality of democratic law-making in conditions of reasonable disagreement, and, more particularly, the law's *public* and *collective* dimension.

3.4. *A First Challenge: The Need for Public Identification*

As Waldron argues, what the normal justification thesis fails to capture from the start is an important dimension of legal and political authority: its public and shared dimension (p. 65). Before an official or an institution can be an authority in an individual case, it ought to be publicly known as such and its procedures be supported by a shared practice of recognition. Only this way can it then be deemed to provide the salient decisions necessary for coordination to take place and hence be able to make a practical difference at the individual level. As Waldron argues,

> ...it may be quite inappropriate for me to regard A as a public authority unless I am sure that many others do in fact so regard it (or are prepared to do so if they see that enough others are prepared to do so if... etc.). (p. 66)

As we saw earlier, Raz concedes this point in his reply to Waldron by adding a condition to the normal justification thesis: the *knowability of*

20 Raz, *The Morality of Freedom*, p. 198; Raz, *Ethics in the Public Domain*, p. 53.

authority (p. 264). This concession implies that, for a public authority to be justified objectively in an individual case, people must be able to find out and decide whether it has the public qualities required to have authority over all of them collectively and not only individually. This leads me to formulate a second challenge which Waldron does not articulate.[21]

3.5. *A Second Challenge: The Need for Collective Decision-Making*

Given the conditions of reasonable disagreement that prevail and the procedural legitimacy of most of our legal decisions,[22] one needs to go even further in the proceduralization of the normal justification thesis. True, in principle, it should be possible to keep the subjective identification of public authority distinct from its objective justification. This does not take the conditions of disagreement and circumstances of politics seriously enough, however. The normal justification thesis should accommodate the fact that democratic authorities make their demands *ex hypothesi* on people who think they have good grounds for believing that the majority is mistaken.[23] In other words, any theory that makes legitimate authority depend on the moral rightness of political outcomes is self-defeating, because it is in many cases precisely because people disagree reasonably about it, and hence about the normal justification thesis, that they need to set up and recognize an authority and engage in democratic law-making procedures.

Of course, as Raz acknowledges, part of the idea of practical authority is that, to protect our individual reasons, we might have to deviate slightly from them through accepting the indirect decisions of an authority that would thus help us comply with them better than on our own. Things differ hugely, however, depending on whether one is considering a private or a public authority. The recognition and hence the establishment of public authority, although it aims eventually at binding individuals, whether in collective or purely individual actions, cannot be about *individually* identifying the best practical authority, by contrast to the recognition of private authority on private matters; it is indeed about *collectively* finding the best way to coordinate diverging opinions on matters of *common concern*. As such, the identification and establishment of public authority necessarily restricts the possibility of respecting a substantive form of normal

[21] This is probably due to his subjective account of the normal justification thesis (pp. 49, 66).

[22] See Waldron, *Law and Disagreement*, p. 96.

[23] See Waldron, *Law and Disagreement*, p. 101.

justification thesis at an individual level. Paradoxically, therefore, the only way we have of complying collectively with the requirements of justice, and the reasons which apply individually to us when we disagree about justice and about how best to respect it, is to abide by the imperfect outcome of a procedure, thus intentionally placing substantive demands of justice second behind our moral interest in coordination.[24]

From the moment we recognize the procedural and collective dimension of the normal justification thesis, there can be no return to a purely substantive and individual account. It would be absurd to emphasize, on the one hand, the dependence of the normal justification thesis on the existence and identification of a public law-making scheme as the only way of complying with the former, while requiring, on the other, that authoritative directives comply individually with reasonably contested substantive standards of justice. Of course, this does not amount to eliminating all objectively substantive elements from the normal justification thesis. As Scott Hershowitz argues, this would make it an empty shell.[25] It should, on the contrary, be conceived as a hybrid of both the procedural and substantive dimensions. In short, this revised account of the normal justification thesis should attribute authority to the outcome of a law-making *procedure*, in which we are intentionally taking part, provided this law-making scheme itself, as opposed to its outcome, is *fair* in each individual case.[26] The law-making procedure's fairness should be assessed by reference to certain minimal objective moral standards, such as the protection of basic procedural equality in a democracy.[27]

---

[24] Of course, coordination implies better compliance with one's individual reasons to coordinate, but these are not the main individual moral reasons at stake in the context of the normal justification thesis. There is indeed a difference between reasons to have an authority and reasons this authority provides us with. This confusion might explain why Waldron does not see fit to go further than the first challenge, although the normal justification thesis, as Raz understands it, is not compatible with his account of natural duties to coordinate in Waldron, 'Special Ties'.

[25] Hershowitz, 'Legitimacy, Democracy and Razian Authority', pp. 219–20: 'So conceived, the normal justification thesis would accommodate all theories of legitimacy that turned out to be true; hence it ceases to be a competitor with other candidate theories of legitimacy.'

[26] In this sense, I think that Hershowitz, 'Legitimacy, Democracy and Razian Authority', p. 220, misses the argument by blaming procedural re-interpretations of the normal justification thesis for diluting the distinction between making better decisions about the matter the directive regards and making better decisions about such questions more generally. See Besson, *The Morality of Conflict*.

[27] See Besson, *The Morality of Conflict*, on this minimal substantive legitimacy of the procedural legitimacy of democratic law. See also Hershowitz, 'Legitimacy, Democracy and Razian Authority', pp. 216ff. See, more generally, J. Rawls, 'Legal Obligation and the Duty of Fair Play', in S. Freeman (ed.), *John Rawls: Collected Papers* (Cambridge MA: Harvard University Press, 1999).

RORTY, THE FIRST AMENDMENT AND ANTIREALISM: IS RELIANCE UPON TRUTH VIEWPOINT-BASED SPEECH REGULATION?

Brian E. Butler

Abstract

In this article I investigate the implications of antirealism, as characterized by Richard Rorty, for First Amendment jurisprudence under the United States Constitution. It is hoped that the implications, while played out in the context of a specific tradition, will have more universal application. In Section 1, Rorty's 'pragmatic antirealism' is briefly outlined. In Section 2, some effects of the elimination of the concept of truth for First Amendment jurisprudence are investigated. Section 3 argues for the conclusion that given the antirealist stance, the Supreme Court's usage of the true/false fact distinction is actually an uncritical allowance of viewpoint-based discrimination into speech protection that has potentially far-reaching and restrictive results for important speech. Finally, in Section 4 Rorty's antirealism is combined with various traditional models of First Amendment analysis to see how it would function. The conclusions aimed at are twofold. First, that Rortian antirealism is compatible with the traditional models underlying First Amendment theory. Second, that a realization that truth is the result of, in Rorty's words, 'intra-mundane' discourse leads to an argument for different and potentially stronger and more far-reaching protections to speech.

Keywords

antirealism, First Amendment, free speech, jurisprudence, pragmatism, Rorty

1. *Rorty's Pragmatic Antirealism*

Richard Rorty argues for a modern self-image based upon an ironic stance towards one's beliefs and a liberal stance towards others. He combines what he thinks to be the best aspects of Dewey, Wittgenstein and Heidegger in order to get to a liberalism that provides (if he is successful in his aims) hope without becoming overly restrictive or, on the other hand, overly hands off in what is allowed government. What is hoped for is a completely de-divinized world of skeptical but sensitive ironic pragmatists/poets. Most important for this article, Rorty combines a thoroughgoing antirealism with an emphasis upon the central importance of discourse to the human self.

1.1. *Antirealism*

First of all, Rorty's stance entails a rejection of what he labels the 'Plato-Kant canon'.[1] This is characterized as a tradition of texts with certain underlying metaphors and a central explicit motivation.[2] These texts all have as an aim arrival at a view from the heights that would 'rise above the plurality of appearances'.[3] This type of aim is possibly best exemplified by Nagel's aim of describing the world from 'the view from nowhere'.[4] All of these theorists, according to Rorty, are looking for a verified unitary position from which to judge everything authoritatively. Rorty, on the other hand, wants us to accept a world without any such privileged vantage point. For Rorty, all these other theorists are wrongly attempting to find 'a language that nature speaks'. He, on the other hand, argues that

> great scientists invent descriptions of the world which are useful for purposes of predicting and controlling what happens, just as poets and political thinkers invent other descriptions of it for other purposes. But there is no sense in which *any* of these descriptions is an accurate representation of the way the world is in itself.[5]

Out of this picture there is clearly a rejection of alternate theories of truth such as 'realism' which is thought to commit one to postulating an unverifiable correspondence between the theory and the world,[6] or 'empiricism' which commits us instead to some type of attachment to only what can be perceived/observed. Such widely diverging theorists such as Fine, Laudan, Kuhn and Putnam have so effectively ridiculed these theoretical stances towards truth that, at least in their simplest forms, they are thought

[1] Richard Rorty, *Contingency, Irony, and Solidarity* (Cambridge: Cambridge University Press, 1989), p. 96. Hereafter all references to this work will be shown as *CIS*.

[2] This side of Rorty's work has great affinity and clear roots in Derrida.

[3] *CIS*, p. 96.

[4] Thomas Nagel, *The View From Nowhere* (Oxford: Oxford University Press, 1986). It is claims that Nagel makes, such as '[w]hat lies beyond our current understanding is not adequately captured in the idea of answers to questions we do not yet know how to ask. It may include things that we or creatures like us could never formulate questions about' (p. 104) that Rorty would take issue with.

[5] *CIS*, p. 4.

[6] Arthur Fine, 'The Natural Ontological Attitude', in Jarrett Leplin (ed.), *Scientific Realism* (Berkeley: University of California Press, 1984), p. 89.

generally questionable or even discredited.[7] For them, as well as Rorty, we are left living in a world where theories and appeals to truths of a technically 'realistic' or 'empirical' nature are highly questionable as to their legitimacy. Of course there are other theories of truth; a couple of examples being the 'disquotational' and the 'coherence' theories. But Rorty's arguments, if accepted, work equally well against these. All theories of truth are intra-mundane just like any truth claim, and therefore are only true for the language-game being used. If this is justified, it turns out that there is no good reason to indulge in epistemology or truth talk at all, and just possibly good reasons to fear it.

For Rorty, these results entail our existence in an essence-less world where we are living within and, ideally, spinning out, alternate linguistic worlds that our lives are lived according to. None of these linguistic worlds are reasonably thought truer than any other. On the other hand, many of the alternate vocabularies can be thought more desirable or better at 'working' in some particularlistic way. This picture of the relationship of truth to language also leads us to a point where it is 'impossible for us to retain the notion that some actions and attitudes are naturally "inhuman" '.[8]

Gone, in Rorty's world, are hopes for an overarching theory that can put the pieces of the world into one coherent and harmonious whole. Gone also is a language that fits the world in some manner traditionally thought of as truth. The conclusion that he comes to from all this is that a modern citizen should, ideally, adopt a stance that he describes as ironism. This stance is characterized as admitting that all of one's most cherished beliefs, social attributes and desires are contingent—they are not any closer to reality than any other.[9] They are to be seen as the product of historical contingency, not of any underlying telos or purpose written into the universe. And they are not to be seen as having any claim to greater validity due to some relationship with the universe than any other alternative vocabulary. An alternate vocabulary may satisfy us more, or serve some purposes better than others, but this does not entail that such a vocabulary is any closer to 'truth'. Because all possible truth claims are internal

---

[7] See, for example, Arthur Fine, 'And Not Anti-Realism Either', *Nous* 18 (1984), pp. 51–65; Larry Laudan, 'Discussion: Realism Without the Real', *Philosophy of Science* 51 (1984), pp. 156–62; Thomas Kuhn, *The Structure of Scientific Revolutions* (Chicago: University of Chicago Press, 1970); and Hilary Putnam, 'Why There Isn't a Ready-Made World', *Synthese* 51 (1982), pp. 141–68.

[8] *CIS*, p. 189.

[9] *CIS*, p. 73.

to a vocabulary, the nature of truth claims become trivial and banal or theoretically circular. This is true of the most simplistic as well as the most sophisticated epistemological stance. An appeal to truth only escapes such banality when it is wrongfully projected as valid outside of the vocabulary it is dependent upon. Then it becomes an attack upon other vocabularies. Because of these realizations the Rortian ironist refuses to 'empower'—all that is left is re-description. Truth, therefore, is an unavailable concept from which to justify any conclusion, aim, adoption of vocabulary, and so on.

1.2. *Discourse*

While Rorty dismisses the hope for a language that nature speaks or that in his words 'mirrors nature',[10] he emphasizes the very important, indeed essential, constitutive nature of language for human life. From his reading of Wittgenstein, Heidegger and Dewey he sees language and life as inseparably intertwined. He describes each culture's and each individual's self as being constituted by their respective 'final vocabularies'. This final vocabulary is 'a set of words which they [the culture or the individual] employ to justify their actions, their beliefs, and their lives'.[11] This language we are living within, and which therefore determines so much about us, is to be seen as 'something that took shape as a result of a great number of sheer contingencies'.[12] The hope for a poeticized culture is a major defining aspect of the ironic liberal citizen. Rorty believes that '[a] sense of human history as the history of successive metaphors would let us see the poet, in the generic sense of the maker of new words, the shaper of new languages, as the vanguard of the species'.[13] This is because 'to change how we talk is to change what, for our purposes, we are'.[14] Ultimately for Rorty our human condition comes down to two claims: (1) '[t]he only things that are really evident to us are our own desires',[15] and (2) '[t]he human self is created by the use of a vocabulary rather than being adequately or inadequately expressed in a vocabulary'.[16] The clear implication of the combination of the antirealism with the emphasis upon the constitutive nature of

---

[10] Richard Rorty, *Philosophy and the Mirror of Nature* (Princeton, NJ: Princeton University Press, 1979).

[11] *CIS*, p. 73.

[12] *CIS*, p. 16.

[13] *CIS*, p. 20.

[14] *CIS*, p. 20.

[15] *CIS*, p. 29.

[16] *CIS*, p. 7.

language is the very high importance of freedom of speech.[17] Protection of alternative forms of discourse becomes vital.

2. *Elimination of the Assumption of Truth—Some Effects on First Amendment Jurisprudence*

Ignoring the greater assumptions and implications of Rorty's antirealism and emphasis upon the centrality of one's chosen vocabulary, a simpler and more specific set of questions may be asked. What would the elimination of recourse to the concept of truth do to First Amendment free speech jurisprudence? Would it change any of the results, or any of the tests? Where would the First Amendment function as before, and where not? These are broad questions and cannot be answered fully in this article. At the same time, a brief investigation of a few areas will show that while the elimination of truth as an operative concept might cause changes in the methods in which the Court goes about deciding such issues, or more importantly the results arrived at, the problems raised do not appear insurmountable.

2.1. *Obscenity*

Some aspects of First Amendment jurisprudence would not have to change at all. For instance, the regulation of obscenity under *Miller*[18] is governed by three requirements. Material will be categorized as obscene if: (1) the average person applying contemporary community standards would find the work, taken as a whole, appeals to the prurient interest; (2) the work depicts in a patently offensive way sexual conduct specifically defined by the state law; and (3) the work, taken as a whole, lacks serious literary, artistic, political, or scientific value. This test does not have need to mention the concepts eliminated such as truth, fact, and so on. Neither community standards, offensiveness, nor the serious value test rests upon the concept of truth. Much First Amendment jurisprudence is, like the obscenity area, without necessary or even implied recourse to the concept of truth.[19]

---

[17] This can be seen very clearly in Richard Rorty's book *Achieving Our Country : Leftist Thought in Twentieth-Century America* (Cambridge, MA: Harvard University Press, 1998), where he argues that the American 'left' has not lived up to its role because of a failure to adopt properly relevant stances within their discourse.

[18] *Miller v. California*, 413 US 15 (1973).

[19] In an area very similar to obscenity—that of profanity—the Court has actually shown some sensitivity to the idea explored later in this article that the form actually creates at least some of the message. *Cohen v. California*, 403 US 15 (1971).

2.2. *Commercial Speech*

Other areas of speech jurisprudence, while using truth as a distinction within the area, might have tools already at hand to develop a truthless (but not toothless) criteria. Take as an example the regulation of commercial speech. In commercial speech there would have to be a clear shift in legal standards. In *Virginia Pharmacy*, the Supreme Court held that truthful, non-deceptive advertising was protected under the First Amendment.[20] Whereas current jurisprudence allows for the regulation of false or misleading statements under *Gertz*,[21] a view that ignored or didn't accept the truth/falsity distinction would have to find another distinguishing point. A decision clearly couldn't hinge upon the truth of the facts alleged, advertised, and so on. But this might not be as problematic as it might initially appear or otherwise raise many difficulties for the legislator or the Court. An alternate standard might be based upon harm to the consumer, for instance. This might be claimed to rest upon matters of fact, but even the most strongly antirealist stances don't dismiss human pain or suffering as not real. Rorty, in fact, explicitly holds out pain from the antirealism critique.[22] The distinction might be described as resting upon the conception of harm that is winning in the marketplace of ideas at the moment.

The recent Supreme Court decision *Liquormart*,[23] which addressed the issue of what regulations are allowed on truthful, non-deceptive advertisements, based the holding on the paternalistic nature of regulations relating to true information. While finding invalid a regulation that prohibited any advertising of the price of alcoholic beverages offered for sale, Justice Stevens, writing for the Court, held that a state could regulate commercial messages to protect consumers. Such regulation is acceptable as long as it is aimed at misleading, deceptive, or aggressive sales practices, or requires the disclosure of beneficial consumer information. Such regulation is allowed because the purpose of its regulation is consistent with the reasons for according constitutional protection to commercial speech. On the other hand, the Court held that if there was a complete prohibition of the dissemination of truthful, non-misleading commercial messages for

---

[20] *Virginia State Board of Pharmacy v. Virginia Citizens Consumer Council*, 425 US 748 (1976).

[21] *Gertz v. Robert Welch, Inc.*, 418 US 323 (1974).

[22] It is a legitimate question as to why Rorty can hold out pain from his critique and the ironist's agenda. But the main point in context of this paper is that one can still worry about issues such as pain without utilizing the word 'truth'. One possible result could be that eliminating truth talk from the discourse would force more awareness of the actual worldly implications of one jurisprudential stance towards speech over another.

[23] *44 Liquormart, Inc. v. Rhode Island*, 517 US 484 (1996).

reasons unrelated to the preservation of a fair bargaining process, then the rigorous review that the First Amendment generally demands is required. While the 'truthful' happens to be heavily implicated in the standard the Court applied, it is clearly watered down by, and combined with, other factors such as 'deceptive' and 'aggressive' as well as 'fair'. If 'truth' cannot be relied on there are, in the case of commercial speech, other tools already available for the Court to use. A balancing test looking only at deception, for instance (defined by looking at the intent of the speaker), might rely only on fairness or other coercive or aggressive tactics. And, once again a standard based upon harm would be available.

2.3. *Libel*

Other areas, such as libel, are almost wholly based upon a true/false distinction. Certainly libel laws would have to change. The controlling case as to public figures, *New York Times*,[24] rests its test upon actual malice based upon knowledge of or reckless disregard for a statement that was false. Falsity would not be an option without the concept of truth to do the work, so therefore some other distinguishing point would have to be selected. Under some theories of the underlying rationale for the First Amendment, the doctrine of privacy could be adopted. This would most likely be a Rorty-type solution to this problem. And in this context this criterion might actually function better than the truth/malice test. The underlying issues animating libel law might be more clearly addressed if it focused upon the harm caused by the speech in question and the public's need for the information it contains over the truth of the statement. For example, it has been argued that the lower protection accorded public figures that are not of a political nature as to libel awards under *Gertz*[25] (compared to non-public or private citizens) should be accorded greater protection than they have currently under modern American libel law. A stance not based upon truth would probably look to a balancing of the harm caused to the person against the need to know of the public—and this almost certainly would give public but non-political figures greater protection.

Another issue under libel law is the so-called 'group libel law' allowed in *Beauharnais*.[26] There the Supreme Court allowed a conviction under a statute that made it a crime to publish criticisms of a group attributing depravity, criminality, or other negative characteristics to a group because

---

24 *New York Times v. Sullivan*, 376 US 254 (1964).
25 See note 21, above.
26 *Beauharnais v. Illinois*, 343 US 250 (1952).

of the speaker's bad motives. This could be seen as similar to problems of discrimination under the Fourteenth Amendment where a defense of 'truthfulness' might actually justify statements because of, for instance, a high statistical correlation between certain races and criminal activity or illegal immigration. If, instead of truthfulness, a harm calculus were adopted under the First Amendment, even true generalities could be libelous.[27] This result has obvious implications for hate speech law. Although libel law would have to change, it appears that there is no real reason why it couldn't do without the true/false distinction.

2.4. *The Clear and Present Danger Test*

What of the central 'clear and present danger test' as developed in *Abrams, Whitney* through *Brandenburg*?[28] One of the virtues of the clear and present danger test is that it really doesn't need the concept of truth to work. Neither the 'clear' requirement, the 'present' or immanence requirement, nor the danger requirement explicitly points to the 'truth'. Holmes's seminal dissent in *Abrams*[29] may mention the word truth—'the best test of truth is the power of the thought to get itself accepted in the competition of the market, and that truth is the only ground upon which their wishes safely can be carried out'. But this can be read fairly as defining truth as what wins in the marketplace of ideas, not that truth, however else defined, will ultimately win in the marketplace. In other words, Holmes defines truth as what wins; he doesn't say an independent truth will win when put into the market. Whichever description wins in the marketplace of ideas is just taken as true. But in this context, 'true' is just equivalent to 'most convincing to the most people given the set of alternative descriptions offered'. Therefore the 'truth' aspect of the statement is expendable. All that is said here is that democratic principles must be adopted. The same can be said of Brandeis' concurrence in *Whitney*.[30] Where he states that '[i]f there be time to expose through discussion the falsehood and fallacies, to avert the evil by the process of education, the remedy is more speech, not enforced silence', this could be taken as an enlightenment-like

[27] I don't wish to get into a debate here as to the wisdom of such a legal standard, but from a very quick glance it appears that the benefits and burdens point in both directions.

[28] *Abrams v. United States*, 250 US 616 (1919); *Whitney v. California*, 274 US 357 (1927); *Brandenburg v. Ohio*, 395 US 444 (1969).

[29] See note 28, above.

[30] See note 28, above.

belief that the truth will arise through dialogue.[31] But on an equally plausible interpretation, what Brandeis could really be saying is 'unless the threat is immediate, whatever discourse is most convincing, given each a chance to speak, wins'. The test then would be one where the main aim is to avoid coercion or physical violence and to encourage democratic deliberation. So, the central test in modern American First Amendment jurisprudence doesn't need, and only tangentially references through its historical sources, the concept of truth.

3. *Non-Protection of Falsehoods as Viewpoint Discrimination?*

If the above brief analysis is correct, then it may be that the protection of speech doesn't really hinge upon the concept of truth. Even so, why make truth an issue if there is no reason to suspect something is wrong with the use of this 'truth' concept? What is wrong with a concept that seems so functional and intuitively acceptable? Why are Rorty and other antirealists so suspicious of the concept of truth?

3.1. *The Intra-Mundane Source of Truth and Fact*

Rorty makes a distinction between 'intra-mundane' discourse and poetic creation. The claim (based upon a Wittgenstinian emphasis upon the concept of 'language-game') is that each final vocabulary or intra-mundane discourse carries within itself a set of criteria for what is to count as a fact. 'Fact' and 'truth' are both constituted by, and reliant upon, the language-game they are embedded within. Any claim resting upon truth or fact, and not admitting this perspectival aspect of such claims, is seen as buying into what Sellars labeled the 'myth of the given'.[32] In Rorty's as well as Goodman's antirealism, on the other hand, 'the given must be acknowledged as taken'.[33] What is argued against is the picture of 'fact' or 'truth' as a neutral standpoint devoid of preconditions and preconceptions.

31 Under this interpretation Jurgen Habermas could be thought to be a descendent of Brandeis. See, for example, Jurgen Habermas, *The Philosophical Discourse of Modernity* (Cambridge: MIT Press, 1987).

32 See Nelson Goodman, *Ways of Worldmaking* (Indianapolis: Hackett, 1978) for an excellent analysis of the problems with taking some objects as given.

33 Probably the most influential statement of such a position is in Kuhn (*Structure of Scientific Revolutions*), for instance—'[t]he distinction between discovery of a fact and invention is one that is "exceedingly artificial"' (p. 52).

The conclusion is that there are no 'self-certifying' facts[34] or truths to be found.

But as there is no neutral viewpoint from which to compare all these competing language-games, there is no neutral arbiter between all the options—and therefore no neutral fact or truth to which to appeal. Once the 'myth of the given' is exposed there is no neutral starting point. A court also has no hope of arriving at a neutral conclusion. And if truth is a concept always necessarily embedded in and determined by the needs of a specific discourse, then truth as a criterion is seen to be a way to entrench the dominant (intra-mundane) viewpoint. The outrage that antirealists feel when confronted with claims based upon the truth of a statement is motivated by the thought that truth can be used as a weapon of those in power and is always determined by the chosen final vocabulary or language-game.[35] That is, truth is the greatest weapon of those using the dominant final vocabulary because it is necessarily a circular appeal to their own internalized (and internal) criteria.

This realization goes hand in hand with Heidegger's statement, 'he who would think greatly must err greatly',[36] and helps to explain his, and more important Rorty's, emphasis upon the importance of the poet. Both fear a restrictive regime of truth, and therefore slavery to the given way of talking. Under this picture of 'truth', fixation upon truth will not set you free; it will just as likely entrap you within whatever vocabulary you are forced or just happen to live with. Appeals to reason, truth, fact, and so on, are just appeals to the status quo. A claim of 'fact' or 'truth', contrary to being neutral or unobjectionable, is just a reification or ossification of dominant ways of thinking. Any such appeal to fact or truth carries within itself no greater claim to legitimacy than what it really is, which is an appeal to 'the way we think'. This appeal to 'we' is not good or bad in itself—it is just deflationary in relation to more substantive stances and beliefs towards what an appeal to 'truth' and 'fact' carries with it in terms of legitimacy or neutrality. But adoption of the shift from a belief in neutral facts to a belief in 'perspectival' of internal facts constituted through the adoption of

---

[34] The 'self-certifying' description is from Wilfred Sellars, 'The Structure of Knowledge', in Hector-Neri Castaneda (ed.), *Action, Knowledge and Reality: Critical Studies in Honor of Wilfrid Sellars* (Indianapolis: Bobbs-Merill, 1975), p. 336.

[35] This is not to claim that this is conscious. Indeed, the most invidious aspect of 'the myth of the given' is that it is mostly unconscious or pre-conscious and therefore all the more difficult to combat.

[36] This is a sentiment that I have come more comfortable with, and have kept near me for solace, since law school.

specific language-games has fundamental implications when placed in the context of First Amendment jurisprudence.

In the antirealist's world (Rorty is the governing example here), facts are unavoidably imbedded within theories and are only explainable by the theory that has produced them.[37] If the antirealist's claim that all facts are created by language use, paradigm immersion, and so on, is adopted, then this distinction between fact and theory has everything backwards. According to these theories, truth is a term that carries with it less of a legitimate guarantee than common sense would allow. What theorists such as Rorty and Feyerabend[38] maintain is that words like reason, truth, and so on, are not neutral in themselves but carry certain loaded conclusions. Therefore, in light of the interest in autonomy and freedom, reference to truth or reason would be better off avoided. In relation to the First Amendment they shouldn't be allowed to carry the weight they are used to carry if the antirealist critique is correct.

3.2. *Truth as a Viewpoint-Based Restriction*

In current First Amendment jurisprudence the greatest suspicion is placed upon viewpoint-based restrictions even if the restriction is deemed modest.[39] This suspicion motivates the Court to apply an almost absolute ban upon such restrictions.[40] On the other hand, the lowest scrutiny of 'rational basis' is placed upon content-neutral restrictions.[41] This insures that content-neutral restrictions are allowed unless the means-end relationship is irrational or the governmental purpose is illegitimate. This distinction between the two types of restriction makes intuitive sense because a viewpoint-based restriction is much more likely to be motivated by

---

37 Of course Rorty would not accept the antirealist label. But I have taken the liberty to describe him as one, and think the label quite warranted by his main claims and attacks upon the philosophical canon.

38 Paul Feyerabend, *Farewell To Reason* (London: Verso, 1987).

39 See, for example, *Schact v. United States*, 398 US 58 (1970), and *Linmark Associates v. Township of Willingboro*, 431 US 85 (1977).

40 '[O]utside the realm of low-value speech, the Court has invalidated almost every content-based restriction that it has considered in the past thirty years. Whether applying an "absolute protection" approach, a "clear and present danger" test, a "compelling governmental interest" standard, or some other formulation, the Court almost invariably reaches the same result—content-based restrictions of "highvalue" speech are unconstitutional' (Geoffrey Stone, 'Content-Neutral Restrictions', *University of Chicago Law Review* 54 [1987], p. 47).

41 See, for example, *United States Postal Service v. Council of Greenburg Civic Associations*, 453 US 114 (1981); *Heffron v. International Society for Krishna Consciousness*, 452 US 640 (1981); and *United States v. O'Brien*, 391 US 367 (1968).

illegitimate reasons and distort public debate (skew the marketplace of ideas). Content-neutral restrictions, on the other hand, have a disciplining and universalizing effect on the legislator even if improperly motivated. Furthermore, there are many legitimate reasons to restrict speech that have nothing to do with the content (an uncontroversial example would be noise restrictions after 1.00 a.m.).[42]

The Court has looked to the fact/idea distinction as one way to separate protected speech from speech undeserving of First Amendment protection. According to *Gertz v. Robert Welch, Inc.*, 418 US 323 (1974), there is no such thing as a false idea under the First Amendment. This stance goes well with the antirealist conclusions discussed above. Ideas are all given a chance to compete for allegiance and therefore are all thought of as high-value speech deserving of great protection. On the other hand, the same case held that there is no constitutional value in a false statement of fact. False statements of fact are thought to have low value at best and therefore are not protected by the First Amendment. While the Court has protected some false speech because of the possibility of chilling debate, the continuing assumption is that there is no real reason other than potential secondary effects to protect false statements of fact. The Court has also explained that in the context of a media libel case the distinction between idea and fact is not necessary for judicial decision-making because falseness of a fact is a matter for the person claiming libel to prove. *Milkovich v. Lorain Journal Co.*, 497 US 1 (1990), and *Philadelphia Newspapers, Inc. v. Hepps*, 475 US 767 (1986). If this is accurate, it may be the case that this is not a distinction the Court needs to make. But this result does not eliminate the underlying, and agreed-upon, conclusion that false statements of fact are not protected by the First Amendment.

Applying the antirealist critique of 'fact' and 'truth' to the Court's reasoning, the Court's unconscious adoption of a common-sense view of fact and truth is very problematic and overlooks the content-based aspects of such a view. According to the antirealist, and in particular Rorty, neither 'fact' nor 'truth' is neutral in content or results when put to such a use. Both are very much in service of whatever vocabulary is being used at the time. The apparent neutrality is, once again, just a result of the inherent circular relationship between what counts as a fact or a truth with the vocabulary these concepts are employed within. Truth, being the result of

[42] For a much more complete analysis of the analytic problems and motivation for the distinction, see Geoffrey Stone, 'Content Regulation and the First Amendment', *William and Mary Law Review* 25 (1983), p. 189.

intra-mundane discourse, is not neutral between ideas; it actually is a slanted concept in service of the dominant world-view of the very same discourse. The distinction between true and false facts, therefore, is a distinction that smuggles in a very biased perspective.

If this is the case, then the Supreme Court, in using the true/false fact test for determining protection of speech has imposed a highly constrictive stance upon First Amendment jurisprudence that has more radical and far-reaching implications for speech than the apparent content-neutrality of the categories would suggest. One way of putting this is to state that by not protecting 'false statements of fact', the Supreme Court has imposed a tax upon extra-mundane discourse (a tax upon the spinner of new vocabularies as opposed to the user of entrenched vocabularies). This imposition of costs upon new or divergent language-games might very well be justified by other considerations than truth or falsity. For instance, Rorty fears what he characterizes as the 'Nietzschean poet' who in service of his or her search for a unique final vocabulary might become 'oblivious to the pain and humiliation' caused to others by the quest.[43] He labels such poets 'mad' and defines them out of protected discourse. Some of these fears are legitimate and such problems might come with the disallowance of the false fact test. But not facing the problem of truth as content and perspective based is not the proper solution. Allowing the fact/truth criterion to make such a distinction in the level of protection afforded, the speech actually will impose a much greater potential limitation of protection to valuable 'experiments in living'. These limitations should not be allowed to be made upon such unconscious distinctions. The exclusion of false statements of fact should be, in this case, viewed as a viewpoint-based distinction and subjected, therefore, to the most strict level of scrutiny. The costs should at the very least be allocated consciously. They should not be allowed to rest where they are by default without being subjected to a reasoned analysis.

4. *The Central Importance of Language: Theories Underlying the Protection of Freedom of Speech*

This emphasis upon the centrality of language provides, ironically enough, a very strong reason for the protection of First Amendment rights even if it is argued that it leaves nothing grounded outside of linguistic usage.

---

43 *CIS*, p. 141.

Rortian linguistic pragmatism emphasizes above all else the importance to individuals of their 'final vocabulary'. It is this use of language that largely makes up what it is to be a person for us. Certainly once the acquisition of language and the sorting out of vocabularies is seen to be so central to the project of having a satisfying life, protection of the domain of speech seems vital. This emphasis upon the centrality of language is more or less compatible with many of the various other theories developed that have historically been thought to underlie the protection of freedom of speech.

4.1. *The Marketplace of Ideas*

As discussed above, Holmes introduces the 'marketplace of ideas' almost at the very beginning of First Amendment jurisprudence. Of course, the Holmsian 'marketplace of ideas' picture of the First Amendment as holding a view of life as an experiment plays right into what Rorty also sees as Millsian experimentalism.[44] Whether Holmes is right to think that this theory is built into the Constitution (as a matter of the history of ideas, I am pretty sure he is not[45]), certainly Rorty's antirealism fits right into a 'marketplace of ideas' picture. Not only does the picture of 'truth' as what wins in the market fit into an antirealist's stance, it is a theory that makes the marketplace concept more coherent and consistent than more substantive ideas of truth would.

It has been argued that both 'the hope that the marketplace of ideas leads to truth, or even to the best or most desirable decision, is implausible'[46] and that '[i]n the long run, true ideas do tend to drive out false ones. The problem is that the short run may be very long'.[47] But both of these worries drop out when the marketplace metaphor is combined with a thoroughgoing antirealism. First of all, in the antirealism version the split seen in the assumption of the first claim between truth and results of the

---

[44] Rorty actually adopts a largely Millsian framework for his project in *CIS*. For example, he states: 'J.S. Mill's suggestion that governments devote themselves to optimizing the balance between leaving people's private lives alone and preventing suffering seems to me pretty much the last word' (*CIS*, p. 63).

[45] The founders were much closer to an 'Enlightenment' picture of discourse as being important in order to clear away prejudices to get at the 'Truth' than might be currently thought. This stance would be much more consistent with the Lockian stance that the founders found so natural with its substantive conceptions of Nature, Property, etc.

[46] C. Edwin Baker, 'Scope of the First Amendment Freedom of Speech', *University of California Law Review* 25 (1978), pp. 974–78.

[47] Harry Wellington, 'On Freedom of Expression', *Yale Law Journal* 88 (1979), p. 1130.

marketplace is unavailable. Whatever the marketplace leads to is 'truth' with a small 't'. For the antirealist, the Platonic picture of a truth standing out to the side of human discourse, waiting there no matter how long people are in error, is clearly misguided. The same picture is driving the second claim—that in the short run false ideas may be arrived at in such a marketplace. This, from the Rortian stance, is also buying into a picture of some type of neutral truth separate from human discourse. Neither of these worries can trouble Rorty. For him, truth is internal to discourse, and therefore the above fears of the marketplace of ideas justification are rendered ineffectual.

A further fear attributed to adoption of the combination of the marketplace justification/characterization and antirealism is that raised by Charles Fried. Fried argues that '[i]f truth is an outcome of social processes, which it is the business of politics to control, the standard of truth can provide no leverage by which to judge politics. But it is just such a point of leverage outside politics that freedom of thought requires to assert itself as a distinct force against the pressures of politics'.[48] But it is hard to see how the conclusion follows from the premises in this argument. The 'marketplace of ideas' theory imposes clear restraints upon government intervention. And Fried's own suggestion of a stance highlighting 'freedom of thought' is certainly compatible with Rorty's Millsian bent. It is very doubtful that 'the denial of objectivity does indeed leave thought vulnerable to political agendas of every sort'.[49] The model of a free exchange of ideas carries with it some powerful limits to legitimate governmental intrusion. This is so whether or not truth is available as an aspect of the justification. The idea of objective truth, on the other hand, as has been discussed above, carries with it substantial dangers of its own.

Furthermore, the Rortian antirealist stance is compatible with other more substantive conceptions of the arrival at truth so long as these conceptions have a strong attachment to procedure. A Rortian would just argue that such conceptions, at their best, do not differ in 'cash value'.[50] That is, he would argue that they result in the same outcome so there shouldn't be any need to argue. Finally, if it is true that '[i]n the

---

48 Charles Fried, 'Perfect Freedom, Perfect Justice', *Boston University Law Review* 78 (1998), p. 731.

49 Fried, 'Perfect Freedom, Perfect Justice', p. 731.

50 This is the way Rorty argues with the picture of deliberative democracy as proposed by Habermas. Rorty claims that while Habermas relies upon Kantian premises and a telos underlying language and Rorty relies upon poetic creation and ironism, since their respective descriptions arrive at the same results there is no real difference between them.

contemporary postmodern world, the notion that there is positive value in the search for truth would strike some as a quaint anachronism... The value that is to be realized is not in the possible attainment of truth, but rather, in the existential value of the search itself'[51] then Rorty's stance is, once again, a helpful one to buy into. It also is clearly compatible with these sentiments. This type of First Amendment justification, when combined with the 'impossibility of complete or immutable truth' actually brings together as compatible such diverse theorists/legal minds as Holmes, Mill, Posner and Rorty.[52]

4.2. *Self-Governance*

The antirealism picture advocated by Rorty is also compatible with the self-governance town meeting picture of the First Amendment as advocated by Meiklejohn.[53] If there is no perfect political organization/solution that can be converged upon once and for all, then democratic deliberation is a plausible solution. Antirealism, much better than hierarchical pictures of truth, can justify just such an appeal to the populace.[54] Rorty's antirealism does, admittedly, take a stance upon justification that is ultimately broader than many of the political speech model advocates would adopt. And this broader stance can be called into question. But this in no way shows any incompatibility of the self-governance model with antirealism. Once again it is actually greatly conducive to such a justification for First Amendment protection.

For instance, Sunstein's advocacy of a 'New Deal for speech' hinges upon a more flexible picture of justification very much in the line of Rortian antirealism.[55] But, in contradistinction to Sunstein's model, which rests upon a conception of 'core' First Amendment speech and political governance to the exclusion of other justifications, the antirealist can both hold to such a justification and allow other reasons greater appreciation than his. Furthermore, the antirealist will not fall into the trap, which

---

[51] William Marshall, 'In Defense of the Search for Truth as a First Amendment Justification', *Georgia Law Review* 30 (1995), pp. 2–5.

[52] Michel Rosenfeld, 'Pragmatism, Pluralism and Legal Interpretation: Posner's and Rorty's Justice Without Metaphysics Meets Hate Speech', *Cardozo Law Review* 18 (1996), p. 134.

[53] See Alexander Meiklejohn, *Free Speech and Its Relation to Self Government* (New York: Harper, 1948).

[54] This might be the proper place to reference Plato's *Republic* where it is shown very clearly what a belief that the truth has been found can justify when related to the populous.

[55] C.R. Sunstein, *Democracy and the Problem of Free Speech* (New York: Free Press, 1993).

Sunstein apparently does, of having an overly clear and relatively uncriticized baseline notion of what the legitimate boundary of the political area is. It is just this sort of essentialism that antirealists fear the most.[56]

A theory that adopted a less procedural conception of truth might find that a correct end-point had been arrived at where more deliberation is unnecessary. It, furthermore, might justify much stronger procedural safeguards for such deliberation than an unanalyzed adherence to truth as an unproblematic concept. An antirealist stance cannot be taken to allow for such a conclusion—for more deliberation is always necessary and desirable. Not only is the adoption of Rortian antirealism compatible with self-governance aims, it would even help strengthen the justification for broad protection under such an aim.

4.3. *Self-Fulfillment and Autonomy*

If the protection of free speech 'derives from the notion of self-respect that comes from a mature person's full and untrammeled exercise of capacities central to human rationality'[57] then seeing the First Amendment as aimed at protection of emerging alternative final vocabularies might just fit the bill perfectly. Rorty's proposal is centered upon self-fulfillment and autonomy interests so it will clearly be consistent with other stances advocating this as its central aim. If, for instance, it is argued that a fuller picture of autonomy interests should focus 'not only on freedom from governmental interference but also on private citizens' relationships with each other',[58] the antirealist's focus upon discourse and language can fully respond. If, as an alternative, it is argued that a Michelman/Radin 'personhood' consideration[59] should be central to First Amendment jurisprudence, Rorty's stance is equally compatible and capable of encompassing such an aim. Certainly it is important as a consideration and central to Rorty's picture. Autonomy interests are easily separated from any truth-based concepts such as authenticity. And this separation, far from weakening these

---

56 Dare I accuse Sunstein of some 'Lochneristic' baseline assumptions?

57 Davis Richards, 'Free Speech and Obscenity Law: Toward a Moral Theory of the First Amendment', *University of Pennsylvania Law Review* 123 (1974), p. 62.

58 Christina Wells, 'Reinvigorating Autonomy: Freedom and Responsibility in the Supreme Court's First Amendment Jurisprudence', *Harvard Civil Rights—Civil Liberties Law Review* 32 (1997), pp. 163–69.

59 Frank Michelman, 'Private Personal but not Split: Radin Versus Rorty', *Southern California Law Review* 63 (1990), p. 1795. While at the time this article was written Rorty might have subscribed to a big split between the personal and the public, I believe his latest book, *Achieving Our Country* (see note 17, above), rightly can be read as discarding this distinction for a more pragmatic and piecemeal approach to the issue.

interests, greatly strengthens their import and the protection needed to further the discourse necessary for their fulfillment.

The Rortian stance brings strong reasons for protecting speech with compatibility among all three justifications investigated above. It also combines them in a manner very similar to a position that has been labeled the 'autonomy/distrust model'.[60] Under this model there is combined an emphasis upon individual autonomy with a 'deep-seated distrust of governmental efforts to regulate public debate'.[61] This stance combines the realization of the vital importance of autonomy interests with a broader picture of necessary protection than those of the self-governance model might allow in a manner that is also consistent with the marketplace of ideas metaphor. This model, once again, does not rely upon truth as a concept necessary for justification of First Amendment protection. All three dominant rationales can be fit within the antirealist framework with minimal loss. And all three actually gain power from the Rortian emphasis upon the importance of discourse and the contingency of all resting points.

Conclusion

In this paper I have been concerned with the combination of free speech issues and Rortian antirealism. My main aim has been to outline what implications antirealism has for First Amendment protection of speech as well as its compatibility with the prevailing justifications for such protection.

Rorty describes a type of antirealism that eliminates the hope of a Platonic-like all-encompassing picture of the world. If there is no 'language that nature speaks', Rorty argues, we should just ensure a continuing discourse among human beings aimed at spinning out more satisfying linguistic worlds. Truth is to be discarded as an unworkable and undesirable concept. All that is left is continuing redescription. At the same time, language is emphasized because language and life are seen to be inseparably intertwined. Our final vocabulary, it turns out, is the central constituent of our self. Protection of alternative forms of discourse becomes vital, therefore, for our search for a satisfying self-image and autonomous activity in general.

---

60 Geoffrey Stone, 'Autonomy and Distrust', *University of Colorado Law Review* 64 (1993), p. 1171.

61 Stone, 'Autonomy and Distrust', p. 1171.

The elimination of truth would have minimal effect upon some current areas of First Amendment jurisprudence, for example obscenity regulations.[62] It would have some effect upon other areas such as commercial speech. And it was seen to entail large changes in standards and results in some areas such as regulation and awards for libel damages. Though changes might be required in some areas it seems as if the law could do without the concept of truth. The conclusion that the central clear and present danger test actually has no recourse to truth at all underscores that ability of disposing of such a concept if this was necessary. The question raised because of this, of course, is why not leave well enough alone? Why not just let 'truth' do the somewhat marginal work it has been doing in First Amendment law?

This question led into a discussion of why antirealists such as Rorty find the concept of truth so objectionable. From a discussion of the 'intramundane' source of truth criteria, the conclusion was reached that all claims of truth or fact are reliant upon, and the result of, the language-game they are embedded within (all claims of truth are intramundane). Once the 'myth of the given' is seen as a myth, the myth of the neutral fact or neutral truth becomes very problematic. This conclusion then has large implications for the mostly non-critical use that the Supreme Court puts the truth or falsity test to. This distinction has been used by the Court to separate speech worthy of protection from that which can be regulated without fear of constitutional implications. But if appeals to truth are seen to be just appeals to the internal criterion of the dominant language-game, any distinction based upon the falsity of a factual statement is just a circular claim without any unquestionable basis. The allowance of regulation of false statements of fact is, from the antirealist perspective, actually a type of viewpoint-based restriction. This has large implications for First Amendment policy because viewpoint-based restrictions are highly suspect and almost universally struck down as contrary to the Constitution. If the antirealist stance is accepted, then the Supreme Court has imposed a highly constrictive stance upon freedom of speech that entrenches dominant final vocabularies over emerging alternatives or less popular existing

---

62 Though this conclusion might appear to be slightly more questionable in light of the Supreme Court's decision in *Ashcroft v. Free Speech Coalition*, 535 US 234 (2002), where the Court found a distinction between 'virtual child pornography' which is not based upon actual models and that which is. But it is interesting that in the Court's reasoning, arguments about potential harm seems to carry more weight than any discussion of truth. Further, if another stance had been adopted, say of harm, much of the tortured and surreal reasoning of the decision might have been avoided.

language-games.[63] Ultimately, the antirealist will argue that allowing the fact/truth criterion to make such distinctions in the level of speech protection afforded will impose unacceptable limitations on potentially valuable experiments in living.

Finally, Rortian antirealism was shown to be compatible with the various underlying theories of justification propounded under the philosophy of free speech. Not only does the importance accorded to our final vocabulary justify the 'marketplace of ideas' picture, but it also encourages strong protection in order to foster debate in ways parallel to the self-government as well as to the personal autonomy models. It results in a theory very similar to what has been called the autonomy/distrust model that combines an emphasis upon individual autonomy with a distrust of governmental efforts to regulate public debate. The antirealist just distrusts the government's ability to sort out speech on the basis of true/false facts. Once the intra-mundane nature of truth is faced, such a distinction just entrenches the currently prevailing viewpoint to the exclusion of others. As all other governmental regulations based upon viewpoint regulation on the basis of falsity are considered highly suspicious given the Rortian perspective, so should those based upon 'truth'. To put it in constitutional terms, 'truth' as a criteria used as means to regulate speech is not narrowly enough tailored.

On a less ambitious level, which I am more disposed to adopt myself, even if the concept of 'truth' is to be retained and antirealism itself is to be looked upon with a skeptical eye, retention of distinctions based upon truth should not be allowed to be combined with a non-critical or foundational stance towards its continuing use in the area of First Amendment jurisprudence. Speech in public and, using a more specific example, in juridical arenas, is clearly one activity where truth claims are disputed; descriptions of the world are put into question and reconstructed. Because of this, a suspicious and critical response to shutting down discourse on the basis of one privileged take on truth, no matter how seemingly correct and concrete, seems more than justified.

[63] A follower of Mill would see this result as grounds for a conclusion that the strongest possible protection should be afforded false statements of fact because they are really better seen as just unpopular stances.

IS THERE A RIGHT TO POLYGAMY? MARRIAGE, EQUALITY AND SUBSIDIZING FAMILIES IN LIBERAL PUBLIC JUSTIFICATION

Andrew F. March

Abstract

This paper argues that the four most plausible arguments compatible with public reason for an outright legal ban on all forms of polygamy are unvictorious. I consider the types of arguments political liberals would have to insist on, and precisely how strongly, in order for a general prohibition against polygamy to be justified, while also considering what general attitude towards "marriage" and legal recognition of the right to marry are most consistent with political liberalism. I argue that a liberal state should get out of the "marriage business" by leveling down to a universal status of "civil union" neutral as to the gender and affective purpose of domestic partnerships. I then refute what I regard as the four most plausible rational objections to offering this civil union status to multi-member domestic partnerships. The most common objection to polygamy is on grounds of gender equality, more specifically, female equality. But advancing this argument forcefully often involves neglecting the tendency of political liberalism (by whatever name it goes in contemporary, complex, multicultural societies) to tolerate a certain amount of inequality in private, within the bounds of robust and meaningful freedoms of choice and exit. Properly understood, polygamy involves no inherent statement about the essential inferiority of women, and certainly not more than many other existing practices and institutions (including many expressions of the main monotheistic religions) which political liberals regard as tolerable, even reasonable. Arguments from the welfare of children, fairness in the spousal market, and the abuse of family subsidies are also considered and found insufficient for excluding polygamy.

Keywords

polygamy, political liberalism, marriage, justification

1. *Introduction: The Slippery Slope and the Slide from Same-Sex Marriage to Polygamy*

If a state with liberal political and justificatory commitments extends recognition and benefits of various kinds to persons forming families, what qualifications may such a state place on the right to access to those benefits?

Proponents of same-sex marriage or civil unions often go to great lengths to argue that same-sex marriage is not susceptible to the slippery slope argument,[1] which holds that overturning discriminatory laws against homosexuals implies allowing "bigamy, adult incest, prostitution, masturbation, adultery, fornication, bestiality, and obscenity."[2] I believe that they are right to take on the slippery slope argument in public and in the context of the American legal system, particularly the assumptions that allowing same-sex marriage can only be a function of moral relativism or turpitude – the unwillingness to make any moral judgments or the failure to make the right ones. However, *must* we resist any further movement down the slippery slope? Why should we stop at same-sex marriage? Why can't we allow polygamy? Or, indeed, marriage between close blood relatives?[3] Just why should the liberal state be in the business of deciding which forms of domestic partnerships are permissible and eligible for recognition? More importantly: what resources do persons with liberal political and justificatory commitments have to answer these questions *in public*, and what constraints do those commitments place on them?

I will make two assumptions for the purposes of this paper. The first is the political and justificatory terrain of some form of *political* or otherwise *non-perfectionist* liberalism. The assumption is that we are considering the resources and limitations of a community of persons who accept

[1] See, e.g., Maura I. Strassberg, "Distinctions of Form or Substance: Monogamy, Polygamy and Same-Sex Marriage," *North Carolina Law Review*, 75 (1997): 1501–1624; James M. Donovan, "Rock-Salting the Slippery Slope: Why Same-Sex Marriage is Not a Commitment to Polygamous Marriage," *Northern Kentucky Law Review*, 29: 3 (2002): 521–590 and Ruth K. Khalsa, "Polygamy as a Red Herring in the Same-Sex Marriage Debate," *Duke Law Journal* 54 (2004–2005): 1665–1693.

[2] LAWRENCE V. TEXAS (02–102) 539 U.S. 558 (2003), Antonin Scalia dissenting, June 26, 2003. Scalia here confusingly combines practices which are presently illegal with ones presently legal in his dissent to a decision which rendered unconstitutional state laws criminalizing sodomy.

[3] I address the question of incestuous unions in Andrew F. March, "Marriage, Sex and Future Persons in Liberal Public Justification: Is There a Right to Incest?" *Journal of Applied Philosophy*, Vol. 27, No. 1, 2010, pp. 39–58.

moral pluralism (if not a specific doctrine like the "burdens of judgment"), some priority for individual freedom, and the obligation to justify public coercion and exclusion in terms accessible and fair to all members of morally and culturally diverse society. The second is that it is justified for a liberal state to recognize some forms of domestic partnerships or families in the first place. It is, of course, possible to imagine the argument that the liberal state gets out of the marriage business by getting out of it entirely – by extending no recognition or positive rights to families whatsoever beyond negative non-interference rights. However, I am interested in the dilemma of a society broadly like existing liberal ones which is committed both to recognizing (and/or subsidizing) families and also to justificatory neutrality (expressed in American constitutional legal terms as the requirement of providing a "rational basis" for unequal treatment).

It seems to me, at least as far as polygamy is concerned, that the conservatives are right, but this is in fact only to say that for many (not all) of the good reasons why same-sex marriage should be legal, so should polygamy.[4] However, as the comparison to same-sex marriage reveals, there are in fact two separate questions at stake. First: should de facto polygamous relationships or family arrangements (continue to) be criminalized even when the adult persons involved do not seek any recognition or subsidy from the state? Second: must a liberal political community which tolerates such de facto relationships also extend to them formal legal recognition as "marriages" and any of the social benefits which are attached to that recognition?

Answering "no" to both questions is certainly coherent. It is not difficult to argue that where there is no evidence of coercion or abuse the state

---

[4] For the purposes of this paper I am defining "polygamy" as a formal intimate relationship involving more than two persons. Thus, where I use "polygamy" it can be assumed that I am addressing all forms of polyamory or group marriage. "Polygamy" is neutral as to the gender of the participants and it is precisely the point of this paper to question whether a liberal state needs to involve itself in the specific affective, emotional and symbolic meaning of domestic life. Treating "polygamy" at this point as the larger set which includes all other forms of polyamory does not imply that the liberal state must in the end endorse this precise term at the expense of other terms which are adopted in order to avoid the hierarchical and inegalitarian associations with "polygamy." In fact, I will argue that a liberal state should avoid, to the extent possible, monopolizing affective terminology, including "marriage" itself. However, the advantage to referring to "polygamy" is that it is certain forms of domestic life which fall under the term "polygamy" which pose the greatest normative challenge. We are no closer to knowing what to do about more challenging forms of polygamy such as polygyny when we seek to defend a strictly egalitarian, non-hierarchical form of polyamory. However, if we can justify a form of group marriage which implicitly allows for the possibility of traditional forms of polygyny then it is presumed that more egalitarian forms of polyamory are also justified.

should not actively interfere with families merely because multiple adults have pronounced themselves "married," but also that there is no prima facie obligation to publicly recognize these unions as "marriages" and to extend to them social benefits. Excluding polygamous relationships from the public status of marriage could be justified on a variety of public policy grounds, for example that recognition would result in numerous foreseeable and unforeseeable legal-administrative complications and that exclusionary laws are needed as a legal device to combat instances where child abuse or coercion is suspected but hard to prove. Liberal theorists could also advance a "reasonable democratic authority" argument that the social institution of marriage is not a primary good but rather something which is legitimately left to a democratic society to define so long as other basic rights and freedoms are respected.

Furthermore, in the case of polygamy we find absent many of the considerations which make the above democratic authority argument so unappealing for many liberals in the case of same-sex marriage. In that case, the state's mere tolerance of homosexual acts and lifestyles while denying public recognition through extending the right of forming legal unions is a form of stigmatization which marks homosexuals as less than equal and often does so on the basis of deeply controversial comprehensive reasoning about morality and the good. An argument compatible with public reasoning could be made, however, that polygamous lifestyles do not make the same demands on our conscience for recognition and thus that decriminalizing polygamy in private while failing to recognize plural marriages limitlessly does not represent a form of stigmatization, disrespect or second-class status. Such an argument might take the following form.

2. *A Case for the Disanalogy between Same-Sex Marriage and Polygamy*

Might a liberal society be entitled to treat polygamous partnerships as a form of "expensive taste," the way that it treats religious commitments? If the logic behind recognizing (and possibly subsidizing) marriage is that forming *a* family is an inherent good both for the parties involved and for the wider society, as well as something a reasonable psychology (or even a reasonable anthropology) expects most people to desire, then this is not tantamount to saying that every choice free individuals make in relation to their conception of family life is entitled to positive recognition. By analogy, recognizing a right to education at public expense is not a right to limitless education nor is a right to a housing subsidy or tax credit a right to the same for multiple properties. Because persons inclined to polygamous relationships *can* form them and enjoy legal protection, failing to formally recognize them *as marriages* is not the same act of disrespect or non-recognition in the way that creating different legal categories for heterosexuals and homosexuals is. Failing to recognize them limitlessly is not an act of disrespect because the reason for not doing so has nothing at all to do with the value or morality of forming polygamous relationships, any more than the failure to subsidize expensive tastes involves a condemnation of all expensive tastes as inherently worthless or immoral.

Furthermore, part of what troubles us about the lack of recognition of homosexuals in the case of denial of marriage rights is that we do not today understand homosexuality as a taste at all, if part of what is meant by "taste" is that it is semi-voluntary, cultivated or transitive (i.e., that it could be satisfied by other, less costly, habits such as heterosexuality). We know homosexuality to be innate and repression of it to be extremely costly in psychological and emotional terms, not comparable at all to the frustration of not being able to act on all of one's expensive tastes. Thus, denial of equal rights and status in this case is troubling for reasons more profound than a mere presumption of freedom. Our present understanding inclines towards a view of homosexuality as an irreducible part of some persons' very selfhood; failure to recognize it is thus much closer to fundamental disrespect of another *tout court* than it is a failure to accommodate someone's expensive taste.

Could the same be said about polygamy? It is possible that some of the same elements of innateness are present, as they are at some level in all drives, inclinations and tastes, but perhaps the same elements of particularity are not. It is perfectly plausible to assume that an inclination toward polygamy can be rooted in natural, non-chosen, non-cultivated traits. Evolutionary psychology would certainly support something like this. In fact, it seems plain that *monogamy* is not so much an innate inclination, the natural state of things, as a social institution to which humans have to accommodate themselves with some difficulty and at some cost. So polygamy, perhaps, is not an arbitrary, self-indulgent expensive taste but rather something with a natural basis.

But this claim may prove too much for the purposes of sorting out our inclinations about rights and recognition. For whereas the point about homo-sexuality is that it is not only natural but *particular* to certain humans (thus giving rise to the need for *recognition* on the part of the majority), the case for polygamy as natural reveals it to be more along the lines of an appetite or *universal* inclination, like the need for sex, comfort or intimacy itself. This understanding, if something roughly like it is accurate, gives strong reasons for tolerating and finding a place for it in society, but simultaneously dilutes the case for recognition of it as a part of someone's personhood or identity since the claim is essentially that it is latent or potential in all humans. What is universal may ground claims for allowance, provision or tolerance, but not for recognition by others. Thus, we understand the inclination toward polygamy as the inclination towards certain human interests and appetites found in other activities as well. It is no more in need of specific recognition than the pursuit of wealth, power, comfort or companionship.

So something like the preceding would be a liberal case for legalizing the practice of polygamy but not necessarily extending the legally recognized status of "marriage" to polygamous relationships. Is there a case, however, for extending the legally recognized status of "marriage" to polygamous relationships and how strong is it?

3. *The Place of Religious Free Practice and Cultural Sovereignty Arguments*

Let me begin by disposing of a few arguments, or variations on one big argument, which I am not using to defend the permissibility of polygamy and/or extension of marriage rights.

These arguments might go under the name of "religious freedom" or perhaps under the banner of "multiculturalism" or cultural relativism.[5]

[5] Most treatments of the problem of polygamy focus on it within the context of religious pluralism or multiculturalism. From the vast literature on multiculturalism, for discussions of polygamy see, for example, Amy Gutmann, "The Challenge of Multiculturalism in Political Ethics," *Philosophy and Public Affairs* 22: 3 (1993): 171–206, Susan Moller Okin, *Is Multicul-turalism Bad for Women?* (Princeton: Princeton University Press, 1999), and Sarah Song, *Justice, Gender, and the Politics of Multiculturalism* (Cambridge: Cambridge University Press, 2007). Bhikhu Parekh considers the case for polygyny and polygamy separately in the context of his broadly sympathetic defense of multiculturalism. He argues that polygyny "violates the principle of the equality of the sexes and has unfortunate consequences, [while] so far as polygamy is concerned, the case is not so conclusive." But since as practiced today, polygamy is associated with unacceptable inegalitarian consequences, "we are right to continue to disallow it." (Parekh, *Rethinking Multiculturalism: Cultural Diversity and Political Theory* (Cambridge, MA: Harvard University Press, 2000, p. 292.) Thom Brooks advances a similar argument in "The Problem with Polygamy," *Philosophical Topics*, Vol. 37, No. 2, pp. 109–122 (2009).

The first would say that citizens have the right to practice their religion and the state intervening to restrict this is an intolerable intrusion on this right. Here what is invoked as valuable is religion itself; either religion is something so valuable in its own right that the state should interfere with it as little as possible, or the *practice* of religion is so valuable, precious, and intimate to the persons involved that the state oppresses them when it stops them from doing what their faith commands.[6] The second would say that we have a moral commitment to celebrate the variety of cultures in the world, that diversity is good per se, that "we" have no right to pass moral judgment on "them" or that failing to make generous cultural accommodations runs the risk of perpetuating domination and oppression of cultural minorities. Who are we to say that some other group's way of living is wrong?[7] But they are really the same argument. If a community wants to uphold its own standards of morality and virtue, then others supposedly have no independent or freestanding intellectual or moral resources to invoke against tolerating those standards.

Both arguments, though, are woefully incomplete for persons with the political or non-perfectionist liberal commitments I am assuming.

---

6 Of course in the United States the question is not so much one of philosophical justification but of a particular legal tradition of recognizing the free practice of religion as a specific right. On the treatment of polygamy as a problem for American constitutional guarantees of religious freedom, see Clark B. Lombardi, "Nineteenth-century Free Exercise Jurisprudence and the Challenge of Polygamy," *Oregon Law Review* 85 (2007): 100–175; Joseph Bozzuti, "The Constitutionality of Polygamy Prohibitions after *Lawrence v. Texas*: Is Scalia a Punchline or a Prophet?" *The Catholic Lawyer* 43 (2004): 409–442; Alyssa Rower, "The Legality of Polygamy: Using the Due Process Clause of the Fourteenth Amendment," *Family Law Quarterly* 38 (2005): 711–731; Michael G. Myers, "Polygamist Eye for the Monogamist Guy: Homosexual Sodomy ... Gay Marriage ... Is Polygamy Next?" *Houston Law Review* 42 (2005–6): 1451–1486; David L. Chambers, "Polygamy and Same-Sex Marriage," *Hofstra Law Review* 26 (1997): 53–83; Elizabeth Larcano, "A 'Pink' Herring: The Prospect of Polygamy Following the Legalization of Same Sex Marriage," *Connecticut Law Review* 38 (2006): 1065–1111. Martha Nussbaum has recently contributed to the polygamy debate, again through the lens of religious freedom and Mormonism and has raised doubts about a convincing rational basis or "compelling state interest" against the practice, should the law guarantee sex equality. (Nussbaum, *Liberty of Conscience: In Defense of America's Tradition of Religious Equality* (New York: Basic Books, 2008), pp. 197–8.)

7 Although this attitude amongst liberals is older than the multicultural turn. In *On Liberty*, J.S. Mill addressed Mormon polygamy not as a form of autonomous experimentation, but as an oppressive practice for women. Yet, he insisted that no community was entitled to carry out a "*civilizade* ... to force another to be civilized." (J.S. Mill, *On Liberty*, in *On Liberty and Other Essays*, John Gray, ed. (Oxford: Oxford University Press, 1991), p. 102.) On Mill's views on polygamy and their insufficiency for a contemporary liberal, pluralist, and feminist approach to illiberal religious communities, see Bruce Baum, "Feminism, Liberalism and Cultural Pluralism: JS Mill on Mormon Polygyny," *Journal of Political Philosophy* 5:3 (1997): 230–253.

The rights to free practice (religious or cultural) in a liberal democracy are obviously not absolute. They are limited primarily for two reasons: free practice cannot involve placing unreasonable burdens on other citizens (the Amish can't endanger the lives of other road users by refusing to put reflective triangles on their buggies) and it cannot involve depriving members of religious or cultural groups of their civil or human rights (what William Galston likes to refer to as the "no free exercise for Aztecs" principle[8] – live human sacrifice is not protected by a liberal state no matter how strong the religious beliefs in question). Furthermore it is not clear that the reason why a liberal democracy protects religious or cultural freedom to the extent that it does has anything to do with the special and inherent authority of religion or culture. Liberals may certainly recognize that religion and culture are valuable (they may even have one or both of them). But if they are protected it is because individual choice and autonomy to pursue a conception of the good life are protected, not some collective entity or particular good like "religion" or "culture." The point is that there is very little force in the following argument: "You are right that the free practice of my religion or culture requires unequal rights and duties for various members of my community and that members of our community do not have the freedoms that you secular liberals prize. But in preventing us from practicing our religion or culture, even to 'protect our vulnerable members' as you love to say, you are oppressing us no matter what the reason." Liberalism does not deny that religion and culture are valuable, but it has no need for their inherent value one way or another: either something is permissible because it involves no unreasonable burdens on others or it is a violation of someone's civil rights *no matter how strong the religious or cultural justification.*

Perhaps these comments do not prove the case against religious freedom and cultural sovereignty arguments for polygamy or other similarly controversial practices.[9] Perhaps a religious rationale for polygamy helps explain why there might be an argument from *recognition* for polygamous marriage, contrary to my earlier argument distinguishing polygamy from homosexuality. A religious or cultural rationale for polygamy might

---

[8] William Galston, *Liberal Pluralism* (Cambridge: Cambridge University Press, 2002), p. 23.

[9] See Sarah Song, *Justice, Gender, and the Politics of Multiculturalism*, Ch. 6, especially pp. 160–164 for an argument for qualified recognition of Mormon polygamy based on multicultural considerations.

help ground the *particularity* which I suggested gives rise to demands for recognition. But as I am not arguing against the permissibility of polygamy and other similar practices I do not have to prove that case. Rather, I am merely *declining* to argue for the permissibility of polygamy and other similar practices on the basis of religious freedom and cultural sovereignty arguments because I feel they are not necessary for it, although it is also the case that I believe that they are not sufficient for it either. In fact, what I will argue for the case of polygamy is that the presence of religious or cultural arguments for the practices may actually count both for and against them.

4. *Should the Liberal State Get Out of the "Marriage" Business? Leveling Down to a Universal Civil Union Status*[10]

I would like to begin by suggesting that asking whether each non-traditional form of domestic partnership has a right to be recognized as "marriage" is an arbitrary way of approaching the relationship between the liberal state and domestic partnerships. Given the commitments of political and non-perfectionist forms of liberalism, I believe that the most justifiable policy on liberal grounds is not the institution of "marriage" increasingly open to new constituent relationships but rather a universal "civil union" status which fulfills the social and moral aims behind recognizing and subsidizing the family[11] but is entirely neutral not only to the gender or even to the numbers of the partners, but also to the affective and emotional content of domestic life and the purposes behind contracting domestic partnerships. I believe that this move to a more neutral language has an intuitive appeal for political liberals. However, I will introduce here a specific positive argument for this move grounded in political liberalism's aim of attenuating social conflict by removing unnecessary philosophical, religious, and linguistic obstacles.

The strongest argument for recognizing same-sex *marriage* beyond mere civil unions when the state offers "marriage" to heterosexual couples is

---

10 Much of this section follows what I write in "What Lies Beyond Same-Sex Marriage?"

11 I am not primarily concerned in this paper with what precise goods and advantages ought to be attached to "civil union" status. It is conceivable that many of the legal rights which spouses confer on one another could be achieved through other legal-administrative devices, and that many of the protections afforded the more materially dependent and otherwise vulnerable members of marriages could be guaranteed whether or not the parties are legally registered as a civil union.

the argument from equality and recognition. The state treats homosexuals unfairly when it denies them access to the same social goods and benefits open to heterosexual couples and fails to treat them fully as equals when it offers them a different public status, even one with the identical package of objective goods and benefits. In fact, conferring a "civil union" status short of marriage (when the latter is available to heterosexuals) publicly marks the unwillingness to extend to homosexuals recognition of them as equal to heterosexuals and is thus a form of stigmatization. Therefore, the only just policy is to level *up* all the way to full marriage rights.

Well, another way of handling the problem of recognition and status is to level *down*.[12] Why not treat "marriage" the way we treat religion: something protected and possibly subsidized in moderate ways by the state but which the state is not in the business of defining, regulating, honoring or distributing other than for reasons of individual rights and legitimate public interests? Religion is left to persons and communities to define and defend. Questions of fairness or recognition *between conceptions of religiosity* arise in this arrangement only rarely and at the margins. Of course, questions of secular versus religious authority arise all the time and the state's authority affects different religions differently depending on their traditional doctrines and practices, but rarely is the question merely the state's obligation to recognize a minority religion *as a religion*[13] but rather the state's right to trump religion for legitimate public reasons. Similarly, then, if *all the state offered to anyone* was legal status as a civil union without making any statement on the true or best definition of

[12] The dilemma of recognition is, of course, one of the areas (another being competitions) identified by Parfit, Scanlon and others as when it is appropriate to level down as part of our commitment to equality, as opposed to priority or welfare. For example, given the choice between giving one of two siblings a gift or privilege and giving it to neither of them, we are strongly inclined to choose the latter so as to avoid favoritism. (See Derek Parfit, "Equality and Priority," *Ratio* 10 (1997), pp. 202–221 and T.M. Scanlon, "The Diversity of Objections to Inequality," in *The Difficulty of Tolerance* (Cambridge: Cambridge University Press, 2003), pp. 202–218.)

[13] Although this is not unheard of. Scientology's claim to religious status has been questioned in various European countries, including in an ongoing fraud trial in France. (See Angelique Chrisafis, "Church of Scientology faces fraud trial in France," *The Guardian*, September 9, 2008.) There was also a controversy in Amsterdam in 1988 when a "Church of Satan" was deemed to be an ordinary brothel and forced to pay taxes on its earnings. Genuine Satanists, on the other hand, were recognized by the Royal Navy for the first time in 2004, thus earning the privileges of performing Satanic rituals aboard ship and to have a non-Christian Church of Satan funeral should they be killed in action. (http://news.bbc.co.uk/2/hi/uk_news/3948329.stm.)

"marriage," then there could be no complaint of unfairness or disrespect by those offered a status less than "marriage."

Furthermore, removing the symbolic good of the word "marriage" from the authority of the state may also appeal to conservatives or the religious. At least part of what troubles them about same-sex marriage (and certainly polygamy and incestuous marriage as well) is precisely the collective, public bestowal of recognition on homosexual relationships as *the same thing* as heterosexual ones. Leveling down, which is essentially the privatization of the commodity of "marriage" as an emotionally and symbolically invested concept, solves this problem. This symbolic commodity can now be the monopoly of every group which wants it. The state doesn't baptize, so why should it "marry"? More accurately, the state doesn't say who can be baptized, why should it say who can be "married"? Conservatives and the religious presently opposed to same-sex marriage can keep the institution of "marriage" and merely have to suffer the knowledge that homosexuals can confer social and economic benefits on one another by availing themselves of the public civil union status.[14] And if neither are satisfied by this (i.e., same-sex marriage advocates still want the official bestowal by the state of "marriage" as an act of public recognition and same-sex marriage opponents still want to monopolize decision-making of those to whom the state extends certain social goods and legally recognized domestic status), then liberals can with a good conscience claim that they are both demanding something to which they are not necessarily entitled.[15]

Thus, the question for this paper becomes whether polygamous relationships ought to be eligible for such a proposed universal civil union status or whether there are victorious public reasons for making a principled distinction between two-member heterosexual and homosexual unions on the one hand and multi-member unions on the other.

---

[14] For a discussion of the same-sex marriage controversy in America which takes seriously the costs of altering the public meaning of the concept (such as "marriage"), see Andrew Stivers and Andrew Valls, "Same-sex Marriage and the Regulation of Language," *Politics Philosophy Economics* 6:2 (2007): 237–253. My proposal also takes seriously the dilemma discussed by Stivers and Valls, but differs from theirs by proposing to remove the linguistic controversy from the hands of the state entirely.

[15] A similar proposal for disestablishing marriage can be found in Tamara Metz, "The Liberal Case for Disestablishing Marriage," *Contemporary Political Theory* 6 (2007): 196–217. Metz's concern, however, is with the liberal concerns for fairness and equality in the private sphere and with our positive reasons for valuing marriage (she thus calls for replacing marriage with an "intimate caregiving union status"). Metz agrees that polygamy would be legal under her scheme (although she does not consider at length any specific arguments related to it).

5. *The Presumption of Permissibility: Starting from the Bottom of the Slope*

My argument for allowing multi-member partnerships to access this civil union status will largely proceed on negative terms, that is, by considering acceptable arguments for stopping the slide down the slippery slope beyond same-sex civil unions and excluding polygamous unions.[16] In a politically liberal society there must be a presumption of permissibility and the burden of justification is on those who would proscribe or who would establish exclusionary grounds for access to a particular good. Once we accept the commitments of justificatory liberalism the emphasis shifts to the reasons which would count as legitimate ones for excluding some persons from access to a good otherwise extended to all citizens.[17] Thus, all of the same commitments which condemn prohibitions on same-sex marriage are presumed applicable to all other cases until shown otherwise. In addition to concerns about arguments from existing cultural practices or religious morality, justification cannot be a rationalization of brute disgust. The less refined feeling that something "is just wrong" but which is based on no deeper reflection than the brute disgust at something alien ought to raise flags for political or justificatory liberals.[18] Sometimes moral "beliefs" really go no deeper than the disgust or revulsion at the alien. The fact that many moral judgments at heart rest on nothing more than a feeling that something – miscegenation or homosexuality, say – disgust us should put us on guard; perhaps even liberals oppose practices (polygamy, incest, Islamic veiling, clitoridectomy) for which they believe they have reasons or rational distinctions whereas in

[16] That is, I accept the distinction advanced by Dworkin between goal-based and rights-based defenses of rights and freedoms, and am obviously concerned about the answer to my question from within the latter strategy. (Ronald Dworkin, "Is There a Right to Pornography?" *Oxford Journal of Legal Studies* 1:2 (1981): 177–212.)

[17] Gerald Gaus refers to this as the core liberal principle (L): "Imposition on others requires justification; unjustified impositions are unjust. ... The basic idea is that freedom to live one's own life as one chooses is the benchmark or presumption; departures from that condition – where you demand that another live her life according to your judgments – require additional justification. And if these demands cannot be justified, then we are committed to tolerating these other ways of living." (Gerald F. Gaus, *Justificatory Liberalism: An Essay on Epistemology and Political Theory* (Oxford: Oxford University Press, 1996), p. 165.)

[18] For the lengthiest treatment of this problem, see Martha C. Nussbaum, *Hiding from Humanity: Disgust, Shame, and the Law* (Princeton: Princeton University Press, 2004) and the symposium on this book in *Journal of Applied Philosophy*, Vol. 25, No. 4, with contributions by William Charlton, John Haldane, David Archard, Thom Brooks and a reply by Nussbaum.

fact they are expressing the same disgust at the unfamiliar which rests at the heart of much opposition to same-sex marriage.[19]

Thus, in the liberal state the question must be "Does this practice intrinsically involve the violation of the rights of someone else or unfair burdens on the wider society?" In other words, the argument for the permissibility of polygamous unions can only proceed by way of an evaluation of the strength of arguments against them. So let us say that there is a *presumption* in favor of the permissibility of polygamy, like the presumption in favor of same-sex marriage.[20] What anti-polygamists have to show is that polygamy is a practice – like clitoridectomy, domestic violence, depriving children of health care, and forced marriage – which is either an *intrinsic* violation of the equal civil or human rights of those involved or an unreasonable burden on others. I believe that there are four main plausible arguments against legalizing polygamy which are compatible with, or at the boundaries of compatibility with, the form of public reason I am assuming in this paper. They are the arguments from (1) female autonomy, (2) damage to children, (3) fairness in the marital market, and (4) the unfair burdening of society.

5.1. *Female Autonomy*

Of course, polygamy in a liberal state would have to be very different from what some Muslims or Mormons presently have in mind. It would have to be regulated through civil law, as opposed to a fully autonomous religious law. Where there are concerns about domination, coercion or child abuse, there would have to be strict measures to ensure that these relationships are voluntary in a fairly robust sense. (Although I think this is not inherently more challenging than the existing debate over religious freedom and rights of exit in illiberal communities. In fact, in most cases it would probably be the *same* debate since there is no reason to believe that

---

19 There is, of course, much psychological research on disgust and the rationalization of moral judgment. See, in particular, Jonathan Haidt, Paul Rozin, Clark McCauley and Sumio Imada, "Body, Psyche, and Culture: The Relationship of Disgust to Morality," *Psychology and Developing Societies* 9:1 (1997), pp. 107–131.

20 Indeed, liberal political theorists have in principle been open to the idea that polygamy could be compatible with justice and equality in certain conditions. See, for example, Gutmann, "The Challenge of Multiculturalism in Political Ethics": "[W]ere we seriously to consider the case against enforced monogamy, as presented by reasonable people who believe in polygamy (for both sexes) .... [p]erhaps we would conclude that the case for state-enforced monogamy is compelling, perhaps not, but our convictions on this score would be better justified were we actually confronted with the case for legalization of polygamy by reasonable proponents of the practice" (204).

patriarchal communities which would gladly avail themselves of polygamy rights are any less patriarchal *now* in the absence of those rights.) And polygamy would have to be defined in neutral terms, which means foremost that it is open to women marrying many men as well or to various combinations of multiple Millian polyamorous experimenters searching for new ways of living. That is, what is under consideration here is polygamy/polyamory and not *polygyny*, the latter being that which exists amongst some Muslims and Mormons. Thus, from a purely formalistic legal perspective there is no particular defense on the female autonomy front that needs to be made. Multi-member civil unions on this scheme would be a form of multi-lateral contract with equal legal status for all members, including the right to refuse entry to new members.

Of course, proponents of the female autonomy objection do not point to the form of the laws in question, but to the *reality* of where polygamous relationships are likely to be created. In reality, the argument goes, polygamy is a practice which will only be popular as *polygyny* amongst deeply patriarchal communities, and allowing it will only give legal cover and political legitimacy to communities seeking to preserve patriarchy, indeed at times radically oppressive forms of patriarchy.[21]

I am sure that this picture of the practice of polygyny – even now on the ground – can be questioned both factually and philosophically.[22] A basic response along the lines of the former would be that the vast majority of polygynous families are not as tyrannical or oppressive as some of the extreme cases known to the wider public. Both good and bad lives are lived within them, just as in monogamous families.[23] A basic response along the lines of the latter is that this objection, put too strenuously,

[21] For a thoughtful formulation of this position, see Brooks, "The Problem with Polygamy."

[22] See Brooks, ibid., pp. 4–6, for empirical studies on the effects of polygamy on the welfare of both women and men. See also Angela Campbell, "Wives' Tales: Reflecting on Research in Bountiful," *Canadian Journal of Law and Society*, Vol. 23, Nos. 1–2, pp. 121–141 (2008) and "Bountiful's Plural Marriages," *International Journal of Law in Context* (Forthcoming) for analysis of women's experiences with plural marriage within Canada's only openly polygynous community, Bountiful, British Columbia. Campbell's research amongst members of the Fundamentalist Mormon community in this town presents a counter-narrative to this common portrayal of the FLDS wife as submissive, silenced, and isolated.

[23] In her defense of legalizing polygamy, Cheshire Calhoun gives numerous examples of how polygamy has been associated with many different kinds of social, economic, and emotional arrangements. (Cheshire Calhoun, "Who's Afraid of Polygamous Marriage? Lessons for Same-Sex Marriage Advocacy from the History of Polygamy," *San Diego Law Review* 42: 1023–42.)

would rest on either philosophically controversial conceptions of free will, or morally controversial conceptions of the level of autonomy and independence needed to live a good life which we do not apply generally to the same extent used to oppose polygamy.

But let us grant the concern. Let us concede that polygamy, if legal, would be most popular not amongst well-educated, autonomous, Millian, polyamorous experimenters but within those traditional, conservative patriarchal communities where concerns about the equality of women are real and salient, such as some FLDS and Muslim communities. Let us also concede that it would, at the very least, facilitate some of the abuses to female autonomy that we are concerned about. I do not even want to counter that legalizing polygamy would, like with prostitution or drugs, possibly alleviate some of the concerns about female autonomy because of the emergent possibilities for regulation and control.[24] (Although this is an important point, it can only enter once we have established the basic point that a practice is itself not unjust but merely commonly associated with abuses. One would never propose legalizing slavery in order to better regulate it (with apologies to Marxists).)

Rather, I would like to consider just how strong the female autonomy objection to polygamy would have to be before it registered strongly on the justificatory scale or became a "victorious" justification (in Gaus's terms). It is not enough to show that many *actual* plural families are unhealthy or distasteful in female autonomy terms, or even that the practice as it exists *now* inclines towards such evils as the domination of vulnerable women. This may be true. (It is definitely true for the situations described in the recent Warren Jeffs and Eldorado, Texas polygyny cases.) But the problem is that this is true in actuality for so many different types of marriage. Are we going to prohibit alcoholics from marrying? People with bad tempers? What about people, including women, who actually *believe* that the proper role for women is one of subordination to their husbands? Is there evidence that life lived under a tyrannical, patriarchal, egomaniacal man is worse as one wife out of four (or 24) than as a sole

[24] Although I am assuming that a multi-member civil union permissible under political liberalism would take care to avoid the dilemmas Brooks discusses of the right of divorce resting in one dominant partner. I do not want to address in this paper what the precise legal-administrative regulations would have to be, but I have in mind something like an association to which all members are equal contractors with rights to refuse new members. It is worth considering whether this feature which liberals would have to insist on would in fact make "liberal polygamy/polyamory" unattractive to conservative religious groups who presently desire the right to polygyny, thus accomplishing much of what liberals, egalitarians, and feminists care about.

wife? Wouldn't the opposite almost have to be true? So, yes, legalized polygamy would lead to lots of legitimate concerns about the safety, welfare, and autonomy of the women who are involved in it; but we have these concerns *now* and in regard to many practices we would not dream of proscribing, such as arranged marriages or even the very fact of marriage within a conservative, patriarchal community. So multiple-member civil unions would have to be as regulated as normal marriage, with special concern for the autonomy, property rights, and freedom of exit for vulnerable women. But these serious concerns are not insurmountable, and they certainly don't make for a victorious moral case against legalizing and recognizing polygamy while we tolerate so many other inegalitarian practices.

Furthermore, because we are not advancing a (positive) free practice or cultural sovereignty justification for polygamy, we are not ceding our right to intervene in cases of child abuse, coercion or severe domination. We are not ceding our right to insist on education for all persons, and on knowledge of the outside world and its laws. That is, the female autonomy objection would have to be *this* strong to do heavy justificatory work: it would have to be the case that poly*gyny* (a subset of polygamy) in any form is such an *intrinsic* violation of female dignity and autonomy that it demands preventing all forms of polygamy (the wider set) just so as to prevent the smaller subset. I do not believe that claim to polygyny's inherent and intrinsic degradation of female dignity and autonomy to be prima facie strong enough to survive doubts grounded in our commitment to moral pluralism, non-coercion, and autonomy. Should that argument succeed, it might be worth considering what else it would claim with it by way of religious or cultural practices and whether this commits us to a form of perfectionist liberalism which seeks to erase as many sources as possible of even freely chosen inegalitarian or heteronomous relationships, consciousnesses and forms of life.[25]

5.2. *Damage to Children, or the "Bin Ladin Objection" to Polygamy*

It is also not enough to talk about the impact on children of living within plural marriages. This is not to deny that it may be worse to be raised as

[25] Thus, I believe that Brooks' rejection of Calhoun's and Nussbaum's limited defense of polygamy is insufficient, because it does not address how polygamy as a "structurally inegalitarian" practice (granting for a moment that it is) differs from other such structurally inegalitarian practices in civil society and when precisely a voluntary structurally inegalitarian practice becomes impermissible under political liberalism.

one child out of 54 than as one child out of two. It may be worse for the children in question, but if plural marriages lead to lots of asocial children running about, this also may create a legitimate public interest in limiting it.[26] But I think here the evidence would not only have to be strong, but overwhelming and unambiguous, more like the effects of child abuse or withholding medical care than maladjustment. Whom else would we prohibit from marrying on the grounds that they are more likely to have asocial, maladjusted or neglected children? Busy people? Poor people? (Poverty is without a doubt a leading stressor on children.) Politicians? People who let their kids play video games too much?

Besides, look at the things that are *like-polygamy-only-worse* which we don't proscribe, such as adultery, and serial divorce and remarriage. (Incidentally, one of the common positive arguments for polygyny in the Islamic tradition is that it reduces the incentive for the husband to divorce and thus may be beneficial for wives and children in this regard.) Note that all of the above concedes that polygamy *probably* leads to bad lives. But what about the things which are *like-polygamy-which-we-don't-even-think-about*: close extended families or multiple families living together in communes or small communities? Perhaps living in a commune with a bunch of friends/half-siblings is not such an inherently bad way to live. Although this paper is interested in exploring whether any arguments for prohibition of polygamy meet the requirements of a justificatory or rights-based liberalism, it would not be difficult to explore how polygamy could fit into all sorts of conceptions of the good, including feminist ones.[27]

5.3. *Fairness in the Market for Partners*

An argument from equality and distributive fairness could be put against legalizing polygamy. The objection would be that legalizing polygamy would privilege the wealthy and unfairly disadvantage the less well-off. Rich men could afford to collect many wives and this would lead to a

---

[26] It has been a periodic theme of popular and academic writers after the September 11, 2001 attacks to speculate on whether the anxiety and alienation of growing up as an excluded and under-recognized child of the Bin Ladin clan might have contributed to Usama Bin Ladin's later radicalization. Thus: the "Bin Ladin Objection" to polygamy. (See, for example, Adam Robinson, *Bin Laden: Behind the Mask of the Terrorist* (New York: Arcade Book, 2002).)

[27] See, for example, Elizabeth F. Emens, "Monogamy's Law: Compulsory Monogamy and Polyamorous Existence," *New York University Review of Law & Social Change* 29 (2004): 277–376. See also Calhoun, "Who's Afraid of Polygamous Marriage," pp. 1037–1042.

shortage for the rest,[28] leaving large numbers of unmarried men ("bare branches") who are then more susceptible to criminality and other forms of anti-social behavior.[29] Such an objection is essentially a form of the Lockean proviso: one must leave "enough and as good in common…to others." It is clearly trying to remain within the bounds of public reason.[30] What can be said in response?

This argument (in the form I presented it) has some of the same features as the "female autonomy" objection. The first is mistaking polygamy for polygyny. But, to repeat, we not are talking about legalizing specifically *polygyny*. There is no need to assume that it is rich *men* who will be getting the privilege of dominating the spousal market since the right will be open to women as well. The second is the assumption that legalizing polygamy will *in fact* mean lots of polygyny and little of other forms of polygamy. It is not obvious that we should assume this, however, except for the earlier assumption about polygyny being attractive mostly to patriarchal religious communities. Perhaps this is true; but it then becomes the case that the risk of unfairness to poorer men is one which afflicts not an entire society but merely particular communities.[31] Thus, at *most*, poorer Mormon or Muslim men (for example) might be disadvantaged.

---

[28] See Richard A. Posner, *Sex and Reason* (Cambridge, MA: Harvard University Press, 1992), Chapter 9. Also, from the blog that Posner shares with Gary Becker: "My view is that polygamy would impose substantial social costs in a modern Western-type society that probably would not be offset by the benefits to the parties to polygamous marriages. Especially given the large disparities in wealth in the United States, legalizing polygamy would enable wealthy men to have multiple wives, even harems, which would reduce the supply of women to men of lower incomes and thus aggravate inequality. The resulting shortage of women would lead to queuing, and thus to a high age of marriage for men, which in turn would increase the demand for prostitution. Moreover, intense competition for women would lower the age of marriage for women, which would be likely to result in less investment by them in education (because household production is a substitute for market production) and therefore reduce women's market output." (http://www.becker-posner-blog.com/archives/2006/10/should_polygamy.html.)

[29] See, for example, Valerie M. Hudson and Andrea M. den Boer, *Bare Branches: Security Implications of Asia's Surplus Male Population* (Cambridge, MA: The MIT Press, 2004) as well as Jonathan Rauch, "One Man, Many Wives, Big Problems," *The Atlantic* (Unbound), April 2006, http://www.theatlantic.com/magazine/archive/2006/04/one-man-many-wives-big-problems/4829/.

[30] I owe this objection also to a personal conversation with no less a defender of public reason and the need for a strict rational, secular basis for discriminating against private sexual and romantic behaviors than Stephen Macedo. That the author of "Homosexuality and the Conservative Mind" (*Georgetown Law Journal* 84:2 (1995): 261–300) does not find it obvious that we are required to move further down the slippery slope suggests the need for public reason liberals to consider the case of polygamy.

[31] Although such excluded men, and boys, may then in turn present various social challenges to the wider society.

Even if true, would this amount to a victorious argument against allowing polygamy?

The only sense in which we have a "right to marry" is that the *state* cannot deprive any citizen of her negative freedom to marry. But marriage is not normally treated as a positive right by liberal theorists in the sense of its successful achievement being guaranteed by the state. Nor is it usually treated as a social good along the lines of education, that is, something which sub-state groups may not conspire to deny some vulnerable members on pain of state intervention. Religious communities do not have the right to deprive their members of primary goods guaranteed by the state, and they do not have the right to deprive their children of such secondary goods as education and information about the wider society which are necessary components of a meaningful right of exit. So the danger in this case is only that a community's practices might make it marginally harder for some *adult* men to find eligible spouses, not to obtain primary goods or other resources for autonomous choices. But, how much harder would it have to be before the state is justified in intervening in a community to the extent of proscribing practices which are not intrinsically oppressive? It would seem to have to give rise to a rather extreme level of deprivation before banning a competitive practice within a sub-state community emerged as the justified response on the part of the state. But it is hard to imagine such a scenario.

Let us imagine that there is a religious community in which 5% of the men were able to monopolize 80% of the female population and in which only heterosexual relations are tolerated. Our concern *at the moment* is for the remaining 95% of the men who have to compete for the remaining 20% of the women.[32] If this community is so authoritarian and tyrannical that there is no realistic right of exit, then what we are talking about in effect is a cult and polygyny is the least of our concerns which might give rise to intervention. But if this community has robust institutions of protest and representation ("voice") as well as rights of exit, then it could be said that men in fact disadvantage *themselves* by not seceding (forming splinter communities) or exiting (apostatizing). If the imbalance in the spousal market were this extreme but the deprived men (and other

---

[32] Of course, overall we are most concerned about the autonomy and rights of exit for the women in the community under consideration, and thus this was the first objection considered in this paper. However, for the purposes of considering "fairness in the marital market" as a *separate* objection to polygamy, we must assume that conditions of autonomy, choice, and rights of exit on the part of women are met in this hypothetical community.

dissenting members, both men and women) had the freedom to form their own splinter community or join another religious group, then we can surmise that they actually deem the choice of leaving that community less favorably than not being able to marry. In this case our intervention would be an intolerable intrusion into persons' moral independence, somewhat akin to forcing the Catholic Church to ordain female priests or Orthodox Jews to *religiously* abolish the institution of the *get*.[33]

Other than religion, are there grounds for fearing that *in practice* men will be the ones marrying multiple women, and in such great numbers as to create a genuine public interest problem? To do so would seem to require strong psychological assumptions. Are women *now* clamoring to be a part of polygynous (one man-many women) partnerships when economic conditions are broadly favorable? In secular, post-traditional societies, do wealthy men feel a strong impulse to legally *marry* (as oppose to form sexual or emotional relationships with) multiple women? I cannot myself think of any reasons to assume that legalizing polygamy would result *in fact* in rich men accumulating multiple wives in *great* disproportion to rich women accumulating many husbands and other possible models of multi-member partnerships. Even if we assume that there will be at least *some* of the latter, then this dilutes the concern about imbalance.[34] Furthermore, any psychological, anthropological or sociological evidence available to us today about likely mating patterns would invariably be tainted by socialization into expectations and desires fostered and facilitated by existing options.[35] But if those options were changed, along

[33] There is an important distinction between insisting that civil law may not recognize radically inegalitarian religious practices and insisting that the religious groups themselves declare those practices to be superseded or abolished whether or not they agree to comply with civil law.

[34] Even Jonathan Rauch, an eloquent and vociferous opponent of legalizing polygamy on the grounds discussed in this sections, acknowledges that in a complex, modernized society "some polygynous marriages would probably be offset by group marriages or chain marriages involving multiple husbands."

[35] Furthermore, such evidence would not only be largely speculative but also potentially self-contradictory. For example, when some people assume that polygynous (one man-many women) relationships would be much more likely for biological or psychological reasons than one-woman/multiple-men relationships, it is common to point not only to existing practice or survey-data but also to evolutionary biology. But if an interlocutor pointed to evolutionary psychology to ground an argument against legalizing polygamy along the lines of the "market fairness" argument we are considering here, presumably one could retort with all sorts of other "truths" grounded in evolutionary psychology: "But women are naturally jealous and would rarely tolerate sharing partners so this will balance out the male proclivity to accumulate partners if women have full civic equality, including the right to refuse polygyny." I think there is good reason to insist on a

with the social costs imposed on them, we cannot be sure – to the extent required for our present justificatory purposes – what kinds of mating patterns might develop.[36]

Furthermore, do we need to assume that legalized polygamy would privilege only the *wealthy*? One might also assume that physically attractive or otherwise more desirable and persuasive people would be able to accumulate multiple partners at the expense of erotic competitors. Should justice be concerned with neutralizing such *natural* advantages that some people have in inducing other free individuals to form voluntary intimate bonds with them? After all, in distributive justice we regard natural advantages as unearned and morally arbitrary, and thus we do not think that all social advantages derived from them are deserved. Why should this be any different with the formation of intimate bonds? Thus, it seems that the question is *Are intimate bonds like wealth or other social goods in that we want to limit the effect of unearned advantages on the competition for their acquisition*?

This seems intuitively misguided. First, I would repeat what I suggested above, that marriage and intimacy are not primary goods, goods which a political community inevitably distributes as part of its basic structure and which it must thus take care to distribute fairly. From a social justice perspective it is not clear that anyone has a *positive right* to intimate relationships (i.e., that some collectivity must provide them), much less a right which must be protected against unfair competition. There are other reasons for doubting that a just society would treat intimate bonds like wealth or other social resources. They are harder to accumulate, even when such accumulation is legal, than money or power. It is harder for

very high burden of proof and generalization before such assumptions about evolutionary psychology play a central role in justification.

36 Dworkin argues on similar lines about the relative weight persons might place on wealth for their own self-esteem and life-satisfaction should they be socialized into his society committed to equality of resources. "It would be a mistake to suppose that the bizarre and mutually dependent attitudes about wealth that mark our own society – the ideas that the accumulation of wealth is a mark of a successful life and that someone who has arranged his life to acquire it is a proper object for envy rather than sympathy or concern – would find any footing in an economic system that is free of genuine poverty and that encourages people, as the initial auction encourages them, to see bank account wealth as simply one ingredient among others of what might make a life worth living. For in our world, these attitudes are sustained and nourished by the assumption that a life dedicated to the accumulation of wealth or to the consumption of luxuries – a major part of whose appeal lies just in the fact that they are reserved for the very rich – is a valuable life for people given only one chance to live. That proposition comes as close as any theory of the good life can to naked absurdity." (Ronald Dworkin, "What is Equality? 2: Equality of Resources," *Philosophy & Public Affairs* 10:4 (1981): 283–345, p. 332.)

accumulation on the part of one person to immediately impact others adversely in a large society. (I do not personally feel the devaluation of my assets and the inflation of female market power because Hugh Hefner has six girlfriends.) And, unlike money, the accumulation of intimate bonds does not so obviously lead to class formation and the bleeding of inequality into political and social domination. But, most obviously, intimate relations require mutual assent. While the exchange of money for labor or goods between two persons requires mutual consent, this is not the consent of the good itself (which is what we are assuming for the moment that spouses are). The money itself doesn't have to consent to be possessed by Wilt Chamberlain as his entitlement. Thus, part of what troubles us about interfering in the formulation of intimate bonds is what troubles libertarians about interfering in *any* free exchange: that it violates people's rights to self-ownership. But whereas libertarians move from self-ownership to a right to all possible goods (and the power they confer) that one can accumulate through free exchange, what is at stake in forming intimate bonds is self-ownership *simpliciter* – the literal allocation of one's personal companionship and attentions. Thus, we don't seem to have to pin our argument to a fundamental moral distinction between advantages in the pursuit of intimate bonds arising from wealth and those arising from natural endowments because it is rather the *intimate bonds* themselves which we don't want to interfere with. Who is to say what one's "fair share" of intimacy is and who is going to impose this fair share at the expense of unwilling persons?

Furthermore, we would need a strong argument explaining why forming *legal* bonds with multiple persons is a serious concern on grounds of fairness, whereas doing so *short of marriage* (what people such as Hugh Hefner are perfectly free to do now) would not be. Here, the comparison with distributive justice collapses entirely. In distributive justice we are not only concerned about the consequences of legalizing *potentially* inequitable exchanges. If anything, the concern is to show why relations which are legal now are not necessarily just. Similarly with discriminatory practices: we are not overly perplexed about the consequences of *legalizing* hiring practices (or policies of membership in groups or associations) which are *in fact* racist or otherwise discriminatory. Philosophical debate focuses directly on whether such discriminatory practices on the part of private associations (such as churches or clubs) are *ever* justified and on the dilemmas of identifying them in practice. Thus, to take seriously the concern about distributive fairness (for the excluded) and the potential for domination (over the "collected" spouses) in the marital market should polygamy be legalized would likely require taking seriously existing inequities, such as certain women monopolizing the affections of multiple men at a time. Who thinks this is part of justice above and beyond the concern that all members of a society have sufficient resources to avoid relationships of domination?

Finally, I would like to register a concern about the type of argument of which the "fairness in the market for partners" objection to polygamy is an instance, which I will call the "if-everyone-did-it" objection. Unlike arguments about equality or fairness in distributive justice, this is not an argument about a general principle to which the distribution of a good must conform. That is, it is not saying that persons who choose wealthy or particularly attractive partners are acting unfairly towards all others with whom they do not enter into intimate bonds. Nor is it even saying that in allowing multiple legal partners the political community is inherently recognizing the greater value of some talents and rewarding them accordingly. What it is saying is that *if many people acted on this privilege, itself possibly innocuous, bad or irrational social consequences* could *result.*[37]

Note first that this is not as strong as the "tragedy of the commons" dilemma which shows how catastrophic results will almost certainly emerge from individuals acting *exactly as we have every reason to expect they will*, i.e., in their own rational self-interest. Rather, it is saying that if many people acted at the same time on this right *which we don't think most will actually find desirable* then this could be *frustrating for an unspecified number of left-out people*. It is using the threat of a *merely potential* future risk of uncertain probability to justify proscribing outright a practice which is not inherently unjust.

This argument is more convincing in other contexts, and it is weak enough there. Perhaps the most common usage of it is in discussions (popular in the early 1990s) on the right to self-determination and secession. One argument against such a right (strongly and crudely put) is that if it were generally acknowledged it would be claimed by every eligible ethnic group and this would lead to widespread international chaos. But there are many rights which if acted upon generally and simultaneously

[37] Hudson and den Boer suggest that the social costs of polygyny reach a tipping point when sex ratios reach roughly 120 males to 100 females, or when one-sixth of all men are surplus goods on the marital market. Rauch: "The United States as a whole would reach that ratio if, for example, 5 percent of men took two wives, 3 percent took three wives, and 2 percent took four wives—numbers that are quite imaginable, if polygamy were legal for a while. In particular communities—inner cities, for example—polygamy could take a toll much more quickly."

would have catastrophic consequences. To give two examples: the right to birth control and the right to withdraw your money from the bank. If everyone always used birth control, the species would die out; if everyone withdrew their money from the bank simultaneously we would have a bank run with deleterious consequences. But in neither case does this deter us from thinking that doing either at any given time is a right we enjoy. In order for the if-everyone-did-it objection to be forceful we either need to doubt that the freedom to do it is a very strong right at all (such as the "right" to constantly create new "financial products" ever more removed from actual economic productivity) or we need some reasonable expectation grounded in psychology or sociology that the natural course of events will lead to the average person acting on the right as much as she can. That is the explanatory appeal of the "tragedy of the commons" dilemma: it is rational for people to consume as much of a common resource as they can and many such common resources are scarce.

The if-everyone-did-it objection to polygamy seems weak: there seems less reason to think that the natural inclination is for people to join harems and that most people would leap at the opportunity the first chance they get than there is to think that they will consume natural resources beyond their fair share or will borrow overly cheap money to finance property speculation in a reckless and unsustainable manner. Thus, while I have argued against the "fairness in the market for partners" objection on its own terms, it also must be said that some fairly controversial psychological assumptions would have to be asserted for the if-everyone-did-it objection to rise to its strongest justificatory level in the case of polygamy, before we factor in economic considerations.

5.4. *Burdening Society, or the Abuse of Privileges Objection*

In societies where the point of civil unions or registered domestic partnerships is to materially subsidize families in various ways, an objection to polygamy could be leveled that the temptation for fraud to access these benefits would be great, or even that the costs of extending them to sincere families would be an unfair burden on others. This is a more plausible form of the if-everyone-(or a-lot-of-people)-did-it objection.

This argument against polygamy would have to show that plural marriages are in fact more costly to a society and, thus, that they amount to an expensive taste. For that to be true we would have to assume (1) that there is only one productive spouse per marriage and (2) that social benefits or subsidies are distributed via legal marriage to an employed person in proportion to his or her number of *spousal* dependents. The first assumption, even if true in some cases, is of unclear moral and even practical significance, and the second seems to suggest a morally objectionable way of distributing social benefits on two accounts. First, it limits access to important goods (such as health insurance) to those who enter into a voluntary relationship which not all persons value in the same way. Second, when (as in the United States) such goods are distributed by employers to the familial dependents of employees, it seems to unfairly and inefficiently burden employers. In fact, the source of the suspicion that polygamy could be an expensive taste liable to abuse of privileges is undoubtedly the association of social benefits with private employment.

Thus, if the second assumption did not hold then it would be hard to see how polygamy (even if the first assumption held) would be any more expensive than non-polygamy (including people remaining single). If, as it seems likely, a politically liberal society would be more likely to adopt the model of European social democracies where citizens as such get directly many of the social benefits that are privileges of employment in the United States, it is hard to see what need or justification there could be for any further subsidy for entering into a civil union per se. That is almost certainly the most just social arrangement, the leveling *up* equivalent in terms of material resources of my proposal (in the introduction) to leveling *down* the public distribution of the symbolic term "marriage." One might argue that there are no justifiable grounds for a politically liberal state to permit economic and health benefits to be provided to some people and not others on the basis of whether they belong to a form of private relationship which has religious origins. Thus, even if a family followed the polygynous model of one employed man and many unemployed women it is hard to see how this is more expensive for society and thus hard to see why one should be concerned about fraud or abuse.[38]

Could one be concerned about general economic efficiency if living in large families allowed people to live more successfully off of their individual subsidies and thus reduced their incentive to join the workforce? I don't think this concern gets us very far. First of all, it is the right of persons to choose to live at a lower level of material welfare if they value other goods. Second, if it does in fact become the case that a society's economically productive members are unable to support efficiently (or generously) its economically non-productive members, then the

[38] I would like to thank Jonathan Quong for forcing me to correct my mistakes in an earlier draft on the idea of polygamy being an expensive taste.

subsidy will of necessity decrease to the amount it can afford (possibly nothing), which would presumably change the incentive structure of those who chose not to work. The welfare state is not a suicide pact.

To this point, I have referred to policies of subsidizing marriage (or civil unions) per se, not the family at large, inclusive of children. Here the concerns are very different; we are no longer dealing with justifying an unfair and irrational way of distributing access to primary goods for adults, but rather subsidizing the maintenance of children. Here it is compatible with public reason to subsidize the family, since the family bears disproportionate costs related to the raising of children. In addition to the direct humanitarian concern in ensuring that all children are minimally well-off, one could argue plausibly that just as a society invests in its future citizens through education it may do so through direct subsidies to the family. If material deprivation from an early age is both unjust in itself and a powerful source of adult asociality, a well-ordered society has a strong interest in preventing this through material subsidy. This would not permit, however, any additional subsidies being extended to childless couples merely because they are married. This approach seems like a logical way of preserving justificatory neutrality but also shows that polygamy per se cannot be viewed as an expensive taste. Therefore, it is hard to see what overwhelming public interest there is in proscribing it or in denying polygamous relationships access to civil union status.

Conclusion

This essay argues that the four most plausible arguments compatible with public reason for an outright legal ban on all forms of polygamy or for excluding polygamous relationships from civil union status are unvictorious. My purpose was not to survey exhaustively the empirical literature on contemporary forms of polygamy, but to tease out the types of arguments political liberals would have to insist on, and precisely how strongly, in order for a general prohibition against polygamy to be justified on grounds of principle.

The most common objection to polygamy is on grounds of female autonomy and equality. But advancing this argument forcefully often involves neglecting the tendency of political liberalism (by whatever name it goes in contemporary, complex, multicultural societies) to tolerate a certain amount of inegalitarianism in private, within the bounds of robust and meaningful freedoms of choice and exit. Properly understood, polygamy involves no inherent statement about the essential inferiority of women, and certainly not more than many other existing practices and institutions (including many expressions of the main monotheistic religions) which political liberals regard as tolerable.

Does this case say anything about our resources and constraints when arguing from public reason? I think at least two points are noteworthy. The first is that arguments from the *free practice of religion* or *cultural sovereignty* not only do not give us special reasons for allowing practices, but may in fact give us reasons for (continuing to) ban them. One of the postulates which allowed me to consider a presumption of permissibility in the case of polygamy was that the nature of the practice in itself is not identical to some of its associated abuses and horrors. We cannot assume that polygamy, if widely legal, would be the same thing as the patriarchal abuse of women from an early age. But if we have reason to believe that these practices would not just be one of many choices for autonomous persons but rather part of a coherent and elaborate patriarchal conception of the good (especially a religious one) then we may indeed have much more reason to fear that certain communities would engage in the shaping of their members' consciousnesses from an early age to expect and tolerate violations of their autonomy and dignity. It is only when we *don't think* that an oppressive form of poly*gyny* is part of a widespread, long-standing and elaborate patriarchal conception of the good that poly*gamy* appears safe.

Second, out of a particular historical and political context public reason has a hard time dealing with arguments from conjecture or contingency of the kinds "this may be fine in theory but not in practice" or "if everyone did it…" or "we need such laws as useful devices to protect people from crimes which are hard to prove." I assumed in this paper that public reason has an assumption of skepticism towards such arguments. They are easily abused, hard to prove and do not tell us anything about the inherent justness of a given act or practice. However, in real life it may be perfectly clear to reasonable people what function a practice or institution serves, what irrational or harmful consequences it has in practice and why a society acts justly or wisely when it proscribes or constrains it as a matter of public policy.[39] For example, I was skeptical of the claim that legalizing and recognizing polygamy is likely to lead to a radical distortion in the spousal

39 Affirmative action is a good example of this phenomenon as well. Race-blind, "merit"-based admissions may be rationally defensible but that rational defense cannot act as a veto against historically justifiable public policies.

market. In a large, morally diverse society during reasonably prosperous times it may indeed be fantastical to argue that legalizing polygamy would have recognizable deleterious effects on society. However, this argument is not meant to pre-empt considerations on the way institutions such as polygamy might function in real world societies where its practice may be entangled with oppressive institutions of property rights, economic distribution or female heteronomy. Nonetheless, it must be insisted upon that in these cases we are dealing with failures of *distributive justice*. It is when a society fails to ensure that all of its members enjoy material independence that they become vulnerable to all forms of domination. Could polygamy be one way in which the wealthy take advantage of the less wealthy? Perhaps, but in a capitalist society where the poor are confronted with countless dangers, vulnerabilities and indignities, the right to contract multiple legal domestic partnerships which guarantee rights to all members does not seem to register very strongly.

Of course, these latter qualifications are not so much a critique of public reason as a defense of it. It *ought* to be flexible enough to accommodate real-world political agents seeking to balance respect for rights with public policy considerations in the full light of their own history and present, and at the same time it ought to be a resource for those actors for discovering what is rational and what is arbitrary in their own inherited institutions.

PART TWO

LEGAL NORMS

THE IDEALITY OF LAW

Sean Coyle

Abstract

Recent works by Nigel Simmonds and Ronald Dworkin offer a challenge to the dominant jurisprudential tradition of legal positivism. Underlying this superficial similarity in aims is a sharp divergence in philosophical outlook. Whereas Dworkin's arguments operate within a body of background assumptions that he shares with his opponents, and which he has done much to shape, Simmonds sees his task as challenging those assumptions. This is particularly evident in the moral philosophies at the heart of each book: Dworkin (I argue) can be seen as offering a Protestant-voluntarist-atheist philosophy; whereas Simmonds resembles a Catholic-conservative-Aristotelian. I explore the implications of these divergent world-views.

Keywords

Dworkin, Simmonds, morality, Aristotle, Protestantism, pluralism, conservatism

Jurisprudence is the philosophical study of the nature of law. But it is also (simultaneously) a reflection on the purposes for which such an enquiry is undertaken. Ought one, for instance, to see such efforts as fulfilling needs that are essentially clarificatory, in that they seek to rid our present understandings of confusions through careful use of distinctions and analysis? Or does Jurisprudence engage in 'analysis' of a different sort, by exploring the richness of current associations in which law is presented to the understanding as a complex moral, political and philosophical idea? In recent times, both Simmonds and Dworkin have challenged the dominant preference for the first of these outlooks (associated with 'legal positivism'). Yet as an examination of these works reveal, each gives a very different meaning to the idea that law embodies a moral ideal. Dworkin himself has done much to shape the agendas that define contemporary jurisprudence, and *Justice in Robes* (consisting of a series of recent essays) reiterates his earlier position and furthers his engagement with various intellectual opponents. Simmonds, by contrast, wishes to challenge those agendas, and to take jurisprudential enquiry in a different direction.

We might begin by considering different ways in which law might be taken to embody a moral ideal. Dworkin's *Justice in Robes*, in the nature of an essay collection, does not seek to advance any single thesis or new idea, but develops his monistic view of the values at work in law. Borrowing a well-known image, he adopts the position of the hedgehog over that of the fox:[1] law, Dworkin argues, is best understood as the expression of a moral ideal of 'political integrity', 'the principle that a state should try ... to govern through a coherent set of political principles whose benefit it extends to all citizens.'[2] It is coherent in that our first aim must be 'to construct conceptions or interpretations of each of these values that reinforce the others', for '[u]ntil we can see how our ethical values hang together [in that mutually supportive way], we do not understand any of them.'[3] In adopting this standpoint, Dworkin rejects the idea that distinct values such as liberty and equality must be understood to conflict. Simmonds likewise criticizes the outlook of the fox, pointing out that the 'necessary' opposition of political concepts to one another depends upon supplying them with rigid identities that are 'invulnerable to the twists and turns [they] can receive in ordinary human discourse.'[4] It is thus only through the adoption of fixed definitions of central political ideas (such as 'freedom') that we are driven to conclude that politics is finally a matter of ungrounded choice between opposing values. But the same search for definitional shortcuts similarly undermines the approach of the Dworkinian hedgehog, for he must define the same political concepts in ways that exclude the possibility of ultimate conflicts. Such definitions will therefore seem convenient and unreal. Simmonds suggests that a reflective understanding, born of a submissiveness towards the kaleidoscopic nature of moral experience, will instead 'reveal complex relationships of mutual support between seemingly distinct values, while also resisting the temptation to regard all sound values as realizable without significant moral cost.'[5] Understanding this, we may come to recognize

[1] 'The fox knows many things, but the hedgehog knows one big thing'. Attributed to the classical poet Archilochus, it was employed as the title of a famous essay by Isaiah Berlin.

[2] RM Dworkin, *Justice in Robes* (Cambridge MA: Belknap Press, 2006), 13 [Hereafter *JR*]. See also Dworkin, *Law's Empire* (London: Fontana, 1986), 92.

[3] Id. 161.

[4] NE Simmonds, *Law as a Moral Idea* (Oxford: Oxford University Press, 2007), 180 [Hereafter *LMI*].

[5] Id.

that 'there are various complex ways in which values can be interdependent yet nevertheless capable of conflict.'

The intellectual distance between these two positions may not at first seem very great. At least, it will not seem so if our focus is upon their rejection of the dominant ideology of positivism. But such a focus disguises a point of great importance. Any set of philosophical debates will serve to structure understanding of the field under investigation, not only in centralizing certain problems whilst marginalizing or suppressing others, but also by the manner in which the main problems are conceived. The question of the moral nature of law has come to be interpreted as that of the relationship between 'law' and 'morals': the extent to which moral values form the basis of legal interpretation, and the sense in which law and morality are 'interwoven'. Despite the obvious inventiveness and originality of Dworkin's arguments, both he and the positivist theorists he is concerned to refute share a basic understanding of the nature of morality. One can only argue about the extent to which law 'embodies' moral values if morality itself sufficiently resembles a body of law-like principles and standards. Dworkin's arguments with legal positivism further entrench these assumptions, the consequence of which is an inevitable narrowing of the field of inquiry. The jurisprudential thought of the present day does not present us with the choice, Dworkin or the mainstream, but rather confronts us with an intellectual landscape in which Dworkin and his opponents (both pragmatist and positivist) share fundamental ideas about the significance and direction of inquiry. This makes it much more difficult to raise questions about the nature of law that do not derive from that shared foundation, questions that will in consequence be viewed by all sides as a distracting irrelevance.

Simmonds has for many years striven to overturn some of the central preoccupations of modern jurisprudence. In *Law as a Moral Idea* he presents a sustained argument that is designed both to weaken the grip on the collective imagination of the juridical conception of morality, and reveal the shallowness of the assumptions which underpin legal positivism. It leaves the impression, however, of being a compromise. Any reorientation of inquiry, Simmonds says, 'must begin from where the discipline currently stands': 'My object [he writes] is not to change the subject by "changing the subject", so to speak, but to undermine a current orthodoxy by direct opposition.'[6] This is, in my view, a mistake. Philosophical

[6] Id, 4.

doctrines are amazingly resilient: they are, for men of ideas, more than a mere set of theses to be studied during the working week. They represent, like all creative things, a form of self-expression in which there is a significant emotional investment. The ultimate bases of philosophical doctrines consist not simply in reason but in belief.[7] As with religious faith, it is sometimes possible to alter belief by bringing to light the tacit assumptions on which the beliefs rest, but very often this is not the case. One senses, regrettably, that a certain defensiveness has prevented Simmonds from giving as full and free an expression to his own fascinating theories as sympathetic readers would wish. It is on these theories of the ethical conditions of modernity that I shall focus in the present essay.

1. *Ideals and Principles*

Let me begin by changing the subject. I have long believed that jurisprudential and political theories possess a significance that is irreducibly eschatological, and that the articulation of the eschatological implications of such theories would be a profitable enterprise.[8] It is possible (for example) to represent human history as a journey from primitive and barbaric beginnings toward the highest state of culture and civility. In so doing, we are naturally inclined to conceive of present arrangements as approaching that end-condition rather than occupying the journey's early stages. Raymond Geuss has drawn attention to the propensity for jurispru dential theories such as that of John Rawls to function as 'compensatory fantasies' in which the shortcomings and injustices of the present are transformed into a theory of the ideal society, essentially similar in its broadest aspects to the society of the moment.[9] Attainment of the ideal is then a matter of refining particular aspects of social institutions and mechanisms of distribution which stand at 'the end of history'.[10] Much the same can be said of Dworkin's jurisprudential outlook: the central problem of legal and

[7] Many philosophers will no doubt deny this. But then what sustains confidence in reason except faith and belief? If the truth of philosophical doctrines were demonstrable, philosophical problems would disappear. For a brilliant account of philosophical belief in this vein, see Michael Oakeshott, *Experience and Its Modes* (Cambridge: Cambridge University Press, 1933).

[8] By 'eschatology' here I refer to doctrines concerning the historical direction and destiny of mankind.

[9] Raymond Geuss, *Outside Ethics* (Princeton NJ: Princeton University Press, 2005), ch 2.

[10] See Francis Fukuyama, *The End of History and the Last Man* (Harmondsworth: Penguin, 1993).

political philosophy is the articulation of an integrated theory of values such as liberty, equality, democracy and justice which shows them to be mutually accommodating. This theory is not to be understood as something to be worked out and then realized through law, but interpreted as a body of principles to some extent already present within the law.[11]

This method of 'constructive interpretation' (as with Rawls's notion of reflective equilibrium[12]) is at once optimistic, in its belief in the open-ended possibilities of human perfectibility, and depressing, for it suggests that present arrangements deny or limit avenues of human flourishing that might otherwise exist if only we had *more* liberty, or *fairer* laws. Each successive approximation to such ideals will therefore seem to fall short of what is required for a fuller flourishing, which remains a postponed good that we are forever doomed to chase. Idealism of this kind, in one sense, serves not to venerate the human condition so much as to express contempt for it: to wish it were other than it really is. More significantly, however, it is a vision of human perfectibility attainable (even if only in principle) within history, and as a result of human efforts. Few, I believe, have paused to reflect upon how far such a vision of the human condition is removed from that offered by Christian eschatology. In Christianity we have a vision in which perfectibility is alien to the human condition, attainable only outside the circles of the world. It is a vision in which salvation is not, ultimately, a human achievement but depends upon a divine judgment that is shaped by the value of mercy.[13] Here, the human

[11] *JR*, 161. Dworkin is of course modest enough to admit that the conjunction of these values may ultimately prove to be of less worth than some as yet undisclosed superior set of values. Yet no thinker whose arguments display such firm sincerity concerning the truth of 'our' values can steadily believe that their falsity is a real possibility, and there is in *Justice in Robes* a pervasive tone of hubristic certainty. In one passage, for example, Dworkin praises the ambition of 'our country's most fundamental contribution to political morality'. 'We have been envied for our adventure [he says] and we are now increasingly copied all over the world, from Strasbourg to Capetown, from Budapest to Delhi. Let's not lose our nerve, when all around the world other people, following our example, are gaining theirs' (*JR*, 138–39).

[12] The similarity of the methods is noted by Dworkin, the crucial difference being 'the equilibrium I believe philosophy must seek is not limited, as his is, to the constitutional essentials of politics, but embraces what he calls a "comprehensive" theory that includes personal morality and ethics as well' (*JR*, 161).

[13] Some versions of Christian belief, drawing a degree of inspiration from Augustine, indeed believe perfectibility to be absent from the ideals at which the Christian must aim, instead centralizing the ideal of love within a fallen state. I am ill-equipped to consider the standpoints of other religions on the matter of salvation. Yet the idea that human perfectibility is not an historical phenomenon seems to me to be present, for example, in the Buddhist belief that one must undergo continual reincarnation until enlightenment is reached; and in Daoist views of meditation as the progressive withdrawal from the snares

condition resembles not a collective journey but a predicament from which human agency alone offers no escape.

I raise these points not as proofs of the falsity of Dworkin's views, but in order to reveal the unsoundness of a pervasive theme of *Justice in Robes*: the idea that anything that may sensibly be said about the nature of morality or law is itself a moral or a legal judgment. Attempts to explore the properties of such judgments from a point of view external to the practice in which the judgments are made is an illusion he calls 'Archimedianism.'[14] Dworkin's lengthiest and most intricate argument against a metaphysics of morals ('Objectivity and Truth: You'd Better Believe It'[15]) is inexplicably absent from the book. Its influence is nevertheless felt throughout, and Dworkin adverts to it many times in the endnotes. *Justice in Robes* contains only briefer expressions of the position, such as the following: 'Legal theorists have an apparently irresistible impulse, however, to insist that [objectivity] must mean something more than is captured in the ordinary opinion that one side had the better argument…'[16] By asking whether legal propositions can be objectively true in a metaphysical sense, Dworkin says, the legal theorists' mistake 'is just Rorty's mistake: Thinking that they can add to or change the sense of the position they want to attack by inserting these redundancies or metaphors in it. There is no perspective from which these inflated and decorated claims can have a sense different from their sense uninflated and undecorated, and that is the sense they have in ordinary legal life'. It is, ultimately, 'not a metaphysical but a legal claim.'[17]

It is unfortunate that Dworkin's more detailed discussion was omitted from the book, because it is a long and complicated argument. Yet its final effect is not to eliminate metaphysical assumptions from moral thought, but merely to suppress them. The effectiveness of the argument depends upon the extent to which it trades on beliefs about the nature of morality that are deeply embedded in modern philosophy: the idea that moral values take the form of law-like principles and standards which are capable

of the world. What unites such views is a rejection of the notion that moral progress is primarily a matter of perfecting the 'external' form of social arrangements.

14 *JR*, 141.

15 *Philosophy and Public Affairs* 25.2 (Spring, 1996): 87–139. Here, Dworkin argues that the question is 'not whether the further claims [concerning the nature of moral propositions] can be translated to make them seem more philosophical or metaphysical, but whether we can understand those philosophical translations as themselves anything but first-order evaluative claims' (100). He argues that we cannot.

16 *JR*, 42.

17 Id.

of generating moral rights, obligations and permissions of various kinds; and the view that moral reasoning must address an intellectual domain of value distinct from that of fact. In a famous passage (quoted by Simmonds), Pufendorf articulates these assumptions as follows: '[T]hat reason should be able to discover any morality in the actions of a man without reference to a law, is as impossible as for a man born blind to choose between colours'.[18] One addresses, as it were, an inert reality which moral judgments then colour in various ways. This encouraged a form of Protestant voluntarism for which moral values (understood as moral *laws*) have their source not in the understanding, but in the will of the 'rational agent'.

Pufendorf's own view was a direct expression of certain positions in Protestant theology which asserted the primacy and freedom of God's will over all forms of natural necessity. Moral laws for Pufendorf were impositions of divine law. Nature, on this view, 'was not the teleologically ordered universe of Aristotle, but something closer to the Baconian or Cartesian understanding.'[19] This served to reinforce a Protestant tradition of reflection upon the intentions of the divine will, the substance of which was revealed not in any facet of nature or worldly events, but only through personal study of Biblical texts. Moral philosophy has preserved this basic framework of thought long after its theological premises were eroded or forgotten. Hence, moral knowledge is generally acknowledged to be of a kind that is irreducibly distinct from worldly concerns, and therefore as inhabiting either a domain of subjective judgment, or (as in Kant's view) an objective and autonomous perspective that is yet somehow connected to the will of the rational agent: 'Inexperienced in the course of the world, incapable of being prepared for whatever might come to pass in it, I ask myself only: can you also will that your maxim become a universal law?'[20]

The notions of 'constructive interpretation' and 'reflective equilibrium' are direct heirs of the Kantian philosophy in this sense. One sees this, for example, in Dworkin's image of 'the heroic Judge Hercules', who thinks,

> not inside out, from more specific problems to broader and more abstract ones, as other lawyers do, but outside-in, the other way around. Before he sits on his first case, he could build a gigantic, 'over-arching' theory good for

---

[18] Samuel Pufendorf, *De Iure Naturae et Gentium* (1688, various editions), I.2.6.

[19] *LMI*, 153. For an alternative interpretation of Pufendorf's significance, see Ian Hunter, *Rival Enlightenments* (Cambridge: Cambridge University Press, 2001).

[20] Kant, *Groundwork of the Metaphysics of Morals* (1785), trans. Mary Gregor in *Practical Philosophy: The Cambridge Edition of the Works of Immanuel Kant* (Cambridge: Cambridge University Press, 1996), 4:403: see *LMI*, 154.

> all seasons. He could decide all outstanding questions of metaphysics, epistemology and ethics, and also of morality, including political morality … He could weave all that and everything else into a marvelously architectonic system. When a new case arises, he would be very well prepared.[21]

The central problem for voluntaristic versions of Protestantism is why, if each will is autonomous, we should ever converge in judgment on universal laws? For the status of such laws as universals is precisely the subject at issue. Any appeal to the 'rationality' of the truly autonomous agent is deeply problematic. Such rationality must either constitute an external standard for judgments of the will, which therefore undermines the will's autonomy in deciding 'for itself' what may be a universal law; or else rationality is itself formed from autonomous judgment, in which case agreeing or converging on what is 'rational' is every bit as problematic as what is 'universal'. Nor can a shared language or history explain the fact of convergence, for these complex products of human association are the very phenomena that must be explained. In such circumstances, belief in the rationality and autonomy of the will must be motivated and sustained by a set of beliefs which define an alternative cosmological standpoint to that of traditional theology. Without such beliefs, there exists no reason for supposing that autonomy can be reconciled with rationality.[22]

Consider, by contrast, the older, Aristotelian tradition of reflection upon the nature of the good life. Though it does not exhibit the same tension between autonomy and rationality, the classical alignment of moral wisdom and experience also depends upon faith in certain cosmological principles. Here, the belief is that 'the good' is realized in ordinary life to some degree. But this basic assumption is more easily and fully integrated into the framework of Aristotelian thought, for Aristotle is addressing his remarks to those already possessed of good character and noble dispositions. Having provided an extensive psychological underpinning for human nature as essentially benign, Aristotle is then in a position to treat the human practices and forms of association which embody that nature as themselves providing a central source of insight into the nature of the good.

---

[21] *JR*, 54. Dworkin explores the significance of this image for 'ordinary lawyers' at 55.

[22] In saying that philosophical arguments are grounded in faith (see note 7 above) I do not of course mean to suggest that philosophical thinking enjoys any well-defined end point: that which is believed may be ultimately mysterious, but belief is not itself inarticulate and sets no final boundaries to the activity of speculation.

Protestant thought, on the whole, lacks a similarly grounded understanding of human nature. For such theories tend to replace detailed investigations of the psychology of human nature with broad and general categories of autonomy, rationality, self-interest and freedom etc. as the basis of an account of moral thinking. As morality becomes progressively detached from its foundation in human character, abstract principles of reason are forced into the role of leading those of suitable bearing towards the good, but they do so in a much more detached and free-floating way: being separated from both human telos and the supposition of external imposition by a divine will, the rational convergence of human wills upon common standards of justice and right becomes a matter of diffuse optimism concerning the 'objectivity' of moral values, and the ability of human minds to apprehend them.

2. *Ideals and Archetypes*

Simmonds's approach is grounded in the older tradition in a number of ways.[23] Understanding of the nature of law, he argues, is a matter of reflecting on an intellectual archetype (sometimes referred to as 'the rule of law') that is both implicit within our practices, and imperfectly instantiated by those practices: 'our practices themselves create the archetype insofar as they are structured by ideas that are best understood as pointing to the archetype.'[24] The proposed inquiry therefore 'lies solidly within the tradition of philosophical reflection upon the *logos*: reflection, that is, upon the world as it becomes clear to us in our speaking of it'.[25] Whilst this may seem to echo Dworkin's own position, the form of such inquiry in fact differs markedly from that suggested by Dworkin.

Whereas Simmonds seeks to illuminate the moral significance of law as a distinctive type of social ordering, Dworkin argues that such significance attaches only to the substance of legal doctrine, no interesting

23 Simmonds is not as forthcoming as he might be about the nature of his intellectual commitments: these include elements of Hegelian thought and aspects of British Idealism, as well as Aristotelianism. The relationship between these strands of thought, and the significance of their union, is not clear. (The bearing of Aristotle on Hegel's thought, for instance, is a difficult philosophical problem in its own right.) I do not mean to imply that Simmonds's position is inchoate; rather that the opportunity to deepen the exploration of this aspect of the theory was missed, perhaps because it would take the argument beyond the more limited aim of 'challenging an orthodoxy by direct opposition': see *LMI*, 4.

24 *LMI*, 58.

25 Id.

philosophical questions attaching to law as a social institution.[26] He thus employs a distinction between a 'sociological concept' of law and a 'doctrinal concept' of law, insisting that only the latter is relevant to an understanding of the moral nature of law. Whereas the doctrinal concept concerns the criteria by which the law within a jurisdiction is identified (and in particular whether moral criteria form part of the truth conditions of legal propositions), the sociological concept examines the idea of law as a distinctive type of social institution.[27] The doctrinal concept therefore represents a philosophical question of huge practical and philosophical importance; the sociological concept, by contrast, acquires importance only against the background of more specific purposes and contexts.[28] Asking whether primitive tribal societies, or the Nazi regime, had a legal system requires us to posit a definition of 'law' which makes sense of such questions: a definition that will derive its significance from whatever purposes such inquiries are thought to fulfill. (For example, we might need, from the perspective of some anthropological investigation, to decide whether a primitive system of custom and compromise counts as 'law'.) But in the more general sense, there is no 'natural distinction that marks off legal structures as having … some essential nature that these distinctions try to capture'.[29]

The idea that questions of the nature of law as a social institution are merely 'sociological' is a quite remarkable view. As Simmonds observes, it holds that there is 'no general philosophical question to be asked about the nature of law as a distinct type of social structure.'[30] It therefore fails to comprehend the significance of a form of association as an object of moral contemplation, and the extent to which morality is itself bound up with forms of association. '[L]egal thought can be itself a matter of deepening by reflection our understanding of the distinctive form of association that we call the rule of law'.[31]

As Simmonds rightly says, 'Any account of the nature of law as a distinct type of social institution will tend to suggest a more general view of the human condition, and of law as a distinct type of response to that condition.'[32] After patient argument, Simmonds concludes that law serves to

26 *JR*, 2–3.
27 Id, 1–5.
28 Id, 2.
29 Id, 3.
30 *LMI*, 27.
31 Id.
32 Id, 30.

introduce a domain of universality and necessity into human affairs, such that each person possesses various dimensions of freedom in which he remains free of the will of others.[33] This illuminates the way in which the law is a set of 'mundane arrangements' but also an ideal. For it consists not only in particular rules and decisions, but a system of rules and general organizing ideas. Our legal understandings are shaped by a complex inheritance, formed from ideas of property, obligation, privacy and so on. Particular rules 'must be integrated within this inheritance before we can clearly discern their law-making effect'.[34] By reflecting upon this intellectual inheritance, we can begin to perceive the justificationary basis of law as something intrinsic to its own nature. Slavery is avoided 'only where the free man is governed by law. If he inhabits a political community governed in any other way, the options he has available to him will be dependent on the will of others'. Thus:

> Law represents the only possible set of conditions within which one can live in community with others while enjoying some domain of entitlement that is secure from the power of others ... The existence of such a domain requires that the law be enforced and therefore the value of such a domain justifies the law's enforcement.[35]

The archetype of law is then a moral idea which is both embodied within established practices, and an immanent critique of those practices. If our moral understanding is to be seen as real, Simmonds argues, it must exhibit this duality: 'it must be bound up with our grasp of the commonplace world, forming part of the realm of socially sustained knowledge that renders us mutually intelligible. The structures of meaning and value that are involved here are inhabited before they are reflected upon'.[36] In this way, our practice 'opens itself to transformation through the very forms of moral perception that it creates'.[37]

The importance of this thought should not be underestimated. It amounts to nothing less than a reorientation of the root-beliefs which underpin and sustain our conceptions of law and government. It grounds those conceptions in a world-view that is at once Catholic and conservative.[38] The Catholicity of the position resides in the thought that the

---

33 Id, 142–43.

34 Id, 12.

35 Id, 143.

36 Id, 141.

37 Id, 149.

38 Simmonds writes as an atheist, and can therefore be expected to oppose the interpretation of the significance of his position that I am about to suggest. We can nevertheless

'commonplace world' is not simply a set of occasions on which we superimpose our understandings; rather it grounds our understandings. Human beings are not free-floating instances of generic 'humanity', for their identities 'depend on the renewal of the particular cultural forms by which they are constituted.'[39] In consequence, our identities (and therefore also our moral characters) are shaped not by the operations of the autonomous will, but by involvement in cultural forms and commonalities from which total separation is impossible. (One's choice to live as a self-sufficient hermit requires both a mature identity and immersion within a linguistic practice. Moreover, such a life comes at a high cost, and this tends to affirm rather than dismiss the value of the commonalities from which one seeks to withdraw.)

Catholicism is not to be confused with shallow universalism, but rejects rather the image, congenial to Protestant ideologies, of the human being as an *ens completum*. The meaning of Augustine's separation of the earthly and divine cities lies similarly in the belief that the religious man must transcend his worldly situation, but can at no point altogether deny or abandon that situation.[40] This deep association of human beings with the shared social world points to truths that go beyond oneself and illustrates that the values to which we are most deeply attached are not necessarily those which are most transparent to understanding. The 'Protestant' features of the modern political world might then come to be exposed as relatively superficial phenomena that move within a richer cultural inheritance.

It should be clear, also, that a Catholic world-view of this kind must imply an attitude of conservatism. The mundane world of imperfect institutions and received practices is not as clay that possesses no intrinsic value until shaped in this way or that. Its value indeed depends not upon its specific form so much as on its familiarity (in terms of that which makes us recognizable to ourselves).[41] For the conservative, '[w]hat is esteemed is the present: and it is esteemed not on account of its connections with a remote antiquity, nor because it is recognized to be more admirable than any possible alternative, but on account of its familiarity: not, *Verweile doch, du bist so schon*, but, *Stay with me because I am attached*

contrast this position with that of Dworkin, who advances a political theory that is avowedly Protestant: see Dworkin, *Law's Empire* (above n 2), 190.

[39] John Gray, *Enlightenment's Wake* (London: Routledge, 1995), 161.

[40] Augustine, *De Civitate Dei* II & XIX.

[41] We must believe this, at least if we believe that we do not inhabit a hell, definitive of identities that are utterly remote from God, or moral virtue.

to you'.[42] To a much greater degree than envisaged by Dworkin, the conservative is sensitive to the loss associated with every change:

> Innovating is always an equivocal enterprise, in which gain and loss (even excluding the loss of familiarity) are so closely interwoven that it is exceedingly difficult to forecast the final upshot: there is no such thing as an unqualified improvement. For, innovating is an activity which generates not only the 'improvement' sought, but a new and complex situation of which this is only one of the components. The total change is always more extensive than the change designed; and the whole of what is entailed can neither be foreseen nor circumscribed.[43]

I stress these implications of Simmonds's position because they invite further reflection upon his suggestion that it is grounded in ordinary semantic intuitions which express inchoate moral insights. As we explore and deepen these intuitions, the world 'becomes clear to us in our speaking of it'.[44] But the tradition of 'reflection upon the logos' is not a simple one. The original, ancient meaning of the term (found in Heraclitus) referred to the divine source and animating principle of the universe, from which the order of things derives. The Gospel of John opens with the identification of Jesus as the incarnation of the *logos* (or Word) by which all was made.[45] Other usages of the term obscure its cosmological connotations. But in the absence of cosmological associations, it is unclear why the world should become 'clear' to us in our speaking. Might the world not, after all, be finally incoherent, exhibiting no clear principles, from which all intelligible order is absent? It is hard to see how any body of knowledge (even science) can claim to understand the world, unless it is rooted in the *logos* in this deeper, cosmological sense.

There is one further sense in which Simmonds's position represents a significant departure from the mainstream of modern legal and political philosophy. Political thought, he urges, should be understood as a

---

42 Michael Oakeshott, 'On Being Conservative' in *Rationalism in Politics* (Indianapolis: Liberty Fund, 1991), 408.

43 Id, 411. Dworkin might conceivably object that his requirement of 'fit' sufficiently anchors change so that the revisionary aspect of his theory is held reasonably in check. This is, I think, an illusion; but more importantly it misses the point. The point is not that the deepest commitments of the present situation are unlikely to be revised, but that his theory obliterates altogether the category of the sacred from human practices (and thus also from human identities). On the connections between conservatism and the sacred, see Leszek Kolakowski, *Modernity on Endless Trial* (Chicago: University of Chicago Press, 1990), 70.

44 *LMI*, 58, 68.

45 See John 1:1.

deepening reflection upon the conditions for the realization of a complex good (one that can only be realized in common). The politics of the modern age, by contrast, concern rather a framework of entitlements governing access to goods that are essentially simple, to be pursued independently by different individuals.[46]

It is possible to regard these remarks as pointing to a distinction between Aristotelian and Platonic images of the state. Aristotle's *Politics* contemplated the ideal form of the state from the moral perspective of the person, seeking the refinement of forms and structures that would facilitate human flourishing and promote excellence-forming habits. The rise of Christian thought preserved this centrality of the person as a moral centre, the ideal here being the quest for the salvation of the individual soul. Platonic images of the ideal state, by contrast, focused upon the quite different ethical notion of the flourishing city, considered as a normative object. This, says Plato (or rather Socrates), is a city in which all individuals are allotted a social role based upon their aptitude to realize dimensions of a communal social life, and not upon their desires or interests.[47] As Adeimantus, one of Socrates's interlocutors, makes clear, such an ethical vision effectively promotes the flourishing of the state at the expense of the flourishing of the human beings within it.

Western philosophy, I would like to suggest, has followed the Platonic image of the state, and has given relatively little thought to the idea at the centre of Aristotle's vision. The central idea of Aristotle's politics is that the nature of society must be apprehended on the basis of a clear conception of 'the good', and that this good is a human good. Politics thus requires a full and proper understanding of the human person as a moral being, and of society as a context of relations between such beings. As such, it depends upon the articulation of a good that is irreducibly complex. By contrast, the Platonic image of the state centres upon a collective good that is intellectually separable from the good of the individual person: those actions, arrangements and institutions that are optimal for the flourishing of the state are not necessarily those which are optimal for the flourishing of its human subjects. Oakeshott brilliantly expounds the underlying characteristic of this philosophy:

---

46 *LMI*, 151.

47 See Plato, *The Republic*, IV, 419a–420. See also the discussion in Geuss, (above n 9), 99. On the appropriateness of modern understandings of the city of *The Republic* as an 'ideal' state, see Eric Voeglin, *Order and History* vol 3 (Baton Rouge: Louisiana State University Press, 1957), 83.

> [It] is the manner in which it divides the life of the individual and the life of society into exclusive areas and so destroys all idea of a whole except as a kind of average condition of being. The individual self can never quite be certain when he is promoting the good of the 'whole' that he will not be forced to exclude himself from that good, and on the other hand, it is always possible that in seeking his own good he may be denying the greatest good to the 'whole'. Now, in place of the 'whole' in this theory, it is clear that we must write the 'rest' ... for a 'whole' which is divided into 'self' and 'others' is no whole at all.[48]

In *Law as a Moral Idea*, Simmonds helps to bring into focus an idea that is obscured by the juridical philosophies of the present day. Such philosophies focus upon the attempt to realize generic ideals (such as 'liberty', 'happiness' and so on) which represent citizenship as a kind of 'average condition of being'. The good being explored is an essentially Protestant one, a set of common standards for a divided world. This notion of the good readily lends itself to exploration in terms, not of 'human nature', but of the various convictions of faceless 'individuals'. We are forced, on this basis, to wander between the notion that society is a mere aggregate of individuals (and therefore averaging of their preferences) and the idea of society as a superstructure distinct from individuals, with its own needs, agendas and goals. Simmonds, by contrast, pursues the Aristotelian thought that state and society form an organic whole in which the requirements of human flourishing flow from reflection upon the embodied human condition as it is manifested by a deep cultural self-knowledge. The complexity of the 'good' being pursued is thus not merely contestable, difficult to articulate and technically problematic, but complex in its very nature, multi-faceted, multi-layered and continuous.

3. *Duty, Order and Aspiration*

I have been exploring two different visions of the ideality of law. Each raises a very profound and problematical set of questions that are all too often excluded from jurisprudential discussion. I would like to use this brief final section to explore the implications of these questions for an understanding of law as (above all) a domain of practical reason.

---

[48] Oakeshott, *Religion, Politics and the Moral Life* (New Haven: Yale University Press, 1993), 51. Oakeshott is here speaking a propos of utilitarianism, and does not connect the idea to what I am calling its 'Platonic' heritage.

There is, as Simmonds points out, a kind of radical subjectivity involved in the idea that the coherence of moral judgment is to be found in (or founded upon) detached principle.[49] Where morality is understood to be a matter of the 'integrity' or coherence of one's conscientious deliberations, what possible basis is there for saying that legal or social practices 'embody' a moral philosophy? Are not practices of law-creation, of the administration and adjudication of law, then (as the positivists said) not essentially inert phenomena open to evaluation according to different, radically detached, considerations? It might remain that one's intellections of those practices and those phenomena are incapable of separation from one's understandings of the practical ends thereby served. But those understandings would be precisely 'evaluations' *of the practices*, i.e. of objects capable of being interpreted and evaluated in different ways. And if so, why should it be imagined that different individuals will (in conscience) ever converge in their judgments of the moral significance of such phenomena? Indeed, that being the case, there is little to justify Dworkin in believing such judgments *must* be those which attempt to place the practice 'in its best light'[50] rather than attempting to interpret other participants' understandings in engaging in and advancing that practice.

The vision of law as embodying an archetype involves a different and more satisfying understanding of moral coherence, as being a matter of the collective intelligibility of discrete and divergent practices that belong to a shared form of life. Observers and even participants in the practices of administering the law could intelligibly choose not to explore the source of this coherence (the 'depth of the ideal' in Simmonds's terms), but pay attention only to the immediate implications of the practices in distributing the needs of material life. In this way contract lawyers (for example) can discuss the various consequences in law of the doctrine of frustration, the justice of its effects on specific litigants on specific occasions, without broadening their inquiry into one concerning the nature or moral ends of contract law as such. They might treat the moral ideas precisely as implications *arising from* the doctrines, rather than as implicit *foundations* of doctrinal ideas, the 'general part of adjudication, silent prologue to any decision at law.'[51]

[49] See Simmonds, 'The Nature and Virtue of Law', 1 *Jurisprudence* (2010), 277–293, 278.
[50] Dworkin, *Law's Empire* (London, Fontana, 1986), 54.
[51] Id. 90.

Is Simmonds nevertheless justified in identifying such implications as *ideals*? Does the archetype of law represent an 'ideal' precisely in being a *moral* 'idea'?[52] Above all, does one not damage or relegate the rule of law in comprehending it as ideal or aspiration, as distinct from 'a stringent moral duty or cluster of duties of justice'?[53] For Simmonds, 'the situation as it confronts us' is the source of understanding that 'calls our moral knowledge into being.'[54] There is indeed a sense in which one's practical deliberations can be said to be shaped by 'the world'. Right action and good practices have no examples to illuminate the mind that are not drawn from worldly contexts, even if those contexts are imagined. In the absence of direct images of perfection it is possible to advance one's understanding of honour (for example), only by contemplating the imperfection of the thousand instances in which honourable action is absent, corrupted, distorted, qualified, incomplete etc.[55] But are our practical deliberations therefore condemned only to moderate the effects of imperfection? Can they never centre upon the determination of duties that demand to be fulfilled even in a world of recalcitrance and corruption? In treating moral ideas as 'ideals', we create the risk of tolerating too readily the abundant failures of governments, judges and citizens to live up to the requirements of justice.

Here I wish to raise a further question in relation to the book's Catholic spirituality, by placing alongside one another two understandings of embodiment: archetype and 'focal meaning.' At a fairly early stage in the book, Simmonds divorces these two understandings (despite 'certain resemblances') due to the fact that focal instances of law (indeed of any concept) are fully instantiated in experience, whereas archetypes are not.[56] This is, I think, incorrect. Reflection on the *logos* is (as Aquinas points out) upon an order incarnated in numerous ways. The concepts employed by the *spoudaios* for the understanding of practical affairs are orientated not only by the intellections human beings have of an order they do not themselves bring about (natural order) nor by the order or coherence of thought itself (rational order), but also by the order introduced into human affairs by the exercise of human powers in reducing aspects of nature to control ('sub-creative order') and that of the very

52 I raise this question in reply to a short but powerful essay by John Finnis, 'Law as Idea, Ideal and Duty' 1 *Jurisprudence* (2010), 245–51.

53 Id, 246.

54 *LMI*, 146.

55 This I take it is the wider intent of Aristotle's doctrine of the mean.

56 *LMI*, 52.

direction and intelligent unification of choice and action.[57] The concepts thus employed will (all of them) apply focally to certain instances of the phenomena in view, and only secondarily (*secundum quid*) to a broader range of instances that are (as Finnis says) 'deviant, marginal, secondary, underdeveloped, etc.'[58] Indeed, the focal meanings will shift as the purposes and reflections of the *spoudaios* shift between the different kinds of order. As a result, instances of law can be understood as focal instances of the very effort to realize dimensions of virtue, or of goodness, freedom, etc. in a world that is in other ways obstructive to, or corruptive of, those efforts.[59]

Simmonds's position can be understood as echoing the darker aspects of Augustine's view of human politics. The demands of true justice are not met at the level of actual political institutions, but only a distortion or corruption of justice.[60] Social order is the relative order of the criminal gang, limited to a 'compromise between human wills about the things relevant to mortal life.'[61] Yet when Augustine castigates the Roman jurists so beloved of his correspondent Nectarius, it is because they have failed to realize the just society except in 'thought and speech'.[62] It is thus supposed by Augustine that (at least) 'learned men' achieve an understanding of the *duties* of justice in speculative thought. Justice is not simply an aspiration, understood only insofar as we are acquainted with its imperfect forms in the here-and-now, but grasped as a set of demands in the cause of which human beings are called to labour.

Aquinas, upon whose account Finnis relies above all others, is willing to go further in this respect. Human societies are not a 'natural condition' of the kind envisaged by Hobbes, but an ordered existence in which justice is in some measure already present. Human practices are not utterly removed from justice, are not completely depraved, but instantiate and participate in justice only incompletely.[63] A similar thought seems to have

---

[57] See Aristotle, *Nicomachean Ethics* X.5–6; See also specifically Aquinas's *Commentary* on the Ethics, I.1.1.

[58] Finnis, (above n 52), 248.

[59] One could reverse the emphasis of Finnis's often overlooked assertion in ch 1 of *Natural Law and Natural Rights*: 'A theory of natural law need not be undertaken primarily for the purpose of thus providing a justified conceptual framework for descriptive social science. It may be undertaken, as this book is, primarily to assist the practical reflections of those concerned to act…' (Oxford: Clarendon Press, 1980), 18.

[60] Augustine, *De Civitate Dei* II.22: '… there never was real justice in the community.'

[61] Id. XIX.17.

[62] Augustine, Epistle 91, 4.

[63] Aquinas, *Summa Theologiae* I-II.91.2, 94.6 & II.57.1.

occupied the mind of the twentieth-century jurist from whom Simmonds derives inspiration: Lon Fuller. In some speaking notes for an address at the University of Vermont in 1959, Fuller is at pains to emphasize that justice is to be achieved through law. The first question to be asked (in his view) is whether in *achieving* justice, institutions or public aspirations are the more important. His answer is that while both are essential, philosophy requires much more emphasis upon institutions. No moral attitude can realize itself directly, without being mediated through (i.e. *realized* by) mechanisms. Thus the writ of Habeas Corpus is wrongly regarded when treated as the 'expression of the spirit' of freedom; it is necessary to realize that 'it *is* freedom in the context of a particular problem.'[64] Indeed the sustaining attitudes necessary for the realization of human goods are not simply attitudes to values such as freedom and dignity, but attitudes *toward* institutions.[65]

What can be drawn from this? Practical reasoning is unduly restricted if it is left to speculate only upon ideas and moral demands as they are imperfectly instantiated in the here-and-now. It must take its direction from moral duties, and from demands of justice that operate (and are capable of operating) fully in this world, however obscured our sight of them, and however short we fall of discharging them. The life of the *spoudaios* as much as that of the Christian is one not only of ideal or of principle, but one that demands the incarnation of principle. Such efforts absolutely require law and other 'mechanisms'. Justice resolutely demands the systematic *administration* of justice. These mechanisms do not always operate as the person of good moral character and practical reasonableness would wish, and in this sense the demands of justice are not independent of aspirations as to how law should be. For one who bears in mind Oakeshott's observation that effected change is always greater than the change envisaged, the task of amending those institutions and mechanisms is at the same time a clarification of moral understanding, of what is being demanded morally. But this implies neither that (i) practical reasoning is guided by aspiration or archetype as the exclusive means of transcending current arrangements, nor (ii) practical reasoning is a process of achieving 'reflective equilibrium' between concrete instincts of justice

---

[64] Fuller, Notes for a talk on 'Traditions of justice among the western peoples', University of Vermont, 13 July 1959, in the papers of Lon Fuller, Harvard Law School Library, Box 11, folder 8. I am extremely grateful to Lesley Schoenfeld and the staff in Special Collections at the Harvard Library for granting access to the papers.

[65] Id. though Fuller adds 'not blind'.

and abstract visions of principle.[66] The reflections of the *spoudaios* are fundamentally reflections upon order, and upon what is demanded for the coherence and perfection of that order. Above all, they are reflections upon the conditions, the duties of justice, that must necessarily be fulfilled if social order is to bring forth the human 'good'.

[66] See John Neville Figgis, *The Political Aspects of St Augustine's City of God* (London, Longmans, 1921), 34: 'The religion of the Incarnation cannot be mere theology - a system of notions developed from certain metaphysical propositions - nor can it be mere ethics, a code of laws on a theistic basis. It has to do with a life on earth, in which Christians hold that in the fullness of time - i.e. at the due moment in history - the eternal reality at the heart of things became self-revealed and self-limited in a living person.'

REVIEW ARTICLE: LEGAL THEORY, LAW, AND NORMATIVITY

Leonard Kahn

Abstract

Joseph Raz's new book, *Between Authority and Interpretation*, collects his most important papers in the philosophy of law and the theory of practical rationality from the mid-1990s to the mid-2000s. In these papers, Raz not only advances earlier theses but also breaks new ground in a number of areas. I focus on three of Raz's topics here: theories of law, separability and necessity, and the normativity of law. While I am generally sympathetic to Raz's thinking on these topics, I raise some room for doubt – especially with regard to his pessimism about finding a uniquely best theory of law and the relationship between law and morality.

Keywords

Joseph Raz, legal positivism, reasons, normativity

Joseph Raz, *Between Authority and Interpretation: On the Theory of Law and Practical Reason*, (Oxford: Oxford University Press, 2009), 413 pages. ISBN 0199562687 (hbk.). Hardback/Paperback $85/$40.

1. *Introduction*

Joseph Raz has, quite reasonably, been called, "the foremost theorist in contemporary English-language analytical jurisprudence,"[1] and *Between Authority and Interpretation* is a collection of his most important papers in the philosophy of law and the theory of practical rationality from the mid-1990s to the mid-2000s. While many of the papers develop ideas that Raz articulated in earlier works,[2] the book is no mere rehashing of familiar

[1] Brian Bix, "Raz on Necessity," *Law and Philosophy* 22, (2003), p. 537.

[2] See especially *Practical Reason and Norms*, Second Edition, (Oxford: Oxford University Press, [1975] 1990), *The Authority of Law*, Second Edition, (Oxford: Oxford University Press,

themes. Raz not only advances earlier theses but also breaks new ground in a number of areas. In fact, there is no possibility of doing justice to the thematic and dialectical richness of a book like this, even in an extended review. Instead of attempting the impossible, I divide the rest of this essay into three sections, each reflecting one of the many topics which Raz addresses in *Between Authority and Interpretation*: the first section focuses on the nature of theories of law, the second turns to separability and necessity, and the third concerns the normativity of law. Sadly, much that is worth discussing must be put to the side here. For instance, I cannot discuss Raz's theory of interpretation, his thinking about civil disobedience, or his so-called "service conception of authority,"[3] and can only touch in passing on one or two aspects of his many instructive disagreements with Ronald Dworkin. These topics will have to wait for another day.

2. *Theories of Law*

According to Raz, a theory of law is a theory of the central concepts involved in legal actions.[4] Moreover, such a theory is (or, at least, can be) "general." That is to say, it can be correctly applied not only to our own society and culture but to other societies and cultures as well, even to societies and cultures with different concepts of law – or with no legal concepts at all. More specifically, theories of law are composed of "theses [that], if true, apply universally, that is they speak of the law, of all legal systems: of those that exist, or that will exist, even those that can exist though they never will" (p. 91).[5] Nevertheless, a theory of law must also acknowledge its locality and temporality. Our own concept of law has developed over time and will continue to do so. As Raz puts it, "Talk of *the* concept of law really means *our* concept" (p. 31, emphasis in the original) – i.e., our concept in the here and now. Since theories of law are "parochial" in this sense, they attempt to explain "a product of a specific culture, a concept which was not available to members of earlier cultures

[1979] 2009), *The Concept of a Legal System* (Oxford: Clarendon Press, 1980), *The Morality of Freedom*, (Oxford: Oxford University Press, 1986), *Ethics in the Public Domain* (Oxford: Oxford University Press, 1995), and *The Practice of Value* (Oxford: Oxford University Press, 2004) but also *Engaging Reason*, (Oxford: Oxford University Press, 1990) and *Value, Respect, and Attachment* (Cambridge, UK: Cambridge University Press, 2001).

[3] *Practical Reason and Norms*, p. 21.

[4] Compare his *Ethics in the Public Domain*, pp. 195–198.

[5] All parenthetical references are to *Between Authority and Interpretation*.

which in fact lived under a legal system" (p. 95). So theories of law, then, are both general and parochial, Raz claims.

Should we find this fact at all puzzling? Would we be warranted in worrying about our theories of law because they are both general and parochial in these ways? Perhaps not. Some humans lived (and live even now) in feudal economies and others lived and continued to live in capitalist economies even though they lacked (or lack) the concepts we deploy in describing such economies. E.g., Geoffrey Chaucer lived under a feudal system while probably lacking anything like the corresponding concept, and Jane Austen plausibly did likewise with regard to a capitalist system. Again, some humans lived (and live even now) in one social class or another without knowing that they did (or do) so. Indeed, it is a truism of sociology that in the United States we have social classes but no real awareness of this fact. And whether or not this is true, it is not a self-contradiction, as it would have to be if the existence of social classes depended on an awareness of their existence.

However, Raz reminds us that law is importantly different from these and many other social phenomena. Following H.L.A. Hart, Raz insists that a theory of law must take "an internal point of view."[6] More specifically, Raz himself says that a theory of law must take a perspective which "is focused on the way the law is understood by the people whose law it is" (p. 93). But how can a theory of law take this point of view if it applies to all times, places, and cultures? *This* question gets at the heart of the dichotomy between the generality and the parochiality of theories of law with which Raz is concerned, and as a result his puzzle comes, I think, into sharper focus.

Raz's solution to the puzzle is to argue that it is not necessary for those who are governed by law to see it as law, *per se*. For law is a kind of social rule. Of course it does not follow – and Raz does not claim – that all social rules are laws or that human society is impossible without laws.[7] He claims only that laws are one among various kinds of social rules. Call this the *Social Thesis*. I say more about the Social Thesis in Section 3, but for now the point on which we should focus concerns Raz's resolution of the generality and parochiality of legal theories, which is as follows: Those subject to a law need only see it as some kind of social rule, not as a law, so they need not have our legal concepts (p. 96).

---

6 H.L.A. Hart, *The Concept of Law*, Second Edition (Oxford: Oxford University Press, [1961] 1996), e.g. p. 96.

7 *Practical Reason and Norms*, p. 163.

This fact puts limits on the ways in which we can understand the role of law in societies that lack (or lacked, or will lack) our concept of law. At best, we explicate "our own self-understanding" (p. 97) of such alien societies, and it might be thought that the role of *self* in self-understanding has relativistic (or even nihilistic) consequences for the philosophy of law. Yet Raz claims that there are mitigating factors which ought to prevent us from reaching this conclusion. We require not only our concept of law to understand other cultures; we also need (at least some of) their concepts as well. Of course, these alien concepts are unlikely to have any currency in our practices; they would hardly be alien if they did. So we will be unable to understand their rules as *they* understood them. But that is not what is required of a theory of law, according to Raz.

If the point of a legal theory is not to understand the law precisely as those subject to it did (or do or will), then what kind of explanations does a legal theory provide? Raz's answer is that a theory gives us necessary truths about the law, for only such truths "reveal the nature of the law" (p. 24), where "the nature of law" and "the essence of law" are understood as co-referential phrases. By putting the matter this way, Raz appears to hold the bar very high, yet he has in fact rather modest hopes for our ability to construct such theories. He warns that "any account of the nature of law will apply to central cases, and will allow for degenerate cases of law" (p. 170). So no theory of law will be entirely free of counterexamples, even if they are marginal ones. Indeed, Raz expresses general skepticism about the usefulness of what he calls the "necessary and sufficient condition requirement" (pp. 56-57) familiar from so much of conceptual analysis. Why? First, it is not the case, Raz thinks, that every set of necessary and sufficient conditions for the correct use of a given concept is either instructive or helpful. Along these lines, Raz mentions Aristotle's famous claim that humans are rational animals. It might well be true that we are, Raz thinks, but it does not follow that our rational nature is any more important than the features of our nature that we share with other animals. Second, some essential features of things are "defeasible," and therefore not subject to necessary and sufficient conditions in the usual way of understanding these terms.[8] Third, excessive worry about necessary and sufficient conditions distracts us from the fact that it is often the place of a concept within a broader "conceptual web" (p. 57) that is of most interest to us.[9] Raz's own thinking about the connections between law and

---

[8] See also *Ethics in the Public Domain*, pp. 250–252.

[9] It is worth comparing Raz's thinking on this point with that of Peter Strawson in his *Analysis and Metaphysics* (Oxford: Oxford University Press, 1992), pp. 17-28. Both Strawson

morality is a good example of this phenomenon.[10] Fourth, Raz maintains that a given concept may have multiple necessary and sufficient conditions for correct application. Yet listing all of them would be no more worthwhile than entries in a telephone book.[11] I return to Raz's pessimism about theories of law at the end of Section 3.

3. *Separability and Necessity*

So what, if anything, *is* essential to the law? Must a standard in some sense be morally legitimate in order to be a law? For much of its recent history, these questions (and questions of this sort) have been the gold standard for work in the philosophy of law. The Social Thesis discussed in Section 2 is part of an answer to this question. Hart provides an influential statement of another part of this answer. According to Hart, "it is in no sense a necessary truth that laws reproduce or satisfy certain demands of morality, though in fact they have often done so."[12] Hart's claim is often called the *Separability Thesis*.[13] Together, the Social Thesis and the Separability Thesis form much of the core of legal positivism.[14] This is no place to rehearse the history of this position and its rivals. It is enough for my present purposes that Raz's name has been, and continues to be, closely associated with the view, especially in its most sophisticated form.[15] While Raz appears to continue to orbit this particular center of gravity, he now thinks that Hart and other positivists were wrong to think that anything like the

---

and Raz clearly reject the project of completely reducing some concepts to other simple concepts familiar from G.E. Moore and still at work in the work of, e.g., T.M. Scanlon. See Moore, *Principia Ethica* (Cambridge, UK: Cambridge University Press, 1903), Chapter 1 and Scanlon, *What We Owe to Each Other* (Cambridge, Massachusetts: Harvard University Press, 1998), Chapter 1.

[10] See Section 4 of this essay below.

[11] It is worth asking whether Raz has in his sights the sort of project for conceptual analysis defended by Frank Jackson, though Jackson goes unnamed here. See Frank Jackson, *From Metaphysics to Ethics: A Defense of Conceptual Analysis* (Oxford: Oxford University Press, 1998).

[12] *The Concept of Law*, p. 182.

[13] Raz defends a version of this position with great ingenuity in, among other places, *The Authority of Law*, p. 46 and *Ethics in the Public Domain*, pp. 210-237.

[14] Sometimes a third thesis is suggested as part of legal positivism – namely, that the validity of laws is, ultimately, a matter of convention. But it is not my purpose to define *legal positivism* in this review, and, at any rate, Raz's relationship to this thesis is somewhat ambiguous.

[15] I do not try the reader's patience with a long list of sources here. Raz's identification with some form or other of legal positivism is simply too well-known for that.

Social Thesis and the Separability thesis come close to exhausting the essential features of law. Other essential features include "that it claims to have legitimate, moral, authority and that it is source-based, and that it claims to have peremptory force" (p. 97). But Raz claims that even these features do not settle the score with regard to the law's essence. We cannot complete Hart's task – discovering the essence of law – simply by conjoining these features, for the law has yet *more* essential features of which we are currently ignorant. We are likely to discover some of these through the fullness of time, but "the list of the essential properties of law is indefinite" (p. 98). So when it comes to the concept of law, we are simply out of luck. Given all of this, it is perhaps not surprising that Raz is rather dismissive about the importance of the usual way of framing debates within the philosophy of law as being between natural law theory and legal positivism (pp. 167-169).

If Raz is right, then, no doubt, he will be responsible for the revision of many syllabi for courses which introduce undergraduates to the philosophy of law. But Raz's cautious approach to the correct understanding of concepts has much deeper implications for the evaluation of theories of law. Raz tells us that "Nothing in my approach implies that there is one best theory of the nature of law ... it strongly suggests the possibility that while many theories are badly defective, there may well be more than one possible ... adequate theory" (p. 10). Part of the explanation of this fact appears to arise from the following considerations: The concepts deployed in the everyday practice of law are not precise enough to develop a theory. So a theorist must give these concepts "sharper focus and definition" (p. 10). But there is no single best way to hone these concepts. Different ways of doing so lead to different theories. Hence, there is no single best theory of the nature of law.

Yet I am not sure we should follow Raz to the very end of this particular limb. Consider a partially analogous situation: No doubt many of the concepts of science are precisifications of other work-a-day concepts. We need think only of mass, force, and acceleration as examples. In one sense, there is no single best way to give these concepts greater precision so that they can serve us in a theory of physics – provided that we limit ourselves to considering the concepts and nothing more. But the theories themselves, which form at least part of the basis of the theory, will have virtues and vices. One theory might be simpler or more generalizable than another. To the extent that these virtues and vices supervene on the precisification of concepts, we can see the precisification itself as being better or worse. As it so happens, without such virtues and vices we would have little to go on when we ourselves are trying to decide which theory to accept. Perhaps one theory would be more deeply entrenched in our practices than another. However, that does not appear to be enough to decide the matter in many cases. We seem to need the idea of a single correct theory of law if we are to engage in theorizing, whether we do indeed have that theory or not.

That said, Raz's open-ended approach to the nature of law is a useful corrective to some other perspectives. Attempts to nail down the essential features of several philosophically important concepts over the last few decades have proved frustrating and are likely to continue to do so. The concept of knowledge is the most obvious example, but it is hardly alone. Perhaps Raz's frankness about providing a partial account of the nature of law strikes the right tone in light of the sometimes frustrating attempts at the full analysis of concepts that have absorbed so much scholarly energy in the profession. However, Raz's skepticism about *ever* being able to settle down on the nature of law appears unmotivated to me. As far as I can see, we have no more reason to think that the list of the essential properties of law is indefinite than we have to think it is definite. A properly balanced approach here requires that we keep an open mind about the nature of law, not that we conclude that a complete understanding of it is forever beyond the reach of sublunary types like us.

4. *The Normativity of Law*

The two main substantive issues discussed in *Between Authority and Interpretation* concern the authority of law and the relationship between law and morality. Raz urges us not to conflate the two of these. Questions about the authority of law are to be understood as questions about its normativity, the manner in which the law constitutes reasons for action. Yet morality is just one variety of normativity. Moreover, "the content of law can be established without resort to moral considerations bearing on the desirability or otherwise of human conduct, or of having particular legal standards" (p. 4), as we have already seen. Nevertheless, on the very same page Raz tells us that "legal discourse is moral discourse." How can *both* of these claims be true?

Raz's answer is subtle. He maintains not only that the law aspires to hold itself to certain standards but also that it is possible for the law in at least some cases to fail completely to meet these standards. More exactly: On the one hand, legal institutions simply take themselves to have moral authority and, therefore, to impose morally binding rights, obligations, duties, permissions, and the like.[16] On the other hand, legal standards can fail to meet these standards, and therefore, fail to be morally justified. "If the law is not morally legitimate then its existence in itself is not a reason for action, though of course, the fact that other people, employers, friends, courts, police are influenced by it may well provide such reasons" (p. 6). But – and this point is vital – even in cases of complete failure, the claimed standards in question do not thereby cease to be laws, Raz claims.

Despite the deft hand that Raz displays in tracing the relations between law and morality, there is room for doubt. Imagine that I take a sword and use it to tap you on both shoulders while saying, "I hereby dub thee knight. Arise, Sir Joseph." Imagine also that I do so not as a joke, not as an attempt to mock the eccentric ways of my host country, nor as any such thing. Now, in attempting to make you a knight, I presuppose a certain kind of authority. But since I am not England's monarch, I lack this authority, and my action misfires. My action is, in J.L. Austin's excellent phrase, "infelicitous."[17] Would we say that my action is nevertheless a knighting simply because I presuppose the relevant authority? Not, I think, if we were pressed on the matter. My words and actions so badly fail to conform to the required standards that they cannot even be called an unauthorized knighting. Nor can we dodge this unfortunate result by claiming that it is a failed knighting, since a so-called failed knighting is simply a failure of an attempt to make a knight and, therefore, not a knighting at all. The same thing, *mutatis mutandis*, can be said in cases where with certain background conditions in place I say, "I now pronounce you man and wife" or "I christen this child Joseph." In both cases I presuppose a sort of authority that I do not have. Yet the first is not an unsanctioned marriage, and the second is not an illicit christening. They are flat-out and unequivocal failures to do the particular intended action. The question, then, is this: Why should matters be any different when it comes to the law? If a legal institution presupposes an authority, then why should we say that it can make laws in cases where it lacks this authority? Why is my failure to secure the required authority even one bit more fatal than the law's?

There are, of course, a number of possible responses. The first of these holds that there really is no difference between *both* cases in which legal institutions lack authority and the cases above in which I lack authority.

---

[16] It is worth stressing the centrality of this idea to Raz's thinking about the law. See *Practical Reason and Norms*, pp. 151–152, *The Authority of Law*, p. 153, *The Morality of Freedom*, p. 92, and *Ethics in the Public Domain*, p. 199.

[17] J.L. Austin, *How to do Things with Words*, Second Edition, Edited by J.O. Urmson and Marina Sbisa (Cambridge, Massachusetts: Harvard University Press, [1962] 1975), p. 25.

This is so because in both cases the lack of authority renders the result, to borrow from Austin once again, "null and void."[18] But it is hard to imagine Raz accepting this result since it would make his own position hard to distinguish from those more sympathetic to natural law theory such as Ronald Dworkin and John Finnis.[19] Even given Raz's skepticism about the importance of the distinction between legal positivism and natural law theory (as discussed in Section 3), his acceptance of something so close to Dworkin's and Finnis' positions on this matter would seem close to incredible, and Raz has certainly gone to some lengths in the past to distinguish his own position from that of natural law and related views.[20]

In the second response there is no difference between cases in which legal institutions lack authority and the cases above in which I lack authority because in *neither* situation does the lack of authority prevent the result from being null and void. That is to say, a law without moral authority is still a law, and a knighting without conventional authority is still a knighting. However, I cannot see why we should be persuaded that this is so. It would be absurd for me to brag about the many people I have knighted, married, and christened, no matter how many times I say the right words with an earnest intention to bring about these states of affairs.

The most interesting response by far is to attempt to find a significant difference between the case of my attempt to make someone a knight and the case of a faulty legal system's attempt to make a law. Several possibilities are on offer, but I contemplate only one here. While nothing prevents me from taking a sword, tapping you on both shoulders, and saying, "I hereby dub thee knight," my social role does not even remotely suggest that I have the authority to make others knights. Likewise, nothing stops me from saying "I now pronounce you man and wife" or "I christen this child Joseph." But the incongruity of my doing so cannot fail to draw one's attention. Being a professor of philosophy has many benefits, but for better or worse the ability to create peers of the realm, marry partners, or christen children is not among them. My presupposition of the necessary authority to do so is completely out of keeping with my role in society.

However, matters appear different in the case of legal institutions. When they attempt to make laws, they not only presuppose the moral authority required to do so, they make this presupposition in a way that

---

18 *Ibid.*, p. 137.

19 Ronald Dworkin, Taking Rights Seriously (Cambridge, Massachusetts: Harvard University Press, 1978) and *Law's Empire* (Cambridge, Massachusetts: Harvard Belknap, 1986) and John Finnis, *Natural Law and Natural Rights* (Oxford: Oxford University Press, 1980).

20 See *Practical Reason and Norms*, pp. 162-170, and *The Morality of Freedom*, pp. 23-37.

seems entirely in keeping with their social role. Along these lines we might ask, if the function of legal institutions is not to make laws, one must wonder what it is and who or what has this authority. Only an anarchist would, I think, object. The bottom line, on this approach, is that the law not only presupposes a certain moral authority; it is the nature of law as a social institution (and nothing else) to do so. This seems consistent with Raz's insistence (discussed in Section 2) that what a theory of law aims at is a true explanation of the necessary or essential features of the law. I cannot pursue this issue any farther here, but a response along these lines seems thoroughly plausible to me. However, we should not let it escape notice that law is not the only institution that necessarily makes claims to such moral authority. Religious institutions seem to do so as well. If they did not, it is unclear how there could be laws in societies that do not have legal concepts, as discussed in Section 2. The upshot is that Raz's case that law is distinct from morality even though "legal discourse is moral discourse" (p. 4) is plausible, though law is not unique in combining these traits. There are other institutions that are distinct from morality, even though there discourse presupposes a kind of moral authority.

Let me turn now to a different point of view on the question of the normativity of law and ask how Raz thinks that the law figures in relation to the question of what, all-things-considered, we should do. One apparently natural way to answer this question is to say that the fact that a law requires us to act in a certain way provides us with a reason to do so, just as other considerations might – considerations such as that it would be pleasant, that it would impress others with our sense of uprightness, or that it would fulfill a long-deferred promise. But Raz rejects this answer. He tells us that the fact that the "existence of a (morally) legitimate law establishing a duty to perform a certain action" (p. 7) is not a reason for doing it, over and above the other reasons for the action in play. Rather, this is "a very misleading and wrong-headed view" (p. 7). Instead, "The law is a special kind of reason for it displaces the reasons which it is meant to reflect" (p. 7). More specifically, Raz tells us that the law provides us with "exclusionary reasons" (p. 144), an idea that has been central to Raz's thinking about the nature of law for almost his entire career.[21] It is in this way that the law is supposed to improve our ability to conform to reason; it overrides those reasons that conflict with it. Given the decisive nature of legal reasons, it must now be manifest why Raz thinks that legitimacy is necessary for the normative force of law.

---

21 See *Practical Reason and Norms*, esp., pp. 35-48, 142-146, and 178-199.

But exclusionary reasons might be more fine-grained than they appear here. First, it is worth noting that Raz treats an exclusionary reason as an all-or-nothing affair. As presented here, a morally legitimate law preempts *all* of the reasons that conflict with it, and a morally illegitimate law does not. Yet it is at least conceivable that some considerations might preempt reasons that arise from certain grounds but not others, e.g., from self-interest or from clannish concerns but not from impartial welfare or from legitimate requirements of fairness. If the law provided exclusionary reasons in this way, it might allow us to explain why it can be warranted to break a law in order to serve the public good but not warranted in doing so merely for our own good. Second, Raz conceives of exclusionary reasons as being *decisive* with regard to other considerations. But again there is conceptual space for other ways of thinking about such reasons. We might think of a morally legitimate law as merely weakening the force of other reasons without necessarily displacing them. The law might be seen as weakening reasons to act contrary to its commands, weakening them enough to displace them in most, but not all, cases.[22] This might explain why the law can require us to refrain from certain actions in the vast majority of situations but not require us to do so if the cost to ourselves is likely to be catastrophic. This is not the place to settle these matters, of course.

5. *Legal Philosophy, the Law, and their Dichotomies*

Perhaps it is not a complete surprise to find oneself comparing Raz's thinking to that of John Stuart Mill. Raz discusses Mill more than any other classical author – including Kant – in some of his earlier works.[23] But make no mistake: I do not mean that Raz shares Mill's well-known commitments to utilitarianism and naturalism – quite the contrary. Nevertheless, when reading *Between Authority and Interpretation* one is often reminded of Mill's thoroughly sensible claim about "popular opinions." According to Mill, such opinions "are often true, but seldom or never the whole truth. They are a part of the truth; sometimes a greater, sometimes a smaller part, but exaggerated, distorted, and disjoined from the

22 I borrow rather liberally here from Dancy's notions of enabling/disabling conditions and intensifiers/attenuators. See his *Ethics without Principles* (Oxford: Oxford University Press, 2003). However, Dancy does not apply these concepts to legal reasoning, and I am not sure he would want to do so. If there is anything wrong with this line of thinking, it is down to my mistakes, not Dancy's.

23 In particular, *The Morality of Freedom*.

truths by which they ought to be accompanied and limited."[24] What Mill thought about popular opinions, Raz clearly thinks about most theories of law. Raz himself begins this book by telling us that "General theories of law struggle to do justice to the multiple dualities of the law" (p. 1). No one has done more to advance this struggle than Raz, and *Between Authority and Interpretation* is yet another exemplary contribution, one that cannot be missed by anyone interested in legal philosophy.

[24] "On Liberty" in *The Basic Writings of John Stuart Mill* (New York: Modern Library), p. 49.

REVIEW ARTICLE: RAZ ON THE SOCIAL DEPENDENCE OF VALUES

Hanoch Sheinman*

Joseph Raz, *The Practice of Value*, with Christine Krosgaard, Robert Pippin and Bernard Williams, edited by R. Jay Wallace (Oxford: Oxford University Press, 2003), 161 pp. ISBN 0199261474 (hbk). Hardback/Paperback. £17.99/–.

The book consists of Raz's 2001 Berkeley Tanner Lectures on Human Values, commentaries by Korsgaard, Pippin and Williams, and Raz's reply. The lectures draw on themes Raz develops in greater detail in *Engaging Reason: On the Theory of Value and Action* (Oxford: Oxford University Press, 1999) (*ER*). They present a picture in which values are socially dependent but not relative. Raz's discussion is ambitious and illuminating. The commentaries and reply are trenchant. On the whole, the book is an excellent instance of its genre.

Raz is not concerned with *which* values there are, but with *explaining* (intrinsic) values and their relation to social practices (pp. 121, 124). The main focus of the lectures is cultural values: 'the values of products of cultural activities' (p. 29), 'values people need to know at least something about and to pursue in order for there to be objects with those values' (p. 33). Raz's favourite example is the value of opera (pp. 30–32).

Raz's '*special social dependence thesis* claims that some values exist only if there are (or were) social practices sustaining them. *The (general) social dependence thesis* claims that, with some exceptions, all values depend on social practices either by being subject to the special thesis or through their dependence on values that are subject to the special thesis' (p. 19). Here I will focus on the special social dependent thesis (SDT) and the values to which it primarily applies—the cultural values.

Raz stresses that SDT is neither reductivist nor politically conservative. There is no evaluation-free way to tell true values from false (pp. 23–24). 'The existence of a sustaining practice is merely a necessary, not a sufficient condition for the existence of some kind of values. [SDT] does not in any way privilege the point of view of any group or culture. It allows one

* This review benefited from the excellent discussions of HEDONS (Houston Ethical Discussions of New(ish) Stuff) during the spring of 2005. Special thanks to Alastair Norcross for valuable comments on an earlier draft.

full recourse to the whole of one's conceptual armoury, information, and powers of argumentation in reaching conclusions as to which practices sustain goods and which sustain evil, or worthless things, which are, perhaps, taken to be good by a population' (p. 25). SDT is not 'conventionalism'—it is not the normative thesis that we should affirm social practices simply because others value them. It is 'a metaphysical thesis, about a necessary condition for the existence of (some) values' (p. 26; cf. p. 127).

A natural way to cash out the claim that value V depends on practice P for its existence is to say that V would exist at time t only if P did. It is a striking feature of Raz's position that he denies this. For all that SDT says, V could exist now even if P did not. 'The thesis is that the existence of values depends on the existence of sustaining practices at some point, not that these practices must persist as long as the value does' (p. 21). Once the values 'come into being, they remain in existence even if the sustaining practices die out' (p. 22; cf. pp. 135, 152). 'The asymmetry between initial emergence and continued existence lies at the root of [SDT]' (p. 22).

Raz intends SDT to capture an intuitive sense in which cultural and other values depend on contingent social practices without espousing 'social relativism', the view 'that the merit or demerit of actions and other objects of evaluation is relative to the society in which they take place or in which they are judged' (p. 16). Relativism conflicts with commonsense morality. 'We take some of our views to be true absolutely, and not qualified by being relative to a perspective' (p. 18; cf. p. 45). Moreover, by confining the validity of values to particular times, places, or perspective, relativism relinquishes the 'resources for criticizing the evaluative beliefs of other societies' (p. 44; for Raz's critique of social relativism, see *ER*, ch. 7).

Raz's explanation of the difference between SDT and relativism appeals to a distinction between the existence of values and their application (or validity). 'Unlike social relativism, [SDT] does not hold that social practices limit the application or validity of values. The test of whether something is valuable or not is in argument, using the full range of concepts, information, and rules of inference at our disposal' (p. 44). '[S]ustaining social practices constitute emergence conditions, and not—as they do according to standard social relativism—application or validity conditions' (p. 135). In a crucial yet enigmatic passage Raz disavows the 'suggestion that what is of value is so only in societies where the value is appreciated' and declares: 'Once a value comes into being, it bears on everything, without restriction' (p. 22).

Raz also distinguishes between the existence of values and *access* to them—the ability to appreciate or engage with values. Since this ability requires the possession of culture-specific concepts, access to values is clearly socially dependent. But SDT is stronger than the social dependence of access thesis: it entails that some values and their attendant excellences would not even *exist* were they never sustained by some social practice (pp. 29–30). At the same time, once a value is created by social practices, it continues to exist even if we lose access to it. The value of opera is a socially dependent value, as the practices that sustain it might have never existed. But since they do, the value will continue to exist even if these practices cease to exist and are forgotten. (Notice Raz's controversial assumption that values whose sustaining practices have become forgotten are inaccessible. After all, people can have the practices and concepts available on record. A clearer case of inaccessibility is one in which the sustaining practices have disappeared without leaving as much as a causally related trace. In this case, should we say that the value has ceased to exist or merely that it is inaccessible?)

Raz thinks that SDT accounts for the 'common belief that there is no point to value without valuers'. 'That an object has value can have an impact on how things are in the world only through being recognized.' Only then can people appropriately respond to values, by respecting them and engaging with them. 'Absent that possibility, the objects [of value] may exist, and they may be of value, but there is not much point to that' (p. 28).

Finally, related to the social dependence of values is their *genre-dependence*. The concept of a genre or kind of value 'defines which objects belong to it, and in doing so it determines that the value of the object is to be assessed (*inter alia*) by its relations to the defining standards of the genre'. The gist of genre-dependence is a two-stage process of evaluation: we first identify the object as a member of some kind of good and then judge it good to the extent that it is good of its kind (pp. 39–40, 138).

Genre-dependence does not collapse into relativism. Raz's view allows for 'detachment', namely 'for transition from good of a kind to good, while retaining the umbilical cord to one's kind as the ground for the detached judgment' (p. 41). If a certain work 'is a good instance of its genre, then it is a good work absolutely, not only good of its kind'. It is good absolutely 'because it is good by the standards of its genre. While the verdict (good, bad, or mediocre) is unrestricted, its ground is always relative to a particular genre' (pp. 45–46).

Unlike Korsgaard and Williams, I am comfortable enough with Raz's talk of values existing. I also think I understand what he means by 'values', at least in broad terms. The value of a valuable object is neither that object itself nor the properties in virtue of which it is valuable. It is, in Korsgaard's terms, the valuableness the object has in virtue of these properties (p. 67). In Raz's terms: 'Values are what those that possess the evaluative properties have in virtue of their possession' (p. 129). But what is it for a value to *exist*? This is important, because SDT is about the social dependence of the existence of values. Raz takes pains to distinguish the existence of values from their *application* (or validity) and from their *accessibility*. A value can exist without applying to anything and without anyone having access to it. What is it for a value to exist unapplied and inaccessible?

One possibility is that values are entities, but a mystifying metaphysics is clearly not what Raz has in mind. Nor does talk of values existing necessitate the postulation of superlative facts. More plausible is to say that a value consists simply of the fact *that* a certain conditional proposition is necessarily true. To preserve Raz's sensible non-reductivism—his insistence that values can only be explained in terms of other normative concepts—we must only make sure the conditional employs normative concepts (at least in its consequent). Here's a general proposal: to say of a cultural value that it exists is to say that, necessarily, engaging in certain activities *would* be valuable *if* certain favourable cultural conditions obtained. Applied to Raz's favourite example: to say that the value of opera exists is to say that, necessarily, engaging with opera would be valuable if the social practices that make operaengaging activities possible or viable were in place.

The trouble is that the proposal threatens to falsify SDT. It is entirely reasonable to assert that writing, singing, or listening to opera would be valuable if the social practices that make such activities possible or viable were in place. But it seems that if that conditional is true at all, it is necessarily true. If it is true now, it was true before opera-sustaining practices emerged—in fact, it would be true even if such practices never existed. Under the proposal, this implies that the value of opera has always existed. Since this contradicts Raz's claim that the value of opera depends on social practice for its emergence, he must reject the proposal. So what is his alternative conception of the existence of values?

Perhaps this. To say that the value of opera exists is to assert *both* that (1) necessarily, engaging with opera would be valuable if the social practices that make opera-engaging activities possible or viable were in place, *and* that (2) these social practices are in fact in place. This proposal vindicates SDT's implication that the value of opera would never come into existence in the absence of some opera-sustaining practices. Alas, it implies that the value of opera cannot exist unless its sustaining practices do. And this contradicts Raz's interpretation of SDT, in which the value of opera might survive its sustaining practices.

Finally we come to a version of the proposal that mirrors SDT. To say that the value of opera exists is to assert *both* that (1) necessarily, engaging with opera would be valuable if the social practices that make opera-engaging activities possible or viable were in place, *and* that (2) these social practices either exist *or existed*.

This final proposal strikes me as implausible. First, both this and the previous proposal seem to ignore the distinction between valuable operas and the value of opera. While it is trivially true that valuable *operas* did not exist before the emergence of opera-sustaining practices, it is not at all obvious that the *value* of opera did not exist then. It seems clear, for example, that had the practices that make opera possible or viable existed in Ancient Greece, it would have been valuable for Socrates to go to the opera. In a natural sense, this implies that the value of opera had existed before the emergence of opera.

Raz could reply as follows: 'It is difficult to deny that opera (the art form) is a historical product that came into being during an identifiable period of time, and did not exist before that. It is therefore also natural to think that *the excellences* [that constitute the value] of operas … depend on the very same social practices on which the existence of opera' depends (pp. 30–31). Perhaps so. But it is *also* natural to resist the inference from the first and undeniable claim to the second. In a perfectly natural sense, the standards constituting the value of opera do not depend on the existence of opera: necessarily, it would be good to meet them if the right social conditions obtained.

But the main problem with the proposal—and hence with SDT—does not depend on the plausibility of thinking that the value of opera existed before Monteverdi. The main problem is the mysterious temporal asymmetry the proposal postulates between the existence of values and the existence of the practices that sustain them. Arguably, the claim that the value of opera is socially dependent owes its appeal to the perceived pointlessness of talking about it existing where opera itself cannot be valuable because it is non-existent. Yet this rationale applies whenever opera does not exist—even if it once existed. To generalize, it is arguable that cultural values depend on practices for their emergence because it is pointless to talk about values existing under unfavourable conditions in which they cannot be meaningfully practiced, appreciated or accessed by anyone. But this is equally a reason to believe that cultural values depend on practices for the *persistence*.

There is an obvious sense in which opera could not exist, let alone be viable, in Athens—the historical and cultural conditions were far from ripe. In that sense, opera could not be practiced, appreciated or accessed—and so could not be valuable—in Athens. And this is why it might be thought pointless to talk about the value of opera existing there. But the exact same consideration applies to some cases in which the sustaining practices have long ceased to exist. There are possibly forms of ancient art or culture that had gone extinct before they could leave us a causally related trace. All the evidence of their existence has been destroyed. There is an obvious sense in which we will never be able to know about, let alone appreciate or practice, these bygone art forms. *If* it is pointless to talk about the value of opera as something that existed in Athens, why is it not also pointless to talk about the value of these long gone and traceless forms of art as existing today—or indeed about the value of opera existing in a possible future world in which it will have been epistemically inaccessible?

Perhaps because unlike the Greek, who could not possibly *rediscover* opera, we can still rediscover the ancient forms of art, and our remote descendents will be able to rediscover opera should it disappear. This line of response is suggested by Raz's comment that values that survive their sustaining practices 'can be known even if exclusively from records. They can get forgotten and be rediscovered, and the like' (p. 22). But this seems to place too much emphasis on a prefix or, what is more likely, equivocate on the relevant notion of possibility. Logically speaking, while opera could not be *re*discovered in Athens, it could certainly be discovered for the first time or created. Had the right historical and cultural conditions obtained, the Greek would have created opera or inherited it from the Ancient Egyptians. More relevant, of course, is the historical or cultural sense in which opera could not have emerged in Ancient Greece. But in *that* sense, long gone and traceless forms of art cannot be rediscovered or reinstated today, either. And opera cannot re-emerge in our imagined future world. If a practice disappears without a causally related trace, the best scientists, archaeologists and historians will never be able to discover *them*. Whatever they might discover will not be the original practices or values.

Now Raz's own example of a value that exists long after its sustaining practices disappeared is that of Greek tragedy (p. 22). But first, this seems to rely on an overly restrictive conception of sustaining practices. It is not obvious that the practices that brought Greek tragedy into existence have disappeared. After all, people still read, perform, and go to see Antigone and Electra. These practices have changed considerably over the years. But are they not still practices *of Greek tragedy*? If so, they surely sustain the value of Greek tragedy? If, on the other hand, we suppose that they are no longer the same practices, what reason is there to believe that the present value of Greek tragedy is the same *value*? (Raz says that '[s]ustaining practices can be identified only in normative language referring to the very values they sustain' [pp. 23–24]. This might explain why social dependence implies nothing about which alleged values are genuine ones. But it does not explain why we should not say of some admittedly genuine value that it has vanished along with its sustaining practice.)

Second and more important, even if we accept a narrow construal of 'sustaining practices', in which the practices that sustained the value of tragedy in Ancient Greece have long disappeared, they have hardly disappeared *without a trace*. Far from it, the modern practices of tragedy are causally related to the ancient. The record is surely there, waiting to be 'rediscovered'. So Raz's example does not speak to the problem. For either it features a value that has never really been lost or else a value that has been lost but is there to be found. Either way, the value has not ceased to exist and temporal symmetry is preserved.

So my objection comes to this. SDT and Raz's distinction between the existence of values and their accessibility might give the impression that a value that has been brought into existence by social practices might continue to exist after the practices vanish without leaving as much as a causally related trace and are no longer discoverable. Raz's comment that a value that has survived the death of its sustaining practices can be rediscovered seems to suggest otherwise (more on this equivocation later). But this need not matter, because Raz is faced with a dilemma: either we can now (re)discover ancient forms of art that have disappeared without a causally related trace, in which case the Ancient Greeks could have discovered opera after all, or else the Greek could not have discovered opera, in which case we cannot (re)discover such ancient art forms, after all. The first horn of the dilemma applies under a strictly logical interpretation of the possibility of rediscovery; the second under a cultural-historical interpretation. Neither horn sanctions the asymmetry at the root of SDT.

I now turn to the relation between Raz's social dependence and relativism. Both the social dependence Raz advocates and the social relativism he rejects say that values are socially dependent in the sense postulated by SDT. But relativism also makes values socially dependent in some other way. So SDT does not entail relativism. But Raz also *rejects* relativism. He does so by claiming that once a value comes into existence, 'it bears on everything, without restriction' (p. 22). This claim is supposed to give us the main difference between social dependence and relativism (pp. 109, 132, 134–35). But how should we read it?

Williams calls attention to the fact that this claim seems to imply that existing values apply to societies in the remote past, and asks whether this in turn implies, for example, that it was a failing on the part of the Romans not to bring the values of liberal democracy into existence. Since his answer is negative, Williams finds it hard to see how existing values bear on everything without restriction (p. 113). It's not that applying our liberal values to Ancient illiberal societies would betray a conceptual confusion. Rather, doing so 'is simply not a very sensible thing to do' (p. 108). Again, 'you can be Kant at the Court of King Arthur if you want to. The question is the extent to which it is reasonable and helpful to do so' (p. 114).

Raz's response is not easy to understand (pp. 131–38, 152). He confirms that 'once a value exists it applies to everything, including to things that took place before it existed' (so Williams was right to read 'bear' in the original formulation to mean 'apply'?), but immediately adds: 'If liberal values do not apply to the Court of King Arthur, this is because they do not apply universally. To be short, though crude, about it, I would say that they apply only to advanced capitalist societies' (p. 152). It almost seems that 'apply' is used here in two different senses: liberal values potentially apply to everything but actually only to capitalist societies.

We can avoid the confusion by insisting on a distinction between values bearing on and applying to things. Once a value comes into existence, it bears on everything without restriction, but its application or validity might still be restricted. But now what does it mean for values to bear on things to which they do not apply? Given the admission that their application (or validity) may well be restricted, what exactly is left of the key idea that once a value comes into existence it bears on everything without restriction? And is it still sufficient to make social dependence a viable *alternative* to relativism?

My own tentative answer is probably not, at least when cultural and political values are concerned. Raz's official statement of SDT hardly reveals all, or even the most important, ways in which he thinks such values are socially dependent.

We have already identified one important way in which Raz seems to qualify SDT in the direction of social relativism. His comment that values whose sustaining practices have disappeared can be rediscovered seems to suggest that a value can survive its sustaining practices only *because* it can still be discovered. If so, the existence at some point in time of sustaining practices is not a sufficient social condition for the existence of values (at t); the existence (at t) of casually related traces that guarantee the epistemic accessibility and discoverability of these practices is also necessary. (But perhaps the comment is not meant to qualify SDT, only to motivate it? [cf. p. 22]. Elsewhere too Raz equivocates: once a socially created good 'has been developed it remains in existence [(1)] forever (*or* [(2)] for as long as it can be—should it be lost—rediscovered)' [*ER*, p. 149, emphasis added]. But as we have seen, the period during which a value can be rediscovered if lost need not last forever. So should we read the first part of the sentence with rider [1] or [2]?) If the comment introduces an additional necessary condition, then SDT may have well read: 'some values exist only if there are (or were) *epistemically accessible and discoverable* social practices sustaining them'. This would massively dilute SDT's importance and blur its difference with relativism.

I now wish to identify another way in which Raz's discussion tends to water down SDT. I have in mind his discussion of how cultural and political values depend on social practices for their application or validity. Consider cultural values first. Raz's 'short, and dogmatically presented, answer' to Williams begins thus: 'Formally once a value has emerged it can apply to everything, without temporal restrictions. Many values are, however, genre specific. Only films can be judged as good or bad films, only parties as good or bad parties. Many values that are subject to [SDT] cannot apply to anything that happened or existed before their emergence. The value of poetry emerged with poetry, the value of marriage with the institution of marriage, and so on. Therefore, there can be neither good nor bad poems, neither good nor bad marriages before the emergence of the values by which they are judged good or bad' (p. 136). This passage appears to contain a relatively modest point but also a significant concession. The modest point speaks to whether there could be good or bad poems before the emergence of the value of poetry. But this is not the question. Of course there could not. After all, Raz thinks the value of poetry did not emerge until the emergence of poems (or poetry-sustaining practices), and there can be no good poems in the absence of poems. The question is whether the value of poetry can apply to things that had existed long before poems appeared on the scene.

The potentially significant concession is in saying that many values that are subject to SDT—presumably, all genre-specific values—'cannot apply to *anything* that happened or existed before their emergence' (emphasis added). So perhaps there is a sense in which the value of opera bears on everything without restriction. But it does not apply to—or is not valid regarding—Egypt, Athens, Rome, the Middle Ages, and perhaps even the Renaissance.

Is this not an obvious form of *social dependence*—of dependence of values on social practices? Genres are socially contingent concepts. They are constituted by standards of excellence that might have been otherwise; they are what they are only because of contingent social and historical facts. Raz does not seem to think that it makes much sense to apply these standards (or take them as valid with respect) to societies and people that had existed long before they emerged. But then what sort of social *in*dependence is marked by saying that they bear on such societies or people?

This impression as regards cultural values is reinforced by Raz's response to Williams's challenge concerning political values. You might expect Raz to bite the bullet and accept the implication that liberal values apply to the remote past. He could then try to account for Williams's intuition that the Romans are not guilty of a 'failing' by appealing to something like the distinction between the moral status of acts and the moral responsibility of agents for their actions. This would be sufficient to explain his agreement with Williams that condemning the High Middle Ages for failing to respect First Amendment values 'is simply not a very sensible thing to do' (p. 108; cf. p. 137). Raz could refuse to condemn the *people* of the Middle Ages but still condemn their acts for failing to accord with liberal values. Instead, he concedes that liberal values do not apply to the Middle Ages in the first place: 'they apply only to advanced capitalist societies' (p. 152). Like Williams, he thinks it makes little sense to apply liberal values to other societies.

The important point is Raz's explanation for this: 'To function well, political arrangements, their institutions and principles alike, have to be suited to the social, cultural, and economic conditions of the societies they govern. Otherwise they are liable to cause more harm than good. Liberal principles and institutional arrangements would have been as counterproductive as they are unimaginable in the Middle Ages' (p. 152). But until we know more about how to interpret this open-ended and potentially extensive social application condition, it is hard to debate it as an alternative to social relativism.

To recap, Raz says that unlike relativism, SDT 'does not hold that social practices limit the application or validity of value'. However, he acknowledges that contemporary cultural and political values often cannot apply to the remote past, and his explanation is thoroughly social. What practices exist in a society substantially limits the application or validity of such values in that society. This is not a consequence of SDT itself, to be sure. It is a consequence of other parts of Raz's account, for example, his genre-specific conception of cultural values or the requirement that political values be suitable for the prevailing social conditions. All the same, it amounts to recognizing a potentially extensive and open-ended dependence of cultural and political values on sustaining practices. This recognition leaves the difference between Razian social dependence and social relativism substantially underspecified and elusive.

Recall now Raz's distinction between the existence of values and access to them. SDT is about existence, not access. But Raz also accepts as 'relatively uncontroversial' the thesis that access to value is socially dependent (p. 30). He takes this thesis to imply that the 'point' of values depends on sustaining practices. Inaccessible values cannot be recognized or engaged with and so are utterly 'pointless' or 'idle' (pp. 30, 36). But first, what exactly is the point of postulating pointless values? What point is served by talking about values bearing pointlessly on things? (Compare Raz: 'what point can there be in the existence of values if there is no point in their instantiation in objects of value?' [p. 29]. Incidentally, Raz claims that '[i]t is *constitutive* of values that they can be appreciated, and engaged with by valuers', and that this supports 'the pointlessness of values without valuers' [p. 29, emphasis added]. If so, why does it not also support the non-existence of values without valuers?)

Second, to echo Pippin's concern (pp. 89, 94), could not the relativist reformulate his claims about values in terms of their point and still say everything he wants to say? Both Raz and the relativist accept that the value of opera exists now but did not in Athens. The only interesting question, it seems, is whether there is a point in applying it now to Athens. If Raz's and the relativist's answers differ, it is not clear how.

Or take Raz's distinction between a value judgment and its 'grounds'. When he says of a value judgment about X that it is genre-dependent, he only means to say that its grounds are sensitive to X's genre. The judgment itself (or its normative force) is 'detached' from its grounds and is 'absolute'. This is why genre-based values 'illustrate clearly the possibility of social dependence without relativism' (p. 42). But can the genre-based grounds of a value judgment fail to affect its force? When I say that X, a novel, is good, I'm not saying that X is a good cookbook. So it might be misleading to say that X is good absolutely (and redundant to say that X is good absolutely as a novel) (cf. p. 45). In constraining the grounds for value judgments about X, it seems, X's genre also constraints the judgment or its force. But the social relativist does not claim that value judgments have no force, only that their force is relative to social practice rather than absolute. Presumably, he could accept that, once relativized to social practice, judgments have absolute normative force. The distinction between a judgment and its grounds simply leaves the difference between social dependence and relativism unspecified.

Finally, what remains of the notion of values bearing on things? One possibility is suggested by Raz's claim elsewhere that 'once a good exists it is true for all that engaging with it is good or valuable, if only they had an opportunity to do so. This is then true even of people who existed before the sustaining practice emerged' (*ER*, pp. 190–91). So perhaps we should say that, if the value of X (e.g. opera, poetry) exists and so bears on everything, then it would be valuable for any person Y to engage with X, if only Y had an opportunity to do so. Now we have already seen that this line of analysis tends to undercut the supposed temporal asymmetry of values. If it would really be valuable for everyone to engage with X if only she had an opportunity to do so, then it would be valuable to do so even if no one has ever had the opportunity to do so—even if, by Raz's existence conditions, the value of X does not exist.

It is also worth noting, however, that the claim in question is exceedingly weak: why would anyone—including a social relativist—wish to deny that it would be good for the Greek to watch romantic comedies if they only had the opportunity, or that it would be good for the Romans to engage with liberal values if only the opportunity arose in Rome? Such counterfactuals seem compatible with a natural reading of the claims Raz uses to characterize social relativism: 'the merits or demerits of actions and other objects of evaluation is relative to the society in which they take place or in which they are judged'; 'evaluative standards...are valid only where they are practiced'; or 'what is valuable is valuable only in societies that think that it is' (pp. 16–18).

Raz's project of stirring a middle course between an objectivist account of values that ignores the plausible intuition that values are sensitive to social practice, on the one hand, and a subjectivist social relativism that fails to account for the objectivity of values and their capacity to ground cross-cultural criticism, on the other, is highly valuable. However, there are two independent reasons to resist his suggested reconciliation. First, the asymmetry SDT postulates between the existence of values and the existence of their sustaining social practices (or between the emergence and persistence of values) is implausible. Second, while the position arising from SDT together with the rest of Raz's claims in this area does not quite collapse into relativism, it also fails to articulate a clearly debatable alternative. The difficulties with Raz's position on the social dependence of values confirm the inherent difficulty of the project.

PART THREE

LEGAL REASONS

LEGAL REASONS: BETWEEN UNIVERSALISM AND PARTICULARISM*

María Cristina Redondo

Abstract

The first part of this work analyses the universalist and the particularist conceptions of reasons. The second part projects this analysis to the legal domain. The author stresses that universalism and particularism regarding reasons are mutually exclusive theories linked to incompatible conceptions of norms, i.e. norms as strict universal conditionals and norms as defeasible conditionals. In giving an account of this tenet, different meanings of universality and defeasibility are explored. A parallel debate regarding reasons can be found in the legal domain, where two contrasting categories of norms are usually distinguished: rules and principles. On this issue the author argues that the conception of legal reasons depends on the way in which this contrast between different kinds of legal norms is shaped.

Keywords

norms, particularlism, reasons, universalism

Introduction

The conception of legal norms as a kind of reason for action has become a common background in many contemporary legal theories. Within this framework, the philosophical discussion about the nature of reasons turns out to be directly relevant to the understanding of law. In this regard, in the first part of my paper, I will analyse two incompatible philosophical models of reasons for action: universalism and particularism. I will show how each model conceives the notion of reason and to what extent their conceptual proposals affect our notions of norm and norm-based reasoning.

* A shorter version of this work was presented at the Internationale Vereinigung für Rechts- und Sozial Philosophie (IVR), World Congress, Lund, August 2003. I am indebted to Ricardo Caracciolo, Riccardo Guastini, Eugenio Bulygin, Mauro Barberis and Marisa Iglesias, who discussed with me a preliminary version of this paper.

First of all, I will distinguish three senses in which universality can be related to norms and reasons and, on the basis of such a distinction, I will criticize those theories that fail to recognize which kind of universality is in question in this debate. Specifically, I will criticize those conceptions that reduce this controversy to a logical discussion about the defeasible or non-defeasible character of norms and normative reasoning. I claim that this reduction is misleading particularly because the defeasible character of norms becomes ambiguous when such norms are analysed as constituting reasons for action. Norms and reasons can be defeated in different senses. These different kinds of defeasibility have been scarcely analysed in either moral or legal theory. However, much in the debate between universalism and particularism depends on them.

In the second part of my paper, some relevant conclusions for legal theory will be drawn from this debate. I will remark that, even if not explicitly, the discussion about the universalist or particularist character of legal reasons has been undertaken by legal philosophers concerned about the difference between two kinds of norms: rules and principles. In this respect, I will try to show that many legal theories which explicitly endorse universalism implicitly reject some of its necessary presuppositions and commitments. In doing so, they are actually offering a non-universalist account of legal reasons.

1. *Universalism vs. Particularism*

1.1. *The Universalist Position*

A reason for (or against) an action x is the content of a relevant consideration for (or against) x. That something (a property or a state of affairs) is relevant to determine what ought to be done means that its consideration is pertinent to our practical reasoning or, in other words, that it has the capacity to make a positive or negative contribution to a practical verdict. This dimension of relevance is unanimously accepted as the central element of the concept of reason. To be a reason is to be relevant to a practical result. In this sense, if something is a reason it has some weight or value and should be taken into account at the time of making a decision.

According to universalism, the relevance of reasons is not necessarily absolute, but it is both uniform and invariable. Reasons mirror norms, and norms are regarded as strict conditionals that correlate certain circumstances or properties with a deontic consequence. In this approach norms establish what ought to be done under certain conditions (the presence of certain circumstances or properties). In doing this, if valid, norms indirectly establish that these conditions are uniformly and invariably relevant to the practical consequence, i.e. they indirectly constitute uniform and invariable reasons. In the universalist approach, we can say that the source of a reason is a universal norm because something is uniformly and invariably relevant only in virtue of a universal norm. In short, within this framework, reasons are norm-based and norms are universally quantified conditionals. With respect to this issue, two important remarks are in order. First, the logical form of universal norms implies nothing about their metaethical status, and second, it is also silent on the question of their specific stringency or force.[1] Concerning their metaethical status, a universalist conception of norms is compatible with realism, anti-realism, cognitivism, non-cognitivism, etc. As far as the weight of a norm is concerned, universal norms may have different strengths or they may be totally irrelevant, i.e. deprived of any force. For instance, unjustified norms lack relevance and they do not constitute any reason at all. Norms with insuperable force are said to constitute absolute reasons that override all other possible reasons. Finally, norms with relative or limited force constitute only *pro tanto* reasons that can be overruled (defeated) by other competing considerations.[2]

It should be emphasized that even if most of the discussion about rules and rule-following behaviour is focused on the notion of absolute rules or norms, universal norms are not necessarily of this kind.[3] In other words, the universal relevance of a norm—which means that it constitutes a uniformly and invariably relevant reason—should not be confused with absolute force—which means that it is a standard with the highest justificatory power. In addition, when the interest is focused on the contrast between a universalist and a particularist conception of reasons the most

---

1 See Russ Shafer-Landau, 'Moral Rules', *Ethics* 107 (1997), pp. 584–85.

2 This position is generally attributed to David Ross, *The Right and the Good*. I am avoiding, on purpose, any reference to the notion of *prima facie* norms, and I do so precisely because of its ambiguity. The *prima facie* character of a norm sometimes is taken to imply its defeasible conditional structure. In this sense, a *prima facie* norm does not admit the strengthening of the antecedent and cannot be the source of a uniformly and invariably relevant reason. In contrast, when the *prima facie* character of a norm refers to its limited or non-absolute force—without implying a defeasible conditional structure—a *prima facie* norm is the source of a uniform and invariable *pro tanto* reason.

3 This particularity is highly important. It means that even if the concept of rule is conceived as necessarily linked to a decision-making procedure, this procedure is not fixed before establishing whether the norm constitutes either a *pro tanto* or an absolute reason. In other words, according to this distinction, expressions such as 'to follow a rule' or 'to apply a rule' are ambiguous. There is not only one way in which an action can be an instance of rule-following or rule-application behaviour. Unfortunately, scholars discuss rule-following behaviour as if rules could only be absolute.

appealing position, or the best situated rival of particularism, is that which conceives rules as universal conditionals constituting only *pro tanto* reasons. A justified (or relevant) norm with limited force (or weight) is still a universal norm if, and only if, every instantiation of its antecedent allows us to detach its consequent.[4] The crucial point here is that the consequent is a non-absolute duty. A non-absolute or *pro tanto* duty may be overridden by other, stronger considerations, but its existence cannot be ignored, since any time that the antecedent conditions of the norm obtain the *pro tanto* duty obtains as well. It always contributes to the conclusive result. Taking into account that absolute force is neither a defining feature of universal norms nor a necessary element of the universalist conception of reasons, in this paper I will not discuss the absolutist version of universalism. At any rate, in a universalist conception, reasons and norms are two faces of the same coin. In virtue of this special relationship the term 'reason' is ambiguous. Sometimes 'reason' means the universal connection established by a certain norm. Sometimes it designates those features that make a norm applicable to a specific situation. Finally, it may also refer to individual situations, i.e. instantiations of the antecedent of such a norm. In other words, reasons can be regarded as norms, properties, or individual normative facts, i.e. facts that can be seen only when a norm is presupposed and applied. Even if it is really difficult to avoid this ambiguity, in this essay I will try to keep the distinction between reasons and norms. In a universalist view, reasons are the facts or properties that become relevant in virtue of a justified norm. In this sense, I have said that, if justified, norms constitute reasons or are the source of reasons.

1.2. *Universal Predicates, Universal Quantifiers and Universal Relevance*

At least three different senses of 'universality' as an attribute of norms must be clearly distinguished. First, 'universality' may mean *semantic generality*. In this respect, a universal norm does not refer to a particular case, but to a class of circumstances. Under this presupposition, the semantic generality of a norm is a gradual property. A norm N1 is more general than a norm N2 when the class of cases regulated by N1 is larger than the class of cases governed by N2.[5]

---

[4] Notice that the relation between the antecedent and the consequent is not merely presumptive. Regarding this point, the analysis here presented does not follow ShaferLandau's proposal.

[5] Regarding this semantic sense of universality see Carlos E. Alchourrón and Eugenio Bulygin, *Normative Systems* (Vienna/New York: Springer Verlag, 1971), p. 78.

There is a second (and more specific) sense in which universality may be regarded as a crucial character of norms. A norm can be universal in a *logical* sense. This occurs when the logical form attributed to a norm is a universally quantified conditional (or a strict implication) as opposed to a defeasible conditional.[6] According to this second sense, a norm establishes a correlation to which it is possible to apply the rules of strengthening the antecedent and factual detachment (or deontic *modus ponens*). To put it briefly, any time the antecedent conditions are satisfied we can obtain the consequence.

These two senses of universality are part of the concept of norm in a universalist outlook. Norms are strict conditionals connecting a deontic consequence to a generic case identified through universal predicates. A third sense of universality refers to the *relevance* of norms in our practical (moral or legal) deliberations. To say that a norm is relevant means that it constitutes a reason for action and makes a contribution to a practical result. A logically universal norm is also universally relevant when it is substantially valid or justified. Validity is not necessarily part of the universalist *concept* of norm but it is a *sine qua non* condition for norms' capacity to constitute reasons for action. A set of properties can be uniformly and invariably relevant only in virtue of a universally relevant norm, and this happens only when the norm is valid or justified.[7] The circumstances or properties mentioned in the antecedent of a universally relevant norm *always* have the capacity to advocate for, or against, a practical outcome.[8]

Consequently, the universalist conception of reasons implies a double commitment. First of all, it assumes a universalist concept of norm. Secondly, it claims that there are some valid or substantially justified norms. Succinctly, this position asserts that there are some universally

6 Regarding this contrast, see Carlos E. Alchourrón, 'Detachment and Defeasibility in Deontic Logic', *Studia Logica* 57 (1996), pp. 5–18.

7 Needless to say that the concept of norm is not always analysed as necessarily related to a reason for action. For instance, according to an externalist conception, a duty—even if established by a valid norm—does not imply the existence of a reason. Only this third sense of 'universality' is related to the classical universalizability thesis discussed in moral philosophy. Cf. Georg Meggle, 'The Universalizability Problem in Moral Philosophy', in Rosaria Egidi, Massimo Dell'Utri and Mario De Caro (eds.), *Normatività, fatti, valori* (Roma: Quodlibet, 2003), pp. 71–87, at p. 71 and p. 79.

8 Notice that the notion of universal relevance includes a temporal reference. The universal relevance of a norm N excludes the possibility that it constitutes a reason at time t and not at time t-1. This feature rules out a probabilistic reading of the relationship established by a norm because it is compatible with the contribution of an instantiation being zero. Cf. Shafer-Landau, 'Moral Rules', p. 585.

relevant norms which constitute uniformly and invariably relevant reasons for action.[9]

As we can see, the core of this proposal regarding reasons is related to the universal relevance of norms, but it is important to note that it also requires the logical universality of such norms. This is so because reasons in this conception presuppose nomological relations and logical universality is a necessary feature of the conditionals expressing such relations. In what follows, each time I refer to 'universal reasons' without specifications I mean relevant properties that have their source in universally justified norms.[10]

1.3. *The Particularist Postition*

Particularism challenges the universalist conception of reasons. No property is uniformly and invariably relevant. One and the same feature may constitute a reason either for or against a certain action, or it may be absolutely irrelevant, depending on the actual setting in which an action must be performed. The context of the action makes the practical difference and explains the changing valency that one and the same property can have in practical reasoning.[11]

It must be pointed out that particularists are not sceptical regarding reasons; rather, they are sceptical about the existence of universal correlations between natural properties and deontic (or evaluative) consequences. There is no hope (or interest) in searching for universal law-like normative relations. Even if we can identify reasons for or against an action in a given context, particularists maintain that this identification does not result from a norm-based process. They defend a contextual-holistic conception of reasons and, from this standpoint, no property has invariant relevance and any property may become relevant depending on the actual traits of individual cases.

Particularism has no reason to discard universality understood as a semantic quality of practical statements or predicates. Moreover, it is

---

[9] From a universalist perspective only a limited number of independent norms may be universally relevant or justified. If this were not the case, that is, if any norm could be considered as constituting reasons for action, this position would collapse into particularism.

[10] The universal relevance of norms implies logical and semantic universality. However, the implication in the opposite direction does not hold. Semantic universality of norms does not imply logical universality (universal quantification), and logical universality (universal quantification), in turn, does not imply universal relevance.

[11] See Jonathan Dancy, *Moral Reasons* (Oxford: Blackwell, 1993), p. 61.

worth noticing that particularists need not reject either logical universalizations or deductive arguments in practical contexts. As a matter of fact they could express their claim in at least two alternative ways.

(1) When the universalist concept of norm is taken for granted and not questioned, particularists are bound to be sceptical regarding the *relevance* of norms. They argue that when we decide how to act, and ask for reasons for or against an action, we do not, and should not, follow norms. In this case, they are accepting a universalist concept of norm, but at the same time they are saying that norms play no role at all in our practical reasoning. In this scenario, particularists would be admitting that a norm is the content of a universally quantified conditional allowing for the application of *modus ponens*. However, the conclusions we can deductively obtain from these conditionals might be totally deprived of weight. *Modus ponens* allows us to obtain conclusions, but a logical conclusion—resulting from a deductive argument—must not be confused with a conclusive reason for action—resulting from a balance of reasons. What is more, nothing ensures that a logical conclusion expresses any reason at all. A statement—be it a premise or a conclusion of a deductive argument—expresses a reason for action depending not on logic, but on a substantive moral theory. According to a particularist moral theory, the relevance of reasons has its source not in norms but in context. In an individual case, we can identify sufficient reasons, and we can obtain a conclusion, but we are not authorized to repeat this reasoning and apply this conclusion to any different case.

This approach sharply separates the logical issues from the practical ones. This would be a way to stress that the particularist view is challenging not a classical conception of logic (deductibility), but a classical conception of morality (generalism or universalism).

(2) However, I believe that this is not the best way to put the particularist conception of reasons. If the dispute actually represents a philosophical (conceptual) disagreement, particularists cannot accept the universalist concept of norm and discuss just the relevance of such norms. They are trying to provide a different way of thinking about practical reasoning; therefore, they have to offer a different understanding of the concepts of both norms and reasons.

When a defeasible conception of norms is accepted, particularists need not be sceptical regarding the relevance of norms.[12] The defeasible

---

[12] See Dancy's view about the default polarity of reasons. Jonathan Dancy, 'On the Logical and Moral Adequacy of Particularism', *Theoria* (1999), pp. 144–55, at pp. 144–46 and 154–55.

conception is appropriate precisely because it allows particularists to show how they can deal with these so-called 'norms' without betraying their substantive moral thesis. In this view, norms are no longer universal law-like relations, but sheer reminders of 'the sort of importance that a property *can* have in the suitable circumstances'.[13] These norms *can* express sufficient conditions for their deontic consequence, in a particular context, but they do not *necessarily* express sufficient conditions for this consequence in every other context. Within a defeasible conception, the properties mentioned in the antecedent of a norm are neither uniformly nor invariably relevant.

Adopting this position particularists are subscribing to a logical thesis that gives support to their substantive practical claims. Under this light, particularists are not sceptical *universalists*, as they seemed to be according to the former presentation. Actually, they are repealing the universalist philosophical (conceptual) proposal. At the same time, they are arguing for a new concept of norm and, consequently, a new logical pattern of norm-based reasoning.

1.4. *Two Senses of 'Defeasibility'*

The contrast between these philosophical conceptions seems both deep and substantial. They maintain opposed theses about important features of our practical rationality. In this regard, it should be pointed out that this contrast cannot be formulated only as a discussion about the logical defeasibility (or universality) of norms.

First, the defeasible conception of norms and reasoning is only *one* of the characteristics necessary to make the existence of relevant norms compatible with a particularist conception of reasons. In fact, from this perspective, norm-based reasoning should not only be defeasible, but also analogical.[14] The defeasible character explains why, even if the antecedent conditions obtain, under certain new or unusual circumstances the norm turns out to be inapplicable. That is to say, we cannot draw a conclusion from it. In turn, the analogical application of a norm shows why, even if the norm's antecedent is not satisfied, when certain similar conditions obtain we can still apply the norm and draw the conclusion. Both attributes are implied in a conception where norms are rules of thumb; that is,

---

[13] Cf. Dancy, *Moral Reasons*, pp. 67 and 70.

[14] See Jaap C. Hage, *Reasoning with Rules: An Essay on Legal Reasoning and Its Underlying Logic* (Dordrecht: Kluwer Academic Publishers, 1997), p. 123.

they are merely useful tools to summarize the properties that are more commonly relevant in certain kinds of circumstances.

Second, I think that characterizing this debate in terms of what kind of logic or logical conditionals are apt to express norms can be misleading. On the one hand, it is true that in order to constitute a uniformly and invariably relevant reason a norm should have the logical form of a universal (non-defeasible) conditional, but it must also be substantially valid or correct. Therefore, it would be a mistake to reduce the discussion about universal reasons to a discussion about universal conditionals. The logical form of a norm, by itself, does not give sufficient information about the kind of reason established by the norm. What is more, it does not guarantee that the norm constitutes any reason at all. On the other hand, It has been correctly emphasized that norms construed as defeasible conditionals do not assure conclusive statements regarding what ought to be done. However, this idea incorrectly suggests that norms conceived as universal conditionals do assure conclusive statements on this matter.[15] Universal normative conditionals, if justified, constitute universal reasons, but these reasons are neither necessarily absolute nor conclusive. Therefore, universally justified norms do not guarantee conclusive statements regarding what ought to be done. Reasons based on universally valid norms—if *pro tanto*—might be defeated by other conflicting reasons. This invites us to distinguish two kinds or senses of defeasibility. The first one is related to the logical form of norms and norm-based practical reasoning. Defeasible norms are not apt to express uniformly and invariably relevant reasons. Their antecedent may be specified through the introduction of new exceptions that modify their identity and prevent both the applicability of the original norm and the constitution of a reason to act in the exceptional situation. This necessarily results in the non-deductive character of the reasoning based on such norms. The second kind of defeasibility, by contrast, is related to the limited force of universal reasons. In other words, it refers to a universally relevant norm, which constitutes a *pro tanto* reason. A *pro tanto* reason is a universal reason that can be overcome by other conflicting considerations in a so-called 'balance' of reasons. A 'balance' of universal reasons is a comparative pattern of practical reasoning which is not reducible to a (defeasible) norm-based one. This is so because universal reasons cannot be expressed through defeasible conditional norms.

[15] This is the case only when norms are conceived as absolute norms (norms constituting absolute reasons).

If conflicting universal reasons bear on the same case it is implied that conflicting universally relevant norms are applicable. However, the presence of a conflicting universally valid norm leaves intact the identity of the one with which it conflicts and it does not prevent the norm from constituting a reason for action.[16]

Briefly put, universalists affirm that behind each reason there is always a justified universal norm that expresses a set of relevant properties. This, however, does not amount to saying that this norm expresses *all* the possible relevant properties of an individual case. The presence of a universal reason says nothing about the presence or absence of other conforming or conflicting reasons, which—if universal—result from the application of further universally relevant norms. Then, in case of conflict of universal reasons, if there is no further universal norm that establishes a hierarchical order, what ought to be done conclusively cannot be determined through the deductive application of *a* universal valid norm, i.e. through a deductive model of practical reasoning. Moreover, this question could not be determined through norm-based defeasible reasoning. As we have already seen, a conflict of universal reasons cannot be treated, on pain of contradiction, as a case of norm-defeasibility where the conflicting factors introduce specifications (exceptions) to a defeasible norm. In such cases, the only way to answer the question about how to act is through a balance of reasons (resulting from the conflicting universal norms).[17]

---

[16] See Hage, *Reasoning with Rules*, p. 124.

[17] A universalist theory of (moral or legal) reasons can hypothesize different kinds of conflicting situations and offer subtle guidelines with which to make a decision, without establishing a formal hierarchy of reasons. A universalist theory of (moral or legal) reasons delimits *a* realm of universal (moral or legal) reasons. This kind of theory, however, neither necessarily exhausts the realm of reasons in general nor excludes the possibility of partial indetermination, that is the possibility that the normative (moral or legal) status of a case is not determined by the universalist theory. In this regard, it is also interesting to note that universal valid norms may be *definitively* formulated, or may be not. In other words, universalists can admit that it is possible to change (specify) the current norm-*formulations* in order to grasp or express a valid norm-*content* better. In contrast, particularists accept the possibility to change valid norm-*contents* (as far as they conceive norms as defeasible conditionals), in order to grasp an individual case better.

A different opinion can be read in José Juan Moreso, 'Conflitti tra principii costituzionali', *Ragion Pratica* 18 (2002), pp. 201–21; Bruno Celano, '"Defeasibilty" e bilanciamento. Sulla possibilità di revisioni stabili', *Ragion Pratica* 18 (2002), pp. 223–39; and José Juan Moreso, 'A proposito di revisioni stabili, casi paradigmatici e ideali regolativi: replica a Celano', *Ragion Pratica* 18 (2002), pp. 241–48. These authors do not distinguish between the revision of norm-formulations and norm-contents. In their view, conflicts of reasons always lead to the revision of norm-*contents*. According to my analysis, this position already implies giving up a universalist model.

The universalist conception of reasons has been correctly connected to a deductive model of practical reasoning. This is so because in an individual case a universal reason exists if, and only if, such a case is an instantiation of the antecedent of a universal relevant norm. We can say that here a deductive syllogism provides an appropriate model to reconstruct the existence of a reason for action in an individual case.[18] However, universalists are certainly not committed to accept only the deductive model of norm-based practical reasoning; they can also admit a comparative pattern of practical reasoning. This is so because they do not reject the possibility that conflicting reasons bear on the same individual situation. In this hypothesis, if there is no hierarchy of reasons, a balance is required in order to decide, all things considered, what ought to be done.

Taking into account these considerations, it would be misleading and partial to equate *tout court* universalism with the rejection of defeasibility and particularism with the rejection of deductibility. Universalists can accept that the reasons constituted by universal norms may be defeasible or *pro tanto*—even if they clearly reject defeasibility as the kind of logical relation established by norms. In turn, particularists can accept deductibility—even if they reject it as an appropriate pattern to identify reasons for action.[19] Finally, both positions may admit that, when conflicting reasons have to be compared and evaluated, deductive reasoning is not a suitable model to determine a definitive answer to the question about how to act.

1.5. *Some Remarkable Consequences*

If this analysis is correct, it is worth noticing some of the consequences arising from it.

(1) The universalist or particularist conceptions of reasons are directly linked to incompatible conceptions of norms. On the one hand, a universalist conception of reasons necessarily implies a universal conception of

---

[18] Von Wright suggests this reconstructive function in several essays where he treats the so-called 'practical inference' as a pattern that allows explaining and understanding intentional action. For instance, see Georg Henrik von Wright, 'On So-called Practical Inference', in *idem*, *Practical Reason. Philosophical Papers*, Vol. I (Ithaca: Cornell University Press, 1983), pp. 18–34, at pp. 18–19.

[19] Further arguments stressing that particularists do not challenge a certain kind of *ceteris paribus* reasoning, and can accept inductive and explanatory generalizations, can be found in Margaret O. Little, 'Moral Generalities Revisited', in B. Hooker and M. Little (eds.), *Moral Particularism* (Oxford: Oxford University Press, 2000), pp. 276–304, at pp. 290–91 and 298–303.

norms and rejects a defeasible one. On the other hand, particularism denies a universal conception of norms and, if it accepts to talk about norms, it calls for a defeasible model. Positions that try to defend the defeasible character of norms preserving the universalist conception of reasons are, at first sight, inconsistent because they are not aware of this fundamental link. I will return to this point later.

As a consequence, the universalist or particular character of a reason is not a gradual but an all-or-nothing exclusive property: a reason either has its source in a universal law-like relation or it does not. This means that regarding a given domain of reasons, you cannot be more or less particularist (or universalist) because it is not a matter of degree.

(2) What is stated above means that universalism and particularism are mutually exclusive. This, however, does not mean they are exhaustive positions. That is to say, these two positions do not exhaust all possible positions in relation to the reasons for action. For example, a sceptical position denies the existence of universally relevant norms, just as a particularist one does, but it also rejects the particularist conception. In this sense, scepticism represents a third possibility rejecting both universalism and particularism.

(3) One of the most significant consequences of the contrast between the universalist and the particularist models is related to the distinction between the existence and the identity of a norm-content, on the one hand, and its formulation and application to an individual case, on the other.

If the idea of a norm independent of the individual cases of application is not viable, then there is no hope for universalism. According to this position, norms govern our behaviour in individual cases precisely because, independently of them, norms establish what properties are relevant in order to decide what to do. If the identity of norms depends on individual cases, it would be rather surprising to say that norms regulate such cases. Instead, from the particularist perspective, the existence of a reason and, if admitted, the identity of a correlative defeasible norm, must be established at exactly the same time in which we are supposed to apply such a norm and decide how to act. In a few words, a universalist conception of reasons presupposes the stability of the norm-contents in which reasons are based. A particularist conception rejects the possibility of stable norm-contents.

(4) This last distinction is tied up to another one, which is also important for this debate: the distinction between the concepts of exception and conflict. Both exceptions and conflicts should be based on reasons.

The crucial difference between them is that reasons bringing about exceptions affect the identity of a norm and its capacity to constitute a reason for action in the exceptional case, whereas reasons bringing about conflicts do not. They leave untouched the reason that the conflicting norm constitutes and compete with it.

While taking into account this difference, it should be clear that a universalist model of reasons could accept the actual context of application as a potential source of conflicting particularist reasons.[20] Nevertheless, universalism could never accept context-dependent exceptions. Admitting contextual exceptions would mean that the norm-content is contextually grounded and this would imply the breakdown of the universal relevance of reasons.

In the legal domain, this difference reveals two ways of dealing with problems arising from demands for equity, that is, individual cases in which the solution established by a norm is unsatisfactory. For those who accept a universalist conception of norms, an equitable decision is suitable, paradigmatically, in a case that cannot be resolved *fairly* by a norm. To be precise, it is a case of conflict between what is demanded by a norm and what is demanded by justice on one particular occasion. In these circumstances, if the requirement of justice prevails, the norm fails to determine what ought to be done. In a defeasible conception, by contrast, norms are appropriate for dealing with equity claims since they are open to the introduction of new conditions of application which will allow these situations to be satisfactorily resolved. Actually, an equity claim makes the defeasible nature of norms explicit. In these situations, a norm need not be left aside; it may be applied once its conditions of application have been revised to adequately respond to the problematic case. It is clear that the content of the norm, from this perspective, is not stable and is fixed at the particular time of application.

2. *Legal Reasons*

It may be suggested that the moral debate between universalism and particularism cannot be legitimately translated into legal terms. Moral philosophy is concerned with the possibility of universal law-like relations between natural and deontic (or evaluative) properties. Legal theory deals

---

20 This means that a universalist conception of reasons may be accepted only for a certain domain of reasons. See Shafer-Landau, 'Moral Rules'.

with institutions, which are man-made realities independent of this metaphysical problem. However, to the extent that the philosophical proposals of universalism and particularism can be seen as providing two rational ideals of decision-making processes, the questions arising from this debate are not only pertinent but also extremely interesting for legal theory.

Applying the former considerations to the legal domain, we can say that a universalist conception should analyse the law as composed of universal norms which are the sources of universal legal reasons. In contrast, a particularist position should claim the contextual character of legal reasons and the impossibility of identifying legal norms that can be universally relevant. Additionally, as we will see, these conceptions could be defended either as general theses regarding a whole legal system, or as limited ones applicable to a specific legal branch.

2.1. *Universalism in the Legal Domain*

The analysis of law in terms of reasons for action is complex because, in this approach, valid legal norms not only constitute, but also presuppose and represent underlying reasons. According to a well-known conception, a valid legal norm constitutes a second-order exclusionary reason along with a first-order ordinary one.[21] I will not discuss here the different models of rule-following behaviour analysed in legal philosophy.[22] In the view I am assuming here, legal norms can be universal in a triple perspective: (1) they can be universal semantic contents, (2) they can have the logical form of a strict universal conditional, and (3) if valid, they are universally relevant, that is, they constitute uniform and invariable reasons resulting from a balance of preexisting underlying reasons.[23] The semantic and practical dimensions of a norm explain why its identity can be analysed as a function of both the meaning of the language in which the norm-content is expressed, and the pre-existing reasons that this content is supposed to represent. To be precise, underlying reasons should be excluded at the time of making legal decisions, but in many cases they are admitted as implicit contents of law that, when made explicit, modify the actual

---

[21] These are called protected reasons. See Joseph Raz, *Practical Reason and Norms*, 2nd edn (Princeton: Princeton University Press, 1990), ch. 2.

[22] See Frederick Schauer, *Playing by the Rules: A Philosophical Examination of Rule-Based Decision-Making in Law and in Life* (Oxford: Clarendon, 1991), especially ch. 5.

[23] Angeles Ródenas, 'Entre la transparencia y la opacidad. Análisis del papel de las reglas en el razonamiento judicial', *Doxa* 21 (1998), pp. 99–121, esp. p. 117. Ródenas is concerned with other problems, but she clearly distinguishes both semantical and practical aspects of norms.

norm-*formulations*.[24] Thus, they are crucial to the question about what the law is.

Leaving aside the underlying reasons, any other relevant consideration which is not part of the justification of a norm should be considered an independent reason. These reasons do not affect the identity of legal norms. They can conflict with legal reasons, and they are obviously relevant to the question about what ought to be done conclusively.

The claim of universalism in the legal domain is that, if there are legal reasons, they are uniformly and invariably relevant. The first implication of this universalist thesis is that the identity of a legal norm (the norm-content) is independent of individual cases. If the content of a legal norm is identified in each context of application, the property of universal relevance vanishes.[25] This is so because, in such a case, legal reasons would completely depend on the decision-making context. As a consequence, a universalist conception of reasons is compatible with most legal theories except with those that accept a radical contextual theory of meaning or interpretation. The second implication of the universalist thesis is that the logical form of a legal norm cannot be a defeasible conditional. Universal legal reasons require the logical universality of the norms on which they are based. Such norms have to be represented through logically universal conditionals expressing a sufficient—though not necessarily conclusive—condition for a deontic consequence.[26] This means that

---

24 These cases of divergence between what is required by the norm-formulation and what is required by underlying reasons have been called recalcitrant experiences of over- and under-inclusiveness. See, Schauer, *Playing by the Rules*, pp. 31–34.

25 The extent to which the norm-contents depend on language, legislator's intentions, underlying reasons, etc. is determined by specific theories of legal interpretation, and it is not part of the universalism-particularism debate. It may be interesting to point out that the rejection of contextual interpretation assumed by universalism does not lead to any specific theory of legal interpretation as it seems to follow from Schauer's analysis. Particularly, it does not lead to Hart's theory of legal interpretation. See Schauer, *Playing by the Rules*, p. 213.

26 I am aware that a significant number of legal theorists maintain that the defeasible character of legal norms may be based only on *legal* considerations. That is to say, legal norms only admit *legal* exceptions and cannot be defeated by moral or other non-legal reasons. Taken literally, these positions are defending a specific kind of legal particularism. However, it is highly probable that even if they talk about the defeasible character of *norms*, they actually refer to the provisional character of norm-*formulations*. Universalism need not deny the possibility of errors in the identification of the norm-contents. Nevertheless, it would be a category mistake to formulate this thesis as a defeasible conception of *norms*. As I have already pointed out, universalism is compatible with the possibility of modifying or changing norm-formulations in order to grasp the universal legal norm-content better.

when a legal norm has been correctly identified it should exclude any new content. If it does not, it would be false to say that the norm has been correctly identified or that it expresses a sufficient condition. Notice that this exclusionary character only regards considerations affecting the *identity* of universal legal norms. It says nothing regarding their force at the moment of deciding what ought to be done conclusively. In this situation, other independent considerations may be relevant, and reasons constituted by universal legal norms do not necessarily exclude independent considerations.

Legal norms, like any other kind of norms, are usually analysed as providing a specific model of decision-making procedure. Such a model is strictly linked to the kind of reasons that legal norms are supposed to create. According to universalism, to follow a legal norm that constitutes universal reasons implies that the decision-maker always takes into account—as uniformly and invariably relevant—the properties established in the antecedent of the legal norm. In other words, a norm is treated as the source of universal reasons if, any time it applies, it commits the decision-makers not to defeat it.

A universalist position does not assign a specific weight to universal legal reasons and it is not bound to a specific theory concerning legal validity. As a consequence, it is compatible with positivist and antipositivist conceptions of law. The central thesis of universalism is that the properties or circumstances established by a valid legal norm—be it the result of empirical facts or a moral reasoning—are uniform and invariable contributors to a legal verdict.

2.2. *Particularism in the Legal Domain*

Important arguments for particularism can be found in the debate concerning the relation between law and morality, especially when the problem of equity is taken into account.[27] However, it is usual to find this moral concern presented as if it were a semantic problem. To be sure, there are also genuine semantic difficulties on which particularist legal theories can rely. In either case, the crucial question refers to the possibility and desirability of identifying (or interpreting) legal norms independently of contextually relevant considerations.

---

[27] See, for instance, Lawrence B. Solum, 'Equity and the Rule of Law', in I. Shapiro (ed.), *The Rule of Law* (Nomos, 36; New York and London: New York University Press, 1994), pp. 120–47.

From the point of view of legal interpretation, all theories that present pragmatical contextual considerations as unavoidable in the correct identification of law are bound to assume a particularist conception of legal reasons. This is so because, except as a rhetorical resort, we cannot state the universal relevance of such reasons once we have said that it is impossible to identify legal norms without taking into account the actual features of each individual case. A theory of legal interpretation is certainly not a theory concerning the kind of reasons legal norms are able to create. However, certain theses regarding legal interpretation can affect or even determine a theory about legal reasons. In this regard, some conceptions of interpretation, as far as they maintain that the law, or some parts of the law, cannot be identified as a set of strict universal norms, imply the withdrawal of the universalist ideal. For instance, this is the case when some kinds of 'realist' thesis are accepted. According to these positions, the law does not bind courts because 'the law is what the courts say it is'.[28] Something similar occurs when radically contextual conceptions of meaning are applied to the identification of legal norms.[29] Moreover, when we assume 'interpretative' or 'hermeneutic' theories defending that the understanding of a legal text—as the understanding of any cultural object from a hermeneutic point of view—is dynamic, it partially depends on the interpreters and should not be fixed before taking into account the whole system to which it belongs.[30]

---

28 Following Herbert Hart, from this perspective, the judge's rulings 'would be both final and infallible—or rather the question whether they were fallible or infallible would be meaningless; for there would be nothing for him to get "right" or "wrong"'. Herbert L.A. Hart, *The Concept of Law*, 2nd edn (Oxford: Clarendon Press, 1994), p. 144. It is interesting to stress that these realist positions are clearly non-universalist but they are also clearly non-particularist. This is so because realists are sceptical regarding the existence of universal norms and they are also sceptical regarding the possibility of determining a right answer based on contextual reasoning.

29 These conceptions should not be confused with those that stress the importance of context, when the concept of context refers to different branches of law, such as civil, criminal, commercial law, etc. These last positions are clearly compatible with universalism. See Timothy Endicott, 'Law and Language', in J. Coleman and S. Shapiro (eds.), *The Oxford Handbook of Jurisprudence & Philosophy of Law* (Oxford: Oxford University Press, 2002), pp. 935–68, at pp. 946–55.

30 Francesco Viola and Giuseppe Zaccaria, *Diritto e interpretazione. Lineamenti di teoria ermeneutica del diritto* (Rome and Bari: Laterza, 1999). A universalist position could admit that the identity of a norm is related to the content of other norms belonging to the same normative system, but it cannot accept that this identity is dynamic or that it depends on the interpreter.

The impossibility of fixing the content of a legal provision before facing an individual case may be defended as a theoretical thesis regarding language (or the law) in general, or may be proposed as a contingent thesis limited to specific parts of a legal system, such as constitutional law,[31] criminal law,[32] or specific kinds of legal clauses expressing highly abstract standards.[33]

From a moral point of view, the commitment to a particularist approach is a consequence of a two-step argument. First of all, it presupposes either a necessary or a contingent relation between morality and the content of law. In other words, it presupposes an interpretative connection between law and morality.[34] Second, but not less important, it requires a particularist conception of moral reasons. In a few words, the thesis that defends the connection between law and morality does not lead to particularism when morality is understood in a universalist way, or when the relationship defended is not interpretative, but ideal or justificatory.[35]

Once again, from this moral perspective, the particularist thesis may have either a global or a local scope, and a necessary or a contingent status. We have a global and necessary thesis when a particularist moral evaluation is conceived as an inescapable step in the identification of a valid legal reason. We have a local and contingent proposal when the consideration of particularist moral reasons is viewed, for instance, as incorporated into law as a matter of fact because of a specific allusion to morality or the presence of a morally controversial concept. When the particularist thesis is defended with local scope, it is implicitly suggested that in order to analyse the law both conceptions of reasons are needed, since sometimes law constitutes universally relevant reasons, and sometimes it does not.[36]

---

31 See Frederick Schauer, 'The Jurisprudence of Reasons', *Michigan Law Review* 6 (1987), pp. 847–70, esp. p. 869.

32 See José Juan Moreso, 'Principio de legalidad y causas de justificación. (Sobre el alcance de la taxatividad)', *Doxa* 24 (2001), pp. 525–45.

33 See Hart, *The Concept of Law*, pp. 131–33.

34 According to some Natural Law theories this relation obtains in every possible world and, in this sense, is conceptual and necessary. According to some versions of Inclusive Legal Positivism the relation holds in virtue of the existence of a social rule of recognition and, in this sense, is conventional and contingent. See Jules Coleman, 'Incorporationism, Conventionality and the Practical Difference Thesis', *Legal Theory* 4 (1998), pp. 381–425, at pp. 403–11.

35 On these different kinds of relations between law and morality, see Carlos S. Nino, *Derecho Moral y Política* (Barcelona: Ariel, 1994). Also Robert Alexy, 'On Necessary Relations Between Law and Morality', *Ratio Juris* 2.2 (1989), pp. 167–83.

36 Schauer, 'The Jurisprudence of Reasons', p. 869.

Only a few legal theories would be willing to call themselves particularists.[37] As a matter of fact, it is difficult to mention examples of legal theories that openly apply the proposals of ethical particularism to the legal domain. However, if my account is correct, the particularist position, though not explicitly accepted, can be considered a non-intentional result of some legal theories concerning legal interpretation and/or the relationship between law and morality.

2.3. *The Debate in Legal Theory*

Within legal theory, the distinction between these two conceptions of reasons has been presented in terms of a contrast between two kinds of norms: rules and principles. In this respect, the thesis presented by Ronald Dworkin has had a high impact among legal philosophers and has set the bases of an ongoing discussion. The debate regarding Dworkin's proposal has brought about various conceptions of principles and the way in which they differ from rules. The characterization of principles gains great importance insofar as it is accepted that they are at the base of any legal system and provide the grounds for its justification. These principles contribute to the identification of the rules and thus affect the reasons established by them. It could therefore be said that the characterization of the reasons that the law is able to create, ultimately depends on the characterization of principles. In the following section I shall limit myself to briefly presenting only three ways of understanding this kind of norm. As will become clear, only one of them is committed to the thesis of the universal relevance of legal reasons and shows a practical difference between two possible ways of regulating behaviour.

(a) Many authors believe that the difference between rules and principles is only a matter of degree, i.e. principles are more abstract, have a wider scope, and—for this reason—determine a result to a lesser extent than rules. This means that they situate the difference in the semantic generality of each kind of norm.[38] Concerning this thesis some remarks are in order. If this approach is correct the distinction between rules and principles has no practical import. The difference in semantic generality has no influence on the kind of reasons that rules and principles are able to create. Therefore, the practical difference between them, if any, is not captured by this semantic divergence.

---

[37] A particularist position is explicitly defended by Solum, 'Equity and the Rule of Law', pp. 120–47.

[38] This position may be attributed to Hart. See Hart, *The Concept of Law*, pp. 259–63.

If the discussion about rules and principles reflects a concern about the different ways in which law can offer reasons for action, the variance in semantic generality, even if it exists, is not only irrelevant, but also misleading. Theories stressing the (semantic) universal status of principles believe that they are still defending a universalist model of reasons. However, it is not the case when principles are considered defeasible norms so dynamic and mutable that they can only be grasped in the face of a specific case.

(b) According to a second approach, both rules and principles are conditional statements that correlate a case (an antecedent) to the normative qualification of a certain behaviour (a consequent). The difference between them is that rules have a closed antecedent whereas principles have an open one. Regarding principles, we cannot formulate a finite or closed list of properties in which they are applicable.[39] This proposal regarding the rules/principles distinction suggests that the practical difference between them should be found in the structure attached to each kind of norm. Rules have closed antecedents and can be treated as strict universal norms that admit the strengthening of the antecedent and deontic *modus ponens*. That is to say, rules may be deductively applied. Principles, by contrast, are defeasible conditionals because their conditions of application are not only vague, they are not even generically determined.

Analysed in this way, principles cannot constitute universally relevant properties. The law's claim to universality, from this perspective, would be based on the existence of logically non-defeasible rules independent from principles. It is important to highlight the need for this independence since, if principles had a bearing on the conditions of application of rules, these would in turn have open antecedents and would be defeasible.

This position suggests that we can preserve a universalist model of legal reasons even if we accept a defeasible conception of the principles which are at the base of the legal order. In my opinion, this belief shows a lack of awareness regarding two important issues. First, it overlooks the necessary distinction between two senses of 'universality' as a property of norms. In this approach, principles are universal contents involving universal predicates but they are not universally *relevant* since, though applicable to an individual case—in virtue of a new condition of application—they

[39] See Manuel Atienza and Juan Ruiz Manero, *A Theory of Legal Sentences* (Dordrecht: Kluwer Academic Publishers, 1998), pp. 8–9. This is only one of the ways in which the authors trace the differences between rules and principles.

can be defeated, left aside and not taken into account. Second, this belief ignores the necessary connection between what I have called the 'two faces of the same coin', that is, that universal reasons presuppose universally quantified norms. Therefore, principles understood as defeasible norms, even if semantically universal, are not the appropriate bases for universal reasons. Defeasible norms cannot constitute universal reasons.

As a consequence of this idea, it is interesting to point out that it is not possible to support a universalist thesis in relation to legal reasons and, simultaneously, admit that they depend on, or may be modified in virtue of, the presence of moral reasons. Regarding the relation between law and morality, we have to accept one of the following incompatible theses. On the one hand, if we seriously claim that the content of legal norms (be they rules or principles) can depend on moral reasons, we should acknowledge that legal norms are not universally relevant and do not constitute universal reasons for action. Legal norms are just provisional formulations of genuine universal norms: the moral ones. When these universally relevant norms are applicable they can modify legal formulations and prevent them from constituting any reason at all. On the other hand, if we do not want to accept this consequence and insist on the thesis that legal norms do constitute universally relevant reasons, we must modify our position and accept that moral norms cannot modify legal ones. That is to say, morality cannot *defeat* legal norms by introducing exceptions or new conditions of application. On the contrary, these moral norms *conflict* with legal ones leaving untouched their identity and force. In either case, if a position defends the universalist character of legal reasons it cannot accept the defeasibility model for legal norms.

At any rate, it should be clear that the universal logical form of norms (or, what amounts to the same, the rejection of logical defeasibility) is a necessary but not a sufficient step in order to defend a universalist theory of legal reasons. Indeed, the admission of the logical universality of norms may be as misleading as the admission of the semantic one. Positions defending the constitutive character of judicial interpretation might stress the universal logical form of legal norms. However (and paradoxically), the reasons established by these universal norms meet exactly the particularist characterization of reasons, insofar as their existence or content depends on each individual context of decision.[40] These positions deny

[40] Following Schauer we can say that, if universal: '...rules entrench the *status quo* and allocate the power to the past and away from present...the allocation of power here is temporal]'. Schauer, *Playing by the Rules*, p. 160. 'Secondly...rules can allocate power

one of the basic presuppositions of the universalist conception of reasons: the stability of norm-contents.

(c) A third characterization of the contrast between rules and principles takes the following two features into special consideration. Firstly, rules are applicable in an all-or-nothing fashion. They are either applicable and determine a decision, or inapplicable and contribute nothing to it. In contrast, principles allow for gradual application. That is to say, while a principle may contribute to determine a result, a rule, if valid, necessitates a particular one.[41] This implies that in the case of a conflict between rules, the final decision can only take one of them into consideration, i.e. only one rule is valid or applicable.[42] In contrast, when principles conflict, it may be possible for all of them to be partially satisfied. The final decision can and should be the result of the balance of all the principles involved. In this sense, it can and should honour them, at least in part.

An additional feature of rules is that only with respect to them—and not to principles—is it possible to admit exceptions.[43] By virtue of its all-or-nothing nature, in an exceptional case, a rule is downright inapplicable; it does not constitute a reason and should not be taken into account.[44] Even if this feature of rules were to be interpreted as a symptom of their defeasible character, the reasons that the law ultimately offers may be universal. This is so only insofar as every exception to a legal rule (i.e. any case of logical defeasibility) finds its basis in a finite set of universal (non-defeasible) principles. In this case, the properties that must be taken into consideration to justify a legal decision are, by virtue of the principles, uniformly and invariably relevant.[45]

horizontally, determining who, at a given slice of time, is to determine what...the "No vehicles in the park" regulation...allocates power away from the park-user and to the rule maker'. Schauer, *Playing by the Rules*, p. 161.

[41] Cf. Ronald Dworkin, *Taking Rights Seriously* (Cambridge, MA: Harvard University Press, 1977), pp. 24–25. See also Robert Alexy, 'Sistema jurídico, principios jurídicos y razón práctica', *Doxa* 5 (1988), pp. 139–51 (143).

[42] Cf. Dworkin, *Taking Rights Seriously*, p. 27.

[43] Cf. Dworkin, *Taking Rights Seriously*, pp. 24–25.

[44] In this sense it could be said that defeasibility is conceptually possible only in relation to rules but not principles. In any case, it is necessary to observe that, for Dworkin, the possibility that rules have exceptions is not a sign of their defeasible nature so much as one of their incomplete formulation. Cf. Dworkin, *Taking Rights Seriously*, p. 25.

[45] It should be obvious that this third characterization of principles reflects Ronald Dworkin's conception only approximately and partially. His proposal takes into account many other features that I have not mentioned here. Some of them, which refer to the identification of principles, could put Dworkin's universalist commitment in doubt. For instance, in Dworkin's theory the stability of universal norm-contents (or principles) is

With regard to this position, the analysis proposed in the first part of this work enables us to extract at least two corollaries:

(1) Principles, insofar as they *are*—or directly constitute—universal reasons, should be formally represented as strict conditionals. The practical universality of this sort of norm presupposes the logical universality of the link between a specific circumstance—or any circumstance—and the relevance of a certain property.

For example: 'Life ought to be respected'. This principle may be represented as a conditional according to which: 'In all circumstances, life is a relevant property'. It is a categorical principle since according to it, life is always valuable and, as such, it must be taken into account every time we make a decision.[46]

Another example: 'In every issue concerning civil law the autonomy of the will must be respected'. This is a hypothetical principle since it has a specific condition of application: the invariable relevance of the autonomy of the will is circumscribed to matters of civil law.

It should be clear that the ascription of a conditional structure to a principle does not mean that its superficial configuration should be that of a conditional statement. Moreover, it does not mean that it is a hypothetical principle, i.e. that its applicability depends on the presence of specific circumstances. In other words, that principles should always have the logical structure of a conditional does not require them to have a conditional formulation and does not prevent some of them from being hypothetical and others categorical.

The strict conditional structure of principles can be easily accepted as long as it is remembered that the consequent of this kind of norm does not qualify an action, i.e. does not answer the question 'What ought to be done (or decided)'. Instead, it confers value to a property which, as a consequence, becomes relevant—i.e. constitutes a reason—and must be considered in the practical reasoning justifying a decision. It is important

---

not assured. If the identity of principles can be changed through interpretation, their universal relevance vanishes.

46 Following Alchourrón, a categorical norm may be logically represented as a conditional with a tautological antecedent. That is to say, accepting O (/) as the primitive deontic opertator, we can define the categorical duty to do A as O (A / T). See, Alchourrón, 'Detachment and Defeasibility in Deontic Logic', pp. 5–7. This characterization is compatible with von Wright's view according to which every norm (including categorical norms) has a condition of application. The condition of application of a categorical norm is 'the opportunity for doing the thing which is its content, and no further condition'. Cf. Georg Henrik von Wright, *Norm and Action: A Logical Enquire* (London: Routledge and Kegan Paul, 1963), p. 74.

to emphasize this feature: in accordance with a principle, what becomes a duty or obligation (if we are to conserve this deontic operator) is this giving relevance to a certain property. This way, principles indirectly have an impact on what ought to be done.

(2) This presentation emphasizes the fact that there are at least two different techniques to guide behaviour. Firstly, motivation may be achieved through rules that establish the deontic qualification of an action and, in doing so, give a direct answer to the practical question regarding how one should act. Secondly, the motivation may also be achieved through principles that establish what properties are relevant for deciding what should be done. Principles, contrary to rules, do not determine an action directly or immediately. Actually, they are or determine reasons for or against an action, and, in this sense, they indirectly guide behaviour. A particularist position holds that these principles are not normative. In fact, they are empirical generalizations that remind us which properties are normally relevant. In contrast, a universalist position holds that principles are a special kind of norm, which establish what properties are relevant, i.e. they establish what counts as a reason when deciding how to act.

Concluding Remarks

Regarding the question about what conception of reasons best explains our notion of legal reasons, I believe it is of utmost importance not to confuse three levels of discussion: the conceptual, the evaluative, and the empirical. Much of the debate on reasons and models of reasoning is ambiguous in this sense and it is not always easy to identify at which of these different levels the discussion is taking place.

In this essay I have provided an outline of the conceptual differences between the universalist and the particularist models. At this conceptual level both models offer a coherent account of the concept of reason and it is difficult to find conclusive philosophical arguments for or against either one of them without presupposing the very conception of reasons we are trying to argue for. This implies that it is logically possible for a legal order to be conceived of as fitting one conception or the other. However, if the question is a descriptive one regarding a specific part of a legal order, it is not possible to ascribe to it both conceptions at the same time. Moreover, it is not possible for a specific legal order to be presented alternatively as some times particularist and some other times universalist. On the one hand, we should remember that these conceptions are mutually exclusive.

On the other hand, we should also keep in mind that stability or temporal invariance of reason is a necessary presupposition of universalism. From this point of view, the thesis according to which we can reconstruct a legal provision—or a whole legal system—in a universalist fashion at one time and in a particularist one at another time is contradictory since it negates a basic presupposition of universalism.

If the question is how we *should* conceive law, it is important to stress that when we decide to treat, or advocate for treating, a public institution like the law as bringing about a specific kind of reason for action, we are committing ourselves to certain values. Universalism is usually linked to the value of certainty, predictability, formal equality, etc. Particularism, in turn, is mainly related with equity, flexibility, fairness, etc. Eventually, in order to choose the best philosophical approach to legal reasons, we have to go into an evaluative level of discourse and explicitly state the values that each model endorses and the advantages and disadvantages we can obtain through its implementation. The particularist or universalist character of legal reasons depends on the way in which legal operators conceive of the law. Provided that both models are logically and empirically viable, it could be a matter of choice. Certainly, a choice linked to important conceptual and substantial consequences.

PART FOUR

LEGAL RIGHTS

CRIMINAL HARMS

Thom Brooks

Abstract

What is a crime? A common answer is that crimes are harms. One particular argument is that morality forms the connection between crimes and harms: crimes are not any kind of harm, but specifically a kind of immorality. This position is consistent with natural law jurisprudence which claims that law and morality are inseparably linked. It is also consistent with standard defences of retribution whereby punishment is justified where deserved and to the degree deserved. Retributivist desert is present for individuals that possess some degree of moral responsibility for causing or attempting to cause evil. The idea that crimes are harms to morals—and so their immorality informs their criminality and the corresponding severity of punishment—has also found favour with so-called 'expressivist' theories of punishment defended by Joel Feinberg, Antony Duff and others. The justification of crimes as harms to morals is part of a venerable tradition that has come to be increasingly seen as discredited. Most academics working in law (and even more practising lawyers) reject natural law jurisprudence and support some version of the separability thesis of legal positivism where law and morality are held to be separable, but not intrinsically and necessarily linked. Yet, curiously, retributivist theories, including expressivism, have been on the ascendency with a growing number of legal philosophers defending the idea of crimes as harms to morals and, therefore, moving in a contrary direction to most others working in law and academic law. I believe this general position is deeply problematic and should be rejected. This chapter focuses specifically on expressivist theories as the increasingly more popular variant of retributivism in academic circles today. The next section provides an overview of expressivism. The following sections argue that it is not compelling both as a view about the criminal law, but also as a theory about punishment. I close the chapter with ideas about criminal harms might be better understood. I argue that crimes might be a kind of harm, but not the kinds of harm endorsed by retributivists and, more specifically, expressivists.

Keywords

crime, harm, Duff, Feinberg, expressivism, communicative, punishment, morality, natural law, legal positivism, legal realism, rights

Introduction

What is a crime? A common answer is that crimes are harms. One particular argument is that morality forms the connection between crimes and harms: crimes are not any kind of harm, but specifically a kind of *immorality*. This position is consistent with natural law jurisprudence which claims that law and morality are inseparably linked. It is also consistent with standard defences of retribution whereby punishment is justified where deserved and to the degree deserved. Retributivist desert is present for individuals that possess some degree of moral responsibility for causing or attempting to cause evil. For example, the murderer deserves severe punishment because he is morally responsible for another person's death and this act is sufficiently evil to warrant severe punishment.

The idea that crimes are harms to morals—and so their immorality informs their criminality and the corresponding severity of punishment—has also found favour with so-called 'expressivist' theories of punishment defended by Joel Feinberg, Antony Duff and others. These theories argue that punishment has an expressivist function of communication public disapproval to criminal offenders for their moral wrongdoings where punishment is proportionate to immorality.

The justification of crimes as harms to morals is part of a venerable tradition that has come to be increasingly seen as discredited. Most academics working in law (and even more practising lawyers) reject natural law jurisprudence and support some version of the separability thesis of legal positivism where law and morality are held to be separable, but not intrinsically and necessarily linked.[1] Yet, curiously, retributivist theories, including expressivism, have been on the ascendency with a growing number of legal philosophers defending the idea of crimes as harms to morals and, therefore, moving in a contrary direction to most others working in law and academic law.

I believe this general position is deeply problematic and should be rejected. This chapter focuses specifically on expressivist theories as the

[1] See Kramer (1999) on the separability thesis.

increasingly more popular variant of retributivism in academic circles today. The next section provides an overview of expressivism. The following sections argue that it is not compelling both as a view about the criminal law, but also as a theory about punishment. I close the chapter with ideas about criminal harms might be better understood. I argue that crimes might be a kind of harm, but not the kinds of harm endorsed by retributivists and, more specifically, expressivists.

1. *The Communication of Retributivist Expressivism*

The Victorian Judge James Fitzjames Stephen presents an early exposition of what I will call *retributivist expressivism*:

> The sentence of the law is to the moral sentiments of the public in relation to any offence what a seal is to hot wax. It converts into a permanent final judgment what might otherwise be a transient sentiment … *the infliction of punishment by law gives definite expression and solemn justification to the hatred which is excited by the commission of the offence.* (1883: 81–82) (emphasis added)

Punishment is the expression of public hatred for a criminal offence communicated to an offender. The public's moral sentiments give rise public anger: it is their moral aversion to a crime that helps justify its criminalization and punishment. Crimes are harms to morals that deserve punishment where an essential role is played by the expression of public anger to offenders through their punishment.

This approach brings together three different ideas. The first is communication. Crime and punishment are matters of public justice to be communicated between the public and offenders. The second idea is retribution. There are many different theories about retribution (Brooks 2012: 15–34). The *standard view* of retribution has been described above: punishment is justified where offenders deserve it because of their moral responsibility for some evil act or omission. Punishment should be proportionate to their moral responsibility and the resulting evil. What justifies criminalization is the immorality of an act or omission; what justifies punishment is the degree of immorality possessed by an act or omission. Murderers and thieves should be punished because each performs evil actions, but the former should be punished more severely because the evil of murder is greater than the evil of theft.

The third idea is expression. Punishment should be communicated to offenders as an *expression* of public disapprobation for criminal wrongdoings. This idea has gained contemporary prominence through the work of Joel Feinberg and his essays 'Doing and Deserving'. Feinberg argues that punishment has a 'symbolic significance' that the idea of punishment as an expression of public anger captures well (1970: 98). Punishment expresses the community's moral condemnation of crime where crime is a harm to morals.

These three ideas might be taken together: punishment is justified as the communication of retributivist expressivism. Punishment is (a) an activity communicated by the state to offenders (b) pertaining to their retributivist desert for moral wrongdoing (c) that is best communicated through the expression of legal punishment.

Some caveats are necessary. First, this justification of punishment understands 'punishment' in a specific way. Feinberg distinguishes 'punishment' from what he calls 'penalties' (1970: 98). Punishment is *only* imprisonment: to speak of the justification of punishment is to address possible defences of hard treatment. Penalties are composed of virtually all alternatives, including monetary fines, verbal warnings and community sentencing. All expressivists (and communicative theorists) are committed to the view that there is a difference in kind between *punishment as imprisonment* and *punishment as a response to crime*. The two are not on a sliding scale and the former warrants additional justification, if it can be justified at all, found only through the expression of public condemnation.

Secondly, there is a curious relationship between the theories of retribution, expressivism and communicative theories of punishment. Each is understood in somewhat different ways although each also presents itself as a distinct alternative to rival theories of punishment. Retributivists do not always accept the view that punishment must require some further justification beyond its being deserved, such as an expression of public disapproval. Expressivists and communicative theorists accept this view, but it is unclear how their views are distinct from retributivists. Expressivists claim punishment is an expression of public disapproval, but only for some disapprovals and not others—and then only in proportion to a specified range of behaviour where public disapproval is relevant. Expressivism, in fact, accepts that only the deserving should be punished and to the degree deserved: therefore, it is difficult to see what work 'expressivism' does for expressivist theories. The communicative theory of punishment, foremost championed by Antony Duff (2001) amongst others, claims that punishment must be 'communicated': whereas expressivists like Feinberg believe punishment is about the expression of public disapproval from the public to offenders, Duff argues punishment should also include the 'communication' of an expression of remorse from offenders to the public. However, communicative theories nevertheless limit the justification of punishment to the deserving and in proportion to what is deserved. While crucial to highlight the stated differences between retribution, expressivism and communicative theories, it is important to note their potential overlap. Indeed, there may be some redundancy in the idea of 'retributivist expressivism'.

This idea has gained in popularity for several reasons. The first is that criminal law has been perhaps the most natural law-friendly area of law. Most traditional crimes are widely consistent with what any reasonable moral theory would disapprove, if not denounce. Crimes such as murder, theft or rape are perhaps the first to come to mind for most people. A natural overlap between the most serious moral wrongs and crimes might suggest some deeper connection between the criminal law and morality and so provide a more welcoming environment for natural law jurisprudence.

A second reason is the concern for providing a more robust justification for punishment within the context of a modern, liberal democracy. Retribution is about the enforcement of some moral perspective on all: we punish crimes as moral wrongs as determined by some viewpoint. But which one? The reassessment of retribution as retributivist expressivism opens up the possibility of a more compelling answer: wrongs are determined by 'us' and expressed through a public communication of disapproval.

The following two sections consider the idea of retributivist expressivism from a more critical perspective. First, I argue that this idea provides a problematic and unpersuasive view about the criminal law. Secondly, I argue that retributivist expressivism does not offer a compelling theory about punishment more generally.

2. *The Criminal Law and Retributivist Expressivism*

Does retributivist expressivism offer a view consistent with the criminal law? It may appear to be consistent at first glance although this is a mistaken impression. For example, most crimes we might think about may include murder, theft, rape or criminal damage. Any reasonable view of morality will disapprove, if not denounce, them all. Different moral theories may disagree on the precise reasons while reaching the same conclusions. The deontologist might denounce murder as a failure to treat persons with the dignity they possess and respect they are owed. Utilitarians might denounce murder as a means to maximise happiness and minimise pain. Reasonable religious believers might claim murder is wrong because of widely shared beliefs about the value of life. Or not. These are only three general illustrations to show how different persons may agree murder is morally wrong and for different reasons. Many other examples could be given.

There is clearly something to be said for the claim that many criminal offences correspond to much of what most of us would find morally problematic, especially in regard to more serious criminal offences. The question is then not whether there is any overlap between crimes and immorality, but a deeper query about the causal link: are crimes harms to morals, such as the examples considered thus far?

This view has defenders among the retributivist expressivists already identified. For instance, Antony Duff argues that 'the criminal law aims to "enforce morality" in the sense that ... it is inconsistent with the central moral values of the political community' (2001: 67). The criminal law, for Duff, enforces public morality through punishment: 'The law "prohibits" murder, rape, and the like because such conduct is wrongful in a ways that properly concerns the law—wrongful in terms of the shared values of the political community' (2001: 58).

H.L.A. Hart was surely correct to say that 'Has the development of the law been influenced by morals? The answer to this question plainly is "Yes"' (1963: 1). But is illegality linked with immorality? The answer to this more fundamental question is plainly 'no'.

Much of the criminal law governs actions and omissions that need not be considered immoral by any reasonable moral view. When we consider crimes in general, our first thoughts may likely to focus on so-called 'other-regarding' harms. These are crimes involving the infliction of some harm to someone, such as murder, theft and rape. Not all crimes have this character. Some are self-regarding, such as drug offences. Other crimes might lack victims or persons wronged (self or other), such as traffic offences.

Consider illegal parking. This is a traffic offence and part of the criminal law. It might not be the first type of offence to immediately spring to mind, but it is an offence that more of us have direct knowledge about: we can normally expect far more instances of illegal parking than murders for most, if not all, political communities.

What does it mean to say this offence is *immoral* or even a *moral wrong*? Perhaps illegal parking through double parking prevents someone who has lawfully parked her vehicle from free movement. Or illegal parking on a narrow street might prevent normal access for traffic to travel. Both cases could be considered instances where the offender demonstrates a clear disregard for the respect for others to some degree.

This need not be true in every case. Illegal parking is not defined by distinguishing the sinful from the virtuous, but often in utilitarian terms: how can traffic move most freely through specific spaces? The fact that a one way street moves in a single direction need not be because this is morally good or desirable, but rather because the road might be narrow and restricting traffic to a single direction maximizes our ability to travel around the vicinity most easily all things considered. So the law might enforce criminal law without any obvious connection with morality. Note that many country roads, such as in my adopted Britain, may be as narrow as any city street, but only the latter might not permit parking on either side and be restricted to one way travel. That we park here or there and drive one direction or another might often be settled almost by chance and luck than morality and virtue. Note further that illegal parking might be morally justified or even morally required depending upon context, such as enabling a life-saving rescue. Illegal parking is not best explained with reference to its immorality, but more often to practicality.

Consider a very different crime, such as treason. Every state criminalizes treason and punishes it with the most severe punishment available to that state. Is treason immoral or morally wrong? The answer is clearly no. Again, there may be cases where treason is morally justified or morally required, such as acts of treason against Nazi Germany or some similar evil state. The criminality of treason is not about moral wrongdoing, but perhaps more practical concerns.

The examples of illegal parking and treason are chosen to identify a spectrum of crimes that any state would include in its criminal law punished relatively small in the case of illegal parking and commanding the most severe sanction in cases of treason. They are also crimes whose 'wrongness' is relatively independent to immorality. If retributivist expressivism cannot account for crimes like these, then it might have a significant problem as a theory of punishment. This is because theories of punishment are theories about practices. Perhaps it is to be expected that there will be some gap between our ideal view of punishment and practices found in any particular state. The fact there is a gap is not the problem; the problem is the size of this gap. Retributivist expressivism runs into trouble not only with crimes on both ends of the scale, but many in between. This is perhaps especially true with so-called crimes involving self-regarding harms. These may include drug offences and (more controversially) prostitution. Few proponents of drug criminalization argue for full legalization of all currently banned drugs. Likewise, few proponents of legalizing prostitution call for full deregulation. So how does the community express its disapproval for acts a person has performed that might cause no harm or inconvenience to the community? How much public anger will stir our collective moral sentiments? The answer is unclear at best.

A serious problem for retributivist expressivism is it is a theory of punishment that rests on a particular foundation consistent with natural law, but at some odds with the criminal law. It is a theory of punishment that can address only some, but not all, crimes we would want to include in the criminal law. None of this is to suggest that crimes are not harmful in any way. But the view of crimes as harms to morality stretches too far beyond the criminal law as we find it and even perhaps as we would want it to be.

3. *Is Retributivist Expressivism Compelling?*

Retributivist expressivism offers a poor match with the criminal law. But is it a compelling theory about punishment?

The idea of expressive communication entails the public speaking with one voice. Offenders receive a message expressed by the public about how much they disapprove of their crimes. However, it is a mistake to argue the public speaks with a single, unified voice in the way suggested. This point is defended well by Hart:

> It is sociologically very naive to think that there is even in England a single homogeneous social morality whose mouthpiece the judge can be in fixing sentence ... Our society, whether we like it or not, is morally a plural society; and the judgements of the relative seriousness of different crimes vary within it far more than this simple theory recognizes. (1968: 171)

Modern society is characterized by the fact of reasonable pluralism (Rawls 1996). No political community possesses one 'social morality' and not others, even if it may privilege one or some. Every community is pluralist and contains reasonable disagreement about moral and political values. One consequence is that there is no single voice from which the community might speak. This is because the political community contains more than one moral view. Perhaps there may be agreement—even an 'overlapping consensus'—that an offender should be punished to some degree, but the reasons for this decision may likely be several and perhaps conflicting.

A more nuanced problem with retributivist expressivism claim that the public can express its disapproval as one voice is that this expression will communicate a particular message. In fact, we may be unable to guard against communicating *unintended* meanings (see Collier 2006: 8–9). It is a mistake to claim that punishment expresses a single message to any messenger, but it may instead multiple messages arising from the reasonable pluralism that exists in any modern political community. Furthermore, we should not insist that punishment expresses only the message (or messages) we intend to express because there may unintended messages communicated as well.

One possible response is offered by Duff. He argues that 'we should not hope to find any criterion, or neat set of criteria, of criminalization' that addresses this concern about what kinds of wrong are to serve as public wrongs deserving of punishment (2006: 98). So perhaps there are many different messages communicated. Criminalization rests on difficult to unpick foundations and his communicative version of retributivist expressivism still remains the most compelling theory.

This is unpersuasive. Supposing there might not be a single standard of 'immorality' derivable from the community's shared values, there remains (*a*) no argument or evidence of what values are shared by our community, (*b*) no satisfactory recognition that the values held by community members may be in conflict nor how such conflicts might be resolved and (*c*) no clear view about the problem of securing the communication of intended meanings while guarding against the expression of unintended meanings.

Retributivist expressivism has a much deeper problem: it is either redundant or incoherent. Retributivist expressivism claims punishment is to be proportionate to the amount of public denunciation appropriate. For example, Feinberg says: 'What justice demands is that the condemnatory aspect of the punishment suit the crime, that the crime be of a kind that is truly worthy of reprobation' (1970: 118). Punishment is an expression of public disapproval. However, not all public disapproval should be expressed as punishment. Only that which is 'truly worthy'—or, in other words, that which is *deserved*—can be the subject of punishment. Punishment is then proportionate to an offender's desert. The problem here is that the degree of appropriate public condemnation need not always be equal to the moral wrongfulness of a criminal offence. After all, we can 'exact retribution ... without denunciation' and 'denounce a crime without exacting retribution' (Cottingham 1979: 238). Expressivists do not argue that, if public condemnation exceeded moral wrongfulness, punishment should be set more severely than deserved. Nor do expressivists argue that, if moral wrongfulness exceeded public condemnation, punishment should be set much lower to bring it closer in line to public disapproval. Note that public disapproval does little, if any, work: punishment is justified when it is retributively deserved and punishment should be in proportion to what is deserved. Expressivism appears to collapse into retributivism.

Now consider Duff's variant on expressivism. Duff argues his communicative view helps to develop retributivism although it is also distinct from it (2001: 25, 30). Retributivists look backward-only to the past crime whereas Duff's theory also looks forward to the future in order 'to persuade offenders that they should repent' (2001: 30). Duff says:

> If he is convicted, his conviction communicates to him (and to others) the censure that he has been proved to deserve for his crime. He is expected (but not compelled) to understand and accept the censure as justified: to understand and accept that he committed a wrong for which the community now properly censures him. His trial and conviction thus address him and seek a response from him as a member of the political community who is both bound and protected by its laws. (2001: 80)[2]

For Duff, imprisonment serves 'the communicative aims of punishment *more adequately* than ... mere convictions or symbolic punishments; a communicative conception of punishment thus provides for its *complete* justification' (2001: 82) (emphasis added). Imprisonment serves communicative aims by providing 'an opportunity' for criminals 'to examine their souls', but not 'invade' them (Duff 2001: 87, see 122–23, 133). We are told 'punishment must go deep with the wrongdoer and must therefore occupy his attention, his thoughts, his emotions, for some considerable time' (Duff 2001: 108). For Duff, the ability to 'go deep' is available only through imprisonment: demonstrating repentance is not enough.

The first problem with his particular theory of punishment is empirical. Imprisonment is said to 'more adequately' satisfy the communicative aims of bringing about a change of heart in offenders than the use of other sanctions. This is an empirical claim for which the only available evidence suggests that, in fact, imprisonment does not perform this task better than alternatives (Brooks 2012: 123–48).

---

[2] See Brooks (2004, 2009) on the criminal trial.

However, Duff is often at some pains to argue that the empirical foundations of his theory of punishment rest on how prison should be rather than how it is. Duff says:

> Such an objection would have force if my claim were that the familiar kinds of hard treatment punishment which are salient in our existing penal systems actually serve to induce repentance and self-reform, but that is not my claim ... My claim is rather that suitably designed and administered kinds of hard treatment should, and in principle could, serve those aims ... it does not depend on proof that our existing penal systems serve those aims. (2000: 420)

The problem with this position is not simply that imprisonment as currently practised fails to satisfy the communicative aims he sets for punishment (and it clearly fails these aims). Instead, there seems no compelling reason to accept—given what we know—that imprisonment will 'always "more adequately"' serve communicative aims better than any alternative approach.

There is a further concern with Duff's theory. Duff says:

> But how can his punishment reconcile him to his victim or the wider community if it is obvious that he is unrepentant and unapologetic? ... The offender has been subjected to what would constitute an appropriately reparative apology if he undertook it for himself. His fellow citizens should therefore now treat him as if he had apologized ... He might not have paid the apologetic debt that he owed ... But something like that debt has been exacted from him, and those who exacted it should now treat him *as if the debt has been paid.* (2001: 123–24) (emphasis added)

What is striking about this passage is that the importance of repentance (and apology) drops out of the picture and appears to do little, if any, work. One concern is that simply serving a length of time in prison is transformed into some 'apologetic debt'. The problem is not simply that there is no evidence that placing offenders in prison is always more likely to inculcate a greater respect for the law than alternatives, but that ultimately it is of no concern whether offenders *do* repent and receive whatever moral communication we had sent, if any. Becoming repentant disappears: 'doing time' is 'repentance' by definition.

For Duff, communicative theories are different from others: expressivism is only about the expression of the public to offenders, but communication includes an expression from the offender to us. But, in fact, no such communication from offender to us may be expressed or perhaps even possible. The 'communicative' theory of punishment may include no actual communication at all and yet its presence is at the heart of its claims about the justification of punishment.

Conclusion: Towards an Alternative

The idea of crimes as harms to morals does not cohere well with current criminal law nor how we might want it changed. Nor do the theories of punishment that endorse this idea offer us a compelling view about crime, morality or punishment. This essay has been critical and now I want to offer a few remarks towards a positive recommendation.

Crime is often considered to be a harm. This may have much to do with the attractiveness of the harm principle whereby an individual is free unless he or she might harm another. Many criminal offences are harms, such as murder or actual bodily harm. However, this perspective captures too much for not all harms are or should be criminal. One example is prize fighting who harm each other when boxing. Few (besides me) believe this should be criminalized. Perhaps all crimes are harms, but not all harms are crimes.

We have considered at some length one attempt to clarify more sharply the idea of crimes as harms in the formulation of crimes as harms *to morality*. We found that this is perhaps too narrow because it omits much of what we would want the criminal law to include. Many crimes are immoral (on various and competing views), but not all are so. Moreover, not all immorality is or should be criminalized: no one (including me) believes telling a white lie to keep a surprise birthday party a secret a wrong in every instance.

Another attempt is the idea of crimes as harms *to rights*. This is a position I defend elsewhere (see Brooks 2012). The criminal law is one part of a wider effort to protect and maintain our rights. Where rights are violated, punishment may be justified as *a response* to crime. All crimes are rights violations and some rights are more central than others. For example, some rights, such as a right against being murdered, is necessary to make possible other rights. Our more fundamental rights may warrant greater protection and, thus, more greater responses via criminal justice.

These remarks are only suggestive, but they are meant to make clear that we need not doubt the existence of 'criminal harms'—crimes can and should be understood as harms—but we have much reason to reject various theories about the kinds of harms that crimes are.[3]

---

[3] An earlier version of this essay was presented to the Oxford Jurisprudence Group. My thanks to the audience and, most especially, to John Gardner, Les Green and Fred Schaeur for their comments.

Bibliography

Brooks, Thom. 2004. 'The Right to Trial by Jury', *Journal of Applied Philosophy* 21(2): 197–212.
Brooks, Thom (ed.). 2009. *The Right to a Fair Trial.* Aldershot: Ashgate.
Brooks, Thom. 2012. *Punishment.* New York: Routledge.
Collier, Charles W. 2006. 'Speech and Communication in Law and Philosophy', *Legal Theory* 12: 1–17.
Cottingham, John. 1979. 'Varieties of Retribution', *Philosophical Quarterly* 29: 238–46.
Duff, R.A. 2000. 'In Defence of One Type of Retribution: A Reply to Bagaric and Amarasekara', *Melbourne University Law Review* 24: 411–26.
Duff, R.A. 2001. *Punishment, Communication, and Community.* Oxford: Oxford University Press.
Duff, R.A. 2006. 'Answering for Crime', *Proceedings of the Aristotelian Society* CVI: 85–111.
Feinberg, Joel. 1970. *Doing and Deserving: Essays in the Theory of Responsibility.* Princeton: Princeton University Press.
Hart, H.L.A. 1963. *Law, Liberty, and Morality.* Oxford: Oxford University Press.
Hart, H.L.A. 1968. *Punishment and Responsibility: Essays in the Philosophy of Law.* Oxford: Clarendon.
Kramer, Matthew H. 1999. *In Defense of Legal Positivism: Law Without Trimmings.* Oxford: Oxford University Press.
Rawls, John. 1996. *Political Liberalism*, paperback edition. New York: Columbia University Press.
Stephen, James Fitzjames. 1883. *A History of the Criminal Law of England.* London.

ON THE NON-INSTRUMENTAL VALUE OF BASIC RIGHTS

Rowan Cruft

Abstract

Basic rights are often of great instrumental value in securing protection for important human needs and interests. The first two sections of this paper defend the thesis that basic rights are also valuable independently of their instrumental role. Taking my cue from Frances Kamm's suggestion that basic rights reflect or express human worth, in the third, fourth and fifth sections I develop the proposal that the non-instrumental value of basic rights derives from their constitutive role in a universal form of community or fellowship. The importance of basic rights' instrumental role is reaffirmed in the final section of the paper, which builds on the earlier sections to offer a 'mixed' theory according to which basic rights have both instrumental and non-instrumental value.

Keywords

basic rights, human rights, non-instrumental value, community, fellowship, friendship, Kamm, Raz, Dworkin

1. *Introduction: Instrumental Approaches to Basic Rights*

This paper examines the non-instrumental value of basic rights. I take 'basic rights' to refer to those morally justified rights that fulfil the following three conditions:

(1) They are of paramount moral importance, where this means both (i) that they take priority over other types of right in cases of conflict, and (ii) that we must make the greatest efforts to avoid violating them.[1]

---

[1] For an interesting discussion of cases where dimensions (i) and (ii) diverge, see F.M. Kamm, *Morality, Mortality, volume II: Rights, Duties and Status* (Oxford: OUP 1996), p. 321.

(2) They exist whether or not they are recognized, demanded, accepted, endorsed, enforced, or complied with by institutions or individuals.
(3) All persons hold these rights, and their correlative duties are binding on all persons and all institutions.

Rights that meet these three conditions are sometimes called 'natural rights' or 'human rights'; by using the phrase 'basic rights' I signal my rejection of the assumptions that these are the rights we would necessarily hold in a pre-social state of nature, and that all these rights necessarily either should be or already are codified in international human rights law.[2]

Many contemporary theorists seem to think that basic rights in my sense, along with all other rights, are justified by their instrumental value. They disagree over what the good ends are for which basic rights are a means: Fabre, Raz, Tasioulas, and Waldron think that a given person's basic rights are justified because they serve that person's *important interests*; utilitarian thinkers like Brandt, Hardin or Talbott take a person's basic rights to be justified by how they serve *the aggregate interest*; Miller, Pogge, and Wiggins see basic rights as justified because they protect their holders' *fundamental needs*; Dagger, Griffin, Lomasky, Nussbaum, and Sen focus in different ways on how basic rights secure their holders' *freedom, capabilities* or *autonomy*; and Rawls takes what he calls 'human rights' to be means for achieving 'a necessary [...] standard for the decency of domestic political and social institutions.'[3] Despite their differences, these

---

[2] Although they are common assumptions, not every theorist assumes that 'natural' rights must be those we would hold in a pre-social state of nature (e.g. this assumption seems to play no role in H.L.A. Hart, 'Are There Any Natural Rights?', *Philosophical Review* 64 (1955), 175–191) or that 'human' rights necessarily ought to be codified in international human rights law (see, e.g. Amartya Sen, *Development as Freedom* (Oxford: OUP 1999), p. 229). For a discussion of the bewildering range of possible meanings of the phrase 'human rights', see Saladin Meckled-García and Başak Çali, 'Lost in translation: the human rights ideal and international human rights law', in their *The Legalization of Human Rights: Multidisciplinary perspectives on human rights and human rights law* (London: Routledge 2006), pp. 11–31). I use the phrase 'basic rights', defined by conditions (1)–(3), to avoid these complications.

[3] The quotation is from John Rawls, *The Law of Peoples* (Cambridge, Mass.: Harvard UP 1999), p. 80. The relevant works of the theorists mentioned are Richard B. Brandt, *Morality, Utilitarianism and Rights* (Cambridge: CUP 1992), esp. Chs. 10 and 11; Richard Dagger, *Civic Virtues: Rights, Citizenship and Republican Liberalism* (Oxford: OUP 1997), esp. Part I; Cécile Fabre, *Whose Body is it Anyway?* (Oxford: OUP 2006), Ch. 1; James Griffin, 'First Steps in an Account of Human Rights', *European Journal of Philosophy* 9 (2001), 396–327; 'Discrepancies between the Best Philosophical Account of Human Rights and the International Law of Human Rights', *Proceedings of the Aristotelian Society* 101 (2001), 1–28; Russell Hardin, *Morality within the Limits of Reason* (Chicago: University of Chicago Press

theorists can be naturally read as sharing the general assumption that the basic rights are justified instrumentally, as efficient means for promoting, protecting or ensuring respect for the theorist's favoured values.

The instrumental nature of these theorists' justifications for basic rights is obscured by the fact that most of the listed theorists would allow that the outcomes these rights produce – in terms of people's *compliance with*, *recognition*, *acceptance* and *endorsement of* them – can have non-instrumental value in the following three ways.

(a) Most would allow that for certain basic rights, the attainment of their immediate objects (where the 'immediate object' of P's right not to be tortured is *P's not being tortured* and the 'immediate object' of Q's right to education is *Q's being educated*) is non-instrumentally valuable. For example, I suspect most of the theorists mentioned would allow that individuals have a fundamental interest in or need for a primary education, whose satisfaction is not only valuable as a necessary means for the individual's attainment of happiness or further goods, but is also valuable independently of its effects. Now according to one understanding, *compliance* with someone's basic right consists not simply in people's attempting to respect the right; rather, genuine compliance consists, at least in part, in the right-holder's successfully attaining the right's immediate object. According to this account, compliance with Jo's right to a primary education partially consists in Jo's receiving a primary education – and that, I have claimed, most theorists would take to be non-instrumentally valuable.

1988); Loren Lomasky, *Persons, Rights and the Moral Community* (Oxford: OUP 1987), esp. Chs. 3 and 4; David Miller, *National Responsibility and Global Justice* (Oxford: OUP 2007), Ch. 7; Martha C. Nussbaum, *Frontiers of Justice: disability, nationality, species membership* (Cambridge, Mass.: Harvard UP 2006), esp. pp. 284–291; Thomas Pogge, *World Poverty and Human Rights* (Cambridge: Polity 2002), esp. pp. 54–59; Joseph Raz, *The Morality of Freedom* (Oxford: Clarendon 1986), esp. Ch. 7; Sen, 'Elements of a Theory of Human Rights', *Philosophy and Public Affairs* 32 (2004), 315–356; William J. Talbott, *Which Rights Should be Universal?* (Oxford: OUP 2005), esp. Ch. 6; John Tasioulas, 'Human Rights, Universality and the Values of Personhood: Retracing Griffin's Steps', *European Journal of Philosophy* 10 (2002), 79–100; Jeremy Waldron, *The Right to Private Property* (Oxford: OUP 1988); *Liberal Rights: Collected Papers 1981–1991* (Cambridge: CUP 1993); David Wiggins, 'Claims of Need', in his *Needs, Values, Truth: Essays in the Philosophy of Value* (Oxford: Blackwell 1987), pp. 1–58. Griffin and Lomasky supplement their autonomy-based accounts with further instrumental considerations; Nussbaum uses the concept of need to explain the central human capabilities; and Raz has recently moved towards a Rawlsian conception of human rights (see Raz, 'Human Rights without Foundations' (2007), available online at http://papers.ssrn.com/sol3/papers.cfm?abstract_id=999874).

(b) In addition, Raz notes that compliance with a given person's basic right can sometimes have further value beyond the value in securing the immediate object for the right-holder. For example, Raz argues that while the immediate object of Jo's right to freedom of expression (Jo's protected capacity to express political opinions publicly, etc.) is of comparatively low value – both instrumental and perhaps non-instrumental – when considered in itself, nonetheless general compliance with the right to freedom of expression borne by all citizens is partially constitutive of an open society of great value.[4] And this open society is arguably valuable, in part, independently of its effects.

(c) As well as *compliance*, several of the theorists listed earlier might also allow that *recognition, acceptance*, and *endorsement* of basic rights has non-instrumental value. For instance, Raz's work suggests that the open society (which is, arguably, partially non-instrumentally valuable) is constituted not only by general *compliance* with people's rights to freedom of expression, but also by widespread *recognition, acceptance*, and *endorsement* of such rights.

Although the listed theorists' views allow that compliance with, recognition, acceptance, and endorsement of basic rights can sometimes be non-instrumentally valuable in the three ways outlined, nonetheless these theorists seem to regard *basic rights themselves* – construed simply as normative requirements existing independently of people's compliance, recognition, acceptance or endorsement – as of purely instrumental value.[5] That is, they all seem to endorse Scanlon's view that the justification of basic rights is:

> backed by something like the following: (i) An empirical claim about how individuals would behave or how institutions would work, in the absence of this particular assignment of rights [...]. (ii) The claim that this result would be unacceptable. This claim will be based on valuation of consequences [...]. (iii) A further empirical claim about how the envisaged assignment of rights will produce a different outcome.[6]

[4] Raz, *Ethics in the Public Domain, Revised Edition* (Oxford: Clarendon 1994), pp. 54–55. Compare *The Morality of Freedom*, p. 191, note 1, for the idea that a right can be justified by an interest other than the interest in its immediate object.

[5] Some might dispute the view that rights are conceptually distinct from acceptance of or compliance with them. For a defense of the thesis that rights are conceptually distinct from their acceptance and compliance, see, e.g. George Rainbolt, *The Concept of Rights* (Dordrecht: Springer 2006), pp. 49–62, or Tasioulas, 'The Moral Reality of Human Rights', in Pogge, ed., *Freedom from Poverty as a Human Right* (Oxford: OUP 2007), pp. 75–101.

[6] T.M. Scanlon, 'Rights, Goals and Fairness', in Waldron, ed., *Theories of Rights* (Oxford: OUP 1984), pp. 137–152 at p. 146.

For the listed theorists, basic rights seem to be justified by their ability to 'produce a different outcome'; basic rights produce this outcome by generating compliance, recognition, acceptance and endorsement, and by motivating enforcement mechanisms that support compliance, recognition, acceptance, and endorsement. This outcome is extremely valuable (both instrumentally and non-instrumentally) in terms of the satisfaction of fundamental interests, the aggregate interest, basic needs, freedoms or decency. It is the value of this *outcome* that – according to the approaches listed earlier – justifies the existence of the basic rights that can secure it.

At least, that is one natural and frequently encountered way of reading the theorists listed. It is not a wholly accurate reading. For example, a close examination of *The Morality of Freedom* reveals that Raz allows that basic rights could be non-instrumentally valuable:

> Some rights may be based on an interest in having those same rights. [...]. A right is a morally fundamental right if it is justified on the ground that it serves the right-holder's interest in having that right inasmuch as that interest is considered to be of ultimate value, i.e. inasmuch as the value of that interest does not derive from some other interest of the right-holder or of other persons. [...] [But it is] very unlikely that all moral considerations derive from people's interests in having rights. Are not their interests in avoiding starvation, in being adequately educated, and other similar interests of moral relevance as well?[7]

This passage suggests, *contra* my reading of Raz's account as 'purely instrumental', that 'morally fundamental rights' are justified by how *the rights themselves* serve their holders' interests, independently of how our reactions to these rights – in terms of compliance with, or acceptance or endorsement of them – serves these interests. Nonetheless Raz goes on to downplay the role of such non-instrumentally justified rights, and those following Raz (including, I think, most of the authors listed earlier) have tended to focus on rights' instrumental value, broadly construed to encompass points (a)–(c).

My aim in this paper is to build on the position sketched in the passage just quoted. In the forthcoming section I defend the thesis that even if they failed to 'produce a different outcome' in Scanlon's terms, basic rights would still be valuable. That is, I argue that *basic rights themselves* are valuable independently of their effects on the world through compliance, acceptance, endorsement, etc. Such effect-independent value must be non-instrumental. In the three subsequent sections I develop an account

---

[7] Raz, *The Morality of Freedom*, pp. 191–192.

of why basic rights are non-instrumentally valuable. My account does not follow Raz in locating basic rights' non-instrumental value in their relation to *interests*, nor do I accept his suggestion that we hold 'fundamental rights' justified *wholly* by their non-instrumental value. Instead, I end by arguing for a 'mixed' account according to which both their instrumental and their non-instrumental value play a part in determining what basic rights we hold.

2. *Reasons for Thinking that Basic Rights are Non-Instrumentally Valuable*

Why might one think that basic rights themselves (rather than compliance with, recognition or acceptance of them) have non-instrumental value? Consider a situation in which some persons' basic rights are wholly ignored: they are violated, with no compensation or apology offered, and the rights are in no other way recognized. One near-example might be the Nazi treatment of Jewish people; another might be slave-holding societies. Let us focus on an imaginary maximally egregious case, in which *nobody* recognizes the basic rights of a certain person or set of persons, nor even shows these people some lesser respect while violating their rights, and these rights will never be recognized in future. In such a situation, purely instrumental approaches would seem compelled to maintain that the violated persons' basic rights have no value, for in such a situation these basic rights are wholly unsuccessful in promoting or protecting whatever ends instrumental theorists select as basic rights' *raison d'être*. This is because, in such a situation, the violated persons' basic rights not only fail to protect their immediate objects, but as these basic rights are in this situation wholly overlooked, they also fail to do anything to serve less immediate ends (such as fairness, efficiency, utility, or their holders' broader interests, needs, capabilities or autonomy). In this egregious case, the violated persons' basic rights achieve nothing for they utterly fail to 'produce a different outcome.' Purely instrumental approaches, like those listed earlier, must imply that the violated basic rights lack all value in this egregious case. Are these approaches correct? We would, I think, judge that the violated persons' basic rights still have value in some respect in the egregious case, even though these rights are in no way recognized and so have no effect on the world. *Contra* purely instrumental approaches, there is something valuable about people having basic rights even here, when they are wholly useless as instruments.

A quick riposte on behalf of purely instrumental theorists maintains that basic rights still have *latent value* in the egregious case, where this means only that in the egregious case basic rights *would be valuable if they were respected or in some way recognized*. The instrumentalist might claim that their theory does not purport to find any 'more-than-latent' value in, nor offer a justification for, a person's *basic rights' existence even when wholly and continually violated*.[8]

This strikes me as an unsatisfactory riposte for three reasons. First, there is indeed a sense in which it seems correct to say that instruments are valuable even when they are not used to achieve what they are means to achieve, and 'latent value' seems appropriate to describe this. For example, it seems correct to ascribe value to a never-used and never-to-be-used shovel forgotten at the back of someone's garden shed; and this seems appropriate because the shovel would efficiently promote our ends if it was used. But it seems to me that this is not the only kind of value that we are inclined to ascribe to basic rights in the egregious case. Basic rights do have latent value in this case, but they also feel valuable in a further way, independently of their potential usefulness. It seems hasty to insist that the idea of 'latent value' can capture all that we value about violated basic rights in the egregious case.

I recognize that this first response simply reports my intuitions. A second response goes further: surely if one knows that something with latent value and no other kind of value will *never* be used, then one can have no reason to create, acquire or favor the existence of this thing. For example, there will be no reason to create, acquire or favor the existence of a car (unless it has some further value (perhaps esthetic or historical)) when the world's car-fuel resources have been exhausted. In this world, it will have become impossible to realize the car's latent value. Similarly, a civil war or other situations of extreme and ongoing violence might make it impossible that a particular person's basic rights could be respected or in any other way recognized now or in the future. In this situation, it would be impossible that the latent value of this person's basic rights could be realized. But it would, I think, still be rational to favor the existence of such rights for this person in this situation (if, *per impossibile*, such detached 'favoring' were an option even though nobody recognized the person's rights). Hence, I suggest, the rights must have more than latent value in this situation, unlike the car in the fuel-free world.

---

[8] Versions of this point were suggested by Antony Duff and Leif Wenar.

Thirdly, basic rights also seem to have value in worlds where they are useless because unnecessary, rather than useless because ignored.[9] For example, consider an altruistic utopia in which each person is incredibly kind to each other person, and motivations to engage in torture, to exclude some from the political process, to ignore those who need an education or not to assist victims of natural disasters, simply never arise. This would be analogous to a world in which we all had shovel-shaped metal hands; in such a world shovels would lack even latent value, because they would not be useful for attaining valuable ends even if they were used. Similarly, basic rights lack both instrumental and latent value in the altruistic utopia: the attainment of what instrumental theorists take to be basic rights' ends (the fulfillment of fundamental interests, needs, utility, etc.) is in this world achieved wholly independently of the existence of basic rights, and *recognition of basic rights would not make it easier to attain these ends.* Nonetheless, it seems clear to me that basic rights are a valuable component of such a world, even though these rights are not needed in order to achieve any results – and the only option appears to be that this value is genuinely non-instrumental (rather than latent or instrumental).

3. *Explaining Basic Rights' Non-Instrumental Value: The Constitutive Approach*

In what ways are basic rights non-instrumentally valuable? It has become common to distinguish between (i) something's being non-instrumentally valuable (or valuable 'for its own sake' or 'finally valuable') and (ii) something's being intrinsically valuable (or 'valuable because of its intrinsic nature' or 'whose value supervenes on its non-relational properties'). For example, Kagan suggests that a unique work of art might be valuable for its own sake, in part because of its relational property of uniqueness; this would be a case of non-instrumental value that was not intrinsic value.[10] My arguments in §(II) suggested that basic rights, construed as normative entities whose existence is independent of compliance with or recognition of them, have more than instrumental value. I shall attempt now to

[9] I am grateful to Kerri Woods for this example.

[10] Shelly Kagan, 'Rethinking Intrinsic Value', in Toni Rønnow-Rasmussen and Michael J. Zimmerman (eds.), *Recent Work on Intrinsic Value* (Dordrecht: Springer 2005), pp. 97–114, at p. 102. See also Christine Korsgaard, 'Two Distinctions in Goodness', in Rønnow-Rasmussen and Zimmerman, pp. 77–96.

explain what this 'final' value of basic rights is. But whether it is 'intrinsic' as well as 'final' will not be my main concern.[11]

One thesis maintains that the non-instrumental value of basic rights consists in their *expressing* or *reflecting* human worth. Kamm writes:

> [T]here may be a type of good that already exists but that would not exist if it were permissible to transgress the right of one person in order to save many lives. This is the good of being someone whose worth is such that it makes him highly inviolable and also makes him someone to whom one owes nonviolation. This good does imply that certain of one's interests should not be sacrificed, but inviolability matters not merely because it instrumentally serves those interests. [...] Inviolability is a reflection of the worth of the person. On this account, it is impermissible for me to harm the person in order to save many in the accident, because doing so is inconsistent with his having this status.[12]
>
> [F]undamental human rights [...] are not concerned with protecting a person's interests, but with expressing his nature as a being of a certain sort, one whose interests are worth protecting. They express the worth of the person rather than the worth of what is in the interests of that person.[13]

These ideas are attractive: it is natural to think that the reason why basic rights are valuable when wholly overlooked (in cases of egregious violation) or when wholly unnecessary (in a utopian world) is because even in these situations basic rights *express* or *reflect* our worth as human beings. We need to explore these attractive but vague ideas.

In what ways can a thing have value because it reflects or expresses something? Reflection gives epistemic access. For example, my reflection in a mirror (even a concave or convex one) gives me some epistemic access to my appearance. It might be argued that basic rights play a similar epistemic role: when I 'see' or recognize someone's basic rights, I thereby learn about the worth of that right-holding person. But in both these scenarios (the mirror, basic rights), the epistemic role of the reflection seems purely instrumentally valuable: the mirror is simply a useful means for enabling me to learn about my appearance; and basic rights,

---

11 But see note 31 below.

12 Kamm, *Intricate Ethics* (Oxford: OUP 2007), pp. 253–4.

13 Ibid., p. 271. Compare Thomas Nagel's similar 'status' view in 'Personal Rights and Public Space', in his *Concealment and Exposure & Other Essays* (Oxford: OUP 2002), pp. 31–52. Compare also dignity-based approaches like that of Nickel (James W. Nickel, 'Poverty and Rights', *The Philosophical Quarterly* 55 (2005), 385–402, esp. pp. 394–395). It is worth stressing that the two quotations from Kamm do not refer to the good of *compliance with* or *recognition* of non-violation, but refer rather to the good of the *normative requirement of non-violation* (i.e. the right) itself.

in their epistemic role as 'reflectors,' are simply useful means for enabling me to learn about human worth. Of course, basic rights have additional instrumental value as protectors of human worth (just as a mirror might also have instrumental value independently of its reflective capacities, for example when used as a shield in battle). But the value of basic rights *as reflectors* seems no more than instrumental, at least if we focus simply on reflection's epistemic role.

Can reflection involve anything more than instrumental value? Sometimes *what is reflected* might be non-instrumentally valuable (a beautiful face, say, or in the case of basic rights, their holders' great worth); but this will not imply that the reflection itself is non-instrumentally valuable. However, sometimes a reflection might be a necessary constituent in a non-instrumentally valuable whole. Consider a beautiful scene reflected in a lake: here perhaps the reflection is a necessary part of a whole that has non-instrumental esthetic value. Some might argue that basic rights play a similar role: the thought would be that *humans plus basic rights* together form a morally satisfying or appropriate whole of which basic rights are a necessary part. This is perhaps similar to the ways that *crime plus punishment* or *virtue plus reward* seem to form morally satisfying or appropriate wholes. We might say that 'the punishment should reflect the nature of the crime' and the occurrence of this form of reflection seems non-instrumentally valuable. But I fear that 'reflection' here does little distinctive work: in the contexts outlined, 'reflecting' seems simply a metaphor for the general notions of 'fitting' or 'deserving.' And to say that basic rights are of non-instrumental value because they are *fitting* to humans, or because humans *deserve* them, is to say little beyond the bare claim that there is non-instrumental value in humans holding basic rights.

We can improve on these thoughts by considering expression. Like reflections, expressions give observers epistemic access, in this case to what the expresser feels or thinks (consider a cry expressing fear or a linguistic utterance). And like reflections, at first glance expressions seem purely instrumentally valuable: my expression 'the tree is over there' seems valuable simply as a means of communicating with others by expressing my thought that the tree is over there; similarly, a cry might seem valuable simply as a means of expressing fear (whether voluntarily or not). But on second glance, this appears simplistic. While *the sounds* I emit in a particular token utterance of 'the Earth is a planet' might be no more than instruments, *the sentence* that I thereby utter (an abstract object identified by its linguistic form) seems to be more than simply a useful means to express a pre-existing pre-linguistic thought. Instead, this sentence shapes or, perhaps, constitutes the thought that it expresses. Similarly, it might be argued that one's cry partially constitutes one's fear, rather than simply expressing it: that is, perhaps without the cry the fear could not be the very type of fear it is, because the cry is part of what constitutes it as this type of fear. It is notable that if these claims are true, and if furthermore the thought or the fear were of non-instrumental value in these cases (I am not sure whether this is true; it is arguable), then the linguistic expression or the cry would have non-instrumental value as *part-constitutive* of a non-instrumentally valuable thought or emotion.[14]

This line of reasoning strikes me as promising for explaining the non-instrumental value of basic rights. In my view, basic rights are not simply useful means, but are also *partially constitutive of* certain relationships (just as expressions partially constitute what they express). And the relationships that basic rights partially constitute are *non-instrumentally valuable*: I argue in §§(IV) and (V) below that they are relationships that bind all humans together in fellowship as members of a shared proto-community. Basic rights gain their non-instrumental value from their constitutive role in this non-instrumentally valuable community.[15]

To build support for this controversial view, we can consider the analogous constitutive role of the duties of friendship. My duties owed to my friend (duties to treat them with concern and compassion by helping them in times of distress, but also by letting them 'make their own mistakes,' etc.) are, I propose, partially constitutive of my relationship of friendship. According to this view, the duties are not simply useful *means* to get me to behave in a friendly manner. Indeed a good friend should not need their duties of friendship in order to motivate them to care for their friend, so the duties of friendship should not operate as instruments in this way. Instead, the duties are a *constitutive part* of friendship: friendship without the relevant duties is an impossibility, not because the duties are necessary to motivate appropriately friendly feelings and actions,

---

[14] Rather than adopting the 'constitutive' account of the non-instrumental value of expressions sketched here, some theorists might instead note that the referents of certain linguistic expressions (such as 'autonomy' or 'human happiness') have non-instrumental value; having noted this, they might argue that such linguistic expressions somehow inherit their referents' non-instrumental value. But this is implausible, and in any case basic rights are not *linguistic* expressions and so lack referents in the relevant sense.

[15] This goes beyond anything Kamm claims. Her notion that basic rights *express* human worth, when coupled with my observation that expressions partly constitute what they express, suggests that basic rights partially constitute human worth. But Kamm does not draw this inference, nor flesh it out with the concept of 'community.'

but because the duties are simply part of what makes a relationship a friendship. If I could feel the same friendly feelings and perform the same friendly acts as a genuine friend, but without having any duties towards my friend to do so, then this would not be genuine friendship. We can support this view by noting that when one wonders whether one is still 'friends with' someone whom one has not seen for years, one of the questions one asks oneself is 'am I still under any special duties to this person?' If the answer is 'no,' then one will conclude that one's relationship with the person is no longer friendship; this is because the duties are part of what constitutes friendship.

My point here differs from the claim (popular among consequentialist defenders of associative duties) that genuine friendship is only *psychologically* possible if friends think about each other in the ways that duties require.[16] Instead, my view maintains that the only *conceptually* possible way to be a genuine friend is for one to be subject to genuine duties owed to one's friend. The relevant necessary constituent of friendship here is not simply *belief in* the existence of such duties, nor simply *compliance with* or *acceptance of* such duties. Rather, the duties themselves – normative entities requiring directed concern for a particular person – are a conceptually necessary constituent of friendship. Without such duties, the relationship would lack the directed normative character necessary for it to be friendship.[17]

---

[16] See, e.g. Peter Railton, 'Alienation, Consequentialism and the Demands of Morality', *Philosophy and Public Affairs* 13 (1984), 134–171.

[17] Raz seems to agree: '[Certain] duties are part of what makes friendship into what it is. They are constitutive of the relationship' (*Ethics in the Public Domain*, p. 41). 'Since friendship consists in part in such duties the existence of the duty is intrinsically valuable if the desirability of friendship itself is, as I shall assume without argument, intrinsic' (*Morality of Freedom*, p. 212). But, despite appearances, I am unsure whether Raz's discussion of friendship is really in agreement with mine. Raz justifies *one's duty to compensate friends for one's faultless harms* by claiming (1) that such compensation expresses concern for the harmed person and (2) that 'friendship is in part the expression of concern' (ibid.). This reasoning appears instrumental: it seems to ground the relevant duties on their value as the *means* to secure the occurrence of something (the expression of concern) that is a component of something intrinsically valuable (friendship). By contrast, I argue – and Raz's passages quoted at the start of this note suggest – that the duties of friendship are valuable not simply as a means to the protection of constituents of friendship, but are themselves *qua* duties part-constitutive of friendship. To support this point, in justifying the relevant duties Raz should have claimed not simply that 'friendship is in part the expression of concern' but rather that 'friendship is in part [*being duty-bound to offer*] the expression of concern' or that a true 'expression of concern' *must itself be part-constituted by duties to offer compensation, rather than simply by compensatory actions and feelings.*

I suggest that basic rights play an analogous constitutive role. They part-constitute a valuable relationship just as the duties of friendship do. But what exactly is this relationship?

4. *Basic Rights as Part-Constituting a Universal Community of Fellows*

If basic rights' non-instrumental value is to be explained by their partially constituting a non-instrumentally valuable relationship – in the way that the duties of friendship do – then it is important to be clear about what the relevant relationship is. Given that basic rights are held by all individual people and are binding on all individual and communal bodies (including governments), such a relationship must be understood as universal in form, binding each individual person to each other individual person (and each communal body) independently of national or other boundaries. Possible candidates for the relevant rights-constituted non-instrumentally valuable universal relationship include the ideas of universal *friendship*, *fellowship* or *community*.

Schwarzenbach has defended the thesis that Aristotelian *civic friendship* should play a role in the modern state: this friendship involves a concern for one's fellow citizens for their own sake.[18] She suggests that this form of friendship finds expression in rights:

> [B]y guaranteeing to each individual – simply on the basis of his or her humanity – a basic set of rights (including due process of law, etc.), and, further, in the repeated effort to uphold these rights and to see them realised in practice, citizens acknowledge and express their general concern and goodwill towards the interests of each particular individual in the concrete. A doctrine of individual rights, far from revealing mere conflict or indifference between citizens, may be seen to embody a fundamental regard – if not love – for the special interests of every human being.[19]

Some of what Schwarzenbach outlines – the 'effort to uphold' rights, the aim to 'see them realized' – concerns the way that *compliance with*, *acceptance* and *endorsement of* rights part-constitute civic friendship. In this respect Schwarzenbach's claims seem similar to Raz's instrumental claims (discussed under (b) and (c) in §(I)) about how compliance with and acceptance of the rights of freedom of expression and freedom of the press

---

[18] Sibyl A. Schwarzenbach, 'On Civic Friendship', *Ethics* 107 (1996), 97–128, at pp. 99–100 and p. 114.

[19] Ibid., p. 114.

part-constitute an open society.[20] But Schwarzenbach can be read – in her stress on the role of 'a basic set of rights' as themselves 'express[ing] [citizens'] general concern,' and on how 'a doctrine of individual rights' itself 'embod[ies] a fundamental regard' – as focusing also on the role of *rights themselves*, construed as normative entities whose existence is logically independent of their recognition. If we take seriously my earlier comments about the constitutive role of expressions, then Schwarzenbach's passage can be read as suggesting that certain rights, because they are expressions of civic friendship, themselves part-constitute such friendship.

Taking Schwarzenbach's cue, should we embrace a broader conception of *universal* friendship as the non-instrumentally valuable universal relationship that basic rights part-constitute? This proposal would not imply that all cases of unfriendly behavior (such as simple rudeness to a neighbor) were themselves basic rights violations. Rather, the proposal maintains that basic rights are *part* of what constitutes a universal form of friendship. This universal form of friendship would be violated by any violation of basic rights; but this form of friendship could *also* be violated in many other ways (e.g. by rudeness or a simple lack of concern) that do not violate basic rights.

In my view, this friendship-centered approach is attractive but a little misleading. It is attractive because it highlights how the universal rights-constituted relationship embodies, as friendship does, a requirement that each party to the relationship be concerned for each other person *for his or her own sake*, rather than simply for some further end. In addition, the concept of 'friendship' seems more appropriate for characterizing this universal relationship than certain rivals such as 'family' (which requires too close a personal concern and suggests too hierarchical a structure) or 'contract' (which wrongly suggests duties that are shouldered voluntarily). Nonetheless, friendship is misleading in this context because, *pace* Schwarzenbach and Aristotle, it is difficult to make sense of the idea of friendships between people who have never met each other and who can

---

20 Raz, *Morality of Freedom*, pp. 253–4 and *Ethics in the Public Domain*, pp. 54–55. See also the similar claim that general *acceptance* of rights against discrimination part-constitutes 'public culture which enables people to take pride in their identity' (*Morality of Freedom*, p. 254). And compare Dworkin's claims about how widespread *acceptance* of the legal rights generated by the principles one's society has chosen for itself can help constitute one's society as a 'community of principle' (Ronald Dworkin, *Law's Empire* (London: Fontana 1986), p. 211).

never meet.[21] Our contemporary concept of friendship is more interactional than this, involving each friend knowing and responding to the other friend, and each recognizing each to know and to be responding to the other. The universal relationship constituted by basic rights binding *everyone* together cannot meet this condition.

Instead, a better concept to illuminate the non-instrumentally valuable universal relationship that basic rights part-constitute is that of a universal *community of fellows*. We are familiar with certain non-universal fellowship communities that can survive without each fellow recognizing and being able to interact directly with all the other fellows: e.g. *fellow citizens* or *fellow employees of a large business*. People live in fellowship with other citizens and co-employees even though they cannot meet or get to know them all. In addition, like friendships, genuine fellowships require each person to be concerned for their fellows *for their own sake* rather than simply for further ends. Furthermore, in my view, the notion of a community of fellows makes especially clear the non-maximizing character of some of the normative requirements that basic rights and their correlative duties comprise,[22] as normative requirements with this non-maximizing character seem to be central to the existence of genuine fellowship. If one was allowed simply to take one's fellows' suffering as something to be minimized in aggregate, rather than as something forbidden by non-maximizing rights, then one's relationship with one's fellows would not be a relationship of genuine community and they would not genuinely be one's fellows.[23]

In sum, if we think of the universal relationship that is part-constituted by basic rights as a *community of fellows*, it follows that (a) this relationship involves a requirement that its members be concerned for each other person *for that other person's own sake*, and (b) this requirement involves

21 See Sandra E. Marshall, 'The Community of Friends', in Emilios A. Christodoulidis (ed.), *Communitarianism and Citizenship* (Aldershot: Ashgate 1999), pp. 208–219 at p. 216.

22 By 'non-maximizing character', I mean the way that your right not to be X-ed can require me not to do X to you even if by doing X I could better minimize the incidence of X overall. For instance, your right not to be tortured can require me not to torture you even when by torturing you I could minimize the incidence of torture overall (e.g. perhaps because you are a torturer's innocent child). For a defense of this 'non-maximizing' characteristic as central to many rights, see my 'Rights: Beyond Interest Theory and Will Theory?, *Law and Philosophy* 23 (2004), 347–397 at pp. 353–354; compare Thomas Nagel, *The View from Nowhere* (Oxford: OUP 1986), pp. 175–180. For the claim that rights to assistance lack this non-maximizing character, see Kamm, *Intricate Ethics*, pp. 254–255.

23 Non-maximizing requirements are perhaps also central to friendship, but to my mind such requirements seem at least as central to *communities of fellows* as they are to *friendships*.

each person in a bilateral non-maximizing normative relationship of '*owing to*' and '*claim against*' vis-à-vis each other person. Basic rights are, I suggest, partially constitutive of this universal human proto-community or proto-fellowship, as we might call it. Furthermore, I argue below that this community of fellows is non-instrumentally valuable. Like personal friendship, it is a good thing, independently of its effects, that the universal human proto-community exists.

5. *The Non-Instrumental Value of the Universal Community of Fellows*

We can come to grasp the non-instrumental value of the universal community of fellows by tackling an objection suggested by Dworkin:

> People cannot be made involuntary "honorary" members of a community to which they do not even "barely" belong because other members are disposed to treat them as such. I would not become a citizen of Fiji if people there decided for some reason to treat me as one of them. Nor am I the friend of a stranger sitting next to me on a plane just because he decides he is a friend of mine.[24]

Building on this, a critic might claim that two people, neither of whom is disposed to treat the other as their fellow, cannot become fellows simply because they are bound together by basic rights with the appropriate directed normative structure. For even mere '*proto-*' fellowship or community to exist, so the critic will claim, the fellows must have some warm feelings towards or desires concerning each other, even if they cannot all know each other. By contrast, I appear in §(IV) to have maintained that basic rights are partially constitutive of a universal proto-community that can exist even without fellow-feelings. In fact, the objector will note, my universal proto-community must be able to survive egregious violations of the basic rights that constitute it, violations that seem to express feelings of hatred. For otherwise the relationship between, for example, a Jewish person and a Nazi, would not constitute a proto-community relationship, and hence the Jewish person's basic rights would in this context lose what I have argued is the source of their non-instrumental value. Given that I claimed, in §(II) above, that basic rights retain their non-instrumental value even in cases of egregious violation, I must therefore maintain that the universal proto-community constituted by basic rights can survive their egregious violation.

---

[24] Dworkin, *Law's Empire*, pp. 201–202.

But the objector will say that this makes my universal proto-community very different from ordinary communities or fellowships. Surely, the objector will claim, German Jewish people in the 1940s were not in community or fellowship with Nazis (barring a few exceptions)? If I persist in insisting that they were in 'community' or 'fellowship' together, but only in a special sense that can coexist with hatred and egregious violation, then the objector will charge that my claim for the explanatory power of this special community or fellowship looks empty. The objector will say that on close inspection the special notions of 'community' and 'fellowship' that I use turn out to refer to no more than *the existence of basic rights* (for such community or fellowship persists wherever basic rights exist, even in cases of egregious violation). This would make vacuous my claim that we can explain basic rights' non-instrumental value by noting their constitutive role in a special form of community or fellowship. This claim would emerge as simply an alternative way of saying that we can explain basic rights' non-instrumental value by noting that they constitute basic rights.[25]

To respond to this objection, we need to paint a picture of the universal proto-community that basic rights part-constitute – a community binding together all people including the violator and victim – in a way that reveals this proto-community to be more than simply a new technical synonym for basic rights.[26] In painting this picture, we shall also illustrate the non-instrumental value of the proto-community.

Developing this response to the objector has three aspects. First, we should note that the universal proto-community that I outlined in §(IV) is not as different from ordinary communities as the objector suggests, even if the universal proto-community can survive violations of the basic rights that part-constitute it, for many communities (and indeed some friendships) survive horrendous violations by their members – and they survive as valuable communities, with even the violator still a member.[27]

---

[25] Compare the similar objection I raised to the claim that basic rights' non-instrumental value can be explained by the fact that basic rights are *fitting* for humans or humans *deserve* these rights (p. 450 above).

[26] An alternative response to the objection maintains that when fellow-feelings are absent, basic rights have merely *latent* non-instrumental value, where this means that they *would* be a component of a form of non-instrumentally valuable universal fellowship *if* the appropriate feelings existed. For reasons against such a 'latent' approach – reasons that apply as much to human rights having latent *non-instrumental* as latent instrumental value – see §(II).

[27] See, e.g. Duff's claims about the convicted criminal as a member of the community (R.A. Duff, *Punishment, Communication and Community* (Oxford: Oxford University Press, 2001)).

In addition (as the examples of co-citizens and co-employees illustrate) I share some ordinary valuable communities with people with whom I have no interactions or shared goals. Similarly, like the universal proto-community, people find themselves in many ordinary valuable communities whether they want to or not, and are not allowed to exit these communities (consider certain national or familial communities). The first aspect of my response notes these similarities between my special notion of universal proto-community and our understanding of many of our ordinary valuable communities.

Secondly, we should also note that the universal proto-community is a much richer concept than, and a different concept from, our concept of basic rights. For instance, the universal proto-community, while constituted by basic rights, is also constituted by other normative requirements, such as a requirement that each person think of other human beings as fellows who share in their common humanity (where this includes, e.g. recognizing other humans as beings with their own perspective, with whom one can argue and reason, and who are capable of loving and being loved). And while the warm feelings of personal friendship are not necessary, a requirement for respectful, sympathetic and polite emotional responses is another normative constituent of the universal proto-community. When people fail to offer such sympathetic or polite responses, or fail to think of others as fellow humans, they do not thereby violate basic rights; but they nonetheless fail to respond appropriately to the universal proto-community within which they live. So basic rights represent just one among a range of normative requirements that together form components of the universal proto-community.

Thirdly, we should note that there is no need to maintain that, even in contexts of egregious violation, the universal proto-community has a bare normative existence entirely independent of people's fellow-feelings. This would mark a major difference between the universal proto-community and all other communities: if the universal proto-community existed independently of people's thoughts and feelings, then the universal proto-community would be very different from other forms of community, all of which are based around some form of fellow-feeling. Yet to respond to Dworkin's objection we do not need to maintain that the universal proto-community that is part-constituted by basic rights exists entirely independently of people's fellow-feeling. Perhaps in a world with *no* fellow-feelings, in which all people had become 'mere machines' to each other, then basic rights – if they still existed – would lack non-instrumental value because the proto-community of fellowship among humans would not exist.

But our world, even when it involves systematic and widespread egregious violation (as under the Nazis, or in slave-holding societies or totalitarian regimes), also necessarily involves people who have some fellow-feelings towards some other humans. For most people such felt responses to some of our species are unavoidable, and this is reflected in the way that many common concepts – e.g. of love, pity, recognition, respect, sharing a joke and reprimanding – can only be understood and appropriately deployed by those who have fellow-feelings towards those humans to which the concepts are applied.[28] These unavoidable feelings constitute a basic moral sensibility involving directed concern for others that is a necessary part of the psychology of most humans. And when a person holds these feelings towards only a sub-set of all humans (as seems to occur in slave-holding or Nazi societies), they form a basis from which wider feelings of universal fellowship can grow.[29]

Such ever-present feelings mean that the proto-community of humankind is never *purely* normatively constituted: relevant feelings and actions will always also help constitute this community, even if they are rare and of restricted scope. In this way, the proto-community of humankind is akin to many bounded communities: many such communities – e.g. those of fellow citizens or fellow employees – are partially normatively constituted and also partially constituted by the feelings and actions of their members, but can survive fairly extensive violations that show that a significant number of their members lack the relevant fellow-feelings or hold such feelings only with excessively restricted scope. I would suggest that a community of fellows can sometimes survive even if the majority of its members lack most of the necessary feelings, so long as they have partial feelings (e.g. a sympathetic response to the hurt of at least some people) that, when appropriately developed, could grow into the feelings of those living in a morally mature fellowship. I propose that enough people have enough feelings that could grow into those required for fully mature universal fellowship, for the proto-community of humankind to bind together even those engaged in and those suffering egregious violation.

To summarize, my response to the objection inspired by Dworkin claims (1) that the idea of a special universal proto-community or proto-fellowship shares many features with our ordinary concepts of

[28] For an elaboration and defense of this claim, see Raimond Gaita, *A Common Humanity*, Second Edition (London: Routledge, 2000), pp. 266–270.

[29] See Gaita's discussion of Orwell's account of the fellow-feeling generated by seeing a fascist soldier running holding up his trousers (ibid., pp. 48–49).

community or fellowship, which allow that communities or fellowships can survive violations by their members, (2) that basic rights are not the only normative requirements that part-constitute the universal proto-community, and (3) that the universal proto-community involves enough fellow-feelings, even if they are partial and under-developed, for it to qualify as a genuine proto-community (in contrast to the purported 'friendship' between me and Dworkin's 'stranger sitting next to me on a plane' for whom I lack the feelings necessary for personal friendship). Points (1)-(3) show that the universal proto-community is more than simply a new technical synonym for basic rights.[30] They also make clear that the universal proto-community of fellows is non-instrumentally valuable. The wide range of normative requirements that constitute this proto-community (requirements focused around demands that people be recognized as fellow humans) and the unavoidable fellow-feelings (e.g. of pity or love) that also constitute this proto-community are clearly of non-instrumental value, even if the requirements are not always respected and the feelings are inappropriately partial and restricted. The world is a better place for their existence, independently of their effects.[31]

6. *Supplementing Basic Rights' Non-Instrumental Value: A Mixed Approach*

Unlike the concepts of personal friendship, family or citizenship, which entail duties with fairly clear and determinate contents (such as the duty

---

[30] See this charge on p. 456 above.

[31] Three issues deserve mention at this point. First, I have argued that basic rights have non-instrumental value as partially constitutive of a non-instrumentally valuable universal proto-community. Is this proto-community also *intrinsically* valuable? Does the community-constituting role of basic rights make them *intrinsically* valuable too? I suspect the answer to the first question is 'yes', because the intrinsic nature of this proto-community, as involving, e.g. directed duties binding on all, is the source of its value as an end. Secondly, I suggest that our relationship to *non-human animals* is a further form of non-instrumentally (and, probably, intrinsically) valuable proto-community, characterized by animal rights that are both instrumentally and non-instrumentally valuable. For an attractive instrumental approach to animal rights, see Nussbaum, *Frontiers of Justice*, Ch. 6; I would supplement this with a non-instrumentalist thesis parallel to but different from my community-constituting view of basic rights. The principal difference is that our proto-community with animals rarely involves reciprocal duties: typically humans owe duties to animals, but animals do not bear such normative 'owing to' relationships to humans. Thirdly, we should also use the constitutive approach sketched in §(IV) to account for the value of the rights and duties that constitute such relationships as the family (which is partially non-instrumentally valuable) and the institution of property (which, I have argued elsewhere,

to listen to a friend in need, the familial duty to assist one's elderly parent, or the civic duty to participate in political debate), I fear we do not have a sufficiently clear pre-theoretical grasp of the concept of the *universal proto-community of humankind* for us to know, without contestable elaboration, which particular basic rights and correlative duties are necessary for this form of community to exist. Instead, the concept of the proto-community of humankind simply tells us that people must be bound together by some network of rights and duties that connects each person with each other person in 'owed to' normative relationships that embody the mutual respect of fellowship. The idea provides *some* constraint on the content of basic rights: a basic right to attack others whenever one wished would be incompatible with the proto-community of humankind. But beyond such constraints, the idea of the proto-community of humankind leaves under-determined whether, for example, basic rights should be predominantly non-interference rights, or should also include assistance rights that place heavy demands on all individuals, or whether basic rights should include property rights and rights to political participation, or should have a different content.[32]

In response to this concern, we should note that my arguments so far have allowed that basic rights are instrumentally valuable in many ways, in addition to possessing non-instrumental value. We can now add that while the non-instrumental value of the proto-community of humankind generates strong reasons for the existence of some universal network of basic rights, further reasons grounded in basic rights' instrumental value determine what the precise content of these rights should be. Thus the instrumental value of basic rights, as protectors of particular interests, needs or aspects of autonomy, still plays an important role in my picture: it determines which particular (among the many possible) universal-community-constituting rights are justified. This 'mixed' approach strikes me as plausible: I do not seek to deny that basic rights have instrumental value; I simply propose that basic rights also have non-instrumental value. Their *instrumental* value can play the central role in determining the rights' precise content.

---

is largely instrumentally valuable (see my 'Against Individualistic Justifications of Property Rights', *Utilitas* 18 (2006), 154–172)).

[32] For a related discussion of the difficulty that 'pure' non-instrumental theories encounter when trying to specify the content of particular rights, see Leif Wenar, 'The Value of Rights', in M. O'Rourke, ed., *Law and Social Justice* (Cambridge, Mass.: MIT Press 2005), pp. 179–209.

Conclusion

The picture sketched in this paper depicts basic rights as both non-instrumentally and instrumentally valuable, their non-instrumental value inhering in their role as binding each person to each other person in a network of directed normative relationships that – together with other normative requirements and unavoidable fellow-feelings – constitutes the proto-community or proto-fellowship of humankind, their instrumental value inhering in their role as protectors of particular important interests or needs of their holders (a role that determines their precise content).

I have focused primarily on explaining basic rights' non-instrumental value, because this aspect of basic rights' value has been overlooked.[33] Recognizing this is essential to a full understanding of the justification of basic rights. We should end by noting that even if the proto-community-constituting account developed in §§(IV) and (V) is rejected, still my arguments in §(II) have established that basic rights have non-instrumental value – the question then will be to explain its nature and source.[34]

[33] Recall §(I)'s discussion of the prevalence of the instrumental approach.

[34] Many of the ideas in this paper developed in discussions at the Universities of Catania, Edinburgh, Glasgow, London, Sheffield and Stirling. I am grateful to all who participated in these discussions, and to the UK's Arts and Humanities Research Council for funding research leave to develop this work.

GROUP RIGHTS AND GROUP AGENCY[1]

Adina Preda

Abstract

On some theories of rights, such as the Choice theory, only agents can have moral rights. The realm of right-holders thus excludes several potential candidates, among which are young children, mentally incapacitated persons, and groups since these are thought to lack the required degree of agency. This paper argues that groups cannot be excluded on purely conceptual grounds. The argument comes in three steps: first, it is argued that full-blown agency or a capacity for autonomy is not required for the possession of Choice theory rights, second, that groups can be seen as agents, albeit in a limited sense, and third, that groups can make irreducibly collective choices in spite of their limited agency. The upshot of this argument is that groups can have rights, provided that they are organised around a coherent decision-making procedure; furthermore, this account can be employed to argue that other creatures of limited agency are possible right-holders.

Keywords

group rights, human rights, interest theory, rights, will theory

Many theories of rights envisage a link between moral rights and agency. This link can occur at either a conceptual or a substantive level. In other

[1] This paper has benefited from detailed written comments and/or discussions with a number of people, for which I am very grateful. Among them are: Jos Elkink, Maria Paola Ferretti, Anca Gheaus, Mihaela Georgieva, Dean Machin, Andrew Shorten, Hillel Steiner, Nicholas Vrousalis, Camil Ungureanu and two anonymous reviewers for the *Journal of Moral Philosophy*. Previous versions of the paper have been presented at a number of conferences and seminars such as the *Theories of Territory Workshop*, London, February 2009, the *Political Studies Annual Conference*, Manchester, April 2009, the SPIRe Visiting Speakers Seminar, UCD, Dublin, November 2008 and the *Human Rights and Political Theory – Conference in Honour of Attracta Ingram*, Dublin, April 2010. I want to sincerely thank the members of those audiences for very constructive comments and criticism, in particular John Baker, Graham Finlay, Cara Nine and Philip Pettit, and to apologise to anyone I may have left out.

words, for some theories the very *concept* of rights makes reference to the notion of agency or choice, while others derive the *content* of rights from the conditions of agency. The latter type of view is popular among human rights theorists, who see agency or personhood as the essential feature of human beings that ought to be protected by rights.[2] In Griffin's words: 'we value our status as human beings especially highly, often more highly than even our happiness. This status centres on our being agents – deliberating, assessing, choosing, and acting to make what we see as a good life for ourselves'.[3] Human rights are thus justified inasmuch as they protect this property of humans.

The former view makes no such normative claim; it is not that moral rights should protect or promote agency but rather that only agents can have rights since the very nature of rights presupposes agency. This paper only discusses this conceptual requirement, which is an integral part of the Choice (or Will) theory of rights. According to the Choice theory somebody possesses a right if and only if s/he has control over the performance of the corresponding duty, that is, if she/he can enforce or waive that duty. It is generally thought that only moral agents have the capacity to exercise the requisite control.

The Choice theory thus excludes from the realm of rights those entities or creatures that are thought to lack the required degree of agency, such as very young children, animals, future generations or indeed groups, which are the focus of this paper. Although we often talk of groups as if they engage in the same kind of purposeful behaviour that individuals do, it is not clear that groups can be seen as moral agents; groups do not have minds and bodies of their own so they cannot possess the same capacities as individual human beings. The reluctance to ascribe rights to groups often boils down to a concern about a group's lack of *ontological* status: the idea that groups do not exist as distinct entities, separate from their members and/or as substances in the world.[4]

This paper aims to show that this concern is misplaced and that the Choice theory can accommodate group rights. The paper has three parts. First, I outline the Choice theory of rights and I argue that the *conceptual*

---

[2] For examples of this kind of theory see James Griffin, *On Human Rights* (Oxford, Oxford University Press, 2007), Alan Gewirth, *Human Rights: Essays on Justifications and Applications* (Chicago, Chicago University Press, 1982).

[3] Griffin, op. cit., p. 32.

[4] I explain further down that this notion can be interpreted in two different ways. See pp. 14–15.

criteria for ascriptions of rights may be less demanding than it is usually thought; Choice theory right-holders need not be full-blown or autonomous agents but have to have a capacity for choice and action, i.e. limited agency. In the second section, I show that a group's lack of ontological status does not preclude it from being seen as an agent, albeit only in this limited sense. In the third and last section, I argue that groups organised around a collective decision-making procedure can act and make genuinely collective choices so they are possible moral right-holders. If this argument is correct, it can also serve to extend the class of Choice theory right-holders to include other creatures that lack a high degree of agency, most notably children.

1. *The Choice Theory of Rights and Agency*

The Choice (or Will) theory of rights is one of the two main theories of rights. According to its main rival, the Interest (or Benefit) theory, rights should be seen as protections of (important) interests. So a necessary and sufficient condition for being a potential right-holder is having an interest of sufficient weight. The Interest theory is thus much more generous in its ascription of rights since moral patients as well as agents can have important interests.

The Choice theory is the less popular theory of rights and it will not be defended here.[5] In this paper, I only aim to show that it can accommodate group rights, in spite of what is commonly thought but this will also suggest some helpful lines along which the Choice theorist can formulate a reply to some objections. It is important to stress, however, that the debate between the Interest and the Choice theories of rights concerns the *nature* of rights. In other words, both theories aim to *describe* the concept of a right, i.e. provide necessary and sufficient conditions for its application, rather than a substantive ground for moral rights. The disagreement between the Choice and the Interest theorist essentially concerns the pairing of duties – legal or moral – with rights and consequently the identity of right-holders.

Thus, on the Interest theory duties correlate with someone's right whenever they are designed to (directly) serve that person's interest.

[5] The best overview of the debate between the two theories of rights can be found in M.H. Kramer, H. Steiner & N.E. Simmonds, *A Debate over Rights* (Oxford, Clarendon, Press, 1998).

By contrast, the Choice theory holds that a duty correlates with someone's right if and only if that person has control over the performance of that duty. A Choice theory right-holder is, in Hart's words, a 'small scale sovereign' over a duty; what this means, more precisely, is that the right-holder is the entity that is empowered to make decisions regarding that duty. In other words, all Choice theory (claim-) rights come equipped with Hohfeldian powers, more specifically with powers to waive or enforce the correlative duty.[6] A right-holder must therefore be able to exercise such powers.

Given this assumption, the Choice theorist has to exclude all unempowerable creatures from the domain of rights so it is more economical with rights than it is perhaps desirable. For this reason, the Choice theory also has some counter-intuitive implications when it comes to identifying the holder(s) of the rights correlative to duties in criminal law. Since individual citizens cannot control the performance of such duties, they are not seen as the holders of the corresponding rights, which is at odds with the widely shared idea that criminal law grants rights to citizens. The solutions proposed to this problem are also somewhat counter-intuitive. For instance, Hillel Steiner argues that the right-holder is the state official who can eventually waive punishment for non-compliance with such duties.[7] The argument presented in this paper implies, however, that if groups can be seen as Choice theory right-holders, Choice theorists might plausibly describe duties under criminal law as owed to the population of a state as a whole *if* the performance of such duties can indeed be controlled by this collectivity.[8] This would be more in line with the common understanding of criminal law.

But in order to be able to ascribe moral rights to groups the Choice theory has to first grapple with the challenge of showing that groups can be agents. In what follows I argue that, in spite of what is generally assumed, ascriptions of rights need not presuppose a *robust* or full-blown sense of agency, which in turn might require a capacity for reflection, reasoning and deliberation; a capacity to act intentionally and make choices is sufficient for ascriptions of rights.

---

[6] For a full description of these powers see H. Steiner, 'Working Rights' in *a Debate over Rights*, p. 240.

[7] See Steiner, 'Working rights', pp. 289 and *An Essay on Rights* (Oxford, UK & Cambridge, USA, Blackwell, 1994), p. 70.

[8] I made some steps in that direction in another paper entitled 'States' rights as group rights: an analytical perspective', forthcoming in Calder, G., Bessone, M & Zuolo, F. (eds.), *How Groups Matter*, Palgrave, 2013.

Carl Wellman is one of the few rights theorists who address in any detail the possibility of group rights[9] and he denies that groups can be seen as agents and consequently as right-holders. His reasoning is illustrates well the kind of assumptions that inform the Choice theorist's implicit rejection of group rights.[10] His argument is seemingly straightforward: since rights involve acting and only agents can act, only agents can possess rights. I will argue in this section that the second premise is false inasmuch as it assumes a relatively robust notion of agency.

My argument is based on a distinction between a *capacity for acting*, or agency in a limited sense, and *full-blown* or *autonomous* agency. We can think of an agent as simply the subject of an action, an *actor*; since acting requires intention, being an agent in this limited sense requires being capable of having an intention.[11] Thus, showing that an entity is an agent in this sense requires showing that it can act intentionally. But being an agent sometimes means more than just being capable of acting intentionally; being an agent often means being the (sole) author of one's life, being in control of one's actions, that is being *autonomous*. This obviously requires a capacity for autonomy or full-blown agency.[12] A capacity for acting is a necessary but not sufficient condition for full-blown agency; in addition, a full-blown agent must be able to choose one's goals, after careful deliberation and reflection and be able to revise them in the light of moral reasons. Autonomous agency thus requires certain capacities that only a conscious, reflective being is capable of. The two senses of agency identified are two ends of the agency spectrum. So agency can come in different degrees, ranging from the most *minimal*, which requires acting intentionally to the most *robust* agency, which is possessed by full-blown agents.

The question is then what kind or degree of agency is required for the possession of rights. Wellman concedes that the kind of agency required

---

9 Two of the main contemporary proponents of the Choice theory, Steiner and Sumner, refer only in passing to the possibility of group rights and while they do not dismiss this possibility outright they both question the possibility of group agency. See W. Sumner, *The Moral Foundation of Rights* (Oxford, Clarendon Press, 1987), p. 211 and Steiner, 'Working rights', pp. 288–289.

10 Wellman is, strictly speaking, not a Choice theorist. In his view, rights confer 'dominion' rather than control on their holders. But this is arguably indistinguishable or at least presupposes choice.

11 An agent is 'the person (or other being) who is the subject where there is action' in Ted Hondrich (ed.) – *The Oxford Companion to Philosophy*, 2nd ed. (Oxford, Oxford University Press, 2005), p. 18.

12 Of course not all agents that have a *capacity* for autonomy are in fact autonomous agents, i.e. exercise their capacity.

for rights is less robust than full-blown agency. However, the notion of agency he employs in his discussion of groups is richer than that warranted by his own assumptions.

Wellman provides three different arguments for the agency condition: the argument from dominion, constituents, and the language of rights. I will focus on his argument from constituents since it is more congenial to the concerns of the Choice theorist than the others. The argument from constituents starts from the typical 'molecular' structure of a Choice theory right; such a right has a Hohfeldian liberty at its core, protected by a claim to non-interference that is accompanied by powers of waiver or enforcement over the corresponding duty. Since a liberty is the absence of a duty, only the kind of entity that can be subject to a duty can have a liberty to the contrary, Wellman claims.[13] This presupposes that the agency conditions for bearing duties are identical to those for (liberty-) rights but it does not point to any specific notion of agency. When it comes to a Hohfeldian power, the agency condition becomes clearer: 'Since a moral power is the ability to effect moral consequences by a specific action performed with a reasonably imputed *intention*, only a being capable of *acting intentionally*, could be said to have a moral power at all. Therefore, only an agent could possess a moral power' (emphases added).[14] The first part of this statement, however, suggests that being able to act intentionally is all that is required for the possession of rights. In order words, minimal rather than full-blown agency appears to be the only necessary condition for the possession of powers/rights.[15]

But in spite of this conclusion, Wellman subsequently claims that a richer concept of agency is required for ascriptions of rights. He thus proposes a 'moderately rich sense of agency', which is 'the same sort that renders one responsible for one's actions: the capacity to act in the light of specifically moral reasons.[16] This in turn presupposes at least the capacities to become aware of the relevant facts, to appreciate their moral relevance, to be motivated by them, and to act in some broad non-moral sense of doing something or other'.[17] This is however a notion of agency that is quite close to the robust end of the spectrum and that may indeed be

[13] C. Wellman, *Real Rights* (New York, Oxford University Press, 1995), p. 108.
[14] Wellman, op. cit., p. 109.
[15] I will argue later that a capacity for *choice*, which is different from a capacity for action, is also required for the possession of rights.
[16] Wellman, op. cit., p. 112.
[17] Ibid., p. 113.

unattainable for groups. It is plausible to think that, inasmuch as these are mental activities, only a conscious being with a mind can possess them. If groups do not have minds of their own they would not have these capacities. But I want to question Wellman's assumption that the kind of agency needed for rights is the same sort of agency that is required for ascriptions of *moral* responsibility.

Wellman claims that: 'if [...] it is inappropriate to ascribe a liberty to any entity incapable of bearing any contrary duty, *then* the conditions necessary for *moral* responsibility are also the conditions for the possession of moral liberties' (emphases added).[18] There two implicit claims here: 1) the conditions for holding rights are the same as those for bearing duties and 2) ascriptions of duties are appropriate only when the conditions for moral responsibility are met. In what follows, I will accept the first premise and question the second.[19]

I submit that being held morally responsible and being held under a duty are subject to different conditions since one can have a duty even when one cannot be held morally responsible for failing to comply with it. An obligation or duty simply requires that its subject acts – or refrains from acting – in a certain way; so as long as one can act, one can have obligations. Being held *morally* responsible for failing to comply with one's duty, which means being subject to *blame* and in some cases punishment, presupposes that the duty bearer not only had the ability to comply with the duty but also that his or her failure to comply was the result of an autonomous decision, one that the agent 'owns'. Thus, ascribing moral responsibility requires a degree of agency close to the robust end of the spectrum, whereas a duty can be imposed on agents with more limited capacities.

Of course, the reason why moral obligations are *typically* imposed on full-blown agents is presumably because we want to hold them morally responsible for failing to comply with their obligations. But the two do not necessarily go together; we can consistently claim that people breach their duties without further implying that they are *morally* responsible for doing so. A child can have and fail to comply with a duty but, under normal circumstance, we would not hold him/her morally responsible and

---

18 Ibid., p. 112.

19 The idea that the same conditions are required for both probably rests on an equivocation between two senses of responsibility: a forward looking notion, equivalent to duty and a backward looking notion, equivalent to accountability. Here I use responsibility to mean the latter.

blame him or her for that.[20] In most legal systems, children under a certain age cannot be subject to a (legal) duty but above a certain age they can be charged and convicted for violating the law yet will not be punished for it. So it is not the case that only autonomous agents can be subject to duties, although a capacity for acting is required for the performance of one's duties.[21] Autonomous agency is a condition for attributions of moral responsibility and blame but not for holding people under a duty.

I have argued that the degree of agency required for ascriptions of duties does not necessarily match the degree of agency required for holding agents morally responsible. But it could be objected that it is unjustified to impose duties on agents without a degree of agency close to the robust end of the spectrum or at least, the *potential* to develop it. In the absence of a capacity for moral responsibility, there may be no good reason, and indeed it may be unfair, to impose duties on agents that cannot be held responsible, except for a developmental purpose. It might be suggested that it is only appropriate to ascribe duties and liabilities for non-compliance to limited agents that have the *potential* for moral responsibility, that is, if they are 'responsibilisable'.[22] This would mean that my argument only applies to those entities that can at least *become* full-blown agents and it is unclear that groups are in this category.[23] I agree that this is the most plausible rationale for ascribing duties – and perhaps rights – to limited agents. This is, however, a *substantive* rather than a *conceptual* requirement. In other words, it may well be the case that normative reasons would militate against holding such agents under a duty but this is not to say that they are incapable of performing them, should they have a capacity to act. So I conclude that a capacity for intentional action is the only conceptual requirement for ascribing duties.

---

[20] It is true that we might sometimes 'punish' children for wrongdoings and punishment normally presupposes blameworthiness but I take it that this kind of action has a developmental purpose and is not genuine punishment nor is it an expression of blame. Needless to say, holding very young children morally responsible for their behaviour and inflicting genuine punishment on them is morally indefensible.

[21] It may be the case that certain types of duty does require full-blown moral agency. I am thinking here of duties of charity or virtue, which are to be performed voluntarily and whose worth comes precisely from engaging an agent's capacity for autonomous choice. In any event, even if this is true it does not affect those duties the performance of which is not a matter of voluntary choice, i.e. perfect duties of justice.

[22] I want to thank Philip Pettit for bringing this point to my attention. See his 'Responsibility incorporated', *Ethics*, 117 (2007), pp. 176–177 and *A Theory of Freedom: From the Psychology to the Politics of Agency* (Oxford, Oxford University Press, 2001), chapter 1.

[23] Pettit accepts that groups have the potential for full-blown agency but I do not want to go that far.

It is important to note here as well that even if groups do not fulfil the conditions for moral responsibility that does not mean that nobody can be held morally responsible for violations of duties or delinquent exercise of rights by groups. For one thing, moral responsibility is not the only type of responsibility that can accompany failure to comply with a duty. For actions that are intended but not autonomously or voluntarily chosen, other notions of responsibility, such as causal or outcome responsibility, may be more appropriate.[24] Furthermore, even if groups are only held strictly liable as a whole for the consequences of genuinely collective actions, moral responsibility can still be distributed to individuals. Genuine collective responsibility is irreducible but that does not mean that it is not *distributable*.[25] In fact, we may find it useful as well as justifiable to hold groups as whole strictly liable for certain actions, while at the same time ascribe moral responsibility and blame to individual members of a group. We might for example hold the Lehman brothers' corporation liable for (some of) the consequences of its actions but we may hold its CEO *morally* responsible and blame him for some of the harm caused. If a group's members acted in morally blameworthy ways, they should be held individually – and criminally – liable. However, this may leave certain 'gaps' of responsibility and the best – or even only – way of dealing with this is by treating groups as responsible agents.

But is there any other reason why ascriptions of rights, rather than duties, require more than a capacity to act? Wellman's argument from constituents suggests that a capacity to act intentionally is all that is required for the possession of rights. But since any Choice theory right-holders possesses a number of Hohfeldian powers that come in mutually exclusive pairs, such a right-holder must be able to make *choices*, that is to select between two options. Since acting intentionally need not imply making a choice, this requirement is a bit more stringent. But once again it does not mean that potential right-holders have to be autonomous or full-blown agents; right-holders must be able to make choices but those choices need not be autonomous or indeed *rational*. Just like in the case of duties, we may have good (normative) reasons for not granting rights to

[24] For a discussion of outcome responsibility see T. Honoré, *Responsibility and Fault* (Oxford & Portland, Oregon, Hart Publishing, 2002) and for a more general exposition of different types of responsibility see P. Cane, *Responsibility in Law and Morality* (Oxford & Portland, Oregon, Hart Publishing, 2003). I take it that outcome responsibility is the moral equivalent or ground for strict liability.

[25] I say more about this in section three, p. 27.

beings that are not autonomous or rational choosers; we probably want rights to be exercised responsibly. But this may be a reason for not granting someone rights not a conceptual reason for arguing that they are incapable of exercising them. Furthermore, the Choice theorist is unlikely to argue that we should withhold moral rights from people who would not exercise them responsibly so it would be inconsistent to argue for a stronger condition when it comes to groups. So, if it can be shown that groups have the capacity to act intentionally and make choices, that is have limited agency, they are potential right-holders. A separate argument, however, is required in order to show that group rights are justified.

The crucial point to take from this discussion is that the necessary conditions for holding rights are not necessarily the same as those for moral responsibility. Thus, we have corrected the assumption that only full-blown agents can have rights and found that and the only conceptual requirement for ascribing rights to groups is a capacity for acting and making choices, that is a limited – though not minimal – degree of agency. It is thus unnecessary to conceive of groups as moral persons of equal standing to individual human agents in order to grant them rights.

But, even if groups need not be full-blown agents in order to qualify as possible right-holders, it is not clear that they are agents even in a limited sense, i.e. that they can act and make choices. Since an action is distinguished from an event by the presence of an intention, one is the subject of an action or the actor, in case one can be attributed the intention with which the action is performed. So in order to show that groups are actors in the very least, we need to show that they can be attributed intentions, more specifically intentions that are not reducible to the intentions of the groups' members. This is the task of the next section.

2. *Groups and Agency*

There is now a voluminous literature on collective intentionality and responsibility.[26] My aim in this section is not to offer a novel account of

---

[26] For different views on shared or joint intention see M. Bratman, 'Shared intention' in his *Faces of Intention: Selected Essays on Intention and Agency* (Cambridge, Cambridge University Press, 1999), M. Gilbert – *On Social Facts* (Princeton, Princeton University Press, 1989) and 'The structure of the social atom: joint commitment as the foundation of human behaviour' in F.F. Schmidt (ed.), *Socializing Metaphysics – The Nature of Social Reality* (Lanham, MD, Rowman & Littlefield Publishers, 2003), L. May, *The Morality of Groups* (Notre Dame, Indiana, University of Notre Dame Press, 1987) and *Sharing Responsibility*

collective intention but only to show that ascriptions of intentions to groups need not imply controversial claims about the nature or moral status of groups. To that end, I will focus on the least controversial case, namely that of organised groups such as corporations, since this the most likely to convince the sceptic.

I will mainly rely on Peter French's account of collective intentionality and I want to support his view that corporations can be ascribed irreducibly collective intentions and can act, but I stop short of endorsing his conclusion that corporations should be treated as 'full-fledged members of the moral community, of equal standing with the traditionally acknowledged residents: human beings'.[27] Scepticism about group rights is motivated precisely by this perceived implication of arguing for group intentionality. In Peter Jones's words, 'sceptics often object to the ontology of groups that they take to be implicit in the idea of group rights. To suppose that groups, like individual persons can hold rights is to suppose that groups can have a being and an integrity that matches that of individual persons'.[28] In other words, the sceptics are concerned that accepting group agency entails the thesis that groups have ontological status, namely that they exist, as entities over and above their individual members. But this claim is interpreted in different ways by different thinkers. Thus, on the one hand, the claim that groups have ontological status could be taken to mean (merely) that a group is more than the sum of its members, that in talking about a group we envisage a referent other than its members

(Chicago & London, University of Chicago Press, 1992) and R. Tuomela - 'Actions by collectives', *Philosophical Perspectives*, 3 (1989), *The Importance of Us* (Stanford, Ca., Stanford University Press, 1995) and 'We-intentions revisited', *Philosophical Studies*, 125 (2005). I will not argue for this here but it seems to me that many of these accounts are not accounts of *genuine* collective intentions. Many of them focus on intentions of individuals that are directed toward a collective goal or that are informed by collective attitudes. For instance, Bratman's, Gilbert's and Tuomela's accounts of 'shared intention', 'shared commitment' and 'we-mode intention' respectively are best seen as accounts of what I would call 'shared' or 'joint' intention rather than collective intention proper. By 'shared' intentions I mean individual intentions that happen to coincide across several individuals; thus, individuals can be seen to act together or perhaps just simultaneously because they have the same goal. By 'joint' intention I mean an intention that individuals may form in light of each other's' intentions thus enabling them to act cooperatively or jointly. Both these types of intention are ultimately reducible to individuals' intentions, in my view.

27 P. French, *Collective and Corporate Responsibility* (New York, Columbia University Press, 1984), p. 32.

28 See Jones, 'Group Rights', *The Stanford Encyclopedia of Philosophy* (*Winter 2008 Edition*), Edward N. Zalta (ed.), URL = http://plato.stanford.edu/archives/win2008/entries/rights-group/, p. 15.

severally, an 'individual' entity.[29] On the other hand, this claim could be interpreted to mean that groups have an 'organic' existence, that they are organisms or metaphysical substances.[30] Let us call the first the weak ontological claim and the latter the strong one, since the latter obviously presupposes the former.[31] The strong interpretation tends to be the one assumed by sceptics about group agency; Wellman, for instance, denies that entities without 'individual substance' can be agents.[32]

But it is sometimes unclear what exactly and/or which of these interpretations the sceptic is concerned about. On the one hand, ascribing ontological status, even in the weak form, to groups can be potentially problematic from a normative point of view. But on the other hand, the sceptic assumes that having ontological status in the strong sense is a necessary condition for ascriptions of agency hence moral rights to groups. But the normative worries are easier to dispel if we accept, as I will argue we should, that seeing groups as agents in a limited sense does not entail the conclusion that they have ontological status in either sense. One can subscribe to an intermediate position whereby only human beings have ontological status, and are the only full-blown agents, but groups can also have a degree of agency.[33] This implies neither that the groups' juridical

---

[29] Pettit argues, for instance, that 'a social integrate is an intentional subject that is distinct from its members – that exists over and beyond its members' and claims that such groups 'deserve ontological recognition as intentional and personal subjects'. P. Pettit, 'Groups with minds of their own' in *Socializing Metaphysics*, p. 184 and 175 respectively. At the same time, he claims that he is not thereby postulating any 'ontological mystery' or an ontologically emergent realm. Thus, he defends a weak form of the ontological status thesis.

[30] For an instructive history of this interpretation, whose roots are to be found in the 'emergentist' tradition of the nineteenth century, see C. List & P. Pettit, *Groups Agents*, New York: Oxford University Press, 2011, pp. 73–75.

[31] This parallels Vincent's distinction between groups as persons, individuals or organic entities. See A. Vincent, 'Can groups be persons?', *Review of Metaphysics*, 42 (1989). He argues that seeing groups as persons does not entail any of the other two views. I found his distinctions very useful but I think he probably overstates the separateness of these claims, in that some of them may imply others but does not elaborate on the possible implications.

[32] See also J. Narveson, 'Collective rights?', *Canadian Journal of Law and Jurisprudence*, vol. 4, July 1991, p. 335 and E. Wall, 'The Problem of Group Agency', *The Philosophical Forum*, vol. XXXI, Summer 2000, p. 195.

[33] Thus, in one sense, I agree with List and Pettit that postulating group agency need not entail an emergent ontological realm but at the same time, I only argue for that view when it comes to groups as limited agents. See List& Pettit, op. cit. I am not offering an argument for the possibility of full-blown collective agency and therefore I am not claiming that robust collective agency is compatible with methodological individualism. Nor am I claiming the opposite. My account is also similar to Copp's and May's but unlike Copp, I do not extend this argument to some unorganised collectives and unlike May, I do not

personality is fictitious nor that they have the same standing as natural persons.

I will focus on Wellman's critique of French, which is a good illustration of some common, yet erroneous assumptions regarding group agency. French argues that corporations can be seen as full-fledged moral agents based on a two-step argument. First, French claims that 'a corporation has a certain kind of unity, revealed by the fact that no statement about a corporation will be logically equivalent to a statement about its members; a certain normative unity is thus in place'. Second, he argues that corporations 'evidence a noneliminable intentionality with regard to the things they do' and this intentionality is created by a corporate internal decision (CID) structure.[34] He therefore concludes that a corporation is a 'noneliminable referent of an ascription of moral responsibility' hence a full-fledged moral person.[35]

Wellman charges French with the offence of having moved from 'the logic of expressions...to a conclusion about the metaphysical status of a corporation'. He claims that although 'a corporation is not identical with a mere sum of human beings, it does not follow, however, that a corporation is an individual substance'.[36] Wellman is correct to point out that semantic or conceptual supra-individualism does not entail metaphysical or ontological supra-individualism, at least not in the strong sense.[37]

But French could reply that no such move was made: if statements about groups are not equivalent to statements about their members, this means that they are non-eliminable referents of ascriptions of moral responsibility. This in turn means that they are full-fledged moral agents. This need not entail that they are 'individual substances'.[38] It is Wellman who assumes that moral agency presupposes 'individual substance'. I already argued against French's second move. While we might plausibly

hold that relations between people in groups have a 'reality' of their own. See David Copp, 'What Collectives Are: Agency, Individualism and Legal Theory', *Dialogue*, 23, 1984 and 'On the Agency of Certain Collective Entities: An Argument from Normative Autonomy', *Midwest Studies in Philosophy*, XXX, 2006 and Larry May, *The Morality of Groups* (Notre Dame, Notre Dame University Press, 1987).

34 The argument is mostly contained in French, op. cit., ch. 3, 'The Corporation as a Moral Person'.

35 Ibid., p. 38.

36 Wellman, op. cit., p. 160.

37 Cf. Schmitt, op. cit., p. 15. Schmitt defines conceptual supra-individualism as the view that 'talk of groups and joint actions cannot be analyzed in terms of individuals, their non-social properties, and admissible composites of them.'

38 French would not in fact reply that but I am claiming that this move is open to him.

argue that (some) groups are full-blown moral agents, this conclusion does not follow from French's argument, which merely shows that groups can have collective intentions.[39] In what follows, I will argue both against Wellman's assumption.

Wellman denies that the second step could be valid without the assumption that groups have ontological status. Now, Wellman's critique here is in part directed at the conclusion that groups are *full-blown* agents and I do not take issue here with that side of the argument.[40] But he also wants to argue that groups cannot act. Here his argument becomes somewhat inconsistent since he accepts that 'the rules that constitute a corporation licence the re-description of certain acts of its members as acts of the corporation'. So he rejects a literal reading of such a statement 'because it would presuppose on ontological commitment': 'If a corporation is not an individual substance, it can only metaphorically be an agent'.[41] I will argue that if non-reductive statements about corporate intentions are true, then these intentions are properly ascribed to the corporation rather than its individual members, although they supervene on their members intentions. This means that the group is an agent although not a full-blown one.

Wellman's argument is based on the implicit assumption that individuals are ascribed actions in virtue of their 'individual substance'. But this notion is somewhat obscure and not clearly defined; however, it seems to include two different requirements: that of substance or *tangibility* and that of individuality or *unity*. It is important to see what does the work in this argument: the fact the human beings are substances, i.e. are embodied, or the fact that they have a certain unity. In other words, is the concern that groups lack *individual* substance or individual *substance?*

Arguably the condition that does the work in this argument is that of unity since there is an obvious sense in which groups have substance since they are composed of individual human beings. Although human beings are themselves complex substances, they possess a body that has 'a real unity consisting in the structure of its composition' and 'on this basis one might plausibly argue that any action of a human being, such as walking cannot be reduced to the sum of the actions of its several members, that

---

39 A valid argument in support of this conclusion would include premises about the rationality and consistency of group reasoning. One such argument is made again by List &Pettit and it implies that only certain groups, namely those that 'collectivise reason' are full-blown moral agents.

40 This is to say, I remain agnostic on whether one can be a full-blown agent without 'individual substance'.

41 Wellman, op. cit., p 161.

is, its right leg moving, its left leg moving, and so on.'[42] So although having substance is necessary for acting, it is not sufficient; it must be a certain kind of substance, possibly indivisible substance. Since the corporation is not a single, separate entity, with *its own* body and mind, it cannot be ascribed a *single*, irreducible action. But what role would unity play in ascriptions of actions to individuals?

One natural thought might be that because a single *mind* coordinates the movements of different parts of one's body we speak of a single action, like walking for instance. Although different parts of the body move separately, they do not move independently of each other since they are coordinated by the same mind by means of a single intention; this is why walking is *one* action. But it seems to me that what is important here is that the movements are coordinated by a single intention rather than by a single mind. One might object here that since an intention is a mental state we cannot ascribe an intention to an entity without a mind, the group in this case.[43] But even if we accept this view of intention, we might reply that the minds of the group's members can host the intention as it were. What is required is that the group be able to form a genuinely collective intention, rather than having a mind of its own. The rejoinder here may be that a single intention requires in turn a separate, collective mind. But is it the case that individual human beings can form intentions because they have a (unitary) mind of their own?

Drawing on findings from psychology, neuroscience and biology, Glen Weyl shows that individuals can be just as divided, and hardly more rational or consistent than groups are.[44] Thus, we can plausibly argue that individuals themselves have more than one mind as it were and these minds often come into conflict. He uses the argument to cast doubt on the liberal commitment to individual agency and responsibility and to suggest that agency is not an appropriate basis for ascriptions of rights.[45]

Weyl's argument can in fact support the points I have been making here: if we still conceive of individuals as agents and hold them

---

[42] Ibid., p. 160.

[43] For the sake of the argument, I will assume here that a mind requires individual substance.

[44] G. Weyl, 'Whose Rights? – A Critique of Individual Agency as the Basis of Rights', *Politics, Philosophy and Economics*, 8 (2009), especially p. 145. I want to thank Hillel Steiner for this reference.

[45] I do not fully endorse Weyl's conclusions. It may well be the case that individuals lack mental unity but this need not undermine liberal commitments since individuals have the *capacity* to be rational, consistent agents. For this reason, it can be legitimate to hold them morally responsible for their choices.

responsible for their actions, in spite of their lack of unity or indeed rationality, there is no reason for denying groups the same kind of treatment. What is more, his argument supports my suggestion that full-blown or autonomous agency is not a necessary condition for ascriptions of rights. Some adult human beings of 'normal' mental capacities are far from being rational or autonomous agents; in spite of this fact we have no difficulty in seeing them as the authors of their actions and ascribing them with such actions. This is in virtue of their being able to reconcile, at least temporarily, their conflicting wills and form an intention that results in action.

It could be objected here that individuals are able to resolve this conflict of wills and form an intention *because* they have one mind, which enables them to make a decision resulting in an intention. But the same role can be played in a group by a collective decision making procedure that can 'unify' the different intentions of a group's members. It is on the basis of this intention that a genuinely collective action can be attributed to the group, just like an action is attributed to an individual on the basis of an intention rather than unity of mind.

The comeback may be that individuals need to deliberate and engage in a process of reasoning in order to form an intention despite their conflicting wills and these are conscious mental processes that require a mind. But, inasmuch as these activities are necessary in order to form an intention, the process of deliberation and reasoning can nevertheless take place among the members of a group. Just like an individual needs to engage in an internal dialogue in order to make a decision, the group members will need to engage in a dialogue in order to reach a single, collective intention. The only difference is that, in the collective case, the dialogue is thought out loud so to speak.

So even if we grant the assumption that a group does not have a mind of its own – because it is not an individual substance – it does not follow that the group cannot form a genuinely collective intention. What may, however, follow is that the group cannot be seen as a conscious or autonomous agent; but that is not a requirement for possessing rights, I argued. So I conclude that unity of mind is not necessary for ascribing intentions hence actions to a group – or to an individual for that matter; intentional unity is however, required.

But it could be objected that I misconstrued the unity requirement. The kind of unity necessary for acting may not refer to unity of mind, or intention, but to unity of mind and body as it were. In other words, it is a *biological* unity that is necessary in order to connect an intention with a bodily movement. It may be the case that the coexistence or continuity of mind and body warrants the ascription of *this* action to *this* individual.

But it is not the case that such continuity is required for ascriptions of actions to human beings. An individual can be the principal or the 'author' of an action performed by someone else, one's agent. If I authorise someone to act on my behalf the action is properly attributed to me; I am the 'author' of the action in case I am the author of the intention with which the action is performed. David Copp argues that collectives can be similarly attributed 'secondary' actions, on the basis of actions of their members.[46] Thus, while it is plausible to maintain that collectives cannot perform 'basic' actions since they do not have bodies, this, according to Copp, does not preclude them from performing actions. These secondary actions are 'constituted' by the actions of their members under relevant circumstances.[47] Given such circumstances, an action of a group's member(s) can be properly attributed to the group as a whole, i.e. it is a collective action, if the intention of that action can be attributed to the group.

Wellman also considers, albeit briefly, Copp's argument and rejects it; he claims that the analogy used by Copp does not hold since in paradigm cases, 'the principal possesses primary agency'.[48] Since the corporation is not a self-sufficient agent, it cannot be a principal, he says. But Wellman (purposefully?) misconstrues Copp's argument. The analogy is only meant to establish that the intention and the bodily movement that form an action need not coexist in one biological entity and that the locus of intention marks the principal. Whether groups can have 'primary agency', as Wellman puts it, is a different issue but there is no reason to believe that primary agency is or requires anything other than the capacity to have intentions. Actions are ascribed to individuals based on their intention rather than the fact that individuals are autonomous agents or embodied creatures.

So *if* groups can be attributed irreducibly collective intentions, they can be ascribed actions, in spite of their lack of ontological status. This is

---

[46] See D. Copp, 'Collective actions and secondary actions', *American Philosophical Quarterly*, 16 (1979) and J. Feinberg, 'Collective responsibility', *The Journal of Philosophy*, 65 (1979).

[47] For a statement of the 'constitution relation' see Copp, *supra* note 41, pp. 182–183. These circumstances include 'all facts about the constitutional rules or laws, laws and by-laws of organized collectives' or 'facts about the composition and dynamics of, or patterns of interpersonal relations within' in the case of unorganised collectives.

[48] Wellman, op. cit., p. 164.

consistent with Wellman's claim that groups do not act 'literally'; it is not the body of the group that acts yet the group is the subject of the action. Thus ascriptions of actions to groups need not presuppose and do not entail controversial ontological claims so (some of) the scepticism about group rights is misplaced.

But accepting that groups can have collective intentions and can act will not convince the Choice theorist that they are possible right-holders. Recall that a necessary condition for being a right-holder is being capable of action as well as *choice*. Since an intention can occur without a prior decision or choice[49] it is not necessarily the case that all the groups that can act intentionally can make choices. In the following section I argue that some groups can make choices that are genuinely collective.

3. *Groups and Rights*

My aim in this section is twofold: first, I want to support the idea that groups can make genuinely collective decisions, that is decisions that are not reducible to the decisions of its individual members and second, to identify the kind of group that can make such decisions. A right will belong to the group *qua* group if and only if the powers associated with it can be exercised by the group as a whole. Thus, if rights ascribed to the group are to be genuine group rights, they should be exercisable by the group as such, rather than by (some of) its members.

What I argue here is that *only* organised groups can be Choice theory right-holders. Some accounts of group intentionality and agency can support the conclusion that even *unorganised* groups or aggregates can have collective intentions and can be seen as actors, that is agent in a minimal sense. But even if some (unorganised) groups could be said to be *acting intentionally* or have intentions *in action*, they cannot be said to have made a decision.[50] Making a choice requires forming an intention to act after a process of selection among alternatives, which presupposes a degree of

---

[49] An intention can be the result of a decision but one can also act intentionally without necessarily choosing to so act. 'Someone may intend to build a squirrel house without having decided to do it, deliberated about it, formed an intention to do it or reasoned about it.' Davidson, 'Intending' in his *Essays on Actions and Events* (Berkeley, University of California Press, 2001), p. 83. See also Bratman, *Faces of Intention*, pp. 31–33. I use decision and choice interchangeably in this paper.

[50] I take no stand here on the question whether unorganised groups can act *intentionally* or have *intentions in action*. I take it that philosophers who argue that unorganised groups can have intentions refer to this type of intention.

awareness on the part of the decision-maker. This will indicate some criteria for identifying the kind of group that can have rights.

In order to make a choice, a group will need a decision-making procedure, that is a way to amalgamate the choices of its individual members; furthermore this procedure should be a public one, that is known to the group's members, in order to satisfy the 'awareness' requirement.[51] Furthermore, we should probably stipulate that a decision-making procedure should be a 'coherent' one, namely one that yields a definite result on a given choice. As it is well-known, collective choices are vulnerable to various impossibility results which show that a majoritarian aggregation of preferences or choices has circular or inconclusive results given certain constraints; nevertheless once these constrains are relaxed, many types of procedure would enable a group to make collective choices.[52] So, we have narrowed down the search for a possible right-holder to groups that are organised around a coherent and public decision-making procedure.

But in order to ascribe rights to the group *qua* group, the choice made by a group should be genuinely collective. So let me clarify what I mean by a genuinely collective choice or decision. A decision is genuinely

[51] I say 'public' instead of formal here in order to include groups that are organised and have a decision-making procedure which is not formal in the sense that it is not 'officially' enacted in written statements or organisational charts. The Mafia is, for instance, such a group but I do not mean to suggest that groups like the Mafia do in fact have rights although it can act and be held responsible. As I mention in the concluding paragraphs, on the Choice theory rights of groups would have to be derived from the rights of their members, so a group can only have rights to act or be treated in certain ways only inasmuch as its members have these rights and transfer them to the group.

[52] The impossibility results that Arrow, for instance, points to occur because of the stringent conditions that the procedure is supposed to satisfy, one set to do with the coherence of the collective decision and the other set, with its representativeness. For an accessible explanation and discussion of the Arrow theorem and related issues see S. Hargreaves Heap, M. Hollis, B. Lyons, R. Sugden & A Weale, *The Theory of Social Choice – A Critical Guide* (Oxford, UK and Cambridge, USA, Blackwell, 1992), pp. 205–215. For other impossibility results and solutions see F. Dietrich & C. List, 'Arrow's theorem in judgment aggregation', *Social Choice and Welfare*, 29 (2007), C. List & P. Pettit –'Group agency and supervenience', *Southern Journal of Philosophy*, suppl., ed. Murray Spindel, 44 (2006) and C. List & P. Pettit, *Group Agents*, chapter 2. My account is not vulnerable to these impossibility results since it prioritises coherence over non-dictatorship; in other words, a decision-making procedure that does not ensure representativeness is entirely acceptable as a collective decision-making procedure although it may be problematic for normative reasons. Furthermore, it seems to me that most of these impossibility results do not affect the kind of choices that are envisaged here, which are *binary* choices while the impossibility results mentioned occur when the choices are between three alternatives. Groups have to choose which of the powers attached to their rights to exercise, which essentially comes down to choosing between waiving and enforcing their rights and I take it that most decision making procedures can yield a conclusive result in this case.

collective when it is not *reducible* to decisions of (some) individual members of a group. In other words, a collective choice is not the sum of all individual members' choices and is not the choice of a few individuals within the group either. Of course the decision reached by a group will probably coincide with the choices of some members; the essential requirement is that it is attributable to the whole group although not necessarily to each and every member. Some members of the group may oppose the decision and yet they can be said to have *made* the decision together with all other members. In short, a genuinely collective choice is one that is attributable to the whole group and is not decomposable into separate decisions.

If this definition of collective choice is accepted, it seems to me that this is precisely what a coherent collective decision-making procedure (CMDP) achieves, namely this transformation of different individual choices into a single and irreducibly collective decision.[53] Any decision reached through a specified procedure is attributable to the whole group without being attributable to each and every member of the group. Of course a CDMP may empower certain members of the group, such as a committee, or even a single person, to decide for the group; in fact, more often than not, CDMPs will do just that; and it might be objected that, if a sub-set of the group's members makes a decision, this decision can only be attributed to that subset, perhaps as a group, but not to the larger group as a whole. The claim I am making here is that, if this sub-set is empowered by the group's procedure, the decision can be attributed to the group.[54] Without such a procedure, the decision is only attributable to those involved in making it. But, as long as the *group's* procedure is followed, the resulting choice cannot be attributed only to those who made it nor can it be attributed to each and every member of the group, as individuals, since some will disagree with it.

From the point of view of irreducibility, it does not matter what the procedure is as long as it specifies that the *group as a whole* decides in that manner. Thus, my department takes some decisions by majority vote, others by consensus, yet others are taken by a committee or by the head of department. All of those are collective decisions and can be attributed to

---

[53] This supports and strengthens French's argument for collective intentionality. He does not adequately explain, I think, why corporate decisions are genuinely collective.

[54] Actually the fact that one person's choice may be decisive over the collective choice supports rather than invalidates, the argument that a group's decisions are genuinely collective rather than a mere aggregation of individuals' choices.

the department as a whole, or indeed to the whole university in case the university's procedures empower the department to make decisions in certain respects. What matters is that the CDMP has the required *authority*; this is to say that only a procedure that was properly instituted and followed can yield a genuinely collective decision because only then the procedure is the procedure of that group.[55] So, a decision-making procedure is required for a group to be able to make a choice and any decision made in accordance with the authorised procedure is a genuinely collective choice.

Now, further objections could dispute my definition of collective choice. One might think that a collective choice should be attributable to *each and every* member of a group, if it is to be the choice of the whole group. This assumption about collective choice probably informs the view that defines collective responsibility as the responsibility of *all* members of a group. On this view, holding a group responsible means ascribing responsibility to all members of a group for the actions of some.[56]

But this kind of view confuses the question of *ascribing* collective responsibility with that of *distributing* it. Collective responsibility proper should be distinguished from the responsibility of each and every member of a group. The special import that collective responsibility has, as well as difficulties associated with it, is due precisely to its irreducible nature. If it is to be a different species of responsibility, collective responsibility has to be understood as the responsibility of the group as a whole rather than responsibility of some individual members for the acts of others. This is not to say that collective responsibility cannot be subsequently distributed to members of the group; although irreducible, collective responsibility can nevertheless be distributed to the group's members though not necessarily in equal shares; the distinctive point as well as challenge posed

---

[55] I do not mean to suggest that only a group's members have the authority to institute the procedure nor indeed that all members should authorize the procedure itself. Depending on the view that one takes about legitimate authority, the source of the procedure itself can differ. A whole group can be the *author* of an action without being the author of the procedure although most liberal views would probably make the former conditional on the latter. If it is thought, for instance, that a monarch has legitimate, probably divine, authority, the monarch's decisions can count as decisions of the whole people s/he represents; similarly the decision procedure followed by the Mafia has the required authority inasmuch as it is instated by someone with the requisite authority. See also D. Copp, 'Hobbes on Artificial Persons and Collective Actions', *The Philosophical Review*, 89 (1980), especially p. 604.

[56] See M. Reiff, 'Terrorism, Retribution, and Collective Responsibility', *Social Theory and Practice*, 34 (2008).

by accepting the notion of collective responsibility is that individual responsibility will not necessarily match individual contributions to collective action although it will probably *track* such contributions.[57] There will be an ascription of responsibility over and above ascriptions of responsibilities to individuals for their own actions and a share of it may accrue to individual members *in addition* to responsibility for their own distinct contributions.

If, for example, the union representing the fire services decides to go on strike, the whole union can be held responsible for any casualties that may occur as a result of this. This is not to say that all members of the union, or indeed all members of the fire services are responsible as individuals, and certainly not to an equal degree: those who voted for strike action will bear a bigger share of responsibility than others, and those who abstained will be more responsible than those who voted against and so on. Nevertheless, the group that made the collective decision and acted accordingly, in this case the union as a whole, can be held collectively responsible.

So a collective choice and the responsibility that comes with it need not be attributed to *all* members of a group but rather to the group as a whole. Individual shares may indeed be apportioned depending on individuals' choices and contributions to the group's decision, but the question of apportioning shares or distributing collective responsibility is separate from that of *attributing* a choice and therefore responsibility.

I therefore conclude that a coherent CDMP is a *necessary* and *sufficient* condition for reaching a genuinely collective choice. Thus, (only) a group that has a CDMP satisfies the *conceptual* requirements for being a right-holder under the Choice theory. This also means, however, that any 'random' group of people that organise themselves around a CDMP is a possible right-holder. But this argument should not be taken to imply that any such group does have moral rights. All I have argued so far is that any organised group is a potential candidate; but in order to argue that groups have certain rights, we need a justification for these rights. I do not propose to offer such a justification here but there is little doubt that a consistent Choice theory account cannot object to rights being transferred from individuals to groups; in other words, any Choice theorist has to allow right-holders to transfer the powers associated with their rights to

---

[57] This is to say that an individual will not only be held responsible for the outcomes of his/her own action, independently of the actions of other but his/her own contribution will nevertheless be the main basis for distributing collective responsibility.

someone else, in which case the new power-holder becomes the right-holder. So any group that acquires powers of waiver and enforcement over its members' rights and is able to exercise them collectively will have the rights transferred to it by its members.

This account may run against some of the popular views in the philosophical literature on group rights, namely those that aim to justify rights for ethno-cultural groups since it is inhospitable to rights for any unorganised groups such as ethnic minorities or immigrants, women, travellers, the working class, etc. This is not to suggest that these groups have no moral rights that pertain to group membership; members of these minorities have rights as individuals and some of these rights may be grounded in their membership of these groups. This should not undermine their claims for legal rights and recognition since individual rights are possibly a stronger currency than group rights and much more easily dealt with by legal systems. Of course any number of individuals can decide to organise themselves around a CDMP and transfer rights to the group as a whole, in which case the group becomes the right-holder. But until then no Choice theory rights can be ascribed to groups simply in virtue of their common identity and/or interests.[58]

This account is consistent with legal ascriptions of rights to groups. Most legal systems and international law grant rights only to organised collectivities with a certain structure and procedures, such as corporations, teams, institutions and states. The main legal persons and right-holders in international law are states. Some legal rights however are also ascribed to other collective entities such as international organisations, national liberation movements and insurgents but these do not have full legal personality. The distinctive feature of all these collectivities is the fact that they are organised.[59] The legal rights of ethno-cultural groups, such as national minorities, are best described as individual rights.[60]

---

[58] It might be argued that such groups can be ascribed collective rights in virtue of their 'shared' interests. The argument I made here is does not foreclose that possibility since it does not presuppose that the Choice theory is the correct one. I do, however, argue elsewhere that genuine group rights cannot be grounded in shared interests. See my 'Group rights and shared interests', forthcoming in *Political Studies*, vol. 61 (2), June 2013, published online September 2012, DOI: 10.1111/j.1467-9248.2012.00975.x.

[59] See A. Cassesse, *International Law* (Oxford, Oxford University Press, 2001), pp. 46–79 and especially p. 76, where he specifies that 'in order to be owners of rights and subjects of obligations, it is necessary for them (national liberation movements) to have an apparatus, a representative organisation that can come into contact, as it were, with other international legal persons'.

[60] Article 27 of ICCPR, which is the only provision in the two human rights covenants relating to minority rights, grants rights to members of national minorities and does not

Moreover, this account is not liable to the charge of high-chauvinism levelled by Thomas Pogge at some arguments for group rights.[61] Since this view does not inquire into the particular characteristics binding the members of a group together, other than a CDMP, it does not discriminate between types of groups.

Conclusions

I argued that the Choice theorist has the conceptual resources to argue for group rights, provided that s/he accepts that groups can make decisions and can act, i.e. that they have limited agency. I also argued that accepting this view need not commit the Choice theorist to any unsavoury ontological claims; in other words, seeing groups as limited agents is consistent with an individualist ontology. In order to be possible right-holders groups have to be organised around a coherent and public decision-making procedure. This implies, contrary to some popular views, that unorganised groups cannot have rights, even if their members share a common identity and/or interests. This need not be an embarrassment for the Choice theory; the aim of the Choice theorist – and indeed any rights theorist – *should* be to be economical with rights since their proliferation can only devalue their currency while not being completely at odds with our intuitions about who should/can have rights.

One advantage of this account is that it can ascribe rights to groups regardless of the unity or identity of a group; thus, whole populations of states can be right-holders without being seen as an organic group with a questionable metaphysical status. Since most of the current states' populations are not homogenous nations but are rather collections of different groups, an account that explains how such a collectivity can have rights is desirable. Furthermore, the account of agency put forward here can be used to extend Choice theory rights to other creatures of limited agency, such as children, human beings who are not fully autonomous, and (some) animals. Inasmuch as these potential right-holders can act and make choices, there is no *conceptual* obstacle to their having rights. But the argument made here provides no substantive justification for granting moral rights to any such creatures.

---

envisage group rights. See also A. Cassese, *Self-Determination of Peoples – A Legal Reappraisal* (Cambridge, Cambridge University Press, 1995), pp. 61–62.

[61] See T. Pogge, 'Group rights and ethnicity' in *Ethnicity and Group Rights – NOMOS XXXIX* (New York and London, New York University Press, 1997).

PART FIVE

PUNISHMENT

STATE DENUNCIATION OF CRIME

Christopher Bennett*

Abstract

In this paper I am concerned with a problem for communicative theories of punishment. On such theories, punishment is justified at least in part as the authoritative censure or condemnation of crime. But is this compatible with a broadly liberal political outlook? For while liberalism is generally thought to take only a very limited interest in its citizens' attitudes (seeing moral opinion as a matter of legitimate debate), the idea of state denunciation of crime seems precisely to be focused on the attitudes expressed in action. In this paper I analyse the elements of the communicative theory of punishment, assessing the extent to which they can be considered anti-liberal. I argue that, understood in a certain way, the communicative theory, though in some sense communitarian, is compatible with at least one central and attractive non-perfectionist strand in liberalism.

Keywords

communicative theory, Devlin, Duff, Hegel, von Hirsch, punishment

1. *Liberalism, Legal Moralism and the Communicative Theory of Punishment*

In this paper I am concerned with communicative theories of punishment of the sort that have been defended by Andrew von Hirsch and Antony Duff.[1] On such theories, punishment is justified at least in part as the

* I presented an earlier draft of this paper to the *Journal of Moral Philosophy* Conference on Punishment, University of Newcastle, 2–3 December 2005. I am grateful to a number of participants who asked helpful questions, especially Fabian Freyenhagen, Antony Duff, Leo Zaibert, Geoffrey Scarre, Matt Matravers, Massimo Renzo and Pedro Tabensky; to the editor, Thom Brooks; and to Leif Wenar.

[1] A. von Hirsch, *Censure and Sanctions* (Oxford: Oxford University Press, 1993); R.A. Duff, *Punishment, Communication and Community* (Oxford: Oxford University Press, 2001).

authoritative censure or condemnation of crime. One question that such theories have to deal with is why this authoritative denunciation has to take the form of punishment rather than some more symbolic way of conveying the message.[2] But I will be looking at a different problem, which arises simply from the notion of authoritative condemnation itself. The question I will be asking is to what extent the communicative theory is committed to a type of legal moralism that liberals ought to regard with suspicion.

Jeffrie Murphy has raised the problem that interests us in a discussion of Joel Feinberg's view that punishment has an expressive, stigmatizing function.[3] He argues that there is a tension, or perhaps a contradiction, between, on the one hand, Feinberg's liberalism and attachment to the Millian Harm Principle and, on the other, his support for a punitive institution that acts coercively against citizens on the grounds of moral failure. The tension arises because, while the former seems to place a fairly narrow constraint on the state's coercive interest in its citizens' attitudes, the latter seems to be based on the view that the state has an overriding interest in the moral quality of its citizens' attitudes.

Consider, for instance, the question whether hate crimes ought to be punished more severely than other crimes. The proposal would be that, where there are two murders otherwise equally deserving of punishment, but where in one of them the motive is racial hatred, this motive should be regarded as an aggravating factor. Heidi Hurd has recently argued that liberals ought to object to making the racial motive an aggravating factor.[4] She claims that liberals ought to recoil from having the state make intrusive inquiries into our motives as a routine criminal procedure. In a liberal theory of criminal law, conditions of culpability ought to be such that they can be determined without prying into the state of the defendant's soul. However, the communicative theory that interests us here points the other way. For if we assume for the sake of the argument that where the racial motive is present the act is morally worse then if our aim in criminal justice is to mete out condemnation proportionate to the gravity of the

---

[2] See e.g. J. Feinberg, 'The Expressive Function of Punishment', in his *Doing and Deserving* (Princeton: Princeton University Press, 1970).

[3] J.G. Murphy, 'Liberalism and Legal Moralism', *Arizona Law Review* 37 (1995), pp. 73–93. Liberal suspicions might also be roused by the Durkheimian history of the expressive view and Durkheim's seemingly overriding concern with social solidarity rather than individual liberty. See the discussion of criminal law in W.D. Halls (trans.), *The Division of Labour in Society* (Basingstoke: Macmillan, 1984).

[4] Heidi M. Hurd, 'Why Liberals Should Hate "Hate Crime Legislation"', *Law and Philosophy* 20 (2001), pp. 215–32.

offence, we ought to condemn racially motivated offences more strongly. Motive is an important factor in determining the degree of condemnation an offence deserves. Therefore, contrary to what Hurd believes the liberal should say, the communicative theory would accept the relevance of motive to culpability. As Murphy argues, on the communicative or expressive view, the conditions of culpability would have to go beyond simply *mens rea* requirements of intending the unlawful action and knowing it to be unlawful: if punishment condemns or denounces then what makes it deserved is 'malice aforethought', that one be blameworthy or morally culpable for the action.

Now Hurd might accept that in a citizen's private life wrongdoing does—or can in the right circumstances—call for condemnation (from appropriately interested parties). But she can point out that it does not follow straightforwardly from this that it is the business of the state to condemn the citizen for moral failure. Whether or not it is depends on what the proper role of the state is, whether the state is an 'appropriately interested party' with regard to a certain wrong. On this point, though, liberals have traditionally held to something like Mill's Harm Principle: that the only good ground for states to invade the sovereignty of their citizens is to prevent harm to others. Whatever the underlying justification they accept, they have wished to grant citizens a right of what Murphy (following Dworkin) talks of as 'moral independence'. In other words, there is a strong presumption in favour of liberty, of leaving citizens to decide for themselves on moral issues. What seems to motivate Hurd's criticism is the idea that it follows from this that whether a citizen engages in immoral conduct is not the state's business; whether he or she engages in conduct that can cause serious harm to others, however, is. This would suggest that 'malice aforethought' is not a good reason for a liberal state to intervene coercively in the life of any citizen.

As Murphy says, this seeming incompatibility raises the following dilemma for someone sympathetic both to liberalism and the theory of deserved condemnation. Either they have to give up their support for their account of punishment or their support for liberalism; or else they have to revise their account of liberalism to explain why it is legitimate for the state to take a coercive interest in some types of immorality. So the question I am interested in is whether this reasoning demonstrates the incompatibility of liberalism and the moral condemnation of crime.

I should point out, therefore, that in what I go on to argue, the question of punishment does not arise. I am not interested in the question of whether the state has a right to inflict hard treatment on its citizens.

What I am interested in is whether the liberal state is within its rights in coercively expressing condemnation to an offender for morally wrong actions, independently of whether this should be expressed through hard treatment.

Now the problem in which I am interested in could be avoided were the censure theorist able to claim that her theory did not require such a strong sense of blameworthiness. For then it would not be necessary for the state to concern itself with the offender's moral character in any deep way. For instance, a theory of punishment might have some role for moral communication even though the conditions that it takes to make the punishment of an offender appropriate fall short of actual blameworthiness. However, a censure theorist could only make this move were she to deny that at least one of the central purposes of punishment is the communication of deserved moral censure to the offender, censure that the offender must be in a position to understand and accept as deserved. The theories I find most promising—such as those of von Hirsch and Duff—place a high degree of importance on the communication of deserved censure to the offender because it is only thus that the offender is taken seriously as a moral agent, a fellow citizen, and not merely as a prop in the criminal justice mechanism. For this reason I think that we should be wary of settling for less than blameworthiness as a condition for meriting punishment. And this means that Murphy's problem is a genuine one that warrants our attention.

2. *The Necessity of Minimal Censure in a System of Law*

My strategy will be to look first of all at two arguments for the claim that authoritative moral condemnation of crime is compatible with the liberal state. The first is based on Hegel's remarks in the *Philosophy of Right* about the need to annul or answer crime. I do not attempt to follow the detail of Hegel's remarks. But I am interested in what he sees as the need, through punishment, for 'the cancellation of crime, which would otherwise be regarded as valid, and the restoration of right'.[5] Now there is a puzzle about how his claim here ought to be interpreted. Hegel's aim is to demonstrate the unconditional (non-contingent) necessity of cancelling the crime. Therefore we should not read his claim that crime has to be punished

[5] G.W.F. Hegel, *Elements of the Philosophy of Right* (trans. H.B. Nisbet; Cambridge: Cambridge University Press, 1991), §99.

since it 'would otherwise be regarded as valid' as the empirical one that, were the state not to respond disapprovingly to crime then people would, as a matter of fact, start to think that these sorts of actions are all right. (A claim that is probably not very plausible for many serious crimes anyway.) But how else are we to interpret it?

My contention is that we can draw up an alternative reading if we look at the symbolic or expressive aspects of crime and punishment. Let us begin by looking at the nature of the state. When it has a legal system, the state, whether liberal or not, claims the right to dictate which actions are permissible for citizens. In other words, by setting up a system of law, the state declares certain actions to be ones that its citizens ought not to perform (I wish to be neutral at this stage as to what this 'ought' involves: it is a bare notion of legal permissibility), and claims to itself sole authority to determine which actions it is that are to be regarded as legally impermissible. Now when a state has laws that are meant to apply to all its members, citizens are expected to act under the condition that their actions are permitted by the laws that hold for all. In this context, one of the symbolic aspects that citizens' actions take on is that of a claim: a claim about what it is or ought to be permissible to do in the state. In other words, action within the state is law-governed action: because of the context in which it occurs, it can be interpreted as legislation for all citizens. This is not to say that the citizen herself thinks of her action as conveying a message that what she does ought to be permissible for all, or that she would agree to such a description if it were presented to her. It is simply to say that in the context in which she acts—that of a community under laws that apply to all—her action has this symbolic meaning. The context in which she acts is one where citizens are supposed to act only in ways that are permissible to all. Therefore her action is appropriately taken as one that presents the claim that this action ought to be permissible to all.

When a citizen's action is law-abiding the claim inherent in it will be valid, from the point of view of the state: that is, it will be consistent with what the state takes to be permissible and therefore no action need be taken. But when an action is invalid, this raises a problem for the state. For it not to take any action would, as Hegel says, be for it to accept the action as valid: this would be for it to accept the claim inherent within the action that this is the sort of thing that citizens ought to be allowed to do. But in this case the claim that the action is 'not to be allowed' is meaningless. The state would not be able to distinguish its claim that the action was impermissible from the claim that it was not advisable, or not recommended. Therefore the way to interpret the Hegelian argument is thus: it follows from the fact that an action has been ruled impermissible that, when such an action is performed, the state must take some action in order to declare the action unlawful: otherwise its claim to have authority to determine what is permissible is empty. There is a necessity that stems from the symbolic meaning of the criminal action rather than its actual or likely effect.

Of course, a sceptic might ask why we should be interested in this symbolism at all: aren't there more important things to be worried about, like human welfare and the prevention of serious harms? The answer to this is that it is simply meant to follow from the fact that law supposedly rules certain actions to be impermissible for all citizens: if valid, the Hegelian argument demonstrates that law is empty if the state does not take action against known or determinable breaches. Therefore our conclusion is that some response that marks the action as impermissible and therefore rejects the claim to permissibility implicit in the criminal action is necessary simply by virtue of the fact that the state claims authority to determine which acts are permissible and which impermissible for its citizens. The claim I am making is therefore meant to rest on one of the presuppositions internal to a legal system rather than on any empirical truths about what the effect of some state action is likely to be.

However, if valid, what the Hegelian argument proves is not the necessity of punishment, or of the rich form of moral denunciation defended by Duff and von Hirsch. If correct, it proves the need for what we might call minimal censure, that the state should do something[6] by way of marking crime as legally impermissible, contrary to the demands of this particular system of law. What the denunciation account holds, by contrast, is that the state should criticize the offender for his or her moral failure. Therefore, even if there is a sense in which any state with a legal system is committed to answering actions that are contrary to law, it does not follow that such states ought to denounce criminal action. Nevertheless, the Hegelian

[6] If one asks what exactly has to be done then I suspect that that depends on what one takes it to mean when one says that an action is ruled 'impermissible' by the state or that citizens are required not to do it. Now there are various things that one might mean by saying that certain actions are 'not to be allowed' in the state. One might think, with traditional legal positivism, that for an action to be prohibited it must be the case that those who perform such actions are liable to be sanctioned for it: this would be so on the view that the only meaningful sense of prohibition is that of 'threats backed by sanctions'. On the other hand, saying that an action is not to be allowed might also be interpreted, say by the censure theory, as the claim that there are strong, perhaps conclusive, reasons against the action, and that anyone who performs it will attract censure. At this stage the point I wish to make is neutral between the positivist and denunciatory interpretations. It simply says that the claim that an action is not allowed is empty unless the authority is willing to do something when such requirements are breached.

argument is clearly helpful to the censure account. For while the censure account no doubt presents a conception of why censure is a permissible action for the state to take, it also needs an answer to the question of why that particular permissible action should be selected for action. It needs an account of the necessity of censure.[7] The Hegelian argument can provide such an account, but, I have argued, needs to be supplemented in order to show why full moral condemnation is an appropriate response to crime.

3. *Two Conceptions of Liberal Political Community*

Let me expand a little on the gap between what has been argued so far and the claims made by the denunciation view. One way of putting it would be to say that the denunciation view sees the state as claiming to itself sole authority to determine, not only what is *legally* permissible, but also the 'official' collective view of that political society on what is *morally* permissible. In issuing moral condemnation the state takes itself as issuing a moral judgement that aims to be authoritative in some way for all citizens: it may not be the case that the state is telling citizens what to think, but it is also not simply offering them advice, or expressing an opinion that it wishes them to take seriously. In condemning crime the state aspires to give voice to a collective judgement, a judgement that all citizens can regard as having a claim on them *qua* citizens. The state presupposed by the denunciation account therefore claims in some manner to be a moral authority: it is not that it must take itself to have greater moral expertise than its citizens, but it must take itself as aiming to formulate and express moral judgements that all citizens could come to recognize as valid constraints.

However, this claim to moral authority may raise some liberal hackles. One source of discomfort, pointed out by Jeffrie Murphy in another paper,[8] concerns moral diversity. The idea that the state can be a moral authority recognized by its citizenry evidently assumes a degree of moral consensus among the population. But isn't our (post)modern condition one of deep pluralism rather than moral consensus? Isn't this diversity one of the

[7] For instance, to counter the criticism of Nigel Walker: 'If the message which expresses blame need have no utility, where lies the moral necessity?' in his *Why Punish?* (Oxford: Oxford University Press, 1991), p. 81.

[8] 'Retribution, Moral Education and the Liberal State', in his *Retribution Reconsidered: Further Essays in the Philosophy of Law* (Dordrecht: Kluwer, 1985), pp. 15–30.

conditions that the liberal state is meant to be particularly suited to addressing? A second, though related, issue is whether the notion of a state authority making judgements about what we should all take to be morally impermissible is compatible with our autonomy or moral independence. One of the founding values of a liberal state is freedom of conscience: the right of citizens to live as far as possible by their own lights and not to have to express allegiance to values they do not personally espouse. Is it compatible with this vision of a free society that we allow the state to express an authoritative opinion in our name on (at least some) matters of conscience?

Now the way in which the censure theorist might attempt to respond to these criticisms is by pointing to an attractive liberal model of the state on which there is scope, or indeed a need, for authoritative moral judgements. What is at issue here, she might say, is whether we want a state that exercises brute power over us or whether we want the exercise of such power to be justified to us in moral terms. If the latter then we do need the state to engage in making—and addressing to us—moral judgements about what justifications are sufficient and compelling. The censure theorist might therefore seek to defend her position by supplementing the Hegelian argument with the claim that the liberal state ought to treat its citizens as moral agents.[9] If the Hegelian argument shows that some intervention is necessary, perhaps the claim that any intervention that is necessary has to be consistent with citizens' identity as moral agents will be enough to justify the censure account and show that it is compatible with the liberal outlook.

In order to see how this argument might work, let us distinguish broadly between Hobbesian and Kantian forms of liberalism.[10] On the Hobbesian view, the reason why, if there were no state, we would need to create one, is that individuals (or perhaps groups) whose incompatible aims would otherwise bring them into constant conflict, need to defer to a supreme collective power in order to secure the peace and stability that is a precondition of each being able to pursue their ends. On this view, each citizen accepts the need to obey a state authority as an unfortunate but necessary

[9] See A. von Hirsch, *Past or Future Crimes: Deservedness and Dangerousness in the Sentencing of Criminals* (Manchester: Manchester University Press, 1985), pp. 54–56 on treating persons as ends not means. This is also a major theme of R.A. Duff, *Trials and Punishments* (Cambridge: Cambridge University Press, 1986).

[10] I should make it clear that, in referring to 'Kantian' liberalism, I make no claim about whether these views about the political community, or anything like them, were actually Kant's.

constraint on their freedom. In these circumstances, the individual parties to the social contract have a common purpose in obeying the dictates of a liberal state (that is, a state in which each is given an equal degree of freedom to pursue their ends), for it is only by doing so that they can give themselves the best chance of achieving their individual ends; but this common purpose derives from a contingent coincidence of interests rather than actually shared ends. Thus although it will generally be the case that what an individual contractor has reason to do is to obey the state—as this will usually give her the best chance of furthering her goals—circumstances may arise (this is the point of the Prisoners' Dilemma) where she can further her goals best by breaking the law.

In criticism of the Hobbesian picture, it has often been pointed out that people are not narrow, amoral egoists, and that the relation between citizen and state need not be taken to be purely self-interested and conditional. It is more realistic to assume, on the contrary, that people have aims that are socially and morally specified (for instance, aims that have to do with the happiness of others, or the success of various social projects, or the sustaining of certain institutions); and that people have a commitment to at least some central moral goals and principles. In fact, some would have us go the whole Kantian hog and say that all citizens have a commitment to treating others as ends in themselves and not merely as means. Once we introduce this moralized view of human nature then a new possibility of political community opens up. For it then appears that it is not just coincidence that citizens have a common commitment to a community in which each is given as much freedom to pursue their ends as is consistent with the same for others: citizens *share* a commitment to this goal because they share an allegiance to the moral principles that such an arrangement embodies.

These different accounts of human nature and political community give us different accounts of the purpose of criminal law. On the Hobbesian view, when someone breaks the law she does something that, by her own lights, seems the right thing to do: it is the best way to pursue her ends. Therefore there is no point in the state sending her any moral message: its wrongness is not something she can be expected to appreciate. What the state can do, however, is to speak to her interests. It can impose something unpleasant on her—taking away her freedom, say—in order to give her an incentive not to do it again. On this Hobbesian view, the state's criminal law can best be seen as a system of threats backed up by sanctions. On the Kantian picture, however, coercive state action is supposed to be grounded in moral reasons that the state takes it that citizens can understand and accept: this Kantian liberal state aspires to the support of a certain (limited and perhaps purely political) moral consensus amongst citizens: it aims to ground its actions in moral reasons that citizens can support.[11] While the Hobbesian might see the state as best being morally neutral, the Kantian liberal state takes certain values to be authoritative for its citizens: it makes the claim that there are values that its citizens ought to accept.

One argument in favour of the Kantian picture of the liberal state has to do with the value of legitimacy, the idea—or ideal—that the principles underlying the coercive action of the state should be acceptable to all its members. The Kantian liberal supports the idea that, where coercive action is taken against citizens, it should be accompanied by a justification that shows how the need for coercion follows from common principles. In this way, coercive state action can be taken to be action on the common purpose of the community as a whole, rather than action taken by one party or faction against another. It is action taken against one of *us*, someone who is expected to understand and accept its necessity, rather than against an outlaw, a renegade, or an enemy. As such, it might be argued, it is only on the Kantian form of liberalism that state power is exercised in a way that treats us as moral agents. The Hobbesian view sees the exercise of state power as a brute form of behaviour control, while the Kantian view takes it as always accompanied by an attempt to convince those affected of its necessity. The Hobbesian view does not do enough to distinguish its treatment of citizens from its treatment of children, animals or psychopaths against whom in some cases citizens may need to be protected.

Now the Hobbesian may argue that the account she offers does not depend on viewing human nature as amoral. She can consistently view agents as having conceptions of the good. The starting point for her account, she might say, is simply a state of affairs in which there is no moral consensus amongst members of a society (no common and overriding principles of Right or fair social cooperation): individuals are bound by no common fabric and therefore are in the situation in which their various projects (for which we can read: moralized conceptions of the good) will inevitably bring them into conflict. Furthermore, she might argue, this is more like the state of affairs in which, in postmodern society, we find ourselves than the simple and harmonious picture assumed by the Kantian.

---

[11] J. Rawls, *Political Liberalism* (New York: Columbia University Press, 1993).

I will not pursue this argument here except to point out that even in conditions of diversity (diversity which can perhaps often be over-stated) parties with differing views about how to live can discover a common interest in agreeing on fair procedures through which to adjudicate conflict. My main point, however, is to pursue the question of whether the denunciation theory is compatible with liberalism. Now it may be argued that in some social circumstances the unifying assumptions of Kantian liberalism (that is, the assumption of rational moral consensus) can be illiberal, and lead to the suppression of legitimate diversity. But while bearing this in mind I will assume that the Kantian form nevertheless represents an important strand of liberal thought and that its idea of the legitimacy is an important ideal that postmodern states ought not to discard lightly.

Does the Kantian form of liberalism have any reason to reject the denunciation account? In grounding its actions in values that citizens are expected to accept, the Kantian liberal sees the political community as in some way bound together by a common morality, however limited, and in which the state is regarded as the authority that expresses that moral consensus in action. Therefore the Kantian liberal cannot argue that it is not the state's job to preach values to its citizens: while it is certainly true, on this position, that in many areas of life the state should leave citizens to decide for themselves, there is nevertheless a political morality that the state can expect its citizens to affirm.

However, although we may have shown that the commitments of the censure account are not inconsistent with the liberal approach, it is not yet clear that the Kantian liberal is committed to what is distinctive about the denunciation account. For the denunciation account takes it, not just that the state can and should address its citizens with moral justifications for its coercive actions, but that action that expresses certain sorts of morally reprehensible attitude (actions that reveal 'malice aforethought' or 'inner wickedness') should itself bring censure on its agent: that at least some, most serious and politically relevant moral failures of its citizenry give us reason enough to have an institution that condemns such breaches. And of course, the Kantian liberal need not be committed to this. The Kantian liberal can consistently hold that only something like harm reduction could provide a compelling general justifying aim of punishment. An obvious reason for rejecting the denunciation account's view of the general justifying aim might be that one rejects its underlying retributivism, or that one thinks such denunciation would do more harm than good. But this would not be to reject it because of any incompatibility with liberal principles, of the sort that Murphy was worried about. The question is whether the liberal who has accepted the Kantian line has grounds for rejecting the denunciation view as illiberal. In order to pursue this question let us look at what the censure theorist is committed to thinking *is* the general justifying aim of punishment and criminal law.

4. *Denunciation and Standards of Behaviour*

Let us pursue this question by sketching what the denunciation view might look like within the liberal state. The liberal state takes it, let us say, that citizens have certain rights, grounded in the moral values of autonomy, liberty and equality, or the idea of society as a fair system of social cooperation. Furthermore, it takes it that these values are supported by some form of moral consensus, and are thus ones that citizens can be expected to accept. As such it declares that citizens have good reason not to violate individual rights. However, the liberal state does not simply recommend the non-violation of individual rights to its citizens: rather, it rules the violation of rights to be impermissible. Thus (from the Hegelian argument) the liberal state is committed to taking some action against anyone who infringes another person's rights, in order to reaffirm the authoritative collective view that this action is not to be performed in the face of the offender's claim that it is or ought to be permissible. Furthermore, within the context of such a state in which laws are taken to be grounded in shared values, the 'claim' that the offender makes through an action that breaks the law is not just that the action should be (legally) permissible, but that it does not offend against the state's fundamental values—or that those values ought not to be the ones that the state takes to be fundamental. Therefore in reaffirming the action as impermissible the state also reaffirms the values infringed as ones that it takes to be authoritative for the political community.

However, remember that on the denunciation view, what the offender is denounced for is 'malice aforethought' or moral failure. It not so much the harm that is caused by what he or she has done as the lack of due moral concern expressed in her action that makes her the proper object of condemnation. In other words, the thing that calls for censure is a moral failure on the part of a citizen, their decision to express in action an attitude that is contrary to the political morality of the state. This means that when the state, on this view, rules certain actions impermissible, it understands 'action' as the expression of certain attitudes. What is legally impermissible is not simply having the attitudes themselves; but neither is it performing the actions accidentally or without the appropriate state of mind: it is performing the actions in such a way that they express a culpable lack of concern for the society's defining values. And I will argue that this suggests, not just that the denunciation view is itself controversial and may be rejected, but that it brings with it a distinctive conception of political community, one that goes beyond what we have looked at so far.

What I want to get at is that the denunciation view shares with Lord Devlin the view that the guiding principle of criminal law ought to be that 'there are certain standards of behaviour or moral principles which society requires to be observed; and the breach of them is an offence not merely against the person who is injured but against society as a whole'.[12] To see how this represents a distinctive conception of the criminal law and political community, let us contrast it with a different approach.

On a common view of the criminal justice apparatus, which we can call the 'economy of threats' approach,[13] the reason why the state prescribes certain rules and backs them up with some sanction or other is in order to protect valuable interests from harm. For instance, if one thinks of human welfare as especially important, then one might take the view that the state ought to grant human beings rights that protect the most important elements of their welfare. Such rights consist at least in part of rules that prohibit certain behaviour and threaten the infliction of some sanction should the rule be broken. By enforcing these rules, states aim to protect individuals and give them a better chance of living free from aggression or other unwarranted external interference. In granting people rights, the state therefore undertakes to do what is within its power (and respecting the limitations imposed by individual freedom) to prevent people being harmed in this way. On this view the state has a primary duty to the protection of its citizens; its prime aim is to ensure as far as possible the prevention of certain avoidable harms. The criminal law is an agency of this type, focusing on harm reduction. The criminal justice apparatus of law and sanction is seen on this view as a complex attempt to control behaviour by offering those who would be tempted to infringe rights in pursuit of their own goals a strong disincentive against doing so.

---

[12] P. Devlin, 'Morals and the Criminal Law', in his *The Enforcement of Morals* (Oxford: Oxford University Press, 1965), pp. 6–7.

[13] Following H.L.A. Hart, 'Legal Responsibility and Excuses', in his *Punishment and Responsibility* (Oxford: Clarendon Press, 1968).

However, the censure view depends on a different view of the criminal law and the polity. On this alternative view, the criminal law has to be seen in the context of a collective attempt to live up to certain standards of behaviour. In other words, rights are seen as principles that citizens have, by their own lights, reason to accept, rather than as tools for the protection of certain interests. Rather than being seen as a technique, something that works to control behaviour indirectly, this account sees the criminal law as setting out a (minimal and partial) set of standards of behaviour that citizens should live up to. Furthermore, this is not just a standard of behaviour, it is a standard of behaviour-expressing-attitudes-towards-values. On this view, the criminal law requires citizens not to perform actions that express reprehensible attitudes. This makes sense in the context of a political community that involves the collective attempt to encourage one another to take certain values sufficiently seriously.[14]

On the censure view, then, what is the general justifying aim of punishment? The central aim is, of course, the communication of censure. But why carry out such censure? The answer cannot be that this is a good way to protect valuable interests: that is not the primary aim, for the deservedness of censure is not contingent on its having good effects. It might be said that it is done for the sake of vindicating the victims of crime; but again this cannot be the whole story, for (a) this doesn't by itself explain why the vindication of victims has to come about through censure coercively directed to the offender, rather than just being asserted about the crime, or about the victim; and (b) it doesn't explain why we ought to censure offenders for 'public wrongs' even when there is no victim. The underlying reason why censure is needed therefore has to be something more focused on the offender and the need to communicate something to *him*. It has to be something like this: the community owes it to the offender (as a participant in the community's shared attempt to live up to certain values) that it take lapses from those values seriously by condemning him for them; to fail to do so would be to fail to take his lapses seriously, and therefore to fail to take him seriously as a participant in that shared project.

[14] Of course, this is not to say that these standards of behaviour have nothing to do with the protection of valuable things. But protecting these things is something that each individual is taken to have reason to do, a reason that provides the criminal law with its content and its rationale; it is not the case that the law is a behaviour modification technique through which individuals can be brought indirectly to act in such a way that these valuable things are protected.

If this is right then the denunciation view is grounded in consideration of the treatment (care or respect) owed to the offender as 'one of us', a participant in a shared project. For this reason the model of censure within a religious community has loomed large in the discussion of the censure model, and particularly in the discussion of the work of R.A. Duff.[15] For it is in the context of a religious community that one most obviously finds a rationale for the existence of the community (or its system of discipline) as a collective attempt to incorporate certain values into its members' lives; and a role for authoritative condemnation of moral failure by way of taking the offender seriously as one engaged in the collective attempt to live up to these values. And this seems like another source of potential liberal concern about the denunciation view. For it might be said that the religious community with its ends of individual moral education and purification is not a good model for liberal political community.

In response to such criticisms, the denunciation theorist can make two points. First of all, she can claim that, while the censure view is, as Duff has written, to be thought of in the context of a normative community 'whose members are bound together by a shared commitment to certain defining values and by mutual respect and concern in the light of those values',[16] it can be the case, as with liberal political community, that these defining values only have to do with limited areas of an individual's life (leaving a wide 'private' sphere within which she is free to act as she sees fit); and that the 'commitment' that is demanded of citizens (especially by the criminal law) can be rather minimal, consisting (negatively) in a determination not seriously to transgress the defining values rather than (positively) an active contribution to the life of the community.[17] Criminal law, on this view, can be seen as being based on a model of the responsible or

---

15 See, for instance, Duff's own use of this analogy in his *Trials and Punishments*, pp. 246–54. See also B. Baker, 'Penance as a Model for Punishment', *Social Theory and Practice* 18 (1992), pp. 311–31; R. Lipkin, 'Punishment, Penance and Respect for Autonomy', *Social Theory and Practice* 14 (1988), pp. 87–104; A. von Hirsch, *Censure and Sanctions*, ch. 8 and 'Punishment, Penance and the State: A Reply to Duff', in M. Matravers (ed.), *Punishment and Political Theory* (Oxford: Hart, 1999), pp. 69–82.

16 R.A. Duff, *Punishment, Communication and Community* (Oxford: Oxford University Press, 2001), p. 46. One of the 'censure' theorists whose views I am particularly interested in, Andrew von Hirsch, would almost certainly reject this 'communitarian' characterization of the commitments of his view. However, it is part of my project here to work out how communitarian the censure account needs to be. My answer to von Hirsch would be that it needs to be more communitarian than he has so far admitted; but that it is not communitarian in a way that should trouble his liberal instincts.

17 Duff, *Punishment, Communication and Community*, pp. 42–48, 66–68.

virtuous citizen, a model that represents an individual with concerns and attitudes consonant with the defining authoritative values of the polity, and which citizens are supposed to see that they have good reason to embody. But this ideal character-type will be only partially made out, and will have only a minimal respect for these values. On this view crimes are serious departures from this model of the responsible citizen. The criminal law therefore enjoins people to live up to this model. People are authoritatively criticized for failing to live up to the standards of behaviour that this model puts forward. But the content of these standards reflects the spirit if not the letter of the Harm Principle: they recognize that their authority is over only a limited area of the individual's life, and over the rest recognizes her as sovereign.

Secondly, the denunciation theorist can try to find a new way of understanding her favoured conception of the relation between criminal law and community that does not rest on the analogy with religious community. For instance, in recent writings, Duff has developed an analogy between political community and *academic* rather than religious community.[18] In (an ideal version of) an academic community, members are taken to have certain responsibilities to one another, responsibilities that are claimed in part because the activity of the community—the advancement and dissemination of knowledge—is an intrinsically valuable one. What I mean by saying that it is intrinsically valuable is that the activity of the community can be seen as something valuable in its own right, having not merely instrumental benefits. When the participants become good at their role in the academic community they have achieved something they can properly regard with pride, a source of self-respect. Therefore the member of the academic community can be expected to—that is, can be taken to have a obligation to—'live up' to the responsibilities of this role. The responsibilities to which the member of the academic community is held can be understood on something more than the 'economy of threats' approach (as those actions that can be influenced by the threat of sanctions in order to protect or promote valuable interests): they can be understood rather as *constitutive* of being a good academic, and being a good academic is an end to which an individual in the community can be expected to aspire. The academic community can therefore be seen as a shared attempt to live up to a certain (partial and limited) model of virtue: the model of virtue that consists in being a good academic. In the

[18] Duff, *Punishment, Communication and Community*, pp. 42–48.

academic community a system of censure or denunciation could reasonably operate, for it makes sense for the community as a whole to express its disappointment in and condemnation of those who fail to live up to its basic standards.

If this analogy is plausible then we have a more attractive model for political community than the religious community. But still, why think that the academic community provides us with an analogy to the political community? Why see the political community too as a shared attempt to live up to the values of some intrinsically valuable activity? Is this not precisely the sort of analogy that will send us back to an anti-liberal communitarianism?

The response to this charge is that some forms of liberal society can be understood in precisely this way. For an example, we need look no further than the Kantian form of liberalism that we have discussed already. On this view, the key ideal is legitimacy. As we have seen, this requires that the state should act coercively only on principles that can be affirmed by all citizens. However, this legitimacy constraint is not meant to apply only to the apparatus of the state. It is meant to provide a model for the public political life of a modern society: it is to apply also to citizens themselves in their public identity, that is, as participants in public political processes. The ideal legitimate society, on this view, is one in which citizens see themselves as participating in a shared attempt to justify to one another the principles that they will use to regulate their living together as a political community. Thus, for instance, when acting as a public official, or engaging in debate about the appropriate exercise of state power, citizens are also meant to respect the legitimacy constraint, acting or making proposals to act only in ways that can reasonably be affirmed by their fellows (that is, their fellows regardless of race, gender, conception of the good, as long as they are also engaged in the process of attempting to find mutually acceptable principles for state action).

Now the importance of legitimacy, on the type of view I am interested in, is not merely instrumental. It is not simply that legitimate states are, say, more stable. Rather, legitimacy is seen as important in its own right: it is a valuable form of relationship in which we interact as co-deliberators, and in which the power by which we are ruled is our own power; it is that state of affairs in which, as a collective, we can be thought of as collectively self-determining rather than being ruled over by one contingently powerful faction or another. In other words, living in and sustaining a state in which the exercise of coercive power is legitimate and can be affirmed by all is a form of shared activity that the Kantian liberal can regard as being intrinsically valuable. This is an intrinsically valuable activity because it puts us into an important inclusive and egalitarian relationship with one another, and allows us freedom through collective self-determination.

Because the ideal of legitimacy can be thought of as a form of shared valuable activity, we can say that there are standards of behaviour internal to it (one might say, standards of excellence). In other words, we could draw up a model of the good citizen, the good state official, etc., the basis of which would be a person in a certain role in the polity who has the appropriate attitude towards the common project of sustaining and respecting legitimacy. We could then go on to say which virtues the person who has this appropriate attitude would exemplify: virtues that would no doubt include specifically political virtues of toleration, civility, self-control, justice (or respect for the rule of law); as well as a host of other non-political virtues such as good judgement, courage, temperance and so on.

However, if the Kantian liberal is prepared to allow this then there is no real barrier to accepting the denunciation view. The denunciation view is rooted in the idea that it can make sense to exhort one's fellow citizens to live up to certain standards of behaviour, and to express extreme disappointment when they neglect or contravene those standards. It involves the view that the collective can hold that the demands of a certain shared project are authoritative for an individual, that it makes sense to ask her to 'live up' to these demands. These demands, on the denunciation view, are—at least in a minimal form—expressed in the criminal law. But the ideal of the state that prizes legitimacy involves precisely this. Such a state demands that its citizens acknowledge a constraint on how they propose to exercise the coercive power of the state: the constraint that they should appeal only to principles that all can be expected to affirm. It holds that the project of exercising only that power over our fellow citizens that can be considered to be the power of all is one that is authoritative for the members of the polity. It holds this because it regards the relationship of co-deliberation or collective self-determination as an intrinsically valuable one, a shared activity constituted by behaviour that meets certain standards of excellence. Although the state's demand that individuals participate in this relationship affects only limited areas of citizens' lives, and although only minimal compliance can perhaps be required of citizens, the Kantian liberal picture shares with the notion of a religious or an ideal academic community the feature of being a shared attempt to live up to certain demands. Therefore it does not seem open to the liberal who endorses such a project to object to the denunciation view as illiberal.

The denunciation view is grounded in a view on which the criminal law codifies the responsibilities that would be taken seriously by the (minimally) 'good citizen', in the way that the responsibilities of academic life can be seen as being based on an idealization of the occupier of a particular academic role. But this view ought to be acceptable to any account that sees political activity as in some way intrinsically valuable activity. In this paper I have used the Kantian liberal approach as an example. However, it is worth noting that I do not mean thereby to tie my colours to this particular mast. For instance, a liberal perfectionist theory could also be compatible with the denunciation account. Indeed in many ways liberal perfectionism is a more obvious home for the denunciation view and its notion of political community as a shared project of living up to certain virtues than non-perfectionism. My aim has been deliberately to look at the non-perfectionist variety and to argue that it has nothing to fear from the idea of state denunciation of crime; but I need not thereby endorse it.

Conclusion

In this paper I have considered whether liberals have good reason to reject the denunciation or communicative theory of punishment on the grounds that authoritative condemnation of the moral quality of an offender's acts is objectionably intrusive. We looked at Heidi Hurd's argument that liberals should reject hate crime legislation for similar reasons: I pointed out that such inquiries into motive would appear to be a necessary part of ascertaining what condemnation is deserved; therefore if such inquiries really are none of the liberal state's business then the communicative theory should indeed be seen as anti-liberal. I have accepted that what the communicative theory envisages is the criticism of an offender's attitudes-expressed-in-action. However, I have argued that the liberal state does indeed have reason to see these attitudes-expressed-in-action as part of its business.

In arguing for this point I have separated and examined the elements of the denunciation or condemnation view. The first element, compatible with a variety of theories of punishment, is the Hegelian argument that any state that prescribes law must in some way and as a non-contingent matter rule actions contrary to law to be impermissible if its laws are to be meaningful or valid. This is not illiberal, but neither does it get at what is distinctive about the censure view. The second element of the denunciation view is that the state must take itself to have the authority to make moral judgements that are judgements of the collective as a whole. This might sound like an intrusion on an individual's right to think for herself, but is actually required by any version of liberalism that thinks that the state ought to be in the business of justifying its actions to citizens in terms that they can be expected to accept. On this Kantian liberalism, the state has to take a view on what values or judgements citizens ought to regard as compelling. This is a central and attractive strand of liberalism; therefore I concluded that this element of the denunciation theory is not anti-liberal either.

The third element of the denunciation view is that it is the fact of moral wrongdoing, and not the causing of harm, that gives the state sufficient reason to have an institution for expressing collective condemnation. This makes sense on a view of the criminal law as part of a collective attempt to live up to certain standards of behaviour, rather than one on which the criminal law is simply an efficient technique for reducing harm and promoting security. However, the description of Kantian liberalism as a collective project of mutual justification and collective self-determination itself involves seeing political society as a shared project to which citizens have some minimal responsibility to contribute. Therefore I conclude that none of these elements of the idea of state denunciation of crime is really in conflict with liberalism.

IMPRISONABLE OFFENSES

Richard L. Lippke*

Abstract

Imprisonment imposes very substantial losses and deprivations on people convicted of crimes. The question for which crimes imprisonment is an appropriate sanction is addressed employing both retributive and crime reduction approaches to the justification of legal punishment. Although there is not complete convergence between what the two approaches imply about its use, it is argued that both would reserve imprisonment for serious offenses, ones that inflict or threaten significant harms with moderate to high levels of culpability. Thus, neither approach supports the current use of imprisonment to sanction a range of lesser offenses.

Keywords

crime reduction, imprisonment, retribution

The United States currently imprisons more than two million of its citizens, a fourfold increase since 1980.[1] Other countries have likewise seen substantial increases in their prison populations in recent years, though none of them comes close to matching the rate at which the US imprisons its citizens.[2] It appears that about half of the people serving time in US jails and prisons have been convicted of offenses involving violence

* I would like to thank Thom Brooks for numerous helpful comments and suggestions on an earlier draft of this paper. I would also like to thank the participants at the conference on punishment at the University of Newcastle, especially Peter Jones, Anthony Duff and Matt Matravers, for comments that helped me to sharpen my discussion of a number of points in the paper.

[1] 'Prison Statistics', US Department of Justice, at www.ojp.usdoj.gov/bjs/prisons.htm. See also Alfred Blumstein and Allan J. Beck, 'Population Growth in U.S. Prisons', in Michael Tonry and Joan Petersilia (eds.), *Prisons*, vol. 26 of *Crime and Justice: A Review of Research* (Chicago and London: University of Chicago Press, 1999), pp. 17–61.

[2] For an overview of international trends in the use of imprisonment, see Roy D. King, 'Prisons', in Michael Tonry (ed.), *The Handbook of Crime and Punishment* (New York: Oxford, 1998), pp. 589–625, especially pp. 590–96.

directed at other persons.[3] Many, upwards of 20 percent, are imprisoned for drug possession and trafficking offenses. Others are imprisoned for property crimes that did not involve assaults on persons or threats made against them. And still others are imprisoned because they in some way violated the provisions of their probation or parole. In other words, many of the people currently imprisoned have neither acted nor threatened to act in ways that substantially injured the lives or health and safety of their fellow citizens. Yet the lives of those imprisoned for crimes will be dramatically affected by their confinement.

Imprisonment imposes losses and deprivations on offenders that are highly stigmatizing and largely unmatched by other legal sanctions. Not only are prisoners separated from society and isolated from friends and loved ones, they suffer very substantial curtailments to their dignity, privacy, freedom of association, autonomy, and abilities to work and earn income. They may, of course, endure much worse than this in many existing prisons. It is not irresponsible to believe that imprisonment is never justified, that its impact on offenders is so horrific that we should find other ways of sanctioning serious offenders. But it is not easy to imagine what these other sanctions would be, especially for offenders who deliberately kill, maim or violently degrade their victims, and who are prepared to continue acting in these ways unless or until the state intervenes.[4] Hence, I assume that imprisonment is a defensible legal sanction, though I would concede that many questions about its character require more attention and debate than they have been given.

There is an enormous philosophical literature on the justification of legal punishment, and a substantial one on whether the death penalty is an appropriate sanction for the most serious offenses. The former rarely focuses sufficient attention on imprisonment as a sanction, though it typically assumes that confinement is the penalty of choice for serious offenders. But a range of questions about imprisonment—for which crimes is it an appropriate sanction, how long prison sentences should be for any given type of offense, what the justified conditions of confinement would look like—are given comparatively little attention in the literature on legal punishment. The death penalty debate, important as it may be, is

---

[3] See Theodore Caplow and Jonathan Simon, 'Understanding Prison Policy and Population Trends', in Tonry and Petersilia, *Prisons*, pp. 63–120 (76). It is worth noting that the distinction between violent and nonviolent offenses is not a sharp one.

[4] Granted, the fact that some offenders will continue engaging in such offenses absent state intervention may be more pertinent to those defending a crime reduction approach to the justification of legal punishment than to those defending a retributive approach.

focused on a criminal penalty that has befallen about one thousand offenders since executions were reinstated by the United States Supreme Court back in 1976.[5] One would think that more attention would be given by penal theorists to a sanction that affects two thousand times as many offenders in a single year.

Granted, there has been considerable philosophical work on the limits of liberty, and more specifically, on what actions should be criminalized. But an account of which acts should be criminalized is not, by itself, an account of how far or in what ways we should criminalize them. There are many sanctions short of imprisonment currently employed by most legal systems. The question of when infractions of the criminal law become serious enough to merit the imposition of imprisonment is thus distinct from the question of which acts the state should criminally proscribe.

My aim is to try to make some headway with the question what constitutes an offense for which imprisonment is an appropriate sanction. It will not be possible to wholly separate this question from those about the appropriate length and character of imprisonment. But I strive to keep these other questions in the background, as much as possible. I discuss the question what constitutes an imprisonable offense in the context of two leading theories of legal punishment. My choice of the retributive and crime reduction approaches is based on two factors. First, though there are other approaches to the justification of legal punishment in the philosophical literature, my sense is that they lack political currency. By this I mean that they appear to have little influence over the legislators, prosecutors, judges and juries who, by a complex series of decisions, mete out criminal justice. By contrast, retribution and crime reduction do seem to loom large in these decisions, though the deeper logic of these approaches to punishment's justification may be little understood or consistently applied by the principal actors in the criminal justice system. Secondly, some of the alternative theories (for example, ones focused on moral education or restorative justice) seem, for various and often different reasons, ill at ease with imprisonment as a sanction. Since I concede that it is a legitimate sanction for certain crimes, my focus is on what the retributive and crime reduction approaches tell us about the crimes for which it is appropriate, and why. Along the way, I consider to what extent the two approaches yield similar answers to the question what constitutes an imprisonable offense.

[5] This figure comes from Amnesty International at www.amnesty.usa.org.

It is important to distinguish the question of what constitutes an imprisonable offense from the question what constitutes an imprisonable offender. To a considerable extent, the answers to these two questions will overlap. But there may be grounds for imprisoning offenders—such as recidivists or individuals who have been convicted of lesser crimes (e.g., property offenses) but who we have good reason to believe are high-rate offenders—who have not been convicted of imprisonable offenses. The complications posed by recidivists and high-rate offenders will receive some attention in the ensuing discussion. Yet my main focus will be on determining the crimes for which imprisonment is an appropriate sanction.

I do not produce an exhaustive list of imprisonable offenses. Philosophical thinking about legal punishment is probably not fine-grained enough to yield such a list, though it can give us crucial guidance in our efforts to determine the crimes for which people should be imprisoned. We should probably not expect to find a sharp boundary between those offenses for which imprisonment is appropriate and those for which it is not. I shall be happy if, in what follows, I can begin to indicate a rough boundary.

I assume that the minimum prison term under discussion is six months. Offenders can be and often are assigned shorter terms of confinement, usually in local jails. At some point, the assignment of very short prison terms will likely merge on the sanction scale with the assignment of lesser, noncustodial sanctions. There is room for debate about where that point is, of course. But I want a significant enough difference between custodial and noncustodial sanctions to make meaningful the discussion of when the former become appropriate.

1. *Retribution and Imprisonment*

The first difficulty to be faced in thinking about what retributivism implies about imprisonable offenses is that there are competing versions of the theory in the contemporary literature on penal theory.[6] Since I cannot

---

[6] Contemporary retributive theories generally split into two camps—unfair advantage and communicative versions of the theory. For the former, see Herbert Morris, 'Persons and Punishment', *Monist* 52 (1968), pp. 475–501; Jeffrie Murphy, 'Marxism and Retribution', *Philosophy and Public Affairs* 2 (1973), pp. 217–43; Wojciech Sadurski, *Giving Desert its Due* (Dordrecht, Netherlands: D. Reidel, 1985); and George Sher, *Desert* (Princeton, NJ: Princeton University Press, 1987), pp. 69–90. For communicative versions, see Jean Hampton, 'A New Theory of Retribution', in R.G. Frey and Christopher W. Morris (eds.), *Liability and Responsibility: Essays in Law and Morals* (Cambridge: Cambridge University Press, 1991),

discuss them all, I shall simplify things in a way that I believe is acceptable given the general thrust of the different theories. Specifically, I assume that any plausible retributive account of the seriousness of criminal offenses is a function of two things: First, the kind and extent of harm done or threatened by criminal acts and, second, the degree of culpability offenders exhibit in doing or threatening such harms. This account of crime seriousness seems plausible whether one believes that punishment deprives offenders of the unfair advantages they have sought or taken, annuls the false moral messages crimes communicate, or censures offenders proportionally with the wrongs they have committed. Showing in detail that this account of crime seriousness fits with these different accounts of the retributive aim of legal punishment would take us too far afield, so I hope readers will take me at my word when I say it could be done.

In lieu of providing theories of either harm or culpability, I will work with some intuitive notions of these that, again, I hope, are at least plausible. Harms, in roughly descending order of significance, include loss of life, physical or psychological injuries that significantly impair persons' abilities to act or enjoy their lives, diminishment of overall health, loss of or damage to property on which persons depend for satisfying their basic needs (both at present and in the future), loss of liberty, loss of dignity, loss of privacy, loss of discretionary property, and inconvenience. Obviously, some of the lower-ranked harms can be worse than some of the higher-ranked ones, depending on their extent. Culpability ranges from the deliberate infliction of harms, to the knowing or reckless infliction of them, to their negligent infliction. Hyman Gross suggests, correctly it seems to me, that the various degrees of culpability reflect the extent to which harms can be attributed to offenders, as opposed to other agents or to chance.[7] Deliberately caused harms can be most directly and emphatically traced to the purposes and intentions of the agents who produced them, and thus are deserving of more of the institutionalized blame legal punishment represents.

To this general account, three complications must be added. First, some crimes do not actually inflict harm, but only attempt, threaten or plan to

pp. 377–414; R.A. Duff, *Trials and Punishments* (Cambridge: Cambridge University Press, 1986); and Jami L. Anderson, 'Annulment Retributivism: A Hegelian Theory of Punishment', *Legal Theory* 5 (1999), pp. 363–88.

[7] Hyman Gross, *A Theory of Criminal Justice* (New York: Oxford University Press, 1979), pp. 77–88.

inflict it. Whether retributivists can justify the punishment of such offenses, and whether such offenses should be punished comparably to ones that actually inflict the harms in question, are difficult questions. I do not say much about the first question in the ensuing discussion, though I say something about the second one. The second complication is that the criminal law in numerous countries prohibits an array of acts that do not inflict, attempt, threaten or plan to inflict any harm. Such prohibitions include ones involving the use, possession and trafficking in certain types of banned substances. They also include what Joel Feinberg terms 'derivative crimes'.[8] These comprise actions that must be regulated if governments are to effectively perform the tasks for which they are constituted. In addition, there are prohibitions on actions the performance of which would make it difficult for citizens to coordinate their activities or gain access on something like equal terms to public spaces and resources. Whether violations of any or all of these prohibitions constitute imprisonable offenses for retributivists are matters that I will return to in due course. Third, crimes often have direct, indirect and remote victims. By 'direct victims', I refer to those individuals who have been murdered, assaulted or stolen from. Indirect victims include the spouses, family members and dependents of direct victims who have their life-prospects diminished by the crimes directed against those they care about or depend upon. Remote victims are other members of the community whose lives may be affected by crimes, especially when they modify their activities to avoid becoming victims themselves of such crimes. Retributivists have not paid much attention to indirect and remote victims of crimes in determining the seriousness of offenses, but I am not convinced that they must or should do so.[9] However, for present purposes, I shall ignore indirect and remote victims.

---

[8] Joel Feinberg, *Harm to Others* (New York: Oxford University Press, 1984), pp. 19–20.

[9] One way to take into account the indirect and remote victims of crimes in sentencing offenders would be to have sentence ranges for each type of offense. Not only would this allow us to assign stiffer sanctions to those whose crimes caused atypical harm to direct victims, it would allow us to punish more severely those whose crimes harmed indirect and remote victims. It might be objected that punishing offenders for the harms caused indirect and remote victims would only be fair in cases where offenders were capable of anticipating such harms and thus the enhanced sanctions that might be assigned to them. This is true enough, but most offenders should be capable of anticipating how their crimes will affect indirect and remote victims. Offenders will presumably know that many direct victims have others who care about or depend on them. As for remote victims, it seems plausible to believe that those who, for instance, commit random acts of violence should be able to anticipate the insecurity, if not terror, that such acts engender in the larger community.

Simplifying a bit, we can divide the harm and culpability components of crime seriousness into three categories: high, medium and low. If we put harm on the left side of a grid and culpability across the top of it, this gives us nine possible combinations of harm and culpability, as illustrated below.

		Culpability		
		High	Medium	Low
	High			
Harm	Medium			
	Low			

High-ranking harms include loss of life and severe physical or psychological debilitation. Medium-ranking harms include loss of property on which persons depend for their subsistence and the infliction of significant, though not permanently debilitating, bodily or psychological injuries. Low-ranking harms include loss of discretionary property and invasions of privacy. Culpability will be greatest for harms that are deliberately inflicted with some degree of prior planning, medium for harms caused by reckless conduct, and low for harms caused by negligence.

My view is that a retributive account of the hard treatment punishment metes out must be keyed to the ways in and extent to which crimes typically harm victims and thereby diminish their life-prospects.[10] In other words, if we do not inflict hard treatment to deter, incapacitate or rehabilitate—options not available to retributivists—then it seems we do so to in some sense match the losses and deprivations wrought by

[10] The notion that sanctions should be keyed, in part, to the harms crimes typically cause their victims is discussed in Andrew von Hirsch and Nils Jareborg, 'Gauging Criminal Harm: A Living-Standard Analysis', *Oxford Journal of Legal Studies* 11 (1991), pp. 1–38 (14). Von Hirsch and Jareborg endorse limited sentencing ranges for offenses, such that deviations from the harms typically produced can be punished somewhat more or less harshly, depending on the features of individual cases.

punishment with the losses suffered by the victims of crime. I shall not pause here to try and explain why doing so is a reasonable course of action.[11] Retributivists should not endorse crude forms of matching sanctions with offenses, such as those entailed by simplistic interpretations of *lex talionis*, for two reasons. First, they must be prepared to reduce the sanctions imposed when culpability for harms is medium to low. Deliberately causing another's death is worse than recklessly or negligently doing so, and legal sanctions, if they are to express proportional condemnation, should reflect this. Second, retributivists must reject sanctions that they have reason to believe will erode or destroy offenders' capacities for moral responsibility, or else punishment will transform offenders into beings that are not appropriate subjects of retributive punishment. But it nonetheless seems that retributivists must be guided in thinking about what penal losses and deprivations to impose on offenders by an understanding of the ways and extent to which various crimes diminish the life-prospects of victims. They must also investigate and analyze the ways and extent to which sanctions affect those on whom they are inflicted.

This brings us to imprisonment as a sanction. Its severity as a sanction will vary somewhat, depending on the type of prison regime in question. At one extreme are the relatively humane forms of imprisonment found in some of the Scandinavian countries, where prisoners are allowed to work, have their own private cells, and go on furloughs or take advantage of liberal visitation policies.[12] At the other extreme are the harsh and restrictive conditions of confinement that are increasingly the norm in many supermax prisons throughout the United States.[13] Granted, imprisonment of any kind inflicts very substantial losses and deprivations on individuals. Yet no retributivist can ignore the different types of prison regimes, since they, along with the duration of confinement, will determine how far or in what ways offenders' life-prospects are diminished by imprisonment. Moreover, in assessing the extent to which imprisonment reduces offenders' life prospects, retributivists arguably should consider the post-prison

[11] For further discussion of this equalizing approach to retributivism, see my 'Victim-Centered Retributivism', *Pacific Philosophical Quarterly* 84 (2003), pp. 127–45, and 'Retribution and Incarceration', *Public Affairs Quarterly* 17 (2003), pp. 29–48.

[12] See Finn Hornum, 'Corrections in Two Social Welfare Democracies: Denmark and Sweden', *Prison Journal* 68 (1988), pp. 63–82.

[13] For description and analysis of supermax prisons, see Leena Kurki and Norval Morris, 'The Purposes, Practices, and Problems of Supermax Prisons', *Crime and Justice: A Review of Research* 28 (2001), pp. 385–424. See also my 'Against Supermax', *Journal of Applied Philosophy* 21 (2004), pp. 109–24.

prospects of inmates, if for no other reason than these too may be affected by the kind of imprisonment to which they have been subjected.[14] As a rough rule of thumb, it seems that the harsher and more restrictive the conditions of confinement are, the harder it becomes for retributivists to justify the use of imprisonment as a sanction in relation to any given type of offense.

Given the ways in which imprisonment substantially diminishes the life-prospects of offenders for some period of time not necessarily co-extensive with the duration of their sentences, it seems that we can quickly eliminate its use as a retributive sanction for a range of offenses. In particular, those on the grid (p. 270) that are low harm/low culpability, low harm/medium culpability, low harm/high culpability and medium harm/low culpability seem unlikely candidates for punishment by imprisonment. Sanctions short of imprisonment would, in such cases, impose losses on offenders commensurate with those their crimes inflicted on victims. Of course, as the harms endured by victims go from low to medium, we would expect the sanctions meted out to offenders to be made correspondingly more onerous. On the other hand, those offenses on the grid that are high harm/high culpability, high harm/medium culpability and medium harm/high culpability are apt to be imprisonable offenses. Such crimes inflict significant losses on their victims and do so in ways that are quite blameworthy. So long as the length of imprisonment for such offenses is appropriate—keyed (admittedly, roughly) to the duration of the diminished life-prospects of victims—imprisonment is a suitable equalizing sanction. The hard cases are the 'middle range' ones, encompassing offenses that are high harm/low culpability and medium harm/medium culpability. With regard to such cases, the character of prison confinement may emerge as a crucial factor. The harsher it is, the harder it becomes to justify its use in relation to such offenses, even though many of them will culpably diminish the life-prospects of victims in substantial ways.

Our thinking about these 'middle range' cases (and perhaps some of those offenses for which imprisonment is more clearly justified) may be complicated by a further factor that is well known to retributive theorists.[15] Many offenders inhabit less than reasonably just societies and

---

[14] For evidence about the effects of supermax confinement on individuals, see Craig Haney, 'Mental Health Issues in Long-Term Solitary and "Supermax" Confinement', *Crime & Delinquency* 49 (2003), pp. 124–56.

[15] See Murphy, 'Marxism and Retribution', pp. 231–43.

have thus grown up and continued to live in socially deprived areas within them. The diminished opportunities to pursue their aims and interests within the law that such offenders experience might lead us to wonder about the degree to which their choices to offend are sufficiently voluntary for purposes of retributive punishment. Worse than this, some of these individuals may experience some stunting or deforming of their capacities for responsible citizenship, capacities that arguably must be realized up to some level of proficiency if persons are to be liable to retributive punishment.[16] These are contentious claims, of course, but suppose that they can be made out in ways that undermine the case for retributive punishment of the socially deprived. There are various ways retributivists might attempt to accommodate such concerns. For instance, they could argue that the victims of social deprivation should receive reduced prison sentences for their crimes.[17] Another way to respond, however, would be to argue that socially deprived citizens who commit 'middle range' offenses should not, for the most part, be imprisoned for their offenses. This suggests that there may be no single list of imprisonable offenses that holds for all societies.

A number of questions and problems with this retributive account of imprisonable offenses remain to be addressed. First, consider crimes that threaten, attempt or plan substantial harms but which do not actually result in anyone's being harmed (or in the case of threats and attempts, which may traumatize those threatened or targeted, produce relatively minor harms). Should retributivists regard such crimes as imprisonable offenses? If one focuses, for the moment, on the nature of the harm threatened, attempted or planned, then the answer might very well be 'yes' in some cases. Culpability for acting in these ways will presumably be quite high, and if the harm to victims would have been medium to high in magnitude, then the case for imprisoning those who engage in such offenses appears formidable. There is, of course, the much-debated question whether those who threaten, plan or attempt harms but who do not carry them out (or succeed in carrying them out) should be punished

---

[16] For further discussion of the effects of social deprivation on individuals and how it should affect our thinking about the justification of legal punishment, see my 'Diminished Opportunities, Diminished Capacities: Social Deprivation and Punishment', *Social Theory and Practice* 29 (2003), pp. 459–85.

[17] For discussion of sentence reductions as a response to diminished responsibility in offenders, see Stephen Morse, 'Excusing and the New Excuse Defenses: A Legal and Conceptual Review', *Crime and Justice: A Review of Research* 23 (1998), pp. 329–406, at 401.

equivalently with those who do (or who succeed).[18] I am inclined to believe that they should not receive equivalent punishments, that there should be some discount for having not actually produced the harm in question. But it should not be a large discount, especially in cases where it is clear that threats of substantial harm were real, attempts to inflict it were completed, or plans to do so went quite a way toward bringing it about. What is puzzling in these cases is this: How can a retributive account of hard treatment that is keyed to matching criminal sanctions with the extent of harm to victims justify punishing offenders who have not actually harmed anyone (or harmed anyone very much)? Though I cannot elaborate the contention here, I believe that this is one of the points at which a purely retributive account of legal punishment founders.[19] I suspect that we punish such crimes to prevent their occurrence. However, I believe that retributivists are right in thinking that the appropriate amount of punishment must be determined with an eye to the character and extent of the harms planned, threatened or attempted.

Second, what does a retributive account of imprisonable offenses imply about crimes with multiple victims, no one of which suffers more than low or low to medium harm? If we focus on the harm to each individual victim, it would seem that such offenses are not of a magnitude to warrant imprisonment, given its impact on offenders. However, the aggregate impact of the offense on many victims may be quite substantial, such that we would want the sanctions imposed to reflect this. The question is whether it is possible for retributivists to defend enhanced sanctions in such cases.[20] I believe it is, since they could argue that

---

[18] For the view that attempts should be punished the same as successes, see Richard Parker, 'Blame, Punishment, and the Role of Results', *American Philosophical Quarterly* 21 (1984), pp. 269–76. For the opposing view, see Michael Moore, *Placing Blame: A General Theory of the Criminal Law* (Oxford: Clarendon Press, 1997), pp. 193–247. See also R.A. Duff, *Criminal Attempts* (Oxford: Clarendon Press, 1996), pp. 348–400, whose arguments shape my own thinking on these matters.

[19] Admittedly, retributive theories that are not, like my own, focused on matching sanctions to criminal harm may not have to incorporate reference to crime reduction aims at this juncture. Communicative versions of retributivism may more easily explain why those who, for instance, attempt harms (but who do not succeed in inflicting them) should be punished. Such attempts can be seen as communicating moral falsehoods that stand in need of nullification or public rebuke. However, I contend that communicative versions of retributivism are unsatisfactory for a number of other reasons.

[20] It is important to distinguish the question under discussion here from the question whether offenders whose crimes have multiple direct victims should serve concurrent or consecutive sentences, with each sentence taking into account the harm done to each

individuals who, for instance, swindle or defraud a large number of people (especially when offenders know they cannot repay them all) are more blameworthy than those who inflict minor to medium harms on one or a few people. Offenders might be able to pay restitution (and thus avoid imprisonment) to a few victims in ways that it is unlikely they can pay it to a larger group of offenders, and they are presumably capable of anticipating this.[21] The harms to indirect victims and social costs of such crimes would also be greater in ways that might be reflected in enhanced sanctions. Perhaps we need a special offense designation (e.g., mass fraud) to cover such cases, so that those who inflict relatively small amounts of criminal harm on many people could be charged with imprisonable offenses.

Third, there are what I earlier referred to as derivative crimes, as well as crimes involving the violation of legal rules and procedures designed to coordinate citizens' activities or fairly allocate the use of public resources of various kinds. What does a retributive account of imprisonable offenses imply about punishing such offenses? For the most part, I believe it implies that they are not imprisonable offenses, since many of them pose little threat of harm to identifiable victims. In a few cases—such as treason or espionage—such crimes will rise to an imprisonable level of seriousness. But in such cases the threat or reality of harm to others is palpable. And there may be some other cases (e.g., serious violations of health and safety regulations) where a retributive account of appropriate sanctions, keyed to the impact crimes have on the lives of victims, may justify the imprisonment of offenders. Yet my sense is that imprisonable offenses in these areas are more the exception than the rule.

Further implications of this retributive account of imprisonable offenses would need to be explored. What seems clear, so far, is that such an account would likely not have us imprison those who commit nonviolent offenses, including most drug offenses and many property crimes. The harms threatened or caused victims in such cases are simply not significant enough, or involve too much victim involvement or participation, to justify imprisoning offenders, even assuming that we continue to

victim. It could be the case, for instance, that the harm to each of the multiple victims is substantial enough to warrant imprisonment. There would remain the question whether the offender should serve consecutive prison sentences or receive some discount due to the cumulative impact of consecutive sentences on his or her life-prospects.

[21] I set to one side the question whether restitution by offenders to victims can serve as a fair sanction, especially where the well-off can pay it without suffering any real setbacks to their interests whereas the poor cannot.

criminalize all of the relevant acts.[22] The impact of imprisonment on such offenders' lives would be incommensurate in such cases with the harms they have threatened or wrought.

2. *Crime Reduction and Imprisonment*

The underlying logic of the crime reduction approach to the justification of legal punishment is broadly consequentialist. Legal punishment, on this approach, promises various good consequences to society—mostly in the form of deterrence, incapacitation and rehabilitation of offenders—which are alleged to be substantial enough to outweigh its negative consequences, which are also considerable. Implicit in this justification is the assumption that other options for controlling unwanted conduct are either not available or have lower benefit-to-cost ratios.[23] Whether and to what extent the institutions of legal punishment actually provide these benefits have been the subjects of considerable empirical investigation and analysis.[24] Complicating matters is the very real possibility that the three primary modes of crime reduction may not, in practice, point in the same direction. For instance, sanctions that increase deterrence or incapacitation may frustrate efforts to rehabilitate offenders. Further complicating matters is the apparent incommensurability of the many benefits and costs to be weighed and balanced in performing the consequentialist analyses this approach to legal punishment requires. I shall ignore these problems with commensurability in what follows, though they are very real and perhaps irresolvable.[25]

There are many things to be said against imprisonment as a sanction on consequentialist grounds, and many people have said them.[26] Prisons are

[22] I am assuming here that people are not 'harmed' in ways that the criminal law properly prohibits and censures by interactions with others that they voluntarily enter into, even if their interests are, in various ways, set back by such interactions.

[23] 'Costs' here should be understood to encompass all of the negative consequences of imprisonment.

[24] Michael Davis expresses skepticism that the utilitarian sentencing project can ever be carried out in light of the abysmal state of our knowledge concerning the comparative effects of different sentencing schemes on crime rates. See his 'How to Make the Punishment Fit the Crime', *Ethics* 93 (1983), pp. 726–52, at 732–34.

[25] But see James Griffin, *Well-Being: Its Meaning, Measurement, and Moral Importance* (Oxford: Clarendon Press, 1986), pp. 75–92, for a useful discussion of the commensurability of seemingly disparate values.

[26] See especially Thomas Mathiesen, *Prison on Trial* (Winchester, UK: Waterside Press, 2000), and Deirdre Golash, *The Case against Punishment: Retribution, Crime Prevention, and the Law* (New York: New York University Press, 2005), pp. 22–38. For an older, but still quite

enormously expensive to build and operate. Imprisonment imposes terrific suffering on inmates, exposes them to violence, predation and degradation, often dehabilitates rather than rehabilitates them, and profoundly diminishes their post-prison life prospects.[27] It also imposes substantial burdens of various kinds on those who care about or depend on offenders, and may, if used extensively as a sanction, further demoralize and impoverish the communities from whence offenders came.[28] Of course, we can imagine various reforms in prisons that might ameliorate some of these negative effects, and supporters of the crime reduction approach might strongly advocate changes in the character of confinement. But many of the negative effects of imprisonment will likely persist even under the most ambitious of prison reform programs.

Crimes also have many negative consequences, and more of them, generally speaking, the more serious the corresponding offense.[29] There are the losses and suffering imposed on direct victims, ranging from loss of life or severe debilitation down to mere inconvenience. Victims may also have medical expenses, lose income from being unable to work, and experience loss of dignity or psychological trauma from having been victimized. Their loved ones and dependents may also suffer various negative effects. Crimes impose burdens on communities and the institutions that govern them, including policing, pre-trial detention, trial, sanctioning and post-sanctioning supervision costs. Those who fear they will be victimized by crimes may purchase insurance, install security devices in their homes, businesses or vehicles, and avoid certain kinds of activities or areas altogether. They may also go on about their activities with more vigilance or wariness, themselves subtle costs of crime.

There is some tendency for those who write about the social costs of crime to ignore its many benefits.[30] There are, first of all, the material and psychological benefits to offenders from their crimes. These, it may be believed, are too morally tainted to count for much, but it is unclear how

useful discussion, see Anthony O'Hear, 'Imprisonment', *Philosophy* 18 (1984 Supplement), pp. 203–220.

[27] I borrow the term 'dehabilitation' from Mathiesen in *Prison on Trial*, p. 53.

[28] See especially John Hagan and Ronit Dinovitzer, 'Collateral Consequences of Imprisonment for Children, Communities, and Prisoners', in Tonry and Petersilia, *Prisons*, pp. 121–62.

[29] See Sam Brand and Richard Price, *The Economic and Social Costs of Crime* (London: Home Office Research Studies, 2000). See also the studies of victim and societal costs discussed in Franklin E. Zimring and Gordon Hawkins, *Incapacitation: Penal Confinement and the Restraint of Crime* (New York: Oxford University Press, 1995), pp. 131–54.

[30] A point made by Zimring and Hawkins in *Incapacitation*, p. 151.

consequentialists can ignore or discount them. But people other than offenders benefit from certain kinds of crimes, especially property or drug offenses. Like it or not, the proceeds from such crimes are parts of thriving underground economies that support people who otherwise struggle to acquire the resources to provide for their basic needs. This will be especially true in impoverished communities where more legitimate means of earning income are scarce or less attractive. It may still be the case that the social costs of certain crimes, all things considered, greatly exceed these kinds of benefits. This will likely be true for crimes involving significant interpersonal violence or the threat of it. It will also most likely be true for crimes involving theft of property on which victims depend for their livelihood. But these are contingent claims, and the existence of such benefits to crime must be reckoned in consequentialist attempts to justify punishment in general, and imprisonment in particular.

We will most want to reduce offenses whose social costs are substantial and the commission of which provided few social benefits. Thus we reach what I term the 'provisional conclusion'. The most obvious imprisonable offenses, on a crime reduction approach, are those that threaten or inflict significant harm on direct, indirect and remote victims. Homicide, rape, terrorism, kidnapping, aggravated assault, armed robbery, and theft of large amounts of property or property on which individuals' livelihoods crucially depend would, as with the retributive approach, appear to be the prime candidates for punishment by imprisonment. The social costs of such offenses are high—direct victims suffer a great deal from them as do indirect ones. The public is especially fearful of such offenses and will want assurance that they will not spread or be committed with impunity. Granted, offenders do, we can suppose, reap some benefits from such offenses. But not only are these benefits likely to be out-weighed by their many costs, one suspects that the benefits are typically confined to offenders themselves (and may be diluted by feelings of guilt or remorse in some cases). Thus, it will be important to establish sufficient deterrent threats to induce desistance from such crimes, incapacitate those most likely to commit them, and rehabilitate those who have committed them. I will, for the time being, bracket the questions whether and to what extent the crime reduction approach can support reduced sanctions for offenses that inflict significant harms but which do so with medium to low levels of culpability.

To what extent or in what ways does the empirical evidence concerning legal punishment's crime reduction tendencies comport with this provisional conclusion? The answer appears to depend on the mode of crime reduction in question—that is, on whether we focus on deterrence, incapacitation, or rehabilitation. Turning first to deterrence, the empirical studies of most relevance to our concerns are those that examine the relationship between sentence severity and general deterrence. These studies focus on whether increases or decreases in sentence severity, usually understood in terms of the length of custodial sentences, are correlated with marginal changes in deterrence. The consensus opinion appears to be that there is very little correlation between increases in sentence length and increases in marginal deterrence.[31] Some argue that there is no correlation at all, and that analysis of what would have to be true of offenders for there to be such a correlation, combined with evidence gleaned from interviews with prison inmates about what they were thinking of when they committed their crimes, explains why criminologists cannot seem to confirm much of a correlation.[32]

It might be objected that such studies are of limited usefulness in determining what constitutes an imprisonable offense, since they tend to focus on changes in the lengths of custodial sentences, rather than the difference between being assigned a prison sentence and not being assigned one. The marginal deterrence effects of the latter difference are what we are interested in.

Perhaps so, but two points are worth making in response to this objection. First, at least one authoritative analysis of the deterrence literature explicitly makes reference to the difference between being assigned a custodial sentence and not being assigned one, still finding a minimal correlation between sentence severity and marginal deterrence.[33] Second, noncustodial sanctions, especially if some combination of them is assigned to offenders, might be roughly equivalent in their disruptive effects on offenders' lives to brief jail or prison terms. This suggests that there is not likely to be a clear line between minimal custodial sanctions and maximal noncustodial ones, such that we should expect to find discernible differences in their marginal deterrence effects. This is important because the alternative to imprisoning offenders is obviously not to refuse to sanction them at all.

---

[31] See especially Andrew von Hirsch, Anthony E. Bottoms, Elizabeth Burney, and P.-O. Wikstrom, *Criminal Deterrence and Sentence Severity: An Analysis of Recent Research* (Oxford: Hart Publishing, 1999), pp. 45–47. See also Daniel Nagin, 'Deterrence and Incapacitation', in Tonry, *The Handbook of Crime and Punishment*, pp. 345–68.

[32] See Anthony N. Doob and Cheryl Marie Webster, 'Sentence Severity and Crime: Accepting the Null Hypothesis', *Crime and Justice: A Review of Research* 30 (2003), pp. 143–95.

[33] See von Hirsch et al., *Criminal Deterrence and Sentence Severity*, p. 6.

Still, it might be hypothesized that as the contrast between noncustodial and custodial sanctions increases—such that if we compare substantial prison sentences to noncustodial sanctions—significant increases in the marginal deterrent effects of imprisonment may emerge. I am not sure to what extent the empirical studies confirm or refute this hypothesis. Even if we grant its plausibility, for the sake of argument, all it may advise us to do is assign relatively lengthy prison terms if and when we assign them. For only such sentences will give us significant crime reduction benefits as compared with their noncustodial counterparts.[34] This does not yet tell us much about which offenses are imprisonable, for any marginal deterrence effects gained by lengthy prison sentences are but one benefit to be factored into a more comprehensive crime reduction analysis of sanctions. Assuming that we must be prepared, as a society, to make good on threats to impose substantial prison sentences for offenses, it would appear that doing so will only maximize overall good consequences if such sentences are employed in relation to offenses high in social costs. Yet this is precisely what the provisional conclusion suggests.

A further complication with regard to deterrence is that most of what we know about sentence severity and marginal deterrence comes from studies performed in societies that are arguably less than reasonably just in certain respects. It could be that the deterrence value of more severe sentences is minimal because many offenders are socially deprived, some of them quite profoundly so. Social deprivation has two effects on people that are likely to weaken punishment's deterrent value. First, it leaves them with proportionally fewer legitimate opportunities to pursue their interests, and thereby tempts them to risk offending. Second, it undermines their allegiance to many of the moral norms underlying key aspects of the criminal law, because they do not see the law as serving their interests in ways or to the extent that it serves the interests of those better off in society. Granted, the threat of truly draconian criminal sanctions might suffice to dissuade the poor against offending, but such sanctions, if actually imposed, would have their own considerable costs and drawbacks. We might speculate that punishment's deterrent value would be greater in more reasonably just societies. All citizens in such societies would have more to lose by risking punishment, and presumably more of them would be responsive to the law's animating moral norms. But as things are in

[34] Daniel Nagin has noted that threats of especially harsh sanctions for certain types of crimes may only lead individuals to shift the kinds of offenses they engage in, not to desist from offending. See Nagin, 'Deterrence and Incapacitation', pp. 356–57.

many existing societies, the threat of harsh legal punishment appears to have surprisingly weak crime reduction credentials.

It might be argued that the threat of imprisonment deters offending in a more subtle way, by reinforcing the strength with which citizens internalize norms against it.[35] By threatening harsh sanctions for offenses, society communicates its strong disapproval of them. Citizens perceive this strong disapproval and respond by more deeply or thoroughly embracing the criminal prohibitions pertaining to certain acts. There does not appear to have been any empirical testing of this hypothesis, but it is plausible to think that state condemnation of certain acts plays some role in shaping citizens' attitudes against performing them. The key question might be how much of a role it plays in this regard. Moral education by parents, schools and churches seems likely to have stronger influence over the beliefs and values held by individuals. If these fail to inculcate proper attitudes toward certain kinds of conduct, state censure of that conduct, one suspects, will be largely ineffective at doing so. It will be especially ineffective if citizens doubt the legitimacy of the state to regulate the conduct in question, as they might if it appears to them that the state is indifferent to the promotion of their welfare in other respects.[36] All of this matters because imprisonment will be a very costly means of attempting to shore up allegiance to the norms in question. If it works to do so at all, it seems we will want to employ it in a discriminating fashion, in order to reinforce those norms violations of which are especially costly to society. But again, this suggests that imprisonment should be reserved for relatively serious offenses.

When we turn to incapacitation, our belief in the benefits of imprisonment might appear to be on more solid ground. Perhaps the threat of imprisonment does not do as much as we would hope to deter offending, but placing offenders in prison surely makes it harder for them to commit crimes. Yet as those who have examined the logic and evidence about incapacitation have shown, the relationship between imprisoning offenders and reducing crime in the broader community from whence they came is more tenuous and complex than it might first seem.[37] For instance, some types of offenses (especially certain drug or property offenses)

35 One version of this argument, defending the use of capital punishment, is offered by Steven Goldberg, 'Does Capital Punishment Deter?', *Ethics* 85 (1974), pp. 67–74, at 70–71.

36 A point made by von Hirsch, et al., in *Criminal Deterrence and Sentence Severity*, p. 40.

37 See Zimring and Hawkins, *Incapacitation*, especially pp. 53–56, and Nagin, 'Deterrence and Incapacitation', pp. 362–65.

tend to be committed by individuals acting in concert with others. If the criminal justice system arrests and convicts only one or some of the members of the group, the rest may continue to commit crimes at roughly the same rate. They may even recruit new members who are more energetic or creative, thus enhancing the group's ability to commit crimes. There are also illegal goods for which there is steady demand. Even if the authorities arrest and convict all those individuals who were formerly supplying the goods in question, others may come forward to supply them anew. The emergence of such criminal entrepreneurs seems more likely in socially deprived communities. Finally, there is the 'aging out' phenomenon. When offenders reach a certain age (though this varies, depending on whether the individuals in question are property offenders or violent ones), their offense rates tend to decrease dramatically or reach zero. This means that if offenders are apprehended and convicted late in their criminal careers, imprisoning them may not yield much incapacitation, since they would have desisted from further offending on their own.

We should not conclude from the complex relationship that exists between incapacitation and crime reduction that imprisonment has few incapacitation effects. Some crimes are not committed by offenders acting as members of groups—many violent crimes, in particular, are apt to be committed by individuals acting on their own or if with others, not as often as members of ongoing criminal enterprises (leaving aside special cases like organized crime). Also, many violent offenders seem less likely to be replaced by others if they are arrested and convicted. In general, there seems to be less demand for things like homicide, rape, kidnapping, terrorism and aggravated assault than there is for drugs or stolen goods. Moreover, there are high-rate serious offenders whose imprisonment, if they can be arrested and convicted early in their criminal careers, would yield substantial reductions in crime. The problem is that only some individuals who are convicted of crimes high in social costs will commit offenses of a similar magnitude in the future. It will therefore not be cost-effective to imprison all who are convicted of such offenses. Do we have the means to determine which of these offenders will reoffend? There is considerable discussion in the incapacitation literature about the feasibility of identifying such high-rate offenders. There are techniques for predicting which convicted offenders will continue to offend at high rates, although there are also doubts expressed about the accuracy of such techniques and the morality of employing them to imprison offenders past the point where they have been proportionally punished for their earlier convictions.[38] My sense is that our prediction capabilities in this regard are not such as to warrant our having strong confidence in them.

We could, of course, err on the side of caution and imprison all offenders who are convicted of having committed crimes high in social costs. Alternatively, we could imprison all of those convicted of committing crimes of certain types that are high in social costs, if there is evidence that those who commit such crimes tend to recidivate. But the more reasonable approach would seem to be case-by-case, where the courts, aided by various professionals, consider the personal and social characteristics of offenders, attempting thereby to determine which of them are the most suitable candidates for custodial rather than noncustodial sanctions. This suggests that it may be more difficult in weighing imprisonment's incapacitation effects to distinguish imprisonable crimes from imprisonable offenders. Still, there is little here to indicate that we should abandon the provisional conclusion, especially by expanding the list of imprisonable offenses to include those low to medium in social costs.

It might be argued, however, that we should be prepared to imprison those who commit offenses that are low, or low to moderate, in social costs if we can identify them as high-rate offenders.[39] Though no one of their crimes, by itself, would constitute an imprisonable offense, the fact that they are likely to commit many such crimes arguably makes them eligible for imprisonment on crime reduction grounds. Notice that this is a possible point of divergence between crime reduction and retributive approaches to the question of what constitutes an imprisonable offense. Retributivists would presumably be unwilling to imprison or even punish individuals based on predictions of their future acts, whereas crime reductionists would have to consider doing so. Again, some believe that we have fairly reliable indicators of high-rate offending, at least with regard to certain types of offenders. Still, the very real possibility that a policy of imprisoning high-rate offenders who commit crimes with low to moderate social costs would produce significant numbers of false positives might temper

[38] For the view that there are promising strategies for predicting continued criminal offending by some types of offenders, see Jacqueline Cohen, 'Incapacitation as a Strategy for Crime Control: Possibilities and Pitfalls', *Crime and Justice: A Review of Research* 5 (1983), pp. 64–74. For skepticism about such strategies, see Kathleen Auerhahn, 'Selective Incapacitation and the Problem of Prediction', *Criminology* 37 (1999), pp. 703–34.

[39] See Edwin W. Zedlewski, 'Why Prisons Matter: A Utilitarian Review', *Corrections Management Quarterly* 1 (1997), pp. 15–24, and *Making Confinement Decisions* (Washington, DC: National Institute of Justice, 1987). For criticism of Zedlweski's analyses, and in particular his estimates of the rates at which individuals offend, see Zimring and Hawkins, *Incapacitation*, pp. 142–47.

the enthusiasm for such a policy among those favoring the crime reduction approach. There would be considerable disutility in imprisoning offenders whose crimes have low to moderate social costs if they are unlikely to commit substantial numbers of future crimes. And usually it would be pointless to imprison those we suspect of high-rate offending if they were close to the point at which offenders generally age out.

Nonetheless, crime reductionists might support large sentence ranges for offenses, so that properly identified and relatively youthful high-rate offenders could be more effectively incapacitated by imprisonment, while those not so identified or not so youthful could be assigned noncustodial sanctions. Whether the case for sentence ranges with harsher top ends is bolstered by deterrence considerations is less clear. Also, the imprisonment of youthful offenders who commit crimes with low to moderate social costs is likely to have deleterious effects on their life-prospects. These would weigh against imprisoning such offenders, and heavily so to the extent that they spur lengthier or more serious criminal careers.

Crime reductionists might also lean more heavily than retributivists toward imprisoning those who commit what I earlier termed 'middle range' offenses if the individuals in question have previous criminal histories. The imprisonment of recidivists whose crimes are low to moderate in social costs might be defended on deterrence or incapacitation grounds—the former if lesser sanctions appear insufficient to dissuade future offending; the latter if our aim is simply to remove from society for some period of time individuals who seem determined to continue offending. Of course, we might be skeptical about the efficacy of such deterrent threats or incapacitation strategies, especially where the offenders in question are severely disadvantaged. As always, there is the question whether alternative courses of action, such as milder sanctions combined with efforts to reduce social deprivation, might not be less costly overall and more effective at reducing crime in the long term. There are complex questions of fact and value to investigate and weigh here. My point is that the crime reduction approach requires them to be investigated and weighed, and it is not clear that the outcomes will jibe with what retributivism tells us about the imprisonment of recidividists who commit middle-range offenses.[40]

[40] Martin Wasik and Andrew von Hirsch argue that retributivists can support somewhat longer sentences for recidivists, especially if sanctioning schemes employ a range of sentences in relation to any given offense. With first- or even second-time offenders, it might be reasonable to conclude that their participation in criminal activity was the result of youth, temporary bad judgment, or undue influence by others. As a result, we might

For the most part, contemporary prisons do not seem well designed to rehabilitate offenders.[41] They generally warehouse inmates under conditions that deprive them of access to work and responsibility, and isolate them from family members and larger communities. We should therefore not be surprised to discover that many offenders come to embrace their outlaw status, identifying more with their fellow inmates and their values than with law-abiding members of society and their values.[42] Add to this the fact that many offenders are resentful of their imprisonment because they are socially and economically marginalized to begin with. Throwing them together with others who feel like them hardly seems a recipe for good outcomes. Furthermore, it is plausible to believe that the longer individuals are imprisoned, the harder it will be for them to make successful readjustments to life in civil society. Thus, if considerations of marginal deterrence and incapacitation do support longer prison sentences for certain types of offenders, there may be some tension between such considerations and that of rehabilitation.

We could reform prisons so that idleness, isolation and passivity were not their hallmarks, and probably on crime reduction grounds we should do so. Even in the absence of such reforms, there is evidence that some types of prison rehabilitation programs reduce recidivism.[43] This may show that prisons need not further incline all inmates toward offending, especially where such programs are adequately funded for appropriate periods of time and offered to all in the prison population. But none of this tells us which offenders to send to prison in the first place. Any potential benefits provided by such programs will have to be judiciously weighed against the negative effects of imprisonment on inmates.[44]

---

assign such offenders sentences at the lower end of the sanction ranges for their offenses. Recidivism evidences that individuals are determined to continue their criminal careers, so doubts about the extent of their culpability for crimes become less sustainable. Repeat offenders might therefore appropriately be assigned penalties at or near the top of the relevant sanction range. See Martin Wasik and Andrew von Hirsch, 'Section 29 Revisited: Previous Convictions in Sentencing', *Criminal Law Review* (1994), pp. 409–18.

41 See Mathiesen, *Prison on Trial*, pp. 27–54.

42 Donald Clemmer referred to the process by which prisoners come to identify with their fellow inmates and embrace their outlaw status as that of 'prisonization'. See his *The Prison Community* (New York: Rinehart and Co., 1958), p. 299.

43 See Gerald Gaes, Timothy J. Flanagan, Lawrence L. Motiuk, and Lynne Stewart, 'Adult Correctional Treatment', in Tonry and Petersilia, *Prisons*, pp. 361–426.

44 It might be suggested that if we are fairly confident that rehabilitation is effective in some cases, perhaps we should imprison youthful offenders whose crimes are low to moderate in social costs so that we can help them before they begin to commit crimes higher in such costs. But this suggestion only makes sense if we have the requisite degree of confidence in rehabilitation, which I doubt we should have. In any case, we would have to weigh

There is, it must be acknowledged, the conjecture that imprisonment may also reduce crime by convincing offenders that remaining within the law is preferable to suffering the sanctions incurred by breaking it. There appears to have been little empirical investigation of this phenomenon of special deterrence.[45] But it is plausible to believe that some offenders find their prison experience to be so unpleasant that they resolve to refrain from further serious offending and act accordingly. Still, the prospects of successful rehabilitation and special deterrence are probably uncertain enough to convince us to modify the provisional conclusion that imprisonment should be reserved for offenses high in social costs. And both effects may be diminished if inmates wind up back in communities devastated by social neglect.

Summarizing, my sense is that the empirical literature on crime reduction generally supports the provisional conclusion reached earlier—that the crime reduction approach justifies the use of imprisonment only for serious offenses whose social costs are quite substantial and whose social benefits are minimal. Imprisonment is unlikely to yield significant deterrent effects, compared to other sanctions, unless the sentences threatened are fairly lengthy, at least in societies with large numbers of disadvantaged citizens. Yet lengthy sentences seem justified on cost/benefit grounds only if they are imposed on offenders whose crimes have high social costs. The incapacitation effects of imprisonment are apt to be weak for drug and low-to-medium-harm property offenders, many of whom will be replaced by others if the benefits from crime are lucrative enough. And given the many costs and drawbacks of imprisonment, including its tendency to harden some offenders, even modest incapacitation effects may not be enough to compensate for its crime-producing effects.

There is the question, deferred earlier, whether the crime reduction approach explains how the culpability of harm-causing agents counts in determining their sentences. At first glance, the case for factoring in culpability seems suspect. The social costs of harmful actions are apt to be the same regardless of the degree of culpability exhibited by those who engage in them. What does it matter to the victim of homicide or others affected

imprisonment's tendency to worsen offenders against any prospects it has for improving them. I do not believe that even the most optimistic views about imprisonment's rehabilitation effects should therefore lead us to abandon the provisional conclusion.

45 Andrew Ashworth remarks that 'relatively little is heard of individual deterrence as a specific aim of sentencing in the modern debate'. See his 'Deterrence', in Andrew von Hirsch and Andrew Ashworth (eds.), *Principled Sentencing: Readings on Theory and Policy* (Oxford: Hart Publishing, 1998), pp. 44–52, at 45.

by it whether the agent who caused death did so deliberately, recklessly, or only negligently? The criminal law might usefully aim at deterring or incapacitating equally all of those who threaten to inflict substantial harms on others. Have we therefore discovered another point at which retributive and crime reduction approaches diverge on the question of what constitutes an imprisonable offense? Probably not, since crime reductionists can argue that those more culpable for inflicting harms ought to receive stiffer sentences than their less culpable counterparts. First, individuals who deliberately act to harm others might usefully be threatened with harsher sanctions because they are more invested in harming than those who injure others out of recklessness or negligence. Those who deliberately harm need stronger disincentives to going forward with their plans. Second, those who deliberately harm others are probably more dangerous, other things being equal, than those who do so out of recklessness or negligence. The fact that the former aim to harm in ways that the latter do not suggests that those who deliberately harm might more usefully be incapacitated.

We should also consider what the crime reduction approach tells us about the imprisonment of those who plan, threaten or attempt harm, or who commit derivative crimes. As we saw, retributivism struggles to explain why we should punish those who plan, threaten or attempt harms but do not actually inflict them. I suggested that a crime reduction aim might have to be introduced to justify the punishment of such offenders. But why should we punish those who have not caused the kinds of social costs actual harms produce? The answer to this question is easiest in the case of attempts, since those who attempt to harm others often succeed in doing so, and even if they do not, they strike fear into their targets and anxiety into anyone in the vicinity of their acts. Where the harms attempted are moderate to high in social costs, there is at least a plausible case for imprisoning such offenders on crime reduction grounds.

Threats of harm, especially where the harm threatened is severe and the means to act on the threat are readily available, also cause fear and anxiety in others and often spill over into the actual infliction of harms—as indeed they occasionally must if they are to succeed. There is also the increased likelihood of mistakes or accidents when the threat involves the use of a weapon such as a gun. We might say that substantial harm is imminent in some threats and, where the social costs of carrying them out would be moderate to high, the case for imprisoning those who make them, so as to reduce the frequency of such costs actually occurring, is stronger. Still, given the many negative consequences of imprisonment, a crime reduction approach might restrict its use to those with histories of making or acting on threats. Such individuals would be greater risks to the community than those who on single occasions make threats on which they do not act. Similarly, those who plan and go some way toward inflicting harms that are moderate to high in social costs might reasonably be imprisoned on crime reduction grounds. This would especially be true if it appeared likely that such planning was not a one-time event, but indicative of a more active malevolence that might recur and come to fruition in the infliction of actual harms.

With derivative crimes, the many negative consequences of imprisonment loom larger and make its justification for such offenses more difficult. Many derivative crimes lack direct victims or even indirect ones, so their social costs may be minimal. Where there are or might be such victims (e.g., in cases of treason or sedition), the case for imprisonment would be stronger, especially if the harms to victims would be medium to high. It might be objected that we would need harsher sanctions for many secondary crimes on deterrence grounds, since the absence of direct victims reduces the moral motives citizens have to avoid such offenses. If it is only the government they are harming with such offenses, then many will have few incentives to avoid them. Perhaps so, though there appear to be significant numbers of citizens who regard government requirements to act in various ways to be sufficient grounds, in and of themselves, to do so. This objection may also exaggerate the deterrent effects of harsher sanctions. And once again, we must consider whether the substantial costs of imprisonment (to offenders, their families, and tax-paying citizens) are worth incurring if the only benefit is engendering slightly higher rates of compliance with government rules and regulations. They might be if the relevant rules and regulations aim at reducing the occurrence of acts high in social costs. But many concern conduct that has, at most, low to moderate social costs.

Concluding Remarks

There appears to be remarkable convergence between crime reduction and retributive accounts of what constitutes an imprisonable offense. For retributivists, imprisonment should be reserved for those who commit offenses that inflict (or threaten) medium to high levels of harm with at least medium levels of culpability, for only such offenses diminish the life-prospects of victims in ways and to an extent comparable to the ways and extent to which imprisonment diminishes the life-prospects of those to whom it is assigned. Similarly, imprisonment is likely to maximize overall good consequences only if it is used to punish those whose offenses are moderate to high in social costs and low in social benefits. Imprisonment has numerous negative consequences for offenders, their families, and society. The marginal deterrence benefits of imprisonment, compared to other, lesser sanctions, appear minimal, at least up to the point where prison terms become fairly substantial. The incapacitation benefits of imprisonment are less reliable than they first appear, especially in relation to many property and drug offenses. The existence of social deprivation makes it harder to justify the use of imprisonment for middlerange offenses on retributive grounds, and weakens the deterrent, incapacitation and rehabilitative effects of imprisonment, even on the somewhat dubious proposition that it can be relied upon to have the lattermost effect.

These conclusions, if correct, have important implications for the current use of imprisonment in many countries. They imply that it is overused, especially in relation to many property and drug offenders. It may also be overused in relation to many who commit derivative crimes or are imprisoned because of technical parole or probation violations but who have not committed violent or socially costly offenses.

It is probably too much to hope that elected officials will soon rethink their tendencies to increase the frequency, duration and harshness of imprisonment as a sanction for offenses. There seems little in the logic of retributivism or crime reduction, if these are properly understood, that supports these recent sentencing trends. Of course, if these theories are improperly understood—as supporting hard, vengeful treatment without any regard for its effects on offenders, their families, or the broader community—then confusion about penal theory may play some role in explaining how we have gotten to where we are today. But I suspect that we will have to look elsewhere if we are to understand what encourages elected officials to persist in their insufficiently discriminating use of imprisonment as a response to criminal offending.

PUNISHING THE GUILTY, NOT PUNISHING THE INNOCENT*

Richard L. Lippke

Abstract

Discussion in this paper focuses on how strongly we should prefer non-punishment of persons guilty of serious crimes to punishment of persons innocent of them. William Blackstone's version of that preference, expressed as a ten to one ratio, is first shown to be untenable on standard accounts of legal punishment's justifying aims. Somewhat weaker versions of that ratio also appear suspect. More to the point, Blackstone's adage obscures the crucial way in which there are risks to be assessed in setting up a criminal justice system – the risk that it will not be effective enough at apprehending and punishing serious offenders, as well as the risk that it will expose innocent persons to harsh punishment. I urge a balancing of such risks, and argue that the salient features of many contemporary criminal justice systems can be plausibly interpreted as attempting to achieve and maintain such a balance. We do not grant criminal defendants a presumption of innocence that the state must overcome with proof of guilt beyond a reasonable doubt in order to institutionally express a strong degree of preference for non-punishment of the guilty to punishment of the innocent. Instead, we do so in order to ensure that institutions of legal punishment have sufficient scope while preserving their ability to accurately sort the guilty from the innocent.

Keywords

criminal trials, deterrence, incapacitation, presumption of innocence, reasonable doubt, retribution

It is well-known that criminal justice systems sometimes fail to do what they are supposed to do – punish the guilty and not punish the innocent.

---

* An earlier version of this paper was given to an audience at the Centre for Applied Philosophy and Public Ethics at Australian National University. I thank those in attendance for their helpful comments and criticisms. Two anonymous reviewers and the editors for the *Journal of Moral Philosophy* also helped me to improve the paper.

According to an old adage, we are to prefer – and indeed strongly prefer – non-punishment of the guilty to punishment of the innocent. The venerable William Blackstone's version of the adage would have us let ten guilty people go unpunished rather than punish one innocent person.[1] There are, it should be apparent, two distinct claims contained in Blackstone's admonition. The first is a preference for non-punishment of the guilty over punishment of the innocent. The other is the degree of that preference, an account of how many guilty people should go free rather than innocents punished. One does not have to search far to find accounts of the appropriate strength of this preference which are stronger or weaker.[2] But they all suggest that we should prefer to let several guilty people go free rather than punish one innocent one.

My contention is that Blackstone's adage is, to a considerable extent, otiose in helping us to confront the question of how to balance punishment of the guilty against non-punishment of the innocent. It is not so much that the ten to one ratio is wrong, though I show that defending it is a dubious project. Nor is it that we will rarely have anything more than very rough estimates of the ratio of guilty to innocent persons punished by any given criminal justice system. It is rather that the real choice we face concerns the risk of non-punishment of the guilty versus the risk of punishment of the innocent. We can structure our institutions to minimize the risk that the guilty will go unpunished, or that the innocent will be punished, or we can attempt to do both. Not surprisingly, perhaps, I argue that the sensible thing is to do both. I also argue that it is plausible to interpret contemporary criminal justice systems as attempting to do so. Such systems give formidable resources and powers to state officials while at the same time adopting procedural and evidence rules that appear to favor criminal defendants. This makes sense if it is a balance that we seek, one in which the risks of non-punishment of the guilty are weighed against the risks of punishment of the innocent. In fact, I suggest that were Blackstone's ratio, or one close to it, really our guiding principle in devising a criminal justice system, we would have to strip police and prosecutors of much of

[1] William Blackstone, *Commentaries on the Laws of England* (Boston, MA: Beacon Press, 1962), p. 420.

[2] See Larry Laudan's *Truth, Error, and Criminal Law: An Essay in Legal Epistemology* (Cambridge: Cambridge University Press, 2006), p. 63, for alternative versions of the appropriate strength of the preference. Alexander Volokh has somewhat irreverently shown that there is little agreement among those who invoke versions of the adage about how many guilty persons should go free before we punish one innocent one, or indeed whether any should. See his '*n* Guilty Men', *University of Pennsylvania Law Review* 146 (1997), pp. 173–216.

their authority and many of their resources. We are unlikely to do anything of the sort because non-punishment of the guilty, especially when their crimes are serious, is a very bad thing.[3] Of course, punishment of the innocent, especially when the sanctions inflicted on them are severe, is also a very bad thing. If I were to offer an alternative to Blackstone's adage, it would be something like this: 'Maximize the number of guilty punished proportionally with the seriousness of their offenses, while minimizing the number of innocents punished.' To this it might be added: 'If push comes to shove, set things up so that non-punishment of the guilty is preferred to punishment of the innocent. But not too strongly.' Granted, as adages go, mine is distinctly lacking in simplicity and dramatic flair.

The discussion is divided into two main sections. In the first, I begin by briefly reviewing the grounds for believing that punishment of the innocent is something that we should strongly seek to avoid. I then take greater pains to demonstrate how non-punishment of the guilty is also quite undesirable, whether one favors a retributive (or desert-based) account of punishment or a crime reduction account.[4] I argue that standard penal theories appear incapable of justifying the strong degree of preference for non-punishment of the guilty to punishment of the innocent that Blackstone's adage recommends. If such theories are understood as normative models for the design of institutions of criminal justice, then they do not support setting up such institutions to so strongly favor non-punishment of the guilty to punishment of the innocent. I also argue, though more briefly, that the distinction between allowing and doing harm cannot be used to support robust versions of the preference for non-punishment of the guilty to punishment of the innocent.

These conclusions will be resisted by those who contend that some weaker ratio can be defended. I make no effort to formulate a more plausible numerical ratio. Instead, I maintain that in the absence of some sense of the probabilities involved – that is, the likelihood that the guilty will go unpunished or innocents be punished – no clear ratio concerning how much the latter should be preferred to the former is apt to emerge.

---

[3] I thus agree with the Laudan's insistence that the importance of punishment of the guilty should not be gainsaid. Laudan does not so much reject Blackstone's ratio as argue that it will not allow us to determine the standard of proof in criminal cases. See *Truth, Error, and Criminal Law*, pp. 73–74.

[4] There are, of course, accounts of legal punishment other than those provided by retributivists and crime reductionists. To the extent that they attempt to justify something akin to existing institutions of legal punishment, I believe it can be shown that they are also unlikely to provide support for Blackstone's ten to one ratio. But I make no effort to support this contention in the discussion that follows.

We must design our institutions of legal punishment based mostly on conjecture about how to achieve and maintain the proper balance between their having sufficient scope, understood in terms of their success at the apprehension and punishment of serious offenders, and accuracy, understood in terms of their separating the guilty from the innocent and punishing the former proportionally with the seriousness of their offenses.

In the second main section, I show how the most salient features of contemporary criminal justice systems can be interpreted as attempts to achieve and maintain such a balance. The account I provide should be understood as a heuristic proposal rather than a history of their origins. In other words, I believe that my account offers a plausible interpretation of the workings of such systems in ways that the Blackstonian adage does not, even if the multitude of agents involved in the design and redesign of such systems did not consciously or continuously aim at achieving a balance between maximizing punishment of the guilty and minimizing punishment of the innocent. Nothing in my account should be taken to deny that improvements in such systems are needed. To the contrary, some contemporary criminal justice systems may be evolving in ways that place too much emphasis on punishment (and, indeed, overly harsh punishment) of the guilty at the expense of non-punishment of the innocent.

1. *Why Blackstone's Numbers Do Not Add Up*

Should we prefer to let ten guilty persons go free rather than punish one innocent one? The first thing to notice about this is what appears to be an implicit assumption about the crimes on the two sides of the comparison. We pretty emphatically should not prefer to let ten guilty murderers go free to mildly punishing one innocent person for receiving stolen goods. Though the innocent person will suffer from the unjust punishment, he or she will not suffer that much, and the crimes that will go unpunished are grave. Surely Blackstone's adage asks us to compare crimes (either left unpunished or punished wrongly) of roughly the same magnitude. So, the claim it appears to make is something more like this: It is better to let ten guilty offenders go free than to punish one innocent person for a similar offense.

It must be conceded that punishment of the innocent, especially for serious offenses, inflicts horrific wrongs on them. Not only do they suffer the public condemnation and stigma that attach to convictions for serious crimes, they will be deprived of their liberty, freedom of association, privacy, and many other things for as long as they serve out their sentences in prison. These are terrible losses, ones that cramp and truncate the lives of individuals, and they are undoubtedly made worse by the knowledge of those who endure them that they are entirely underserved. Once the innocent are released from prison, assuming that they are, their suffering is apt to continue in the form of social scorn, inability to find work, and the emotional scars inflicted by long years of confinement. Importantly, most of those wrongly punished will have loved ones and dependents who suffer along with them, not only as they are being punished but afterwards when gainful employment and social re-acceptance are hard to come by. The profound tragedies such cases represent should not in the least be gainsaid, even when they are the products of legal error rather than intentional wrongs inflicted by callous or reckless state officials.

Part of the allure of Blackstone's adage may come from the ease with which we imagine ourselves or others as the recipients of unjust punishment, and thus deprived of the exercise of moral and legal rights that we are normally entitled to. Such punishment is a paradigmatic case of the abuse of state power, and Blackstone's adage, if nothing else, captures in a vivid way the extreme caution that we want the state to employ in exercising its power. I do not dispute the need for such caution – in fact, I argue that some of the key features of contemporary criminal justice systems are grounded in it. Yet it is important to not lose sight of the fact that it is also terrible to be the victim of a serious crime. The harms such crimes inflict include loss of life, significant loss of physical or psychological function, loss of dignity, and the loss or destruction of property on which individuals depend for their future welfare. Even those victims who do not lose their lives may struggle for years to overcome the injuries they experience. In some cases, the quality of victims' lives is permanently diminished. Moreover, since most contemporary legal systems adjust the sanctions meted out to those found guilty of crimes according to the culpability with which they acted, there likely will be cases in which the perpetrators of such harms, even when punished proportionally with the seriousness of their offenses, do not suffer as much or for as long as do their victims. For instance, although the victims of manslaughter or negligent homicide will have lost their entire lives, those punished for inflicting such losses will retain theirs, cramped and truncated though they might be because of their having to endure punishment for some period of time. Also, crime victims will rarely suffer alone, since they will have loved ones or dependents who must endure the anguish and hardships of having individuals close to them deprived of their lives or physical or psychological welfare.

In some cases, victims and those who care about them will have to cope with the additional burden of having those who wronged them escape punishment altogether. That is, one suspects, a profound source of disappointment and despair for victims and their loved ones. Indeed, since Blackstone's adage invites us to compare persons wrongly punished with persons who wrongly escape it, we must, it seems, factor into our evaluation of the adage the additional anguish experienced by crime victims whose victimizers escape all punishment.

It is not apparent how we are to meaningfully compare the disvalue of individuals wrongly punished against the disvalue of criminal victimization. But supposing that we can make such comparisons, is it really plausible to believe that undeserved punishment, terrible as it is, is so bad that we should prefer to let ten offenders guilty of serious crimes go unpunished rather than inflict serious punishment on one innocent person? It is, I believe, difficult to make sense of such a claim on standard accounts of legal punishment's justifying aims. Consider retributive or desert-based theories, according to which legal punishment aims at sanctioning the guilty proportionately with their criminal ill deserts. It is fairly straightforward, on such theories, to explain why we should have a preference for letting one guilty person go free rather than punishing one innocent person, especially if we assume that the crimes on each side of the comparison are roughly equivalent. For retributivists, if an innocent person is punished for a crime, then two individuals do not get what they deserve – the innocent person punished and the actual culprit who is not punished.[5] If a person who is guilty of a crime is not punished, then only she does not get what she deserves. It would seem, other things being equal, that we should prefer the state of affairs where one person does not get what she deserves to one in which two people do not.[6] Or, if one prefers, we could say that the state of affairs involving one evil should be preferred to that involving two. It might be objected that when the guilty are not punished, then there are actually two people who do not get what they deserve – the guilty person and her victim (assuming there is one) who does not, as it is

[5] It is possible to imagine cases where a judge or jury convicts two people for a crime, believing them both guilty of involvement in it, where only one of them is, in fact, guilty. In that presumably rare case, only one injustice occurs, namely, punishment of the innocent person.

[6] It might be objected that this way of putting things gives retributivism too much of a consequentialist cast. But I do not see why retributivists should not be able to compare two states of affairs, judging one worse than the other, without thereby becoming full or even half-fledged consequentialists.

sometimes said, 'receive justice'. Although this is said of victims whose victimizers go unpunished, there do not appear to be two separate desert claims here, since both will be satisfied if the guilty person is punished. The victim's claim, if she has one, seems wholly derivative from the guilty person not getting what she deserves.

Important as the preceding point is, things are much less straightforward when we consider Blackstone's ten to one ratio. If ten guilty people go free, then ten do not get what they deserve, and it is hard to see how a retributivist would regard that as preferable to two people not getting what they deserve, as occurs in cases of punishment of the innocent. Are we to believe that being innocent and being punished is five times worse on some metric of desert than being guilty and not being punished, assuming, again, equivalent crimes on the two sides of the comparison? That seems a most unpromising position for a retributivist to defend. Things do not improve if we consider diminished versions of Blackstone's adage, according to which we should let five or three guilty persons go free rather than punish one innocent one. Indeed, it is not clear why letting even two guilty persons go free should be preferred, on grounds of desert, to punishing one innocent one.

This point appears to hold regardless of the kind of retributive theory in question. Competing retributive theories offer different accounts of why the state should punish the deserving, whether it is to deprive offenders of the unjust advantages they have gained,[7] nullify the false moral messages their crimes communicate,[8] censure offenders proportionally with the seriousness of their offenses,[9] or encourage them to develop a penitent understanding of their crimes.[10] On all of these theories, the state is implicated in two wrongs if it punishes the innocent, but only one if it fails to punish the guilty. Yet if it chooses to let ten or five or three guilty individuals go free rather than punish one innocent one, then it is implicated in

---

[7] See Herbert Morris, 'Persons and Punishment', *Monist* 52 (1968): 475-501; Jeffrie Murphy, 'Marxism and Retribution', *Philosophy and Public Affairs* 2 (1973): 217-43; Wojciech Sadurski, *Giving Desert its Due* (Dordrecht, Netherlands: D. Reidel, 1985); and George Sher, *Desert* (Princeton, NJ: Princeton University Press, 1987), pp. 69-90.

[8] See Jean Hampton, 'A New Theory of Retribution', in R.G. Frey and Christopher W. Morris (eds.), *Liability and Responsibility: Essays in Law and Morals* (Cambridge: Cambridge University Press, 1991), pp. 377-414, and Jami L. Anderson, 'Annulment Retributivism: A Hegelian Theory of Punishment', *Legal Theory* 5 (1999): 363-88.

[9] See Andrew von Hirsch, *Censure and Sanctions* (Oxford: Oxford University Press, 1993), and von Hirsch and Andrew Ashworth, *Proportionate Sentencing: Exploring the Principles* (Oxford: Oxford University Press, 2005).

[10] See R.A. Duff, *Trials and Punishments* (Cambridge: Cambridge University Press, 1986), and *Punishment, Communication, and Community* (Oxford: Oxford University Press, 2001).

ten or five or three wrongs, and it is hard to see how that is supposed to be better than its being implicated in two.

Crime reduction approaches to the justification of legal punishment can also make a persuasive case for preferring non-punishment of the guilty to punishment of the innocent. The burdens and costs of punishment of the innocent will usually be considerably greater than those of non-punishment of the guilty. When the innocent are punished, they and others who depend on them suffer (and suffer enormously if the punishment is severe), while the actually guilty person remains free to commit further crimes, which is obviously a potentially serious cost. There are some complications here for crime reductionists, since punishment of the innocent may have some marginal deterrent effects (as critics of the approach have long argued) and incapacitation effects if the person wrongly punished is prone to offending.[11] Still, the actually guilty person is the one who seems more likely to commit future crimes, other things being equal, and if he commits serious offenses, then the costs of his being free to do so will be quite substantial. With regard to the guilty who go unpunished, we cannot say that there are no negative consequences that result, especially if they go on to commit other serious offenses. However, as we have just seen, such negative consequences also exist when the innocent are punished. And those negative consequences are compounded by the sufferings of the innocent and those who depend on them, and by the burdens on the public of having to pay for the punishment of individuals who are less likely to commit further offenses. All of this seems sufficient to warrant a clear preference for letting one guilty person go unpunished to punishing one innocent person, at least if we assume, once again, that the crimes on both sides of the comparison are roughly the same.

Yet can the ten to one ratio expressed by Blackstone's adage be sustained on a crime reduction approach? There are, as we have seen, portents of difficulty even when we are comparing one innocent person being punished with one guilty person going unpunished. Punishment of the innocent is not always a pure loss with respect to deterrence or incapacitation.[12] Worse than this, punishment of the guilty may not reduce

[11] It will not work for crime reductionists to argue that the contribution to deterrence made by punishing an innocent person is marginal, since that is also true when a guilty individual is punished. It is, if anything, punishment in the aggregate that deters.

[12] This will especially be true in cases in which the police have focused their attention on individuals with past criminal records in their efforts to solve crimes. Such 'rounding up of the usual suspects' may result in the apprehension and punishment of individuals who

crime in the communities from when they came, and there are conceivable cases in which it will not make its marginal contribution to deterrence.[13] If this is not worrisome enough, it is clear that once we start adding to the number of guilty who are to go unpunished, the likelihood that some of them will go on to commit other serious crimes increases significantly. True, punishment of the innocent is a very bad thing, especially when it involves imprisonment, or worse, the loss of life. But again, being the victim of a serious crime is also a very bad thing, and presumably a worse thing when one's victimizer goes unpunished and one does not receive the satisfaction that justice has been done. To this we might add that victims in such cases will receive no restitution from those who victimized them, should that be an option. Worse still, some who have already been victimized may be victimized again by individuals who go unpunished and are thus not incapacitated, deterred or rehabilitated by punishment. In short, there seems little reason to believe that Blackstone's number ten strikes the optimal crime reduction balance, when all of the good and bad consequences of non-punishment of the guilty are weighed against those stemming from punishment of the innocent. And we might doubt whether a five or even three to one ratio could be sustained in the majority of cases.

In fairness to Blackstone and others who express the strong degree of preference, the ten to one ratio may have been more defensible in historical contexts in which the sanctions employed by the criminal justice system were uniformly harsh. If the only sanctions available to those convicted of felonies are the death penalty or lengthy prison terms, it might make sense to prefer to let a significant number of guilty people go free rather than punish one innocent one, especially if the guilty have committed only moderately serious offenses. The numerous injustices of the guilty going unpunished would then presumably not outweigh the enormous injustice of punishment of the innocent. Yet, as the crimes committed by the guilty become more severe, the number of them that we would prefer to allow to go unpunished would presumably dwindle. And this defense of a strong preference for non-punishment of the guilty to

---

are innocent of the crime in question but prone to offend. For discussion of this police practice and its effects on the innocent, see Richard O. Lempert, Samuel R. Gross and James S. Liebman, *A Modern Approach to Evidence Law* (St. Paul, MN: West, 3rd edn, 2000), pp. 327-28.

[13] On the tenuous relationship between incapacitation and crime reduction, see Franklin Zimring and Gordon Hawkins, *Incapacitation: Penal Confinement and the Restraint of Crime* (New York: Oxford University Press, 1995), pp. 43-56.

punishment of the innocent will have considerably less appeal in criminal justice systems that, like most of them in the world today, have scaled sentencing schemes according to which crimes are punished proportionately with their seriousness.

Instead of interpreting Blackstone's adage as a principle that any defensible theory of legal punishment must accommodate, we might attempt to cast it as a more general principle of morality. There has been vigorous debate about whether doing harm is worse than allowing it.[14] For the sake of argument, let us suppose that it is. It might then be claimed that what Blackstone's adage says is that it is considerably worse for the state to punish the innocent than for it to allow the guilty to go free. The former actively inflicts harm on innocent parties; the latter merely allows harm to go unpunished or otherwise unaddressed.

This way of defending Blackstone's adage is not very promising. Leave aside, for the moment, the plausible objection that inflicting harm is unlikely to be ten times, or even five times, worse than allowing it. Two other difficulties bring this defense of the adage to its knees. First, we should probably assume that the state agents in question neither intentionally punish the innocent nor intentionally let the guilty go free. When these things occur, they are, let us suppose, inadvertent.[15] State officials are simply adhering to rules of the legal system that foreseeably, though unhappily, produce such outcomes. But then not only is it unclear whether inadvertently causing harm is worse (let alone ten times worse) than inadvertently allowing it, it would have to be shown that we accurately characterize what state officials are doing when they inadvertently punish the innocent as 'harming' them. True, such officials impose losses on the innocent. Yet they do not act unjustifiably in doing so, at least if they act pursuant to their proper authority. Similarly, when they let the guilty go unpunished, it may not be clear in what sense they are 'allowing harm'. Second, state officials arguably have an affirmative obligation to track down and punish the guilty.[16] If they fail to fulfill that obligation, then

[14] See, among others, Samuel Scheffler, *The Rejection of Consequentialism* (Oxford: Clarendon Press, 1982); Shelly Kagan, *The Limits of Morality* (Oxford: Clarendon Press, 1992); and Phillipa Foot, 'The Problem of Abortion and the Doctrine of the Double Effect', reprinted in P. Foot, *Virtues and Vices* (Berkeley, CA: University of California Press, 1978).

[15] If they are not inadvertent – if state officials are actively attempting to frame and punish the innocent – then the problem that we face is a very different one and not, I would argue, the one referred to by those who invoke some version or other of Blackstone's adage.

[16] Jeffrey Reiman makes a similar point in the essay he co-authored with Ernest van den Haag, titled, 'On the Common Saying that it is Better that Ten Guilty Persons Escape

they are not in the same position as ordinary citizens who let harms occur when they could have prevented them.[17]

It might nonetheless be suspected that some weaker version of the ratio is defensible. Perhaps we should not prefer to let ten guilty murderers or rapists go free rather than punish one innocent person for murder or rape. But surely as the number of guilty who are to go unpunished decreases, we might at some point prefer that result to the severe punishment of an innocent person. More generally, does not Blackstone's adage capture something of significant import – namely, our sense that we should prefer not to bring every guilty person to justice if this means that, along the way, we must punish an unacceptably large number of innocent ones?

The latter way of putting things comes closer to the heart of the problem we face. In setting up and maintaining institutions of legal punishment, we know that we are creating some risk that innocent persons will occasionally become ensnared in them, despite our best efforts. What is misleading about the Blackstone ratio, and indeed about all attempts to revise the ratio, is that they make it seem as if we have a simple choice to make: How many guilty who go unpunished are equivalent to one innocent person being punished? Yet not only are we likely to be unsure about how to make such comparisons, this way of setting things up crucially ignores how probabilities will affect our evaluation of the relevant ratios. Should we prefer to let two guilty murderers go unpunished rather than punish one innocent person for murder? The answer might initially seem to be 'yes'. But once probabilities are introduced, things quickly become murkier. Suppose that the risk that the two guilty murderers will go unpunished is 95 percent, whereas the risk that one innocent person will be punished for murder is 0.05 percent. Is it still so clear that we should prefer risking letting the two murderers go unpunished to risking the punishment of one innocent person? It seems not. And yet the choice we face in designing and maintaining institutions of legal punishment is one involving just this sort of weighing and balancing of risks, ones the exact

---

Punishment than that One Innocent Suffer: Pro and Con', in Ellen Frankel Paul, Fred D. Miller, Jr. and Jeffrey Paul (eds.), *Crime, Culpability, and Remedy* (Oxford: Basil Blackwell, 1990), pp. 226-48, at 229.

[17] Vidar Halvorsen develops a version of this argument in 'Is it Better that Ten Guilty Persons Go Free than that One Innocent Person be Convicted?' *Criminal Justice Ethics* (2004): 3-13, at 11. Halvorsen employs an analogy in which one lifeguard drowns a person by holding his head under water, while another lifeguard simply allows a swimmer who is floundering in the water to drown. Halvorsen plausibly suggests that the former is worse than the latter. But his analogy seems flawed, since state officials presumably do not

magnitudes of which are likely unknown and perhaps unknowable. My hunch is that, at best, we will have to grapple with crude ballpark estimates of the figures on both sides of the comparison – how many guilty are going unpunished under an existing set of institutions and how serious are their crimes versus how many innocents are being convicted and for what kinds of offenses?[18] There are, as we have seen, powerful reasons involving justice and the reduction of suffering to see to it that the guilty are punished, especially when their crimes are serious. These justify us in giving state authorities ample resources to apprehend, try, and punish criminal wrongdoers. Against this we must weigh the risks created by the malfunctioning of such institutions or the misapplication of their operative rules and procedures. We might have some empirical data which will help us determine the success or failure of our institutions at managing both of these tasks, and we can modify the institutions in ways that seem likely to improve their performance. But it is their general tendencies, and thus the risks that they create both ways, that we can usefully attempt to evaluate. The application of fixed ratios of any kind are likely to be unhelpful in this task, because they suggest that it is known certainties that we must choose between rather than crude projections of probabilities.

2. *Balancing Scope and Accurate Sorting*

In the previous section, I argued that what we must attempt to do is balance the criminal justice system's tendency to capture and punish the guilty against its tendency to wrongly punish the innocent. In short, we want our institutions of criminal justice to maximize punishment of the guilty and minimize punishment of the innocent. In this section, I begin by suggesting that a useful way to think about criminal justice systems is in terms of their adherence to two imperatives that are potentially in conflict.

First, we want a criminal justice system to have sufficient scope, by which I mean that it must do a tolerably effective job of apprehending,

---

deliberately intend to punish the innocent, or allow the guilty to go free. Yet Halvorsen's lifeguards both deliberately intend the outcomes in their respective cases.

[18] For one attempt to estimate the wrongful conviction rate in the United States, see D. Michael Risinger, 'Innocents Convicted: An Empirically Justified Factual Wrongful Conviction Rate', *Journal of Criminal Law and Criminology* 97 (2007): 761-806. Interestingly, though Risinger believes that the wrongful conviction rate is too high, he does not offer an optimum rate, preferring instead to propose various suggestions about how to bring the rate down.

charging, convicting and punishing those individuals who are guilty of criminal offending. It might seem, at first glance, that it is crime reductionists who can most readily accept this imperative, as a criminal justice system's having sufficient scope will be crucial in its maintaining a credible deterrent effect and incapacitating those apt to commit further offenses. But retributivists also have an interest in the scope of criminal justice, since it will presumably be counted by them as a good thing if more rather than fewer offenders receive their just deserts, at least other things being equal. In that case, more rather than fewer offenders will have their unfair advantages taken from them or their false moral messages annulled. This concern with sufficient scope might be more pronounced when the crimes in question are serious ones. For retributivists, such crimes create greater injustices, whereas for crime reductionists, they cause victims more suffering and create greater burdens of various kinds for others. Moreover, the criminal justice system will inevitably have to compete with other institutions in society for scarce resources. We do not and should not pursue criminal justice come what may, but instead seek to balance its pursuit against, among other things, the need to maintain a common defense and provide citizens with education, health care, and eldercare. Hence we might want to modify the scope imperative accordingly, saying that we want the criminal justice system to punish more rather than fewer offenders, and especially the more serious ones.[19]

If the criminal justice system is to have sufficient scope, then certain individuals within it must be given the resources and authority to pursue offenders. We need police to apprehend suspects, investigators to gather evidence concerning their alleged crimes, prosecutors to charge and pursue adjudication of charges against individuals, and courts to which the charges and accumulated evidence can be presented. Importantly, it is the job of police, investigators, and prosecutors to get the ball rolling, so to speak, and, within limits, we do not and should not object if they provisionally regard and treat some individuals as likely guilty of having committed crimes. Such officials probably cannot do their jobs effectively if

[19] In fact, there is evidence that contemporary criminal justice systems do expend more resources on apprehending and punishing those who commit the more as opposed to less serious offenses. Offense clearance rates (that is, the rates at which law enforcement agencies arrest and prosecute at least one person for an offense) are considerably higher for violent personal crimes such as murder or aggravated assault than for property offenses such as larceny or burglary. See, for instance, the statistics on clearance rates in the United States cited by the Federal Bureau of Investigation at http://www.fbi.gov/ucr/cius_02/html/web/offcleared/03-NC.html.

they must refrain from such provisional judgments. The trick is to devise adjudicative procedures that rigorously test those judgments. For the second crucial thing we want the criminal justice system to do is to systematically sort the guilty from the innocent and punish the former in accordance with their crimes. Retributive support for this concern with accurate sorting is particularly strong – individuals are not treated in accordance with their deserts if they are punished when they are actually innocent, or not punished when they are actually guilty, or over or under-punished given the severity of their offenses. Crime reductionists have often been accused of giving accurate sorting less weight in specific cases, but it seems clear that, given the suffering and burdens legal punishment creates, they cannot generally be indifferent to the accuracy with which state authorities separate the guilty from the innocent and punish the former in accordance with their crimes.

It would be misleading to say that the scope and accurate sorting imperatives are necessarily in conflict with one another. The resources and authority that we grant state officials in the pursuit of criminal justice are not granted with an eye toward expanding the scope of punishment come what may. We do and obviously should encourage the relevant officials to investigate crimes carefully, look for and take seriously exonerating evidence in relation to given suspects, and to pursue cases only when it appears reasonably likely that they can secure convictions. It is, after all, the guilty who we want the authorities to apprehend and punish.[20] Doing so requires them to perform a delicate balancing act – ensuring that a sufficient number of serious offenders are apprehended and punished while at the same time attempting to preserve the accuracy of punishment. We could stipulate that they only investigate or charge individuals who they 'firmly believe' are guilty, or who they are 'fairly certain' are guilty. But this would hamstring them too much, at considerable cost to the scope of punishment. This means that the set of individuals investigated and charged will, in all likelihood, exceed by some considerable (and largely unknowable) margin the set of individuals who are actually guilty. We might be prepared to live with this if we have confidence in the accuracy with which our adjudicative procedures then separate the guilty from the innocent. The problem, I believe, is that we have powerful reasons for believing that they are not always successful, that achieving and maintaining the proper

20 Indeed, the resources that we give police and prosecutors will aid accurate sorting in a variety of ways. Police and prosecutors provided with adequate resources will presumably make fewer mistakes.

balance between scope and accurate sorting is chronically difficult. My conjecture is that we attempt to ensure that balance by structuring the adjudicative process in ways that appear to favor criminal defendants, and perhaps to strongly favor them.

Contemporary legal systems typically grant criminal defendants the presumption of innocence and require the state to establish their guilt to the exacting standard of 'beyond a reasonable doubt'. Following Larry Laudan, I interpret the former as directing judges or jurors to view defendants as if nothing has been established concerning their guilt simply by their having been charged with crimes.[21] The burden is on the state to prove their guilt and the standard of proof is stringent. That standard, which Laudan usefully abbreviates BARD, should be understood as requiring the state to not only provide clear and convincing evidence of a defendant's guilt but also discredit any evidenced alternative explanation for the crime that shows a defendant to be innocent.[22] The state need not rule out merely fanciful alternative explanations, but it must show evidenced ones to be implausible. If it does not, then defendants should be found innocent (which is not to say, of course, that they are materially innocent).[23]

To see just how defendant-friendly this combination of the burden and standard of proof is, contrast it with five other possible combinations of the two:

(1) Defendants have a presumption of guilt that they must rebut with evidence convincing beyond a reasonable doubt.
(2) Defendants have a presumption of guilt that they must rebut with evidence that is clear and convincing.
(3) Defendants have a presumption of guilt that they must rebut with a preponderance of evidence.
(4) Defendants have a presumption of innocence that the state must rebut with a preponderance of evidence.
(5) Defendants have a presumption of innocence that the state must rebut with clear and convincing evidence.

Understanding the presumption of guilt is fairly straightforward. Defendants have the presumption of guilt if their merely being charged with

[21] Laudan, *Truth, Error, and Criminal Law*, p. 94.

[22] Here I draw on both Laudan's *Truth, Error, and Criminal Law*, pp. 82-83, and Alex Stein's *Foundations of Evidence Law* (Oxford: Oxford University Press, 2005), pp. 178-79.

[23] Laudan usefully distinguishes defendants' 'material innocence', or lack thereof, from their 'probative innocence', that is, the failure of the prosecution to establish their guilt BARD. See *Truth, Error, and Criminal Law*, p. 96.

crimes is taken to provisionally establish their guilt. This is consistent with the presumption's being rebuttable. The alternative standards of proof require more explanation. On probabilistic accounts, BARD is met if evidence is presented showing that a conclusion of guilt is true at a level of at least 90 percent probability. The clear and convincing evidence standard (which Laudan abbreviates CACE) is met if the evidence shows a conclusion to be true at a level of at least 75 percent probability. The weakest standard, a preponderance of evidence (which Laudan abbreviates PoE), requires only that the evidence show a conclusion to be true at a level of 51 percent probability. There is debate about whether these probabilistic accounts are perspicacious.[24] Hence, we might prefer ones that emphasize the quality of evidence in addition to (or in place of) its quantity. BARD was explicated along these lines previously. It tells us that we should regard a conclusion regarding a defendant's conduct as true if the evidence for that conclusion is clear and convincing and alternative evidenced explanations of the defendant's conduct have been discredited. The PoE standard, by contrast, warrants our drawing a conclusion if there are more reasons for it than against it, or perhaps if there are stronger reasons for it than against it. The CACE standard is somewhere in between PoE and BARD. I will interpret it as warranting the drawing of a conclusion if there are considerably more reasons for it than against it, or if there are considerably stronger reasons for it than against it.

Especially when contrasted with the first two combinations, the combination of a presumption of innocence for defendants and imposition of the BARD standard on the state appears enormously favorable to defendants. It might therefore seem that the way in which the criminal justice system is structured makes little sense in the absence of something like a Blackstonian strong degree of preference for non-punishment of the guilty to punishment of the innocent. In particular, we might wonder why the fifth combination, involving a presumption of innocence for defendants and imposition of the CACE standard of proof on the state, is not sufficient to protect most innocent defendants. Is not the insistence on BARD overkill, particularly in the absence of a strong aversion to punishing the innocent? Moreover, there are other features of many contemporary criminal justice systems that seem to strongly favor defendants. There are various exclusionary rules concerning probative evidence, which is thus kept from judges or juries because it is thought too prejudicial to defendants or

---

[24] See Laudan, *Truth, Error, and Criminal Law*, pp. 44-47, and Stein, *Foundations of Evidence Law*, p. 178.

improperly attained by state authorities. There are testimonial privileges that prevent witnesses with various kinds of relationships with defendants from testifying against them, in spite of their having damning evidence against such defendants.[25] And so on. How can we make sense of all of this if not in terms of the Blackstone ratio, or something close to it?

The answer, I contend, is that we recognize (implicitly, if not explicitly) that the resources and authority we grant state officials in order to pursue and prosecute offenders, and the motivations that their occupations engender, tend to favor expanded scope over accurate sorting. In the first place, when prosecutors level charges against defendants, especially in cases where the offenses alleged are serious ones, the effect is powerfully stigmatizing. Regardless of the fact that under most contemporary criminal justice systems there is an official presumption of innocence for criminal defendants, solemn public accusation arguably undermines – or worse, rebuts – that presumption. For one thing, it is natural to assume that prosecutors would not level charges if they did not have substantial evidence demonstrating the guilt of those accused. For another, prosecutors, in announcing charges, rarely cite the presumption of innocence. Instead, they typically seek to convey their utter confidence that they 'have the goods' on the accused. In part, they no doubt do this to assure the public that they are not wasting time or resources on frivolous prosecutions. But there seems little doubt that part of what they also seek to do is convince the public that establishing the defendant's guilt is a mere formality (which is something that prosecutors may actually believe, of course). It is defense attorneys who must remind the public that the accused are innocent until proven guilty. Yet defense attorneys, in most cases, seem at a decided rhetorical disadvantage compared to prosecutors. Defense attorneys are hired by the accused to represent them, so of course they must say that their clients are innocent. Unlike prosecutors, who represent the public and are public employees who are trusted with authority and surrounded by the aura of it, defense attorneys are apt to be seen as little more than hired guns.

It might be objected that the preceding amounts to little more than speculation unsupported by empirical evidence. Moreover, we might hope that the judges or juries who actually decide the guilt or innocence of defendants do take the presumption of innocence more seriously than do members of the general public, even assuming that most members of

---

[25] For an overview of these procedural and evidentiary rules, see Laudan, *Truth, Error, and Criminal Law*, pp. 136-37.

the public do not do so. But in the first place, jurors are drawn from the general public, and though they may try to set aside their beliefs about accused individuals as they decide guilt or innocence in particular cases, we might reasonably worry about how successful they will be at doing so. There is, in fact, evidence from those who study juries suggesting that many jurors do not really understand or accept the presumption of innocence. A substantial proportion of them instead appear to believe that defendants are guilty until proven innocent.[26] Are judges apt to do better in this regard? Perhaps, but their greater familiarity with the criminal justice system will inform them that most accused individuals are guilty and most who go to trial will be convicted.[27] In addition, as we will see, there are other pressures and constraints on judges that might in various ways work to undermine their willingness to see to it that the state meets its strong burden of proof in criminal cases.

The stigmatizing effect of public accusation may be sufficient, all by itself, to explain and justify our insistence on the presumption of innocence for criminal defendants. The laying of charges against individuals makes their conviction more likely, regardless of their actual guilt or innocence. We therefore reasonably seek to counterbalance its impact in order to enhance accurate sorting. Unfortunately, the presumption of innocence's impact in this regard may be less that what we would hope for. But our aim in insisting upon it is arguably not to thereby bring the criminal justice system in line with Blackstone's ratio, or anything like it. Instead, our aim is to slow the rush to adverse judgments against innocent defendants that might otherwise occur with more frequency. This is consistent, I would maintain, with our steadfastly wanting the criminal justice system to convict the guilty.

Secondly, in their efforts to apprehend and punish the guilty, prosecutors have formidable resources at their disposal, ones that are apt to exceed, by some considerable margin, the ones most defendants can call

26 See Mitchell J. Frank and Dawn Borschard, 'The Silent Criminal Defendant and the Presumption of Innocence: In the Hands of Real Jurors, is Either of Them Safe?' *Lewis & Clark Law Review* 10 (2006): 237-85, at 249-51, and Keith A. Findley and Michael S. Scott, 'The Multiple Dimensions of Tunnel Vision in Criminal Cases', *Wisconsin Law Review* (2006): 291-397, at 340-341.

27 Findley and Scott make this point in relation to prosecutors, but the same presumably holds in relation to trial judges. See 'The Multiple Dimensions of Tunnel Vision', p. 330. Moreover, as Thom Brooks points out, judges will in some cases have had access to evidence that juries are denied – evidence that though it is inadmissible, strongly suggests the defendant's guilt. Brooks questions whether judges will be able to put such evidence out of their minds in rendering verdicts. See his 'The Right to Trial by Jury', *Journal of Applied Philosophy* 21 (2004): 197-212, at 200-201.

upon.[28] Prosecutors have the police force to investigate crimes and uncover evidence and typically have numerous assistants to which they can delegate various tasks. Granted, these are far from unlimited resources, and prosecutors may find themselves beleaguered by caseloads that they can reduce only by resorting to plea agreements with defendants or their attorneys. But it still is the case that relatively few defendants will be able to hire and retain counsel who (with assistance) spend long hours investigating charges, filing motions to challenge evidence, or preparing elaborate trial defenses. Moreover, the relative edge most prosecutors have is enhanced by their ability to employ various tactics to motivate witnesses to testify or otherwise provide evidence against defendants. Prosecutors can strike plea agreements with some defendants to secure their help in building cases against other defendants. Or they can threaten to prosecute or agree to drop charges against individuals to gain their compliance in the prosecution of charges against others. Defense attorneys have no comparable resources at their disposal, though they can attempt to impeach the testimony of witnesses (which prosecutors can likewise do with defense witnesses) or challenge the admissibility of evidence.

Thirdly, prosecutors will often have an edge in the expertise they bring to bear on cases. Not only are they dedicated professionals, but all they do is prosecute criminal cases. We should assume that they become quite adept at this, experienced in the intricacies of criminal procedure and thoroughly familiar with the tactics they must employ to achieve convictions on those (rare as it turns out) occasions in which they go to trial. Moreover, if they are good at what they do, they will no doubt build up some respect and good will from the judges before whom they try cases. This is not to suggest that judges will be partial to prosecutors, but only to say that they will often be familiar with them and perhaps somewhat disposed to give them the benefit of the doubt when difficult decisions must be made. Of course, there may be judges who do not like or trust prosecutors, or who bend over backwards to not let their familiarity with and respect for prosecutors cloud their judgment. But as we will see, judges too have incentives to not be too hard on prosecutors. By contrast, it is reasonable to believe that defense attorneys will be a decidedly more mixed lot when it comes to their expertise in criminal cases, especially

[28] One recent estimate of US expenditures on policing and prosecuting crimes puts the figure at about $90 billion per year. Of course, that enormous sum must be spread over thousands if not hundreds of thousands of cases. Still, it is an impressive amount. See David A. Anderson, 'The Aggregate Burden of Crime', *Journal of Law and Economics* 42 (1999): 611-42.

when they are appointed to serve indigent clients. They may also be less well-known to the judges before whom they must bring motions, and this may work to their disadvantage. Only when defendants are able to hire and compensate adequately local, experienced criminal defense lawyers will the advantages prosecutors tend to have in this regard be effectively counterbalanced.

Fourthly, and quite importantly, police and prosecutors will often have more potent incentives to amass convictions than to do justice – to value the scope of the criminal justice over its accuracy.[29] They will know that their perceived success (and the many benefits that go with it) crucially depends on their achieving convictions. Their failures to catch and punish the guilty will tend to loom larger than their failures to separate accurately the guilty from the innocent or punish the former for the crimes that they have actually committed. Granted, there will be occasional cases in which individuals who have been found guilty are subsequently exonerated. Even in such cases, however, the public may not blame police or prosecutors for miscarriages of justice. And most of those wrongly convicted will be presumed guilty and quickly forgotten. By contrast, failures to arrest or convict anyone, especially when the crimes in question are serious ones, will not be as quickly forgotten by the public or crime victims. It is hardly surprising, then, that police and prosecutors tout their arrest and conviction records. Not only do they have nothing to gain by publicizing their failures, they have little to gain by publicizing their decisions to drop or not pursue charges, even though in some of these cases they will be doing precisely what we want them to do from the standpoint of accurate sorting.

Many defense attorneys, by contrast, lack comparable incentives to mount elaborate defenses of their clients. Not only will many of them be court appointed or have clients of modest means, but most of them will rightly suspect that the vast majority of their clients are either guilty or likely to be found guilty should they go to trial.[30] This means that many defense attorneys will not be motivated to probe the prosecution's case very deeply or rigorously, preferring instead to encourage their clients to strike plea agreements.

---

[29] See Findley and Scott, 'The Multiple Dimensions of Tunnel Vision', pp. 323-27, who argue that police often jump to conclusions about the guilt of suspects and then, unwittingly in many cases, ignore exculpatory evidence or evidence pointing to other suspects. See also p. 328, where they discuss the tendency for prosecutors to adopt a 'conviction psychology'.

[30] Findley and Scott, 'The Multiple Dimensions of Tunnel Vision', p. 331.

Fifthly, as I have already hinted, judges in criminal cases may also act in ways that subtly give the state some advantage in the prosecution of crimes. They may be vulnerable to political pressure, especially in jurisdictions in which they are directly elected.[31] Even appointed judges might be wary of being perceived as 'soft on crime'. Though some judges might be relatively indifferent to public perceptions of their conduct, it seems unlikely that they would have wound up on the bench in the first place if they were political radicals inclined to question the prevailing status quo when it comes to matters of criminal justice. As a result, they might not worry too much about the inadequate defenses often received by the accused, and they seem unlikely to tolerate for long efforts by defense attorneys to exonerate their clients based on evidence or testimony concerning the pervasive structural inequalities that we have good reason to believe precipitate much criminal activity.[32] Most judges will instead enforce existing procedural and evidentiary rules designed to keep trials focused on the narrow question of whether defendants committed the offenses with which they are charged, thereby eschewing questions about why they acted as they did. Yet it seems clear that the implicit exoneration of the political and economic status quo in criminal cases works to the state's advantage, since it effectively eliminates issues that might otherwise complicate determinations of guilt or innocence in criminal cases. This will especially be true in countries such as the United States where criminal responsibility for actions is generally all-or-nothing, and thus where defenses of diminished responsibility are more the exception than the rule.[33]

There may be other features of contemporary criminal justice systems that work in the state's favor, but my view is that the preceding list of state

---

31 See Brooks, 'The Right to Trial by Jury', p. 203.

32 Evidence for the claim that judges are not overly concerned by the quality of defense received by criminal defendants in many cases is, admittedly, indirect. In the United States, there is considerable evidence of gaping holes in the indigent defense system. Given that the majority of defendants are indigent, and that their cases are more or less routinely processed by the courts, it certainly does not seem likely that judges are closely scrutinizing the legal representation that such defendants receive. Efforts to do so would clog the courts in ways that would quickly come to be regarded as intolerable. On the state of the indigent defense system, see Mary Sue Backus and Paul Marcus, 'The Right to Counsel in Criminal Cases, A National Crisis', *Hastings Law Journal* 57 (2006): 1031-1130.

33 For discussion of how the criminal law in the United States is binary in character, and thus generally hostile to claims of partial or diminished responsibility, see Stephen Morse, 'Deprivation and Desert', in William C. Heffernan and John Kleinig (eds.), *From Social Justice to Criminal Justice: Poverty and the Administration of the Criminal Law* (New York: Oxford University Press, 2000), pp. 114-60, at 144.

advantages in public perception, expertise, resources, and incentives to convict is enough to justify our burdening it with a stringent standard of proof in criminal cases.[34] If we did not do so, we might well find ourselves with a criminal justice system that had impressive scope but insufficient accurate sorting – both in terms of separating the guilty from the innocent and convicting the latter of the crimes that they actually committed. Since it is easier to see how conviction of the innocent would occur in systems without the presumption of innocence and a stringent burden of proof on the state than it is to see how inaccurate sorting of the other kind might result, it is worth pausing to explain this.

Consider what might happen if we required the state to only prove a defendant's guilt by a preponderance of the evidence. The state would then have to demonstrate that there were more reasons to believe the defendant guilty of the crime with which she is charged than to believe her innocent. Alternatively, the state would have to only show that there were stronger reasons to judge her guilty than there were to judge her innocent. Now, suppose that though a defendant is charged with second-degree murder, she is really only guilty of manslaughter under the law. With PoE as the standard of proof, the state may well succeed in convincing a judge or jury of her guilt on the more serious charge. After all, there might be some reasons to believe her guilty of the more serious charge, and enough of them to outweigh the ones suggesting otherwise. By contrast, if BARD is used, the greater weight of reasons for believing the defendant guilty rather than innocent should not suffice to convict her. Simply put, BARD's higher requirements force prosecutors to match the charges they file against individuals more closely to the evidence that they can muster. Over the long run, this means that BARD will produce more accurate linkages between convictions and what guilty individuals have actually done.[35]

---

[34] Keith Findley and Michael Scott argue that numerous other procedural rules in criminal cases, as well as common judicial practices, work to the state's advantage in convicting defendants and making such convictions stick. For instance, appellate judges are generally reluctant to scrutinize judgments of fact made by trial courts. This means that the vast majority of convictions will be upheld unless there is some procedural or constitutional defect in the trials that produced them. Findley and Scott contend that in the rare cases in which judges do scrutinize the factual basis for convictions, they are apt to affirm the trial court decision in the absence of glaringly bad decisions by the judge or jury. In addition, many jurisdictions impose severe restrictions on the introduction of new evidence during appeals, even where that evidence casts substantial doubt on the guilt of those convicted. Yet such restrictions systematically work against accurate sorting in some cases. See Findley and Scott, 'The Multiple Dimensions of Tunnel Vision', pp. 348-49.

[35] Nonetheless, it must be conceded that, in some cases, given the higher standard of proof BARD represents, prosecutors will be forced to forego or drop charges for which they

Still, the preceding arguments might be deemed insufficient to account for employment of the BARD rather than the CACE standard. Since CACE likewise requires the state to meet a high burden of proof, it might be argued that our choice of the BARD standard does betray a strong degree of preference for non-punishment of the guilty over punishment of the innocent. However, I am not convinced that such a preference is why we prefer BARD to CACE. For one thing, it is not clear whether the CACE standard would require prosecutors to rebut alternative, evidenced explanations of the events in question that exonerate defendants in the way that BARD does, on my interpretation. Though the differences between CACE and BARD appear none too precise, it might be that the former would be satisfied if the state presented many more (or stronger) reasons for believing defendants guilty than believing them not guilty, whereas BARD more positively demands the refutation of evidenced alternative accounts of what happened when they appear to exonerate defendants. Beyond this, a further reason for preferring BARD to CACE cites the possibility of misuse or abuse of the resources and authority we give police and prosecutors to investigate crimes and bring charges against citizens. The powers that we bestow on such officials are profoundly worrisome, even if they are used properly. Not only is the potential for misuse or abuse of such powers always present, we have considerable evidence that this potential is realized on numerous occasions. Sometimes state officials are simply incompetent at or relatively indifferent about discovering the truth in criminal cases. At other times, their actions evince corruption or more active malevolence. The catalogue of official sins is both familiar and disturbingly lengthy: The police focus prematurely on one suspect to the exclusion of other equally suspicious ones. They ignore exculpatory evidence in relation to their target suspect, or worse, destroy it. In what we hope are rare cases, they plant incriminating evidence on suspects or in their homes or automobiles. They pressure suspects to confess during interrogation and witnesses to implicate the suspects who are deemed guilty of the crime in question. For their part, prosecutors might not properly vet the evidence that they are given by the police. Prosecutors may also withhold exculpatory evidence from defense attorneys. Sometimes

believe the evidence is weak, even though the defendants in question are, in fact, guilty of the charges. A weaker standard of proof, by contrast, would enable prosecutors to go forward with and gain convictions on more charges. It may be that we assume (or hope) that the number of cases in which mistaken punishment of the innocent is averted by our having the higher standard is greater than the number of cases in which mistaken non-punishment of the guilty occurs.

prosecutors offer attractive plea bargains to defendants who they know to be equally if not more guilty of the crime in question in order to induce them to testify against other defendants. Worse than this, they offer sentence reductions to jailhouse snitches to provide testimony against defendants when they should strongly suspect their witnesses of lying to advance their own interests. Prosecutors may also pursue more serious charges against defendants than the evidence supports to advance their political careers or to pursue personal vendettas.[36]

One of the things that the BARD standard gives us is an extra measure of protection against such misuses and abuses of power, thereby ensuring more accurate sorting. Granted, even the BARD standard cannot prevent the most extreme abuses of the authority and resources that we grant state officials in the investigation and prosecution of crimes. If those officials are bent on framing the innocent, there is probably nothing we can do to prevent them from succeeding. But insistence on the BARD standard can be construed as a strategy to reduce the frequency of the more mundane misuses and abuses of power by state officials.

Blackstone no doubt recognized the potential for such miscarriages of justice, living in a time in which there were fewer procedural protections for criminal defendants and more awful sanctions awaiting those convicted. Perhaps he can therefore be pardoned for his rhetorical overkill – his exaggeration of our preference for non-punishment of the guilty to punishment of the innocent. Nonetheless, things have not changed so much since Blackstone's era that we can comfortably drop our guard and accept the lower burden of proof that the CACE standard represents.[37] Given the powerful stigmatizing effects of legal punishment and the significant losses and deprivations it doles out in cases of serious offenses, insistence on the presumption of innocence and the BARD standard puts us in a position to say truthfully to those innocents who are convicted that we have done our best to set things up so that this injustice did not befall them.

---

[36] For a vivid illustration of many of the ways in which police and prosecutors can go off the rails in criminal cases, with devastating results, see John Grisham's nonfiction work *The Innocent Man: Murder and Injustice in a Small Town* (New York: Doubleday, 2006).

[37] It might be suggested that we should ease off on the BARD standard in trials for minor criminal offenses, employing CACE instead, since the consequences of inaccuracy in either of its two forms in such cases will not be as profound. True enough, though I do not believe that the distinction between major and minor offenses should be understood to correspond with that between felonies and misdemeanors. Misdemeanor convictions are sometimes punished with jail sentences of up to one year, which is a substantial imposition by any reasonable standard.

Indeed, were we to accept and act on Blackstone's ten to one ratio, I believe that we would have to do much more than stubbornly insist on the presumption of innocence for charged defendants and adherence to the BARD standard. If we literally preferred to let ten murderers, rapists, or thieves go unpunished rather than wrongly punish one innocent person for such crimes, then the sensible thing to do would be to starve police and prosecutors of the resources that they need to successfully pursue and punish serious offenders. Blackstone's ratio would surely be more consistent with a considerably weakened state criminal justice apparatus, one that was calculated to let many serious offenders go unmolested so that no innocent individuals would be mistakenly punished. The resources and authority that we grant criminal justice officials make more sense on the assumption that we are not prepared to tolerate such lax enforcement of important legal standards. Hence we grant state officials such powers, realizing the risks that they create, and attempt to counter those risks with various legal protections designed to minimize punishment of the innocent.

3. *Objections and Replies*

As already noted, many contemporary criminal justice systems also have other seemingly defendant-friendly features – rules excluding certain kinds of probative evidence or exempting certain witnesses from testifying against defendants. It might be suggested that these other features, when combined with the presumption of innocence and the BARD requirement, make sense only if our legal system is designed to express a strong preference for non-punishment of the guilty over punishment of the innocent.

In response, I would point out that some of these further features of contemporary criminal justice systems may instead be predicated on our desire to render the pursuit of criminal justice consistent with other important values. This is probably true with exclusionary rules concerning illegally obtained evidence – by which we attempt to ensure that police powers do not intrude illegitimately upon the privacy of citizens. And it is arguably true with regard to rules exempting certain individuals from testifying against defendants – by which we attempt to balance the pursuit of criminal justice against the preservation of certain crucial types of relationships among individuals.[38] With regard to other procedural or

[38] Though see Laudan's criticisms of such exclusionary and testimonial rules in *Truth, Error, and Criminal Law*, pp. 213-33.

evidentiary rules, I would argue that they should be considered on a case-by-case basis in order to determine whether or how they affect the balance of scope versus accurate sorting. My claim is not that all of the current procedural and evidentiary rules are equally important in helping to maintain the appropriate balance between the two. Instead, I have defended the more limited claim that the two most salient features of contemporary criminal justice systems need not be understood as grounded in a strong preference for non-punishment of the guilty to punishment of the innocent.

It might also be objected that my account of what we are attempting to achieve with the presumption of innocence and the BARD standard depends in crucial ways on a number of contingent claims about how the authority and resources that we grant criminal justice officials tend to play out. But what if they played out very differently? More specifically, what if we were convinced that state officials no longer possessed an edge in public image, resources, expertise, and motivation? Would it not follow that, based on my account, we would have to consider altering either the presumption of innocence or the BARD standard? And is it not pretty clear that we ought to reject doing so, precisely because the combination of the two expresses an appropriately strong degree of preference for non-punishment of the guilty to punishment of the innocent?

Although I believe that it is unlikely that the state's many advantages in criminal cases will be absent in most real-world contexts, it is possible to imagine scenarios where they would be. Suppose that we found ourselves living in a society the government of which had very weak legitimacy. When individuals were charged with crimes, the stock response of the citizenry was shock and skepticism, rather than the suspicion that those charged were guilty. Suppose also that police and prosecutors were provided so few resources that their abilities to arrest and bring to trial even those guilty of the most heinous offenses were badly compromised. Suppose also that when prosecutors did manage to charge and try individuals, they inevitably found themselves up against suspects who were very ably defended and whose attorneys were given wide leeway by judges to introduce exonerating social circumstances at their trials. And suppose, finally, that the general distrust of the public toward the state extended to the jury box, which was thus populated by individuals who would acquit unless the case presented against defendants was overwhelmingly convincing. In circumstances such as these, we would expect the scope of the criminal justice system to be quite limited. It would not often convict the innocent, but that is because it would not often convict anyone. Would it, then, be reasonable for us to consider altering the structure of the criminal justice system, by denying defendants the presumption of innocence or lowering the burden of proof on the state, or both?

I believe that it might be, though given the apparent indifference of the citizens in the society just sketched to the existence of serious criminal offending in their midst, we might doubt the feasibility of such alterations. Attempts to saddle defendants with a presumption of guilt would likely be rendered moot by the general skepticism among citizens toward the state – just as in our own very different circumstances, the presumption of innocence is dealt a severe blow by the stigmatizing effects of public accusation. Also, a weakened burden of proof on the state would probably excite even greater distrust in a citizenry inclined to regard the actions of state officials with suspicion. Officials in such a hypothetical society would probably do better to consider alternative ways of expanding the scope of punishment.

The important point is that our preference for a presumption of innocence combined with a strong burden of proof on the state would be far from ideal in such circumstances. All that this shows, I believe, is that our preferred way of doing things presupposes a very different set of background conditions, ones that are much more often the norm in existing societies. In fact, a persuasive case can be made for the view that recent statutory changes and court rulings have expanded the powers of prosecutors in alarming ways, ones that tend to promote the scope of criminal justice without sufficient regard for its accuracy.[39] But such claims involve complex assessments of the tendencies of state powers and how these tendencies interact with procedural and evidentiary rules designed to protect criminal defendants, especially innocent ones. There is, of course, room for reasonable disagreement about the risks – of non-punishment of the guilty and punishment of the innocent – that modifications in existing rules and practices would create. But my view is that we do and ought to care about both kinds of risk and thus seek a balance between them.

When push comes to shove, someone might ask, should we not prefer one set of institutional arrangements over another if the two give us equal scope and the former gives us somewhat more accuracy? Of course we should. Should we continue to prefer the first set over the second if the first gives us slightly less scope but somewhat more accuracy? Perhaps. But what if the first set gives us significantly less scope combined with

---

[39] See Bennett Gershman, 'The New Prosecutors', *University of Pittsburgh Law Review* 53 (1992): 393-458.

somewhat greater accuracy? Then what? Those who subscribe to Blackstone's adage, or something like it, would apparently see this as an easy call: The first set of arrangements is to be preferred. I am not so sure. Much depends on how serious the crimes are that would go unpunished under the first set of arrangements, and how much more accuracy it would provide us. Again, my contention is that it is an elusive balance that we seek, one whereby we maximize punishment of serious offenders and minimize punishment of the innocent for serious crimes. Beyond that, I am not certain that anything more precise can be stated or defended.

'WHO'S STILL STANDING?' A COMMENT ON ANTONY DUFF'S PRECONDITIONS OF CRIMINAL LIABILITY

Matt Matravers*

Abstract

Antony Duff has argued that an important precondition of criminal liability is that the state has the moral standing to call the offender to account. Conditions of severe social injustice, if allowed or perpetuated by the state, can undermine this standing. Duff's argument appeals to the ordinary idea that a person's own behaviour can sometimes negate his standing to call others to account. It is argued that this is an important issue, but that the analogy with individual standing is problematic. Moreover, Duff's account of standing needs to address two interconnected issues: first, when and in what way the state can lose its standing to call offenders to account, and second, over what range of offences.

Keywords

criminal liability, Duff, punishment, social injustice

One of the traditional concerns of legal philosophy is whether law that emanates from an unjust state is really law at all, and so does or does not command obedience (or, perhaps, require disobedience). Such debates often take the form of asking whether Nazi laws, or the laws of Apartheid South Africa, are laws and ought to be obeyed. As part of these discussions, the issue of whether punishment can be justly applied in such conditions arises, but only as a subsidiary of the main issue.

In contrast, contemporary penal philosophers have in general not been much concerned with the consequences of general injustice for their 'ideal' theories of just punishment. The topic seems to surface once in a

* This paper was first given at a conference on punishment at Newcastle organized by Thom Brooks. I am grateful to Thom both for the invitation and for his comments on the paper. I am also grateful to Antony Duff and to the other participants for their searching comments.

while, but it fails to command widespread attention. There are exceptions, though. Jeffrie Murphy's 'Marxism and Retribution'—a paper that is strangely titled given that almost the only connection with Marxism contained within it is in Murphy's use of the work of a self-avowed Marxist, Willem Bonger—argues forcefully for the relevance of distributive injustice for so-called 'fair play' theories of punishment.[1] More recently, Antony Duff has raised the issue in *Trials and Punishments*; *Punishment, Communication, and Community*; and in a number of papers, and it is with his arguments that this paper is concerned.[2]

1. *Duff on the Consequences of Distributive Injustice for Penal Justice*

Antony Duff has developed and defended an account of punishment as moral communication. Ideally, the communication induces penitential repentance in the offender, and penal hard treatment provides a vehicle for that penance.[3] Such an account, of course, depends on conceiving of the state as a fairly rich moral community. It also depends on the state being in a legitimate position to 'speak'—to communicate censure based on reasons to the offender—and on the offender being in a position to 'hear' and understand the reasons for the censure.

In *Trials and Punishments*, Duff offered a rather gloomy prognosis for penal justice in present circumstances. The problems he identified included the absence of genuine moral communities, deficiencies in the trial process, and the dire state of penal institutions. The cumulative effect of these problems was, in Duff's view, such that our community (and, by extension, those like it) could not convey the proper message in punishment; even if it could, it could not sensibly expect the offender to hear the message; and even if both of those things could be addressed, the community did not provide means of punishment that would

[1] Jeffrie Murphy, 'Marxism and Retribution', *Philosophy and Public Affairs* 2 (1973), pp. 217–43.

[2] Antony Duff, *Trials and Punishments* (Cambridge: Cambridge University Press, 1986), ch. 10; *Punishment, Communication, and Community* (New York: Oxford University Press, 2001); 'Who is Responsible, for What, to Whom?', *Ohio State Journal of Criminal Law* 2 (2004), pp. 441–61; '"I Might Be Guilty, But You Can't Try Me": Estoppel and Other Bars to Trial', *Ohio State Journal of Criminal Law* 1 (2003), pp. 245–59; 'Answering for Crime', *Proceedings of the Aristotelian Society* CVI (2005), pp. 85–111. I have also discussed the problem in the context of a general theory of the justification of punishment—Matravers, *Justice and Punishment: The Rationale of Coercion* (Oxford: Oxford University Press, 2000), but here I want to focus on Duff's account.

[3] Duff, *Punishment, Communication, and Community*.

enable the criminal 'to repent his crime and to redeem himself'.[4] Duff's conclusion was that 'we should…look back to a deterrent system of punishment'[5] as the only one capable of communicating *reasons* to criminals and potential criminals. These would be prudential rather than moral reasons, and so the system would not be ideal, but at least a scheme based on deterrence would treat the offender as a reasoning being.

By the time of *Punishment, Communication, and Community*, some of Duff's gloom had lifted and the account given there is generally more upbeat.[6] The reasons for this seem to be both negative and positive. On the negative side, Duff is more impressed with the objections to a deterrence system than he was in the earlier book.[7] On the positive, Duff seems to think that more good will be achieved by sticking with the ideal system of punishment as a goal, and working incrementally towards it, than by substituting an entirely different, second-best, rationale for punishment.

In addition, *Punishment, Communication, and Community* also introduces an important distinction that Duff has used to discuss the problem of doing penal justice in conditions of injustice. 'A normative theory of punishment', Duff writes, must identify 'the conditions given which the punishment of a particular offender or the punishments imposed by a particular system are justified'. However, it also needs to do more than this: it needs to identify the *preconditions* of just punishment. That is, the 'conditions that must be satisfied before we can engage in this practice [the practice of just punishment] and before we can discuss the legitimacy of particular actions taken or policies pursued within the practice'.[8]

Duff considers a number of preconditions of criminal liability, but the one upon which I want to concentrate is that those who call the alleged criminal to account must have the *standing* so to do. This issue is critical for Duff given his communicative, penance-based, justification of punishment. Nevertheless, one need not accept all of Duff's wider theory for the issue to bite. At a minimum, one must think that to be held criminally responsible is (at least in part) to be held *answerable* and that the criminal trial is (again, at least in part) a forum in which the alleged offender is challenged to answer for his alleged offences. However, since these are fairly minimal claims, and since Duff has provided compelling evidence for them, there are no reasons not to accept them.

---

4 Duff, *Trials and Punishments*, p. 292.

5 Duff, *Trials and Punishments*, p. 298.

6 See particularly ch. 5.

7 Duff, *Punishment, Communication, and Community*, p. 178.

8 Duff, *Punishment, Communication, and Community*, p. 179.

1.1. *Duff on Standing*

To understand what motivates Duff's concern for the standing of the court (or, more generally, of those who attempt to call the alleged offender to account), consider the example he gives of 'an academic institution that lays down strict rules for its students concerning their academic behavior...rules that are justified in terms of the values that define the institution as an academic institution'. It is worth quoting at some length:

> [The rules] require the students to treat other members of the institution with honesty and respect, to attend classes, to produce essays on time, and so on. These rules are applied and enforced by the academic staff, who are given the authority to call students to account and to penalize them for breaches of the rules. But suppose that the staff themselves treat their students with persistent dishonesty and disrespect. They regularly fail to appear for classes that they are due to give, or they appear late. They mark essays carelessly, or they mark them months after they were written. Such behavior may not breach any formal rules of the institution; or if it does breach the formal rules, those rules are never enforced against members of staff. If a student is then called to account by members of staff or by an official committee for an alleged breach of the rules, she might with justice reply that they lack the moral standing thus to call her to account or to judge her: not because she is not bound by the institution's rules (she would be prepared to answer for breaches of them to her fellow students or to members of staff who behaved appropriately towards her) or because she thinks her conduct was justifiable or excusable (that is not the question she is addressing); but because those who would call her to account have themselves, in their behavior towards her, shown no respect for the values they accuse her of flouting.[9]

There seems to me to be something deeply compelling in all this. The response, 'who are *you* to say that?', does, as Duff says, seem to speak to the preconditions of answerability. Moreover, if one believes that the proper function of the criminal system (or one of its proper functions) is to hold people answerable, then the question 'to whom is the alleged offender answerable?' must be answered and this, in turn, leads to questions about the standing of those identified. Nonetheless, for the reasons discussed below, I do not think the issue straightforward and I do not think analogies with our ordinary practices of moral criticism and accountability always apposite.

---

[9] Duff, *Punishment, Communication, and Community*, pp. 185–86.

2. *More on Standing*

There is clearly a difference between criticizing and calling to account, although at times they may be hard to distinguish. Thus, President Mugabe of Zimbabwe may criticize the absence of democracy in Florida during the US Presidential election of 2000, and he might make disparaging remarks about a system that allows critical electoral decisions to be made by the brother of one of the candidates. In response, one might think 'who is he to criticize' or (more colloquially) 'it is a bit bloody rich coming from him', but those kinds of thoughts do not seem to negate the criticism. Similarly, a negligent member of the academic staff in Duff's fictional university might criticize a student who is months late with an essay. Again, the student might think, 'well, it is a bit rich coming from you', but that does not seem to blunt the criticism. The essay is late and the student is rightly criticized. That thought does not seem to need the further question 'but, is she rightly criticized *by him*' answered in order to be complete.

Criticizing someone, then, is not *just by itself* calling them to answer for their conduct. However, often the two do come together, and an account of when they do so may support Duff's account. To see this, imagine the student talking to her roommate after having been criticized. She might say, 'he told me off for my essay being late, but I wasn't going to explain myself *to him*'. The thought here, which is surely familiar and understandable, is that the student felt that she did not owe an explanation to this particular member of staff; she did not feel answerable to him for precisely the reason Duff gives (that by his conduct he has forfeited the standing to call her to account). Similarly, the brothers Bush might say that they are not going to discuss democracy with a tin-pot tyrant and we would understand what they meant even if we thought the substance of Mugabe's claims correct.[10]

However, if we focus more closely on the details of Duff's example then an issue arises that does not seem to be captured by these cases. The academic staff, Duff writes, 'are given the authority' to call lax students to account. Let us assume that the university, and its values, are generally admirable and that the authority of the academics is properly conferred on them. A student fails to hand in an important essay by the deadline (as it happens, the content of this essay has not been affected by the lax

---

[10] The Mugabe example also brings in issues relating to the need for the parties to be bound by the same laws and (possibly) institutions (Duff, *Punishment, Communication, and Community*, pp. 181–84), although these are not dealt with here.

standards of the academic staff). A sub-committee of the department is convened to call the student to answer for her conduct (which includes, of course, the possibility that she has some good answer such that she should not be penalized). The members of staff placed on this sub-committee happen to include (and I don't think it makes a difference if it is true of all of its members) academics who routinely miss deadlines for handing back student work.

Consider now how we respond if the student refuses to attend the committee, or refuses to engage with it, because she believes she is not answerable for her conduct to these particular members of staff. We might, I think, sympathize with her if she thought the staff hypocritical (she might think 'they shouldn't sit on *that* committee'); we might even sympathize with her thinking 'it is a bit bloody rich coming from them', but I do not think we can allow that she is not properly called to account by the committee. The critical difference between these academics individually criticizing the student when they, too, are lax, and these academics together constituting a committee whose function is to bring students to account is, of course, that in the latter case the academics take up a particular *role*, which (*ex hypothesi*) is appropriate.

It is important to note that that is not to say that the university, or the department, is wise to staff this committee with these people, but that is a separate matter. It would be inappropriate for the student's mother, should she happen to be an academic in the department, to sit on the committee, but no similar bar seems to apply to lax academics (even if their appointment is inadvisable). Being late yourself does not bar you from being a good and impartial judge of others' pleas of mitigation or excuse for lateness.

In short, the academics sit as representatives of the department or the university and its values, not as individuals. The student, then, cannot appeal to the behaviour of the individuals who happen to constitute the committee unless she intends to show that they cannot be relied upon to judge properly. However, I cannot see any reason why simply by virtue of sharing the fault in question one's judgement should be improper (although, of course, there may be all sorts of other reasons why those who judge should try to maintain high standards). It is surely for this reason that magistrates who commit minor traffic offences are not thrown off the bench.

For the student case to have any bite, then, it seems that we must alter our interpretation of the case in one of two ways. In both, the point is to cast doubt on the moral standing of the *institution* rather than on that of the individuals who happen to staff it. One possibility would be to alter the example so that the university itself is said to be corrupt or to express wrong, or repugnant, values. So, for example, a student might attend a university that publicly promises to protect academic freedom and freedom of thought when it is, in fact, funded by Southern Baptist churches and committed to the discussion of only that which follows from a literal interpretation of the Bible. In such a case, a student called to account for an essay in which she discusses evolution could, I think, claim that the university has no standing to call her to account (not because it is committed to fundamental Christianity, but because the institution itself is implicated in hypocrisy).

A less radical adjustment to the example might be this. Consider, as Duff asks us to, a department that has rules that apply to both staff and students. However, violations of those rules by staff are routinely ignored by the department and the department is complicit in allowing staff to violate its rules. At the same time, violations of the rules by students are vigorously policed and prosecuted. Again, what is put into question by this is the integrity of the institution and not that of its individual representatives.

In these two cases, Duff's thought that the preconditions of liability are not met is an attractive one. There is surely *something* wrong in being held to account by an institution that is itself in violation of the values to which it appeals in its calling the alleged offender to answer for her actions. However, even these cases become problematic on closer examination.

One issue that arises is whether it makes a difference that the value that the alleged offender is said to have violated is the same as the value that the institution violates. Consider again the Southern Baptist university. Imagine that this university violates a number of academic values; it only hires staff with particular viewpoints; it sacks staff who do not toe the line; it actively discourages freedom of thought, and so on. However, it does not tolerate plagiarism by staff or students. Now consider that the student is charged with plagiarism. Is it really the case that the student can properly say 'I will answer to a university that respects (all these other) academic values, but not to this one; it does not have the standing to ask me to answer for my (alleged) plagiarism'? It seems to me that this case is a great deal less persuasive than the case in which the institution condones, or is complicit in, plagiarism committed by its staff whilst it prosecutes the same offence when done by its students.

In response to this kind of problem, Duff might insist that I am confusing two different things: the wrong done and the-wrong-done-for-which-the-person-is-answerable-to-this-institution. That is, for Duff, the issue of whether plagiarism is a wrong (it is) is separate from the question of whether it is, in the circumstances, a wrong for which *this* person must answer to *this* institution. However, Duff's conceptual distinction (which I accept) does not by itself do the trick because the substantive issue of when an institution loses standing remains. That said, when it comes to that substantive issue it is not clear to me that one can do more than trade intuitions about the point at which, and scope over which, an institution loses standing.

Consider one last example: assume that the current UK Government lied about the intelligence regarding weapons of mass destruction in Iraq and about when it knew that the US Government was intent on invading Iraq and changing the regime there. If these things were true, one might think they go to the heart of the general moral standing of the Government given the significance of going to war. Nevertheless, even if true, these facts seem to me to be irrelevant if I am charged by that Government with attempting to defraud my insurers by lying about the value of the goods stolen from my house in a robbery. Serious loss of standing in one area does not seem to translate in any straightforward way into loss of standing in another.

3. *Doing Penal Justice in Conditions of Distributive Injustice*

I have spent a great deal of time on Duff's account and example for three reasons: first, his discussions, in both *Trials and Punishments* and *Punishment, Communication, and Community*, of the problems raised by the injustices that surround us have a philosophical depth and humanity that is unmatched in the literature. Second, it must be right that if we think of the trial, for example, as calling the alleged offender to answer for his (alleged) conduct then we ought to examine whether the court has the moral standing to demand an answer. Duff is right, I think, that this is not a question that is faced often enough. Third, the thought 'I'm not answering *to you*' is a familiar and powerful one. Does it, though, translate in the way Duff thinks to the contemporary punishing state?

3.1. *Some Background*

To simplify matters, I intend to stipulate certain things. Consider only a state that is, in some fairly loose sense, legitimate all things considered (states that are wholly illegitimate seem to me to raise different questions). The state, though, contains extensive distributive injustice such that it makes sense to talk of the social exclusion of the poor. The extent of this injustice is not so great as to mean that the relationship between the state and its citizens is fatally damaged. By this I mean that, in common with thinkers as diverse as Hobbes and Rawls, I think there is a point at which the state fails to function to such a degree that its citizens can properly think of themselves as having returned to a state of nature. At that point, all legal (and, I think, moral) bets are off (that is, no legal [and, I think, moral] obligations obtain). Unlike Hobbes, I am unclear about how to theorize the relevant tipping point, but assume that none of this applies to the state under discussion here. Finally, assume that normal legal boundaries apply. That is, the citizen is answerable only to the state in which he lives and by whose laws he is bound.

3.2. *Trying to Make it Work*

Consider an example offered by Duff: 'an impoverished single parent steals clothes from a supermarket for her children'.[11] One possibility is that the degree of impoverishment is such that no legal obligations obtain between the state and the single parent. In this case, as Duff says, the woman cannot be held to account for this, or any other, action.[12] However, I have stipulated that this is not the case. The issue is whether the state *in this case* has the standing to hold the woman answerable for her actions. For Duff, it is critical to ask whether the woman can properly deploy the argument that she is not answerable to this state given its treatment of her. How might she do this? One way would be to try to show that the state has violated the very same values that it now appeals to in calling her to account.

This, though, is quite difficult. Grant that the woman is impoverished as a result of distributive injustice that the state does nothing to correct. Unless the account of that injustice involves something like the thought that 'all property is theft', the connection between the value flouted by the shoplifter and that flouted by the state will only hold at some fairly abstract level. The state, it could be said, has violated the value of equality—or of equal respect—in allowing an unjust distribution of social and economic goods, and that has *some* connection with the value violated by the shoplifter, but the precise relationship is unclear.

The problem of relating the actions of the citizen to the standing of the state (and its institutions) is recognized by Duff in a discussion of the idea

11 Duff, *Punishment, Communication, and Community*, p. 182.

12 Duff, *Punishment, Communication, and Community*, p. 184.

that the court may lose standing in relation to some crimes, but not all. He writes,

> Even if the court lacks the right to call the defendant to account for some crimes, those involving values that the political community has failed to respect in its treatment of him, it surely still has the right to call him to account for other crimes: for murder or for rape, for instance, since his life and sexual integrity have not been attacked by the community.[13]

Far from accepting this, however, Duff continues:

> But, first, we must ask how far the political community and its institutions have respected these values in their dealings with this person or the group or community to which he belongs. If, for instance, the police or the courts have not taken criminal attacks on members of this disadvantaged group seriously, this failure undermines their standing to call members of this group to answer for attacks that they commit, since it shows that the community does not treat the members of the group as fully sharing in those values. Second, the question is whether this person is answerable as a citizen to his fellow citizens: but if their collective treatment of him has effectively excluded him from many of the rights and goods of citizenship, if they have collectively failed to treat him as a citizen, how can they now call him to account as a fellow citizen?[14]

Of course, Duff recognizes that the rapist is answerable to someone (paradigmatically, his victim), but it is clear that he thinks it (at least) problematic to hold the disadvantaged rapist answerable to the state.

The second response in the quotation given above can be put to one side. As I said, I am not concerned with cases where the entire relationship between the state and the citizen has broken down. Moreover, Duff accepts that there are cases that fall short of complete breakdown, but which still raise the issue of standing. So, it is the first part of the quotation with which we should be concerned.

Duff admits that he does not pursue the question of just how serious the exclusion or disadvantage suffered by the alleged offender has to be to have an impact on the standing of the courts. The account given above, though, surely goes too quickly. Imagine (and sadly it is not too difficult to do) that the police generally take offences committed against Afro-Caribbean men living in the UK less seriously than they take offences committed against white women. Does that really mean that the state has

---

13 Duff, *Punishment, Communication, and Community*, p. 187.

14 Duff, *Punishment, Communication, and Community*, pp. 187–88.

lost its standing to call to account an Afro-Caribbean man charged with rape?[15]

I am not sure how one could go about answering this question in a systematic and consistent way. The worry, then, is not just that people will differ in their responses to different cases, but that the analysis is unworkable. In the UK, for example, it is true that the social and economic disadvantages endured by some people results in their having shorter—and less healthy—lives than those enjoyed by the relatively affluent. Now, even if one thinks that the UK is blighted by significant distributive injustice, it is surely not, at least yet, the case that the situation is so bad that general legal and moral obligations between citizens and between citizens and the state have broken down. However, the fact that under one description the state fails to take seriously the values of life and bodily health of some of its citizens would seem to mean, for Duff, that the state has lost all standing to hold those affected to answer for any crime (since I take it that all crimes from the most serious down can be related in some way to the values of personal and bodily integrity).

In short, I think the space that Duff wants to carve out—a space with which all penal theorists should be concerned—expands to cover too much. Distributive injustice that falls short of returning us to the state of nature can always be described in ways that relate it, or its effects, to any and all criminal activities. Yet, if our concern is with how to practise penal justice in the real world, it cannot be the case that any degree of distributive injustice renders the state impotent with respect to criminal justice.

Conclusion

Towards the end of Duff's discussion of these matters, he comments that there are good reasons to think that the preconditions he has been considering are not 'adequately satisfied for many of those who appear before our criminal courts'.[16] The thought behind this comment is surely widely shared. In the UK and USA (and in many other parts of the world), the overlap between those unjustly treated by the system of distributive justice and those who appear in the system of criminal justice is both worrying and depressing. It is appropriate, I think, for us to ask ourselves whether

[15] There are connections here with the debate between McDermott and Brooks on capital punishment. See Thom Brooks, 'Retributivist Arguments against Capital Punishment', *Journal of Social Philosophy* 35 (2004), pp. 188–97.

[16] Duff, *Punishment, Communication, and Community*, p. 188.

in the current circumstances we are in any position to demand answers from those who, having fallen foul of distributive injustice, then violate some value the demands of which we, in truth, have also failed to live up to. The practical answer to that question is that standing is an all-or-nothing affair and, unless all has been lost, we are in such a position.

What follows from this? One way to answer is to compare the position tentatively arrived at here with the conclusions reached by Duff after his discussion of these matters. Duff writes with respect to the problem of calling the disadvantaged to account:

> One way to see the point here is to imagine ourselves as jurors and ask ourselves whether we could honestly look this [disadvantaged] person…in the eyes and condemn him for his crime. What we have to ask ourselves in that imagined situation is not merely whether the evidence we have heard suffices to prove his guilt, but whether we, as the jurors who are supposed to judge this defendant as our fellow citizen, have the right or moral standing to do so; and the answer to that question depends partly on whether we, as members of the polity of which we and he are supposedly fellow citizens, have treated him as a citizen.[17]

As should be clear by now, I think this runs together three important issues: whether the crime for which the defendant is charged is directly related to the value that the polity has failed to respect in relation to that defendant; whether the state of the polity is so parlous that 'all bets are off' or whether we are in an unjust situation short of the state of nature; and finally it confuses the individual standing of the jurors with the standing of the polity. It is not for the jurors to ask whether they, individually, can judge. Rather, they should ask whether the polity, which they represent, has the standing to judge.

However, and finally, it should be said that the position arrived at in this paper faces exactly the same challenge as that faced by Duff's account. This is to give some suggestion for how these worries should translate into practice. In my case, what is needed is both an account of the tipping point that returns us to the state of nature and an account of whether anything can be done in circumstances of injustice short of this. Standing, for me, may be all or nothing, but that does not mean that injustice should have no consequences for criminal liability. Given that, it is possible to end on a note of agreement. As Duff says:

---

[17] Duff, '"I Might Be Guilty, But You Can't Try Me"', p. 258.

We cannot hope to do adequate penal justice, penal justice to both victims and offenders, until we come closer to achieving political and social justice. Meanwhile, and in a properly humble and cautious spirit which recognizes how far from clean our collective hands and consciences are in this context, we must seek to develop more nuanced and complex legal procedures that could at least recognize, even if they cannot do adequate justice to, the claims and complaints of both victims and offenders.[18]

[18] Duff, "'I Might Be Guilty, But You Can't Try Me'", p. 259.

THE PARADOX OF FORGIVENESS

Leo Zaibert

Abstract

Philosophers often claim that forgiveness is a paradoxical phenomenon. I here examine two of the most widespread ways of dealing with the paradoxical nature of forgiveness. One of these ways, emblematized by Aurel Kolnai, seeks to resolve the paradox by appealing to the idea of repentance. Somehow, if a wrongdoer repents, then forgiving her is no longer paradoxical. I argue that this influential position faces more problems than it solves. The other way to approach the paradox, exemplified here by the work of Jacques Derrida, is just too obscure to be by itself helpful. Yet, I argue that what I take to be its spirit is on the right track. I recommend distinguishing between (1) the definition and the justification of forgiveness, and also between (2) forgiveness understood as (a) a mental phenomenon and (b) an overt, communicative act. These distinctions are not given their due in the specialized literature, and I expose the nefarious consequences of this neglect. By focusing on forgiveness as a mental phenomenon I seek to analyze the root of the talk of paradoxes which surrounds the discussion of forgiveness. Finally, I present an analysis of forgiveness as a pure mental phenomenon, and argue that this analysis is the most important step in understanding forgiveness in any other sense. While my analysis reveals interesting aspects of forgiveness, it reveals, too, that forgiveness is not quite as paradoxical after all.

Keywords

blame, condonation, definitional stop, forgiveness, justification, punishment

Recent contributions to the literature on forgiveness often begin with a lamentation to the effect that philosophers have not given the phenomenon of forgiveness enough attention. Typically the philosophers' lack of attention is all the more poignant in 'comparison to the attention they give the related concept of punishment'.[1] While this lamentation is, precisely in light of the wealth of recent discussions of the phenomenon, somewhat passé, much remains to be clarified regarding the analytical contours of forgiveness. What is not passé is to see forgiveness as an extraordinarily complex, indeed a philosophically paradoxical phenomenon, in spite of the fabulous success of (self-help) books which simplemindedly hype forgiveness as the solution to all sorts of vicissitudes.[2] Philosophers—in contrast, it seems, to the general public—agonize over the nature of forgiveness, and they allude to a veritable 'paradox of forgiveness'. By way of introducing the problem that shall occupy my attention, I would like to address, in turn, two different ways of formulating the paradox of forgiveness.

The first way is Aurel Kolnai's. Kolnai died before presenting his 'Forgiveness' to the Aristotelian Society, but the version of this piece included in the *Proceedings* has proven extremely influential. In this article, which Kolnai considers to be 'chiefly *logical*',[3] he presents the following paradox:

> [either] forgiveness is objectionable and ungenuine inasmuch as *there is no reason to forgive*, the offender having undergone no *metánoia* ('Change of Heart'), but persisting in his plain identity *qua* offender[4] ... [or] at the other end of its spectrum, forgiveness seem to collapse into mere *redundancy*, or the mere *registering* of moral value in the place of moral disvalue.[5]

Kolnai's formulation of the paradox, without further clarifications, is not immediately enlightening. In fact, some have concluded that 'the [Kolnaian] paradox might move some to conclude that the concept of

---

[1] Berel Lang, 'Forgiveness', *American Philosophical Quarterly* 31 (1994): 105–17, at 105. Similar laments are found at the outset of Claudia Card, 'On Mercy', *The Philosophical Review* 81 (1972): 182–207; in R.S. Downie, 'Forgiveness', *The Philosophical Quarterly* 15 (1965): 128–34; P.F. Strawson *Freedom and Resentment and Other Essays* (Oxford: Methuen, 1974), *passim*; Joram Graf Haber, *Forgiveness: A Philosophical Study* (Boston: Rowman & Littlefield, 1993), *passim*, and in many other influential works.

[2] Consider a small sample of best-selling books on forgiveness: *Forgiveness Is a Choice: A Step-By-Step Process for Resolving Anger and Restoring Hope; Forgiveness: How to Make Peace With Your Past and Get on With Your Life; Forgiveness: The Greatest Healer of All; The Gift of Forgiveness*; *The Art of Forgiveness, Lovingkindness, and Peace; Forgiveness: A Bold Choice for a Peaceful Heart.*

[3] Aurel Kolnai, 'Forgiveness', *Proceedings of the Aristotelian Society* 74 (1973): 91–106, at 91.

[4] Kolnai, 'Forgiveness', p. 97.

[5] Kolnai, 'Forgiveness', p. 98.

forgiveness is internally incoherent'.[6] Schematically, at first, Kolnai's paradox can be brought into sharper focus by considering the famous request that Jesus made in the cross: *Father, forgive them; for they know not what they do.* The paradox is then the following: if, on the one hand, they really did not know what they were doing, and assuming that this ignorance was not itself culpable, then surely they should be *excused*, not forgiven. Forgiveness, as a matter of sheer logic, presupposes (perceived) culpable wrongdoing. On the other hand, if they did know that they were doing something wrong, then presumably they should have been *punished*, and, again, not forgiven. (This presumption's strength is tied to the strength of retributive intuitions.) In other words, putative cases of forgiveness are either not cases of forgiveness at all, or else they seem to be cases where forgiveness is presumably unjustified.[7]

Thus, the Kolnaian paradox has two parts. The first part is indeed 'chiefly logical': putative instances of forgiveness are in fact spurious, since they are instances of other sorts of phenomena: often what looks like forgiving is something else: excusing, exonerating, forgetting, exculpating, or, crucially for Kolnai, condoning. The second part of the paradox, however, is not 'chiefly logical', since it relates to the robust normative discussion concerning the justification of forgiveness. The tension between normativity and description shall occupy my attention throughout, for, as we shall see, the conflation of the merely definitional (descriptive) and the justificatory (normative), complicates the already difficult discussion of forgiveness.

The second way of formulating the paradox is Jacques Derrida's, whom I would like to pit against Kolnai. In his characteristic style, Derrida states that in order to understand

> the very concept of forgiveness, logic and common sense agree for once with the paradox: it is necessary ... to begin from the fact that, yes, there is the unforgivable. Is this not, in truth, the only thing to forgive? The only thing that calls for forgiveness? ... One cannot, or should not, forgive; there is only forgiveness, if there is any, where there is the unforgivable. That is to say that forgiveness must announce itself as impossibility itself. It can only be possible in doing the impossible.[8]

---

[6] Jean Hampton, 'Forgiveness, Resentment and Hatred', in Jeffrie G. Murphy and Jean Hampton, *Forgiveness and Mercy* (Cambridge: Cambridge University Press, 1988), p. 42.

[7] The reference to the biblical passage merely seeks to illustrate a philosophical problem; this article approaches forgiveness in a wholly secular way.

[8] Jacques Derrida, *On Cosmopolitanism and Forgiveness* (London: Routledge, 2001), pp. 32–33.

Not surprisingly, perhaps, Derrida is led to the sort of grandiloquent statement for which he is (in)famous: 'Forgiveness is thus mad. It must plunge, but lucidly, into the night of the unintelligible'.[9]

The main reason why I pit Kolnai and Derrida against each other is that that the former is primarily interested in what is widely known as 'conditional forgiving', whereas Derrida can be seen as primarily interested in 'unconditional forgiveness', and the opposition between these two views of forgiveness shall prove important for my purposes. As we shall see, Kolnai 'resolves' the paradox of forgiveness by appealing to the idea of repentance (*metánoia*, in the preceding quotation): what renders forgiveness 'genuine and unobjectionable' is that the wrongdoer has (in the forgiver's eyes, at least) repented—as we shall also see, this is a rather influential view. In what follows, I shall criticize the Kolnaian move, arguing that the appeal to repentance does not help us overcome the paradoxical nature of forgiveness.

In contrast, by linking forgiveness to the unforgivable, Derrida simply refuses to 'resolve' the paradox of forgiveness; and he, rightly in my opinion, suggests that the phenomenon of forgiveness chiefly worth our attention is independent of whether the wrongdoer repents or apologizes. I will argue that forgiveness is also independent of many things with which it is usually considered (even by Derrida himself) to be essentially linked. Unfortunately, however, Derrida's formulation of the paradox is yet more unhelpful than Kolnai's, as Derrida fails to adumbrate, even in rough outline, what the analysis of this forgiveness-without-repentance which he describes could turn out to be, and thus I cannot defend his position on the matter. I think, however, that, if I understand him correctly, I will here defend the *spirit* of the Derridian position (or at least part of it). Going beyond Derrida, I shall present an *analysis* of the sort of forgiveness I think he has in mind. Such analysis comes in the last section of this article—much needs to be clarified before getting there, and in particular, much needs to be said about the infelicities of conditional forgiveness. But, merely to fix ideas, let me sketch the position that I will defend later in this article: to forgive is to deliberately refuse to punish. This account sounds, perhaps, too broad, and while it may still sound problematically broad after I defend it below, I hope to be able to dispel doubts about the potential infelicities concomitant to this breadth.

---

[9] Ibid., p. 49.

1. *The Unforgivable and other Methodological Preliminaries*

Derrida's style may be unique, but in the passage quoted he commits a rather ordinary mistake. The error has to do with the ambiguous use of the term 'unforgivable'. Although there is great obscurity as to what exactly this locution means, it typically seeks to suggest that some wrongs are of such immense gravity that they *should not* be forgiven. Nazi atrocities, say, or child molestation, are customarily held to be in this sense unforgivable; arguably the point being made is that these very serious wrongs *should* be punished, and *should not* be forgiven.

To be sure, it is only by assuming that Derrida uses 'unforgivable' in the sense of 'ought not to be forgiven' (and not in the sense of 'cannot (logically) be forgiven') that his quoted views make sense. Forgiveness presupposes, on my interpretation of Derrida, that the act to be forgiven is, *prima facie* at least, something that we *should not* forgive. For if we *ought* to forgive a given act, then, and indeed paradoxically, this act would no longer be as interesting a case for being forgiven (it will often just be a case in which the alleged wrongdoer is excused, justified, not really a wrongdoer, etc.). What Derrida means by 'there is only forgiveness ... where there is the unforgivable', is, then, that forgiveness can only occur as a response to something that should, in principle, in some sense, not be forgiven.

As a matter of sheer definition, forgiveness is a way of reacting to 'the guilty as guilty', to use R.G. Collingwood's apt phrase (which Derrida uses elsewhere as well).[10] This phrase captures an important point about forgiveness, and to which I shall return in the next section. For now, I will just offer a one-liner of my own, which I hope helps to unpack the importance of Collingwood's: to 'forgive' the no longer guilty is no longer to forgive.

There is, then, a purely analytic connection between punishment and forgiveness worth our attention: only what is punishable is forgivable, and only what is forgivable is punishable. Not merely wrongdoing, however, but *culpable* wrongdoing, is a logical precondition of both punishment and forgiveness.[11] As Hannah Arendt, amongst others, would have it:

---

[10] R.G. Collingwood, *Essays in Political Philosophy*, ed. David Boucher (Oxford: Clarendon Press, 1995), p. 127. The theme of the 'guilty as guilty' runs throughout Derrida's *Cosmopolitanism and Forgiveness*, but he uses the very expression on p. 34.

[11] My account of punishment differs in significant ways from the standard account found in the literature. For my purposes here, the main noteworthy peculiarity of my account of punishment is that it sees punishment as a manifold phenomenon. The punisher, on my

we 'are unable to forgive what [we] cannot punish'.[12] Now, this thesis entails neither that (1) whenever we blame someone for her wrongdoing, we must either punish or forgive her, for punishment and forgiveness are not jointly exhaustive—not only can we do other things too, but we can refuse to do anything at all, as we shall see in due course, nor that (2) if we do punish the culpable wrongdoer, then we cannot forgive her (or vice versa). While I will eventually suggest that punishment and forgiveness are mutually exclusive (synchronically), the analytic connection just uncovered does not by itself support the mutual exclusivity thesis.[13] My suggestion thus far is strictly this: (perceived) culpable wrongdoing is a necessary condition for the very possibility of forgiving X, just as it is for punishing X. Strictly speaking, then, whatever *on these grounds* cannot be forgiven cannot be punished either (and vice versa)—of course, something may, *on some other grounds*, be unpunishable but forgivable (and vice versa). But whether something *should* be punished or forgiven is a different discussion. The paradox, again, is that sometimes an act which presumably ought to be punished (and which, therefore, is simultaneously punishable and forgivable), somehow ought to be forgiven as well.

The term 'unforgivable' is thus ambiguous: it refers (in its strictest sense) to the impossibility of forgiving, and also (in a looser but much more widespread sense) to the inappropriateness of forgiving. To fail to distinguish the two senses is to be guilty of committing the same very famous mistake that John Stuart Mill committed as he equivocated between two different senses of 'desirable'.[14] The error, in effect, is to confuse descriptive and normative enterprises, which I noted at the outset. In dealing with the paradox of forgiveness we must be particularly careful, for the paradox of forgiveness reveals the difficulties facing, on the one hand, an *account* (or definition, or description, or theory) of the phenomenon of forgiveness itself, and the difficulties facing a *justification* of the phenomenon, on the other.

---

account, need not have the authority to punish, need not wish to communicate anything to the punishee, and so on. For more on my account, see my *Punishment and Retribution* (Aldershot: Ashgate, 2006).

[12] Hannah Arendt, *The Human Condition* (Chicago: University of Chicago Press, 1958), p. 241.

[13] See Christopher Bennett, 'Personal and Redemptive Forgiveness', *European Journal of Philosophy* 11 (2003): 127–44, for a defense of the possibility of punishment and (one peculiar form of) forgiveness coexisting simultaneously.

[14] See John Stuart Mill, *Utilitarianism* (London: Longmans, Green & Co., 1901), pp. 52ff.

Both Kolnai and Derrida, however, like most authors, lump together these issues, as they in the same breath refer to 'objectionable and ungenuine' forgiveness (Kolnai), or to what 'we can or should do' in connection to forgiveness (Derrida). This is terse to a fault. We can bring to bear a lesson from the philosophy of punishment to the discussion of forgiveness: our understanding of punishment, qua phenomenon, has not been advanced by the recalcitrant tendency to confuse the problem of its definition with the problem of its justification. Indeed many justifications of punishment are misleadingly advertised as if they were theories of punishment.[15] This error in the philosophy of punishment, which goes back at least until Plato,[16] has, however, recently been offered as the beginning of wisdom by one of today's most insightful forgiveness and punishment theorists. This is how Jeffrie G. Murphy puts it:

> The Question 'What is Forgiveness?' cannot after all be sharply distinguished from the question 'How is forgiveness justified?' ... We cannot define forgiveness and *then* ask what moral reasons make it appropriate.[17]

Later I will have more to say about Murphy's illuminating views on forgiveness, but for now I just wish to focus on the fact that this amalgam of definition and justification is inconvenient in the case of forgiveness (just as it is famously inconvenient in the case of punishment). Murphy, sensibly, disagrees with a certain widespread view of forgiveness according to which forgiveness is the simple overcoming of resentment. Thus Murphy suggests that forgiveness is 'foreswearing resentment on moral grounds', and that forgiveness is something we do 'for a moral reason'.[18] I think that

---

15 See, e.g., the (largely unheeded) warning in Antony Flew, 'The Justification of Punishment', *Philosophy* 29 (1954): 291–307, especially at 297. This is not to deny that sometimes, particularly regarding value-terms, the relationship between definition and justification is very close. (See, on this, Gerald Dworkin, *The Theory and Practice of Autonomy* [Cambridge: Cambridge University Press, 1988], pp. 1–33, and Hilary Putnam, *Reason, Truth and History* [Cambridge: Cambridge University Press, 1981], pp. 201–216.) My point is merely that there is a way of confusing definitional and justificatory enterprises which is famous in the case of punishment, and which, although not at all famous, is also present in the case of forgiveness.

16 See Plato, *Protagoras* 324a–b, in W.K.C. Guthrie (trans.), Edith Hamilton and Huntington Cairns (eds.), *The Collected Dialogues of Plato* (Princeton: Princeton University Press, 1989), pp. 308–52.

17 Jeffrie G. Murphy, 'Forgiveness and Resentment', in Jeffrie G. Murphy and Jean Hampton, *Forgiveness and Mercy* (Cambridge: Cambridge University Press, 1988), p. 23.

18 Murphy, 'Forgiveness and Resentment', p. 24. For some interesting modifications (which do not affect the substance of my concerns in this article) of Murphy's views see his 'Remorse, Apology, and Mercy', *Ohio State Journal of Criminal Law* 4.2 (2007): 423–53, and

these remarks are fundamentally correct. Yet, they do not, I think, entail quite what Murphy thinks: namely, that we cannot separate the definition and the justification of forgiveness. Consider an analogous example, that of 'white lies': these are lies we tell for a moral reason, say, kindness, or benevolence (that is, in fact, part of what distinguishes them from 'normal' lies), but this is by no means to *justify* white lies. There is a difference between asking 'Why do you do X?' and asking 'Why should you do X?'

In spite of the fact that a given white lie is *motivated* by benevolent reasons, the question as to whether or not one is *justified* in lying (even whitely) remains pertinent. The fact that one always forgives for a moral reason—as Murphy correctly has it—does not entail that this moral reason is a good, or definitive one. Furthermore, even if it were true that whenever someone tells a white lie, she herself, at least, would have to believe that she is justified, this would not entail that she in fact is justified. In other words, it is one thing to define a white lie, and another to justify it—even if in defining we refer to some (moral) reasons that the white liar has for lying. Similarly, one thing is to describe what it is that we do when we forgive and another thing is to justify our forgiving—even if in the former enterprise we refer to the (moral) reasons that the forgiver has for forgiving. Forgiveness, like punishment, is the sort of phenomenon that stands in need of justification, and independently of issues of motivation which may be built into the very definition of the phenomenon.

Confusing the definitional and the justificatory enterprises is of no help in answering the justificatory question. In particular, we should resist the following move regarding forgiveness (itself a parallel to a very famous move regarding punishment): forgiveness which is not (believed by the forgiver) to be deserved is not forgiveness. That is, just as some have built retributivism into the very definition of punishment, some may wish to build (something akin to) retributivism into the very definition of forgiveness. Elsewhere I have argued against this move in the case of punishment—a move which in effect caricaturizes the justification which is incorporated into the definition of punishment.[19]

---

his American Philosophical Association presidential address, as published in his 'Legal Moralism and Retribution Revisited', *Criminal Law and Philosophy* 1.1 (2007): 5–20.

[19] In addition to Zaibert, *Punishment and Retribution*, see Leo Zaibert, 'The Fitting, the Deserving, and the Beautiful', *Journal of Moral Philosophy* 3.3 (2006): 331–50.

While it remains to be seen whether forgiveness can ever be *deserved* (maybe granting forgiveness is always supererogatory),[20] the arguments against building the justification of punishment into its definition do apply to forgiveness as well. For the problem here is not with desert itself (it just happen to be the case that the only justification which is customarily built into the definition of punishment is desert-based retributivism), but with the general smuggling of justifications into definitions. The objection, broadly, is against the thesis that asserts that a punishment which is not believed by the punisher to be the right thing to do is not punishment. And, similarly, we can object to the thesis that asserts that forgiveness which is not believed by the forgiver to be the right thing to do is not forgiveness.

The most decisive objection to this sort of move is captured by H.L.A. Hart's famous discussion of what he dubbed 'the definitional stop'.[21] One cannot simply evaporate deep moral questions *deus ex machina*, by turning them into merely conceptual questions. Turning retributivism into a merely logical thesis, à la Antony Quinton (et al.),[22] and then saying that punishment which is not deserved is simply not punishment has not convinced any retributivists, and it has not advanced the normative debate between retributivists and consequentialists. Similarly, claiming that simply as a matter of definition, forgiveness which is not motivated by X (X being whatever reason, moral or otherwise) is not forgiveness is not likely to solve any interesting question as to whether or not we *should* forgive.

In the next section I shall elaborate on how the amalgam of the descriptive and the normative plays out within the specific context of requiring repentance in order for forgiveness to be possible (or to be morally appropriate). In closing this section, I would like to refer to one more general unfortunate side-effect of this amalgamation of definition and justification, namely a view whereby punishment and related phenomena are (mostly or usually) bad, whereas forgiveness and related phenomena are (mostly or usually) good—or, at the very least, that the two families of

---

20 On the relation between retributivism and forgiveness see Kathleen Dean Moore, *Pardons: Justice, Mercy, and the Public Interest* (Oxford: Oxford University Press, 1989), pp. 89–165.

21 H.L.A. Hart, *Punishment and Responsibility: Essays in the Philosophy of Law* (Oxford: Clarendon Press, 1968), pp. 5ff.

22 Antony Quinton, 'On Punishment', *Analysis* 14 (1954): 133–42.

phenomena are radically opposed.[23] Hastings Rashdall, for example, openly opposes the 'ethics of forgiveness' to the 'irrational', 'immoral' (and 'wholly unchristian') ethics of (retributive) punishment.[24] This sort of assumption is visible even in some of the most valuable recent contributions to this discussion found in the specialized literature. Claudia Card, for example, begins her influential 'On Mercy' claiming that: 'Mercy [and with it forgiveness] and retribution have been thought to presuppose fundamentally different ethical orientations',[25] and a corollary to these views which she diagnoses (a corollary which she does not endorse) is that one of these orientations is good whereas the other one is bad. Similarly, Martha Nussbaum opposes the mildness and gentleness of *epieikeia* (equity, leniency, or mercy—all related to forgiveness), with the harshness and rigidity of *dike*, justice or retribution, or retributive punishment.[26] While few authors would deny that some instances of punishment are good and that some instances of forgiveness are bad, there nonetheless exists a certain pattern of approaching these issues whereby punishment and related phenomena are to be shunned and forgiveness and related phenomena are to be celebrated.

One noteworthy exception to this simplistic view, particularly useful for my purposes, is Collingwood, who eloquently disagrees with views asserting the moral superiority of punishment over forgiveness, and vice versa. Oddly, however, Collingwood concludes that 'punishment and forgiveness are thus not only compatible but identical; each is a name for the one and only right attitude of a good will towards a man of evil will'.[27] But, for the reasons just canvassed, Collingwood's thesis is also to be rejected. His is, after all, but another way of conflating the justificatory and the descriptive enterprises. Collingwood is right, of course, in that the *motivation* behind forgiving and behind punishing could be identical, but this does not render forgiveness and punishment themselves identical phenomena.

---

[23] Consider the title of Martha Minow's famous book: *Between Vengeance and Forgiveness* (Boston, MA: Beacon Press, 1998); or, similarly, the title of Trudy Govier's *Forgiveness and Revenge* (London: Routledge, 2002).

[24] See, e.g., Hastings Rashdall, 'The Ethics of Forgiveness', *International Journal of Ethics* 10.2 (1900): 193.

[25] Card, 'On Mercy', p. 182.

[26] Martha Nussbaum, 'Equity and Mercy', *Philosophy and Public Affairs* 22 (1993): 83–125, 85ff., and *passim*.

[27] Collingwood, *Essays in Political Philosophy*, p. 132.

2. *Repentance and Forgiveness*

The widespread claim that forgiveness requires repentance is often hard to assess because it is not clear whether what is meant is that, as a matter of logic, it is impossible to forgive the unrepentant, or, rather, that as a normative matter, forgiving the unrepentant is objectionable. This is not only the result of the looseness with which many authors shift between descriptive and normative enterprises which we have just discussed. For, as we have also seen, the very paradox of forgiveness which occupies our attention has a part which is purely descriptive and a part which is to an extent normative. I shall now try to show how the appeal to repentance is unsuccessful in resolving the paradox.

Although there are numerous defenses of the thesis that forgiveness requires repentance, the best starting point for this discussion is Kolnai's seminal article, to which I referred at the outset. In this article Kolnai forcefully argues that if so-called forgiveness were to be granted to the unrepentant, then it would not really be forgiveness, but, at best, mere *condonation*. Kolnai's distinction between forgiveness and condonation occurs in the context of distinguishing forgiving from all sorts of related phenomena, such as pardoning, absolving, forgetting, and the like. Surely this is a salutary enterprise, which by now has become rather common.[28] In fact, Kolnai's distinction is particularly valuable in that it also contains a rather enlightening account of the terms used to refer to forgiveness and related phenomena in different languages, thus avoiding the insularity of some 'ordinary language' analyses.[29]

The project of distinguishing forgiveness from related phenomena is not, however, without risks, and I think that one of these risks materializes in Kolnai's distinction between forgiveness and condonation. The main risk is the abuse of stipulation: to draw sharp analytic distinctions between allegedly diverse phenomena by mere fiat. Again, the philosophy of punishment offers illustrative examples: the infamous use of the 'definitional stop', or the common attempt to distinguish punishment from revenge (or from monstrosities, or from barbaric cruelty), are illustrative cases.[30] Of course, to define any entity, is, ipso facto, to admit the

[28] See Haber, *Forgiveness*, pp. 11ff., 59ff., and *passim*; Lang, 'Forgiveness', pp. 113–15.

[29] The linguistic distinction between 'pardon' and 'forgiveness', in English, for example, does not have currency in some other languages, like French, as Kolnai points out—and indeed not, either, in romance languages in general. The general point is that the peculiarities of this or that natural language *need not* be philosophically meaningful.

[30] See Zaibert, 'Punishment and Revenge', *Law and Philosophy* 25 (2006): 81–118.

existence entities other than the one being defined. Not all 'definitional stops' are vicious or to be avoided (if they were, then all definitions would be vicious). I will argue that Kolnai is guilty of employing the definitional stop in a vicious way—as are, too, many of those who require repentance for the definition (or the justification) of forgiveness.

Kolnai defines condonation as a state of affairs whereby someone 'deliberate refrains from any retributive response' to the wrong, even though he sees it as a wrong, and does consequently disapprove of it.[31] Now, this refraining can be motivated by a variety of reasons, although they are not as varied so as to render condoning indistinguishable from 'indifference', 'laziness' 'light-mindedness', 'exculpation', 'absolution' and other phenomena. In Kolnai's view, the way in which the condoner '*acquiesces* in the offence' differs from the way in which the indifferent, the light-minded, the lazy, the exculpator, the absolver, etc., deal with the offence. Unlike all these other forms of refraining from inflicting punishment, condonation constitutes for Kolnai 'a more consciously decisional act [more than the other ones just mentioned] and so far closer to a *simulacrum* of forgiveness proper'.[32] Interestingly, then, while Kolnai's central thesis is that condonation and forgiveness are dramatically different, condonation is still closer to forgiveness than all these other related phenomena—indeed condonation is, in an unexplained sense, a 'simulacrum of forgiveness'.[33] Yet, Kolnai and followers seem to forget this very point: that condonation is in fact rather similar to forgiveness[34]—a point to which I will return in the last section of the article.

In Kolnai's opinion, condonation differs 'sharply' from forgiveness, however, in that 'it does not presuppose and nullify the original retributive position'.[35] Sadly, however, Kolnai says precious little as to what this retributive position is, or about how it is that forgiveness *alone* nullifies it.

31 Kolnai, 'Forgiveness', p. 95.

32 Kolnai, 'Forgiveness', p. 96.

33 It could be argued that the similarity between forgiveness and condonation that I am emphasizing is merely structural, and thus not too interesting. So, my argument resembles the claim that a lie is more a similar to a truth than are groans or exclamations. But this argument is not persuasive, since the other phenomena which Kolnai analyzes share that similar structure too, and since the similarities Kolnai admits between forgiveness and condonation are, in any event, not merely formal.

34 As evidenced, for example, by the fact that more than one of the quotations which the *Oxford English Dictionary* presents as illustrating the meaning of 'condonation' equate it with forgiveness.

35 Kolnai, 'Forgiveness', p. 96.

Surely it is part of the logical structure of forgiveness that it is a response to (perceived) *culpable* wrongdoing—and with this Kolnai agrees, although he has not shown that this need be different regarding condonation. In fact, Kolnai hardly discusses the reasons why the condoner condones. Abruptly, and somewhat gratuitously, Kolnai tells us that: 'condonation is ... virtually "conniving" and immoralistic; in its gravest forms, it is not only undignified and self-soiling but unfair'.[36]

Not only is this dismal opinion of condonation odd in light of the fact that by his very own admission, condonation is more like forgiveness than are the host of other related phenomena which he discusses, but also in light of the fact that Kolnai asserts that:

> to condemn *all* condonation might, however, amount to over-severity; for it seems plausible that without condoning *some* faults we could not possibly live together, nor, for that matter, with ourself.[37]

Maybe it is true that we cannot possibly live together or even in peace with our very selves if we did not do some undignified, self-soiling, or unfair things. But if condonation in some cases allows us to live with others and with ourselves, and these things are valuable, then we should pause before we flatly condemn condonation. And yet, condemning condonation flatly is precisely what Kolnai does. He further distinguishes condonation from forgiveness in that the latter is 'supposed to contribute to the eradication of wrongdoing' whereas the former somehow contributes 'to the fostering of it'.[38] This familiar amalgam of the justification and the definition of forgiveness (and of condonation) should by now be admitted to be clearly problematic. It is not clear that forgiveness contributes to the eradication of wrongdoing, or that condonation does not.

The standard view is that punishment (and not the refusal to punish—of which *both* forgiveness and condonation are instances) contributes to the eradication of wrongdoing. Whether or not punishment indeed contributes to the eradication of wrongdoing, however, says little about the logical structure of the phenomenon of punishment itself; similarly, whether or not condonation and forgiveness would differ as to their effects vis-à-vis the eradication of wrongdoing is not to pick out a difference in the structure of the two phenomena. Kolnai, however, summarily and

---

[36] Kolnai, 'Forgiveness', p. 96.
[37] Kolnai, 'Forgiveness', p. 96.
[38] Kolnai, 'Forgiveness', pp. 97–98.

facilely decrees that condonation and forgiveness are 'sharply' different, and he confidently moves along, focusing on the 'unobjectionable and genuine' forgiveness which occurs only when we forgive the sincerely repentant.

A one-line summary of Kolnai's position is that (the disposition) to forgive (the repentant) is a good thing, whereas the mere condoning of the unrepentant is not—which is problematically reminiscent of the sort of simplistic moves (discussed above) regarding the goodness of forgiveness and the badness of punishment, except that now the culprit is not punishment but condonation. Kolnai's move is, I submit, just 'old wine in new skins': it is a vicious appeal to the definitional stop. If a certain behavior is a 'consciously decisional' response to wrongdoing, independently of whether or not the wrongdoer repents, it is condonation *and a bad thing*; if the consciously decisional response is the result of believing that the wrongdoer repents, then it is forgiveness *and a good thing*. Thus, it problematically turns out that acts of forgiveness are, as a matter of definition, good—provided that we are justified in believing that the wrongdoer really repents, we cannot be mistaken in forgiving her.

Nowhere does Kolnai tell us how it is that something—condonation—which, by his own admission, resembles forgiveness so closely, can nonetheless be so bad, in spite of the fact that forgiveness is a good thing. This reeks of gratuitous stipulation, and, in the last section of the article I shall suggest that the difference between condonation and forgiveness is much more tenuous and much more complicated than Kolnai (and others) take it to be. For now, I wish to discuss other problems facing the thesis that forgiveness requires repentance.

The essential reason why repentance is taken by Kolnai and others to be so important is that, by repenting, the wrongdoer somehow distances herself from her act. Thus, Kolnai and others think, repentance facilitates forgiveness, for the forgiver can simultaneously condemn the wrong and forgive the wrongdoer. That is, they urge, there is a difference between what we do *to* the wrongdoer, and what we do *about* the wrongdoing. As a matter of fact, the repentant wrongdoer can join forces with the forgiver in condemning the wrongdoing—to repent means, in part, to condemn the wrong one committed. This idea includes the 'hate [and blame, and punish] the sin but love [and forgive] the sinner' line, whose lineage goes back to Saint Augustine—a position still much en vogue nowadays, for example, in the Catholic church's attitude regarding homosexuality.

Kolnai sensibly disagrees with this suspicious and overly 'neat separability between the sin and the sinner', which he in fact dubs 'fictitious'.[39] Yet, Kolnai does endow repentance with this alchemistic property of rendering the repenting wrongdoer significantly different from the unrepenting wrongdoer, and from herself before she repented—and thus somehow worthy of forgiveness. Similarly, Murphy admits that, in principle, 'it is, of course, impossible to hate the sin and not the sinner', but he admits that there is at least one exception to this 'impossibility': the case in which the sinner is no longer 'intimately identified with his sin'.[40]

Thus, for Kolnai, Murphy, and others, the most important way in which a wrongdoer can separate herself from her wrongdoing is through repentance. But this suggestion presupposes a problematically communicative account of wrongdoing and of forgiving. For example, Murphy assumes that one important reason why we resent instances of wrongdoing (in fact, one important reason why these acts are wrong) is that they are '*messages*—symbolic communications. They are ways a wrongdoer has of saying to us 'I count but you do not', 'I can use you for my purposes', or 'I am here up high and you are down there below'.[41] These messages are disrespectful, and it is mainly this disrespect that we resent.

While sometimes wrongdoers may wish to send those messages, or sometimes certain actions *mean* (independently of the wrongdoer's intentions) sending this or that message, sometimes things are otherwise. In fact, while Murphy comes close to tacitly admitting that his model really applies only to intended wrongdoing,[42] he seems to fail to see the implications of this admission. For surely unintended culpable wrongdoing exists, and as such it is both punishable and forgivable, even though, presumably, these instances of wrongdoing do not constitute or entail sending the messages that Murphy describes as one important reason why we resent these wrongs. Moreover, as Garrard and McNaughton have perspicuously suggested, the communicational view of wrongdoing fails even in cases of fully intended wrongdoing:

---

39 Kolnai, 'Forgiveness', p. 97.

40 Murphy, 'Forgiveness and Resentment', p. 24.

41 Murphy, 'Forgiveness and Resentment', p. 25.

42 See, e.g., Murphy, 'Forgiveness and Resentment', p. 25: 'Intentional wrongdoing *insults* us and attempts (sometimes successfully) to *degrade* us'. Some forms of unintentional wrongdoing, say borderline cases of extreme recklessness, can also send messages, buy they tend to be messages of indifference rather than of a directly *insulting* or *degrading* nature.

> if my car is stolen by someone wholly unknown to me, it would be odd to say, without a special context, that I resent it, and this is because it would be odd for me to regard myself as being personally slighted [and wrong for me to think that the wrongdoer was communicating anything whatsoever—to me or to anybody else]. The unknown car thief does not pick on *me* [or on anyone else] (any car would do, mine just happens to be there).[43]

Still, for the defenders of the forgiveness-requires-repentance thesis, the wrongdoer who had initially sent messages along the lines Murphy sketches, as she repents, she then sends different messages, to the tune of 'I no longer stand behind the wrongdoing, and I want to be separated from it. I stand with you in condemning it'.[44] It is in virtue of this message of repentance, then, that we forgive her. In light of the limitations arising from the fact that this sort of view is a non-starter in cases of unintended wrongdoing, and that it does not work either in the many cases resembling Garrard and McNaughton's example, then, even if Murphy and Kolnai were correct, it would still be true that their account/justification (their amalgam) of forgiveness would only work in a rather limited number of cases. And yet it is a perfectly common occurrence to forgive unintended wrongdoing, and wrongdoing of the sorts described by Garrard and McNaughton.

But there is more which is problematic in the communicative view of wrongdoing and forgiveness presupposed by the forgiveness-requires-repentance view. If wrongdoing need not involve communicating anything (as I have glossed over Garrard and McNaughton's example in order to emphasize), why should repentance perforce involve communication? Why, moreover, should what the repentant wrongdoer experiences, even if she wishes to communicate it, have the force to perform the alchemist trick of turning what would otherwise have been merely bad condonation into good forgiveness (or, indeed, the force to make punishment somehow inappropriate)? Lurking in the background of these views is the additional view whereby forgiveness itself is communicational: by forgiving we send a message to the forgivee to the effect that she is now welcome back into our community, or that we no longer hold any grudge against her, etc. The same questions regarding the communicational analysis of

---

43 Eve Garrard and David McNaughton, 'In Defence of Unconditional Forgiveness', *Proceedings of the Aristotelian Society* (2003): 39–60, at 42–43.

44 Murphy, 'Forgiveness and Resentment', p. 26. Murphy admits that there exist legitimate moral reasons for forgiving other than repentance, but he is emphatic in that repentance is 'the clearest way in which a wrongdoer can sever himself from his past wrong'. Ibid.

wrongdoing and of repentance are pertinent in the case of the communicational account of forgiveness: Why should forgiveness communicate anything at all? Could we not forgive privately, even in secret?

The mystery surrounding the quasi-magical powers of repentance is not solved by looking at the important role that repentance has in many different religions. As is well known, the idea that true repentance on the part of the wrongdoer requires that the aggrieved party forgives her is 'fundamental to Judaism [and to other religions as well]'.[45] As Haber points out:

> Under Rabbinic law, on the eve of Yom Kippur, wrongdoers are obligated to ask forgiveness from those they have wronged. Should their request be denied, they are obligated to ask two more times, at which point, should their request be denied, it is the victim—not the wrongdoer—who is morally to blame.[46]

It would be interesting to see how many rabbis would truly forgive, say, Hitler, after he sincerely apologized three (or three thousand) times, and why, if some would indeed forgive him, this would be the right thing to do. Some people would compellingly refuse to forgive certain acts, again, say Hitler's acts, no matter how sincerely (or often) he repented—Hitler's acts could be seen as unforgivable, in the sense that they should never be forgiven. Yet, the question as to what exactly this awesome power of repentance is remains unanswered. Unfortunately, the defenders of the forgiveness-requires-repentance thesis say precious little of help in answering this question. Merely to assert that repentance is communicative along the lines that these defenders sketch is not to explain why this communication has the effects that they claim it has.

There are, of course, immense epistemological limitations regarding our ability to know when someone else's (or even our own) repentance is full and sincere. But, putting these limitations aside, I suggest that there are two options (one of which is further subdivided) as to what repentance may entail, none of which is useful for Kolnai, Murphy, and other endorsers of the forgiveness-requires-repentance thesis.

On the one hand, if the repenting wrongdoer would merely, and in more or less jejune ways, 'feel bad' about what she has done, then it seems to be more or less inadequate to grant forgiveness—to forgive in this case would be an instance of what Dietrich Bonhoeffer calls 'cheap grace'.[47]

---

[45] Aaron Lazare, *On Apology* (Oxford: Oxford University Press, 2004), p. 241.
[46] Haber, *Forgiveness*, p. 103 and *passim*.
[47] Quoted in Lazare, *On Apology*, p. 241.

If merely feeling bad about my wrongdoing were sufficient for being forgiven, it is hard to imagine how forgiveness could possibly be conducive, as Kolnai believes it is, to the eradication of wrongdoing. On the other hand, however, even if the repenting wrongdoer displays a robust, sobering owning up to her own wrongdoing, in such a way that she *deeply* suffers for having behaved as she did, this will still be problematic. For now two further alternatives suggest themselves. First, if someone really repented this maturely, arguably she would punish herself, and, at any rate, she may not accept to be forgiven, for otherwise she would rightly see this as the cheap grace of the previous case. Second, it is possible that this suffering is by itself constitutive of punishment. But if this is so, then so-called forgiveness turns out to be, again, spurious: we are not quite forgiving this wrongdoer, we are merely refraining from *victimizing* her, given that she has already been punished (even if she punished herself) for what she did.

As it turns out, invoking repentance does not resolve the paradoxical nature of forgiveness, for, after much fancy footwork, we remain in roughly the same place we started. Either putative instances of forgiveness are spurious (in the case of the truly repentant wrongdoer who has already punished herself), or, when the putative instances of forgiveness are not spurious, then they seem more or less like 'cheap grace', more or less unjustified. Thus, resolving the paradox of forgiveness via the appeal to repentance seems doomed. I thus turn to the discussion of the type of forgiveness worth our attention: pure forgiveness.

3. *Pure Forgiveness and Treating the Guilty as Guilty*

Some (unbridled retributivists) have asserted that culpable wrongdoing is *sufficient* (not merely necessary) for the justified punishing of X. These influential authors (say, Immanuel Kant or Michael Moore)[48] would then have difficulty admitting that forgiveness is ever possible (or ever justified). Most contemporary authors seek to justify punishment combining retribitivist and consequentialist rationales. Independently of the success

---

[48] See, e.g., Immanuel Kant, *The Metaphysical Elements of Justice*, trans. John Ladd (New York: Macmillan, 1965), *passim*; Michael Moore, *Placing Blame* (Oxford: Clarendon Press, 1997), *passim*. Moore is more nuanced than Kant in his discussion of conflicts of duties, but if these nuances allowed him to tolerate forgiveness, then they would create other problems for his views. See my *Punishment and Retribution*, pp. 173ff., where I discuss unbridled retributivism.

of these mixed justifications of punishment (about which I am rather skeptical),[49] it is clear that the force of retributivism is irresistible: a wholly non-retributive justification of punishment is not very attractive. And yet retributivism is, in some sense, at odds with forgiveness. Thus, while forgiveness poses a much more serious problem to unbridled retributivist positions, it nonetheless poses problems to any justification of punishment that contains a retributivist element.

I am unaware of philosophers who flatly assert that culpable wrongdoing is sufficient for the justified forgiving of X, but if there are, then there surely would arise the 'paradox of punishment' along the lines of the paradox of forgiveness.[50] What seems downright inconsistent is for someone to assert that culpable wrongdoing is sufficient for *simultaneous* justified punishment and justified forgiveness. In any event, even if one does not endorse extreme positions, in some cases at least we think that punishment is the right thing to do, and then it seems that in those cases forgiveness would perforce not be the right thing to do. In some cases at least, 'either punishment is right and forgiveness wrong, or forgiveness is right and punishment wrong', as Collingwood would have it.[51] And yet, it seems that it is precisely in cases where punishment is or seems right that forgiveness would be interesting.

In fact, I think this is part of what describes the sort of case that Derrida has in mind when he talks about 'pure forgiveness' or 'unconditional forgiveness'. Derrida distinguishes between an 'economic' type of forgiveness and another 'aneconomic one'; only the latter is 'pure' in his sense. Derrida opposes, and in my opinion rightly, the view that forgiveness is conditioned by certain actions by the wrongdoer, in such a way that if the wrongdoer does not engage in those actions forgiveness would be logically impossible (or, in other formulations, that it would be unjustified). As Derrida puts it:

---

49 See, e.g., Zaibert, *Punishment and Retribution*, ch. 1.

50 The famous biblical passage 'If someone strikes you on the right cheek, turn to him the other also' (Matthew 5) may be seen as suggesting that wrongdoing is indeed sufficient for the justified forgiving of X. Assuming, somewhat plausibly but by no means certainly, that the turning of the other cheek involves forgiving, will not quite turn this into an objection to my claim that there is no paradox of punishment. For these sorts of claims need to be understood within the context of the view that the reason why we are to turn the other cheek is because it is God himself—not us—who would do the punishing (see, e.g., Romans 12). So, punishment is not really eliminated in favor of forgiveness; rather we are ask to engage in inaction (it is an interesting question whether this inaction is indeed to forgive), insofar as God will act (on our behalf).

51 Collingwood, *Essays in Political Philosophy*, p. 124.

> I would be tempted to contest this *conditional* logic of the *exchange*, this presupposition, so widespread, according to which forgiveness can only be considered *on the condition* that it be asked, in the course of a scene of repentance attesting at once to the consciousness of the fault, the transformation of the guilty, and the at least implicit obligation to do everything to avoid the return of evil.[52]

In contrast to this 'economic' sort of forgiveness (the term 'economic' suggests the idea of 'transaction' or 'exchange' in the case of conditional forgiveness; the term 'aneconomic' describes unconditional forgiveness, in which this transaction or exchange is absent), Derrida describes pure forgiveness as:

> the *unconditional*, gracious, infinite, aneconomic forgiveness granted *to the guilty as guilty*, without counterpart, even to those who do not repent or ask forgiveness.[53]

For analytic purposes, I would like to steer clear of the discussion of grace or of infinitude, and focus exclusively on the idea of forgiveness without repentance (or apologies). This strategy, moreover, allows me to remain in close contact with the *secular* literature on forgiveness.

I think that turning towards something akin to what Derrida calls pure forgiveness is crucially important if we wish to better understand the paradox of forgiveness. Derrida is emphatic about the primacy of his version of pure forgiveness:

> despite all the confusions which reduce forgiveness to amnesty or to amnesia, to acquittal or prescription, to the work of mourning or some political therapy of reconciliation, in short to some historical ecology, it must never be forgotten, nevertheless, that all of that refers to a certain idea of pure and unconditional forgiveness, without which this discourse would not have the least meaning.[54]

And yet, I think that Derrida does not go far enough in isolating pure forgiveness, and in separating it away from these other reductive manifestations. For example, in the second to last quotation he talks about pure forgiveness being *granted*, and this seems to me to be unnecessarily close to precisely those sorts of economic transactions which he wishes to avoid. Moreover, as he discusses the right of grace (and executive

52 Derrida, *On Cosmopolitanism and Forgiveness*, p. 34.
53 Derrida, *On Cosmopolitanism and Forgiveness*, p. 35.
54 Derrida, *On Cosmopolitanism and Forgiveness*, p. 45.

pardons),[55] he refers to a 'personal head-to-head or face-to-face [encounter], which one could think is required by the very essence of forgiveness'.[56] And Derrida does not distance himself from the necessity of a 'face-to-face' encounter between the wrongdoer and the forgiver—in fact, Derrida problematizes cases in which language may render this encounter moot, namely, when the wrongdoer and the forgiver do not speak the same language, or even when they do not share the same values. Given Derrida's interest in pure forgiveness, it is puzzling to see how in his book, *Cosmopolitanism and Forgiveness*, he discusses forgiveness in connection to political phenomena which, though surely important, are not 'pure' in his sense.

Thus Derrida, in my opinion, does not sufficiently distance himself from conditional forgiveness. Granted, he distances himself from one of those conditions, in fact from the commonest of these conditions (in terms of its treatment in the specialized literature): repentance. But he does not get around to analyzing this pure forgiveness which he thinks is so important. And while it is true that the distinction between conditional and unconditional forgiveness is drawn up in terms of whether or not one requires that the wrongdoer repents, this is, logically speaking, obviously not the only condition that may be imposed on forgiveness.

Some of the most important defenses of unconditional forgiveness are in fact defenses of the morality of forgiveness without repentance, and only tangentially touch upon those purely conceptual or analytic aspects which I discuss here.[57] That is, they limit themselves to claiming that forgiveness need not be conditional on the wrongdoer's repentance (or on her apologies) in order for it to be 'morally permissible'.[58] Moreover, defenders of unconditional forgiveness typically do not address the issue of whether or not even what they call unconditional forgiveness needs to be *granted*, or *communicated*, to the wrongdoer. In contrast to these standard moves, I wish to emphasize two aspects of my account. First, I am not primarily interested in the morality of forgiveness (except for those moral aspects which may be necessary to resolve the paradox); my 'defense' of unconditional or pure forgiveness is simply an attempt to show how it can

---

[55] See, for more on Derrida's treatment of forgiveness in connection to public policy, Austin Sarat, *Mercy on Trial: What it Means to Stop an Execution* (Princeton: Princeton University Press, 2005), pp. 71ff.

[56] Derrida, *On Cosmopolitanism and Forgiveness*, p. 48.

[57] The best defense of unconditional forgiveness in the recent literature is, in my opinion, Garrard and McNaughton, 'In Defence of Unconditional Forgiveness', pp. 39–60.

[58] Garrard and McNaughton, 'In Defence of Unconditional Forgiveness', p. 39.

exist. Second, my account of pure forgiveness is non-transactional through and through; it is wholly aneconomic, to deploy Derrida's term—it need not be granted or communicated at all, and thus it is irrelevant for my purposes whether or not the forgiver and the wrongdoer speak the same language, share the same values, and so on.

My pure forgiveness is thus *purer* than even Derrida's pure forgiveness. Furthermore, my account of pure forgiveness is not quite identical to what authors in the literature mean by unconditional forgiveness. For example, as they discuss Gordon Wilson's reaction to the death of his daughter as a result of the IRA's infamous Remembrance Day Bombing on 8 November 1987—he forgave the assassins—commentators typically assert that this is an instance of unconditional forgiveness, simply because it was not conditioned by the requirement that the assassins repented.[59] And yet, quite obviously, this case could have been conditioned by all sorts of other considerations, such as the belief, on Wilson's part, that such an explicit and sensational case of forgiveness may have contributed to the end of violence, the attainment of peace, and so on. That is, it is often summarily assumed that forgiveness given without requiring repentance is thereby unconditional—although it is obvious that, in addition to repentance, there could be all sorts of conditions placed upon forgiveness.

My account of pure forgiveness is related to my own work on punishment theory, where I have urged that, in order to understand the phenomenon of punishment itself, it is advisable to focus on cases purer than the one that tends to monopolize the attention of specialists (criminal punishment carried out by the State). This suggestion is not at all motivated by the view that criminal punishment carried out by the State is not a very important topic (undoubtedly it is), but by the view that the discussion of such a type of punishment is contaminated by all sorts of (again, terribly important) discussions pertaining to political philosophy, thus obscuring the phenomenon of punishment itself, qua phenomenon. Thus, with this eidetic reduction of sorts, I have tried to analyze what happens when a person punishes, independently of whether this person has the authority to do so, wishes to communicate anything, is doing the right thing, and so on. Here I wish to apply this method to the analysis of forgiveness.

---

[59] See Garrard and McNaughton, 'In Defence of Unconditional Forgiveness', p. 39; see also Bennett, 'Personal and Redemptive Forgiveness'. Similarly, both Garrard and McNaughton and Bennett praise Wilson's forgiveness, and in fact the former authors explicitly assert that 'it is always admirable to forgive' ('In Defence of Unconditional Forgiveness', p. 40). For reasons which by now should be clear, that I am not discussing the morality of what Wilson did.

When analyzing punishment, I have suggested a much tighter connection between punishment and blame than is typically acknowledged. To punish is to do something about what we find blameworthy. And then the obvious question suggests itself: blame is to punishment is like _____ is to forgiveness? Notice that blame, punishment, and forgiveness are all responses to wrongdoing. Notice, too, that if the forgiveness-requires-repentance thesis were correct, forgiveness would not be a response to wrongdoing simpliciter, but rather to wrongdoing-which-is-repented; presumably, adherents to this thesis would also say that punishment is not a response to wrongdoing simpliciter, but rather to wrongdoing-which-is-not-repented. But insofar as punishing is to go beyond mere blaming; the question remains: what is that more basic phenomenon regarding which going beyond entails that one is forgiving? Or is the question rather: blame is to punishment like forgiveness is to _____? The fact that it is not clear whether the blank in these questions should be to the left or to the right of 'forgiveness' suggests the answer: the blank, in either case, should be filled by repeating the very term 'forgiveness': blame is to punishment like forgiveness is to forgiveness.

In other words, the term 'forgiveness' is ambiguous—and this ambiguity is not customarily noticed. The ambiguity is between forgiveness as a pure mental phenomenon, and forgiveness as the communication of this mental phenomenon. To be sure, that there exists something like private forgiveness and something like communicative forgiveness is not an entirely novel thesis. Solomon Schimmel, for example, presupposes a distinction between 'private' and 'interpersonal' forgiveness, which in some ways resembles my distinction.[60] Christopher Bennett has recently interestingly distinguished between 'redemptive' and 'personal' forgiveness; a distinction which also bears resemblance to Schimmel's distinction and to mine. Some of the main differences between my distinction and others (such as Schimmel's or Bennett's) shall become apparent below, as soon as I present my analysis of each of my two types of forgiveness. But some important differences between my views and similar theses stem from their emphasis on the healing power of forgiveness, its power to restore relationships, and with the sorts of considerations regarding the loss of status that we suffer when we are wronged, and which I discussed above, in connection to Murphy's communicative views.

---

[60] Solomon Schimmel, *Wounds not Healed by Time: The Power of Repentance and Forgiveness* (Oxford: Oxford University Press, 2002), pp. 42ff.

For example, Bennett believes that to 'grant' personal forgiveness (while at the same time withholding redemptive forgiveness) to the unrepentant wrongdoers is rather admirable. I do not make such pronouncements; and I suspect that this alleged admirableness would have to be determined on a case-by-case basis. Moreover, these other forms of 'personal' or 'private' forgiveness are not the sort of purely mental phenomena with which I am interested, insofar as they tend to require that through 'personal' or 'private' forgiveness, the forgiver may come to 'treat the wrongdoer as an equal'. In fact, as Bennett examines the possibility that what he calls personal forgiveness be not forgiveness at all, he concludes that it must be forgiveness insofar as (1) 'it involves the overcoming of hostile feelings towards the wrongdoer occasioned by the wrongdoing' and (2) 'it involves the resumption of relations between two individuals'.[61] While I agree with Bennett's thesis that personal forgiveness is indeed forgiveness, I do not find these reasons compelling (as will become clear immediately—I believe we can forgive without overcoming hostile feelings, and without necessarily wishing to resume any relationships).

Thus, my distinction between pure and communicative forgiveness is different from similar extant distinctions. Moreover, to focus on the dangers of the ambiguity inherent to these two types of forgiveness which nonetheless go by the very same name is not terribly common. That is, those authors who admit that there are different types of forgiveness are not primarily interested in explaining the ambiguity that I am exposing here. Less common yet is the attempt to see the connection between this ambiguity and the paradox of forgiveness.

Hopefully, it is immediately clear that regarding the pure mental phenomenon of forgiving, few limitations obtain (fewer, in any case, than regarding the phenomenon of its communication). For example, I may forgive, as a pure mental phenomenon, wrong acts which have not harmed me in any way, and in this sense I can forgive dead people, myself, and so on; whereas, for obvious reasons, it is not clear whether this is possible regarding forgiveness as a communicative phenomenon. The analyses of each of these phenomena should make these differences explicit. These analyses are extensions of my account of blame (which I have defended elsewhere).[62] A blames B for Xing, when:

---

[61] Bennett, 'Personal and Redemptive Forgiveness'.

[62] Leo Zaibert, *Five Ways Patricia Can Kill her Husband: A Theory of Intentionality and Blame* (Chicago: Open Court, 2005).

(1) A believes that X is wrong,
(2) A believes that X is an action of B,
(3) A believes that B is a moral agent,
(4) A believes that there are no excuses, justifications or other circumstances which would preclude blame,
(5) A believes that the world would have been a better place had B not done X.
(6) A believes that the world would be a better place if something would happen to B, something which would somehow offset B's Xing.
(7) B's having Xed tends to make A *feel* something negative, i.e., a reactive emotion, like outrage, indignation or resentment.

A forgives B (as a pure mental phenomenon) when, in addition:

(8) A believes that the world would in fact be a worse place if *she* did something to B in response to her wrongdoing, and thus she deliberately refuses to try to offset B's wrongdoing.[63]

A forgives B (in the communicative sense) when, finally:

(9) A communicates to B, or to someone else, that she has forgiven (in the sense of a pure mental phenomenon) B.

If instead of (8) and (9), I would simply write (8'): 'A does something to B, which A believes it is painful for B to endure, as a response to B's having Xed', and leave it at that, then we would have an analysis of punishment.[64] Since it is obvious that one cannot consistently satisfy (8) and (8') simultaneously, then it is clear that, on my analysis, to punish and to forgive are indeed mutually synchronically exclusive. Of course, one may at one time satisfy (8) and at another time satisfy (8')—one can, indeed, oscillate between these two states. What one cannot do, on pain of irrationality, is to satisfy both (8) and (8') simultaneously. To concentrate on forgiveness itself, the first thing that my analysis brings out is that while the two types of forgiveness have a lot in common, the purest form of forgiveness is mental forgiveness; for whether or not we should communicate our forgiveness is to add a new dimension to the analysis. I will thus concentrate only on what goes on in someone's head when she forgives, though much of what I say may apply as well to communicative forgiveness.

---

63 The appeal to the world being a 'better (or worse) place' is very general; for more on what this appeal entails see my *Punishment and Retribution*, *passim*.

64 Again, for a defense of this admittedly broad account of punishment, see my *Punishment and Retribution*, *passim*.

There are several peculiarities of my analysis of pure forgiveness, beyond the by now obvious point that it is not conditioned in any of the usual senses, and certainly not conditioned by the wrongdoer's repentance, her apologies, or indeed by any behavior on her part. Of course, the account may be seen as 'conditioned' by the fact that the wrongdoer acted, that her action is wrong, and that she is not excused, justified, etc.—but these are merely innocuous matters of logic, not smuggled normative issues.

My account of forgiveness makes explicit that merely to claim that forgiveness, like punishment, as a matter of sheer logic requires wrongdoing, or even culpable wrongdoing, is not to go far enough. We can only forgive, just like we can only punish, that which we find *blameworthy*. This realization has important implications. In contrast to the overwhelming majority of views, my account shows that not only is it possible to forgive and continue to blame, but that this is the most natural form of forgiveness, at least in the sense that it is the one that happens first. To come to believe (8) in no ways entails ceasing to believe any of the elements contained in (1) through (7). Moreover, and since my account of blame includes an emotional component (feelings of resentment, outrage, or indignation), it follows, too, that we can forgive and continue to resent, continue to hold (emotional) grudges against the forgivee. In addition to the mental phenomena described in (1) through (8) above, a forgiver may also wish to get rid of the emotional component described in (7), or may come to cease to believe some of the elements contained in the analysis, but this is by no means necessary in order for forgiveness to exist. All that is necessary, given that A blames B, is that A would also comply with (8), and this compliance does not entail (nor preclude) the abandonment of any of the other elements in the analysis.

The overwhelmingly standard view, in contrast, has it differently: to forgive is, explicitly, to overcome resentment (even if this overcoming is done for a moral reason). That is, on this standard understanding of forgiveness, as you forgive, you no longer hold on to anything resembling my condition (7). This is not necessarily to say, however, that you must believe that as you forgive, insofar as you cease to resent, you also cease to blame, since it is not necessarily the case that your account of blame involves this emotional component, as mine does. (Bennett, for example, believes that as you grant personal forgiveness, you cease to resent, though he believes that this does not entail that thereby you also cease to blame.)[65] Still, the

[65] Bennett, 'Personal and Redemptive Forgiveness'.

standard line is that as you forgive you cease to resent and to blame, and indeed you cease to believe anything resembling my condition (6) as well.

The interplay between conditions (6) and (8) in my analysis deserves close attention. On first approximation, it may look as if for A to believe (6) and (8) simultaneously would be inconsistent. While I do not think it is inconsistent at all (as I will show immediately), it is to an extent understandable that it may appear odd, since this is, I submit, the root phenomenon giving rise to all the versions of the paradox of forgiveness: the forgiver believes that if a certain bad thing would befall the wrongdoer, this would be an acceptable state of affairs, and yet she refuses to bring about this state of affairs herself.

Imagine that a friend of yours has forgotten that today is your birthday, and that you wish she had not; you may find it acceptable if a common friend reminds your forgetful friend of your birthday, while at the same time refusing to remind your friend of it yourself. I am neither defending your position in this example nor tackling the problem of what the reasons justifying your position may turn out to be: I am merely arguing that this peculiar relation between (6) and (8) is not an uncommon phenomenon. We may want (and expect) people to treat us kindly, even if we do not think it appropriate for us to be telling others what kindness is; Socrates may have thought that the world would have been a better place had he not been convicted, but not if he would personally engage in certain actions; A thinks that it would be a better place if B pays his debt, and yet she refuses to remind B about the existence of the debt, and so on. Consider some of the peculiarities of forgiveness.

Imagine that A experiences the series of mental phenomena described in (1) through (8); imagine further that although A refrains from intervening in making sure that B's wrongdoing is offset, somehow the exactly offsetting event occurs (that is, an event that makes B suffer the exact amount which would, in A's estimation, offset her wrongdoing). Would A be sad or disappointed as a result of what happened to B? It seems to me that unlike the standard accounts of forgiveness, my account allows us to answer this question negatively. Standard accounts, after all, assume that A no longer blames, or resents, or believes that the world would be a better place if something offsetting B's wrong would happen to B, and thus, that whatever suffering may afflict B, A would regret. But on my account the only inappropriate thing would be for *A, herself,* to inflict the suffering upon B—and not simply for B to suffer. Imagine A has come to conclude that B deserves to undergo an immensely painful experience, as the only way to offset her similarly extraordinary wrongdoing. A may nonetheless refuse to engage herself in actually making sure that B suffers so dramatically, though she may welcome, or perhaps be indifferent, if this suffering befalls B through other causes.

Many views on forgiveness presuppose that to forgive someone is to behave as if the wrongdoing would in a sense not have happened—the images of wiping the slate clean, or of turning the page, etc., all seem to capture this idea. But on my account this is not a plausible thesis. Imagine two people, Charles and Duncan; imagine that Charles has done you wrong, though you have come around to forgive him, whereas Duncan has, in your estimation, never done wrong to you or anyone else. Further imagine that each of them suffers a perfectly quantifiable amount of pain, and that this amount of pain was exactly what you thought would offset Charles's wrongdoing. I think that you would find Duncan's suffering more tragic, more upsetting, than you would Charles's—even though you have forgiven Charles. I am not suggesting that you will necessarily celebrate Charles's suffering; rather, I am suggesting that your reaction to it must *differ* from your reaction to Duncan's suffering, though it would *differ*, too, from your reaction to Charles's suffering had you not forgiven him. And this difference is connected with the requirement (8): *you* will not punish, but if someone else punishes you may not be upset.

Yet, it may seem that my account of forgiveness is still too broad (indeed too similar to what Kolnai calls condonation), in that the term forgiveness should be restricted to those cases in which refraining from punishing is commendable, when the refraining from punishing is caused by a moral reason, along Murphy's lines. However, I think that rather than constituting a problem, and independently of the problems facing Kolnai's distinction between forgiveness and condonation, the breadth of my account is one of its strengths.

After all, the more limited scope of standard accounts of forgiveness is based on the appeal to moral reasons, which, though plausible, is not entirely convincing. Consider the sort of case that Card discussed: refusing to punish a powerful gangster due to fear that his associates would hurt innocent people seems not to be truly to forgive the gangster.[66] But is this not a moral reason? Why is this not to forgive the gangster? If this is indeed a moral reason, then standard accounts may have difficulty showing that this is *not* to forgive the gangster. Much work remains to be done in further specifying the *type* of moral reason which is peculiar to forgiveness,

---

[66] See Card, 'On Mercy', p. 187.

given that not just *any* moral reason seems to suffice. I think that my account allows me to argue that this is not to forgive the gangster, in that if I refuse to punish the gangster in order to avoid harming innocents, I would want others to refrain from harming innocents too. In other words, it is not that the world will be a worse place if *I* punish the gangster: insofar as punishing him will harm innocent people, this is not a matter of a difference between myself and others—no one should punish him.

Moreover, it is simply not the case that any instance of not punishing a wrongdoer will on my account count as forgiveness. For not only do I require that this refusal to punish be *deliberate* (thus limiting considerably what the candidates to forgiveness could possibly be), but this deliberation is linked to the admittedly complex realization that while the world would be better if the wrongdoing were somehow offset, this offsetting should not come from oneself. Thus, refusing to punish a wrongdoer who deserves to be punished because one has a plane to catch, or because one is lazy, or because one loves (or fears) the wrongdoer, or because by punishing her we would harm innocent people, etc., are not, on my account, necessarily instances of forgiveness. In cases like these, either the belief contained in (8) or the deliberate refusal tied to this belief also contained in (8) (or both) are absent.

But, via this deliberation, I may be lapsing into Murphy's appeal to moral reasons after all. This is not a serious problem, insofar as I said at the outset, on *this* point, i.e., on the importance of specifying the type of reason which is relevant for forgiveness, I agree with Murphy. My account differs from his in that mine is indeed liberally broad as to the reasons which it would allow as leading a person who satisfies (1) through (7) to also endorse (8), whereas he focuses more than I do on repentance. (An additional difference I mentioned above is that the concern with reasons, which I share with Murphy, does not lead me to suggest that the definition and the justification of forgiveness are not sharply distinguishable.) That reasons to forgive are variegated, and that some are good and some are bad, distinguishes my account from the sort of forgiveness-requires-repentance accounts that I have discussed above, of which Murphy's is an example. After all, the forgiveness-requires-repentance thesis is usually accompanied by the repentance-justifies-forgiveness, or the repentance-precludes-punishment corollaries. And I have argued that these sorts of corollaries are problematic in that they are vicious instances of definitional stops.

In sum, my account of pure forgiveness does limit what counts as forgiveness: it is not the case that any and all instances in which we fail to punish someone whom we deem blameworthy are, willy-nilly, instances of forgiveness. But, admittedly, my account does allow a variety of reasons to enter someone's deliberation as she is about to forgive. I do this, however, precisely in order to avoid the sort of definitional stop visible in the forgiveness-requires-repentance views whereby all instances of forgiveness are, *eo ipso*, instances of justified, or otherwise appropriate, forgiveness. The comparatively large scope of my account of forgiveness allows us to judge that some instances of forgiveness are morally objectionable while others are admirable. This is, I think, an advantage of my account over the forgiveness-requires-repentance/repentance-justifies-forgiveness approach.

Can, on my account, one of the reasons for forgiving be that the forgiver believes that the wrongdoer has repented? Perhaps. The problem with presenting a straightforward affirmative answer to this question is the following. If repentance is endowed with the sorts of wholly expiatory powers with which it is typically endowed, it is hard to see how the alleged forgiver could possibly meet requirement (6). That is, if repentance is understood in this way, then the repentant person is no longer blameworthy, and thus, as a matter of sheer logic, no longer forgivable. If repentance is understood differently, then it may be a reason for forgiveness in my account—though it importantly remains an open question whether it would be a good reason.

In contrast, then, to the 'forgiving' of the initially-guilty-but-through-repentance-no-longer-guilty (or at least no-longer-as-guilty) with which Kolnai, Murphy, and others are concerned, mine is an account of the forgiving of the guilty truly as guilty. Admittedly, it sounds odd to say things to the tenor of 'I forgive you, but I still resent you and blame you for what you have done', but that something sounds odd is not a reason to reject it. There are, moreover, problems with the opposing, widespread view that to forgive means, or entails, that one *eo ipso* no longer resents or blames. I have not discussed how common cases in which we forgive while we continue to resent and/or blame are; my claim is only that these cases are possible—sometimes the forswearing of resentment sets in gradually, and it takes place *after* one has forgiven. In recognizing this possibility, my account of forgiveness avoids the pitfalls of other accounts. Why we may sometimes be justified in forgiving the guilty as guilty is an issue that I have not discussed either; and it surely involves discussions of moral positioning and distance, of aesthetic valuation, and of fittingness, which are beyond the scope of this article. But I hope to have succeeded in exposing the shortcomings of those 'solutions' to the paradox of forgiveness which are linked to repentance, and that thus render forgiveness *definitionally* good.

I hope to have succeeded too in showing that the paradox of forgiveness emanates from a purely mental phenomenon: that we think that it would be good if a certain wrongdoer would suffer (by way of offsetting her wrongdoing), and yet we think that it would be wrong for us to inflict this suffering ourselves. While surely an interesting and under-researched phenomenon, this is not at all an uncommon situation in which to find oneself; it is not 'mad', and it is not quite to 'plunge, but lucidly, into the night of the unintelligible'.[67]

[67] With thanks to the Alexander von Humboldt Foundation for supporting my research, and to the participants of my seminar on forgiveness in the Spring of 2007. Thanks are due, too, to Christopher Bennett, Thom Brooks, Antony Duff, Pierre Grenon, Ingvar Johansson, Jeffrie Murphy, Gerhard Øverland, Anna Schur, Jonathan Simon, Barry Smith, Aaron Snyder, and the two anonymous referees for this journal, for comments on earlier versions of this article.

BIBLIOGRAPHY

The *Journal of Moral Philosophy* originally published the essays in this collection. This bibliography lists the full contents of all articles published since the *JMP* was launched in April 2004. The *JMP* acceptance rate is about 5%.

Allen, Robert Francis, 'Robust Alternatives and Responsibility', *Journal of Moral Philosophy* 1(1) (2004), pp. 21–29.

Alm, David, 'Deontological Restrictions and the Good/Bad Asymmetry', *Journal of Moral Philosophy* 6(4) (2009), pp. 464–81.

Anderson, Scott A., 'Of Theories of Coercion, Two Axes, and the Importance of the Coercer', *Journal of Moral Philosophy* 5(3) (2008), pp. 394–422.

Andreou, Chrisoula, 'Standards, Advice, and Practical Reason', *Journal of Moral Philosophy* 3(1) (2006), pp. 57–67.

* Reprinted in Thom Brooks (ed.), *Ethics and Moral Philosophy*. Leiden: Brill, 2011.

Bazargan, Saba, 'The Permissibility of Aiding and Abetting Unjust Wars', *Journal of Moral Philosophy* 8(4) (2011), pp. 513–29.

* Reprinted in Thom Brooks (ed.), *Just War Theory*. Leiden: Brill, 2013.

Bedi, Sonu, 'Expressive Exclusion: A Defense', *Journal of Moral Philosophy* 7(4) (2010), pp. 427–40.

Bennett, Christopher, 'Forgiveness and the Claims of Retribution', *Journal of Moral Philosophy* 1(1) (2004), pp. 89–101.

Bennett, Christopher, 'State Denunciation of Crime', *Journal of Moral Philosophy* 3(3) (2006), pp. 288–304.

* Reprinted in Thom Brooks (ed.), *Law and Legal Theory*. Leiden: Brill, 2014.

Besser-Jones, Lorraine, 'Personal Integrity, Morality and Psychological Well-Being: Justifying the Demands of Morality', *Journal of Moral Philosophy* 5(3) (2008), pp. 361–83.

Besser-Jones, Lorraine, 'Drawn to the Good? Brewer on Dialectical Activity', *Journal of Moral Philosophy* 8(4) (2011), pp. 621–31.

Besson, Samantha, 'Democracy, Law, and Authority', *Journal of Moral Philosophy* 2(1) (2005), pp. 89–99.

* Reprinted in Thom Brooks (ed.), *Law and Legal Theory*. Leiden: Brill, 2014.

Bittner, Rüdiger, 'A Horse in the Basement: Nietzschean Reflections on Political Philosophy', *Journal of Moral Philosophy* 7(2) (2010), pp. 321–33.

Brake, Elizabeth, 'Rawls and Feminism: What Should Feminists Make of Liberal Neutrality?' *Journal of Moral Philosophy* 1(3) (2004), pp. 293–309.

* Reprinted in Thom Brooks and Fabian Freyenhagen (eds), *The Legacy of John Rawls*. New York: Continuum, 2005.

Brock, Gillian, 'The Difference Principle, Equality of Opportunity, and Cosmopolitan Justice', *Journal of Moral Philosophy* 2(3) (2005), pp. 333–51.

* Reprinted in Thom Brooks (ed.), *Global Justice and International Affairs*. Leiden: Brill, 2012.

Broome, John, 'Does Rationality Consist in Responding Correctly to Reasons?' *Journal of Moral Philosophy* 4(3) (2007), pp. 349–74.

* Reprinted in Thom Brooks (ed.), *Ethics and Moral Philosophy*. Leiden: Brill, 2011.

Brown, Stephen, 'Naturalized Virtue Ethics and the Epistemological Gap', *Journal of Moral Philosophy* 1(2) (2004), pp. 197–209.

Butler, Brian E., 'Rorty, the First Amendment and Antirealism: Is Reliance upon Truth Viewpoint-Based Speech Regulation?' *Journal of Moral Philosophy* 1(1) (2004), pp. 69–88.

* Reprinted in Thom Brooks (ed.), *Law and Legal Theory*. Leiden: Brill, 2014.

Carens, Joseph, 'The Integration of Immigrants', *Journal of Moral Philosophy* 2(1) (2005), pp. 29–46.

* Reprinted in Thom Brooks (ed.), *Global Justice and International Affairs*. Leiden: Brill, 2012.
Carter, Alan, 'The Evolution of Rawls's Justification of Political Compliance: Part 1 of The Problem of Political Compliance in Rawls's Theories of Justice', *Journal of Moral Philosophy* 3(1) (2006), pp. 7–21.
Carter, Alan, 'Political Liberalism and Political Compliance: Part 2 of The Problem of Political Compliance in Rawls's Theories of Justice', *Journal of Moral Philosophy* 3(2) (2006), pp. 135–57.
Casal, Paula, 'Global Taxes on Natural Resources', *Journal of Moral Philosophy* 8(3) (2011), pp. 307–27.
Casal, Paula, 'Rejoinder to Pogge and Steiner', *Journal of Moral Philosophy* 8(3) (2011), pp. 353–65.
Clark, Michael, 'Retribution and Organic Unities', *Journal of Moral Philosophy* 3(3) (2006), pp. 351–58.
Choi, Yoon, 'Revisiting Kant's Ethics: Two Challenges to the Status Quo', *Journal of Moral Philosophy* 5(1) (2008), pp. 137–49.
Cholbi, Michael, 'A Kantian Defense of Prudential Suicide', *Journal of Moral Philosophy* 7(4) (2010), pp. 489–515.
Christie, Tim W., 'Natural Separateness: Why Parfit's Reductionist Account of Persons Fails to Support Consequentialism', *Journal of Moral Philosophy* 6(2) (2009), pp. 178–95.
Clayton, Matthew, 'Equality, Justice and Legitimacy in Selection', *Journal of Moral Philosophy* 9(1) (2012), pp. 8–30.
Coyle, Sean, 'The Ideality of Law', *Journal of Moral Philosophy* 6(4) (2009), pp. 521–34.
* Reprinted in Thom Brooks (ed.), *Law and Legal Theory*. Leiden: Brill, 2014.
Crisp, Roger, 'Ethics Without Reasons?' *Journal of Moral Philosophy* 4(1) (2007), pp. 40–49.
* Reprinted in Thom Brooks (ed.), *Ethics and Moral Philosophy*. Leiden: Brill, 2011.
Cruft, Rowan, 'On the Non-instrumental Value of Basic Rights', *Journal of Moral Philosophy* 7(4) (2010), pp. 441–61.
* Reprinted in Thom Brooks (ed.), *Law and Legal Theory*. Leiden: Brill, 2014.
D'Agostino, Fred, 'The Legacies of John Rawls', *Journal of Moral Philosophy* 1(3) (2004), pp. 349–65.
* Reprinted in Thom Brooks and Fabian Freyenhagen (eds), *The Legacy of John Rawls*. New York: Continuum, 2005.
Dancy, Jonathan, 'Defending the Right', *Journal of Moral Philosophy* 4(1) (2007), pp. 85–98.
* Reprinted in Thom Brooks (ed.), *Ethics and Moral Philosophy*. Leiden: Brill, 2011.
Debes, Remy, 'Emotion, Value, and the Ambiguous Honor of a Handbook', *Journal of Moral Philosophy* 8(2) (2011), pp. 273–85.
DeGrazia, David, 'Moral Vegetarianism from a Very Broad Basis', *Journal of Moral Philosophy* 6(2) (2009), pp. 143–65.
de Muijnk, Wim, 'Thinking about Normativity: Ralph Wedgwood on "Ought"', *Journal of Moral Philosophy* 7(1) (2009), pp. 133–44.
Deonna, Julien A., 'The Structure of Empathy', *Journal of Moral Philosophy* 4(1) (2007), pp. 99–116.
Dietsch, Peter, 'Distributive Lessons from Division of Labour', *Journal of Moral Philosophy* 5(1) (2008), pp. 96–117.
Dobos, Ned, 'Consistency in the Armed Enforcement of Human Rights: A Moral Necessity?' *Journal of Moral Philosophy* 8(1) (2011), pp. 92–109.
* Reprinted in Thom Brooks (ed.), *Just War Theory*. Leiden: Brill, 2013.
Dorsey, Dale, 'The Hedonist's Dilemma', *Journal of Moral Philosophy* 8(2) (2011), pp. 173–96.
Elster, Jakob, 'Scanlon on Permissibility and Double Effect', *Journal of Moral Philosophy* 9(1) (2012), pp. 75–102.
Enoch, David and Ehud Guttel, 'Cognitive Biases and Moral Luck', *Journal of Moral Philosophy* 7(2) (2010), pp. 372–86.

Eylon, Yuval, 'Just Threats', *Journal of Moral Philosophy* 6(1) (2009), pp. 94–108.
Flikschuh, Katrin, 'Duty, Nature, Right: Kant's Response to Mendelssohn in *Theory and Practice III*', *Journal of Moral Philosophy* 4(2) (2007), pp. 223–41.
Friedman, Alex, 'Intransitive Ethics', *Journal of Moral Philosophy* 6(3) (2009), pp. 277–97.
Frowe, Helen, 'Self-Defence and the Principle of Non-Combatant Immunity', *Journal of Moral Philosophy* 8(4) (2011), pp. 530–46.
* Reprinted in Thom Brooks (ed.), *Just War Theory*. Leiden: Brill, 2013.
Fuller, Lisa F., 'Poverty Relief, Global Institutions, and the Problem of Compliance', *Journal of Moral Philosophy* 2(3) (2005), pp. 285–97.
* Reprinted in Thom Brooks (ed.), *The Global Justice Reader*. Oxford: Blackwell, 2008.
* Reprinted in Thom Brooks (ed.), *Global Justice and International Affairs*. Leiden: Brill, 2012.
Goddu, G.C., 'More on Blameworthiness and Alternative Possibilities', *Journal of Moral Philosophy* 3(1) (2006), pp. 69–75.
Gosseries, Axel, 'Equality and Non-discrimination in Hiring – Introduction', *Journal of Moral Philosophy* 9(1) (2012), pp. 3–7.
Grau, Christopher, 'Moral Status, Speciesism, and Liao's Genetic Account', *Journal of Moral Philosophy* 7(2) (2009), pp. 387–96.
Green, Michael, 'Social Justice, Voluntarism, and Liberal Nationalism', *Journal of Moral Philosophy* 2(3) (2005), pp. 265–83.
* Reprinted in Thom Brooks (ed.), *Global Justice and International Affairs*. Leiden: Brill, 2012.
Hall, Timothy, 'Doing Harm, Allowing Harm, and Denying Resources', *Journal of Moral Philosophy* 5(1) (2008), pp. 50–76.
* Reprinted in Thom Brooks (ed.), *Ethics and Moral Philosophy*. Leiden: Brill, 2011.
Harcourt, Edward, 'Crisp's "Ethics Without Reasons?": A Note on Invariance', *Journal of Moral Philosophy* 4(1) (2007), pp. 50–54.
Hassoun, Nicole, 'Free Trade, Poverty, and Inequality', *Journal of Moral Philosophy* 8(1) (2011), pp. 5–44.
Hausman, Daniel M. and Matt Sensat Waldren, 'Egalitarianism Reconsidered', *Journal of Moral Philosophy* 8(4) (2011), pp. 567–86.
Hayward, Tim, 'Thomas Pogge's Global Resources Dividend: A Critique and an Alternative', *Journal of Moral Philosophy* 2(3) (2005), pp. 317–32.
* Reprinted in Thom Brooks (ed.), *Global Justice and International Affairs*. Leiden: Brill, 2012.
Hendrix, Burke A., 'Authenticity and Cultural Rights', *Journal of Moral Philosophy* 5(2) (2008), pp. 181–203.
* Reprinted in Thom Brooks (ed.), *Global Justice and International Affairs*. Leiden: Brill, 2012.
Hills, Alison, 'Practical Reason, Value and Action', *Journal of Moral Philosophy* 4(3) (2007), pp. 375–92.
* Reprinted in Thom Brooks (ed.), *Ethics and Moral Philosophy*. Leiden: Brill, 2011.
Hirose, Iwao, 'Aggregation and Non-Utilitarian Moral Theories', *Journal of Moral Philosophy* 4(2) (2007), pp. 273–84.
Hofmeyr, Benda, 'The Power Not to Be (What We Are): The Politics and Ethics of Self-creation in Foucault', *Journal of Moral Philosophy* 3(2) (2006), pp. 215–30.
Holroyd, Jules, 'Substantively Constrained Choice and Deference', *Journal of Moral Philosophy* 7(2) (2010), pp. 180–99.
Hookway, Christopher, 'Ethics and the Pragmatist Enlightenment', *Journal of Moral Philosophy* 3(2) (2006), pp. 231–36.
Hutton, Eric, 'Han Feizi's Criticism of Confucianism and Its Implications for Virtue Ethics', *Journal of Moral Philosophy* 5(3) (2008), pp. 423–53.
* Reprinted in Thom Brooks (ed.), *Ethics and Moral Philosophy*. Leiden: Brill, 2011.

Hyams, Keith, 'When Consent Doesn't Work: A Rights-Based Case for Limits to Consent's Capacity to Legitimise', *Journal of Moral Philosophy* 8(1) (2011), pp. 110–38.
James, Aaron, 'Rights and Circularity in Scanlon's Contractualism', *Journal of Moral Philosophy* 1(3) (2004), pp. 367–74.
* Reprinted in Thom Brooks and Fabian Freyenhagen (eds), *The Legacy of John Rawls*. New York: Continuum, 2005.
John, Stephen, 'Security, Knowledge, and Well-being', *Journal of Moral Philosophy* 8(1) (2011), pp. 68–91.
Kahn, Leonard, 'Legal Theory, Law, and Normativity', *Journal of Moral Philosophy* 9(1) (2012), pp. 115–26.
* Reprinted in Thom Brooks (ed.), *Law and Legal Theory*. Leiden: Brill, 2014.
Kaufman, Alexander, 'Rawls's Practical Conception of Justice: Opinion, Tradition and Objectivity in Political Liberalism', *Journal of Moral Philosophy* 3(1) (2006), pp. 23–43.
King, Matt and Peter Carruthers, 'Moral Responsibility and Consciousness', *Journal of Moral Philosophy* 9(2) (2012), pp. 200–28.
Kirchin, Simon, 'Moral Particularism: An Introduction', *Journal of Moral Philosophy* 4(1) (2007), pp. 8–15.
Kirchin, Simon, 'Particularism and Default Valency', *Journal of Moral Philosophy* 4(1) (2007), pp. 16–32.
Knight, Carl, 'Egalitarian Justice and Valuational Judgment', *Journal of Moral Philosophy* 6(4) (2009), pp. 482–98.
Knight, Kelvin, 'MacIntyre's Progress', *Journal of Moral Philosophy* 6(1) (2009), pp. 115–26.
Kristjánsson, Kristján, 'A Utilitarian Justification of Desert in Distributive Justice', *Journal of Moral Philosophy* 2(2) (2005), pp. 147–70.
Laden, Anthony Simon, 'Taking the Distinction between Persons Seriously', *Journal of Moral Philosophy* 1(3) (2004), pp. 277–92.
* Reprinted in Thom Brooks and Fabian Freyenhagen (eds), *The Legacy of John Rawls*. New York: Continuum, 2005.
Landemore, Hélène, 'Politics and the Economist-King: Is Rational Choice Theory the Science of Choice?' *Journal of Moral Philosophy* 1(2) (2004), pp. 177–96.
Landrum, Ty, 'Persons as Objects of Love', *Journal of Moral Philosophy* 6(4) (2009), pp. 417–39.
Lang, Gerald, 'Luck Egalitarianism, Permissible Inequalities, and Moral Hazard', *Journal of Moral Philosophy* 6(3) (2009), pp. 317–38.
Lee, Win-Chiat, 'Cosmopolitanism with Room for Nationalism', *Journal of Moral Philosophy* 9(2) (2012), pp. 279–93.
Lefkowitz, David, 'Partiality and Weighing Harm to Non-Combatants', *Journal of Moral Philosophy* 6(3) (2009), pp. 298–316.
* Reprinted in Thom Brooks (ed.), *Global Justice and International Affairs*. Leiden: Brill, 2012.
* Reprinted in Thom Brooks (ed.), *Just War Theory*. Leiden: Brill, 2013.
Lenard, Patti Tamara, 'Motivating Cosmopolitanism? A Skeptical View', *Journal of Moral Philosophy* 7(2) (2010), pp. 346–71.
* Reprinted in Thom Brooks (ed.), *Global Justice and International Affairs*. Leiden: Brill, 2012.
Lenman, James, 'How to Live, What to Do: A Critical Study of Allan Gibbard, *Thinking How to Live*', *Journal of Moral Philosophy* 3(3) (2006), pp. 359–69.
Levy, Neil, 'A Role for Consciousness After All', *Journal of Moral Philosophy* 9(2) (2012), pp. 255–64.
Liao, S. Matthew, 'Time-Relative Interests and Abortion', *Journal of Moral Philosophy* 4(2) (2007), pp. 242–56.
* Reprinted in Thom Brooks (ed.), *Ethics and Moral Philosophy*. Leiden: Brill, 2011.
Liao, S. Matthew, 'The Basis of Human Moral Status', *Journal of Moral Philosophy* 7(2) (2010), pp. 159–79.

* Reprinted in Thom Brooks (ed.), *Ethics and Moral Philosophy*. Leiden: Brill, 2011.
Liao, S. Matthew, 'The Genetic Account of Moral Status: A Defense', *Journal of Moral Philosophy* 9(2) (2012), pp. 265–77.
Lippert-Rasmussen, Kasper, 'Publicity and Egalitarian Justice', *Journal of Moral Philosophy* 5(1) (2008), pp. 30–49.
Lippert-Rasmissen, Kasper, 'Intentions and Discrimination in Hiring', *Journal of Moral Philosophy* 9(1) (2012), pp. 55–74.
Lippke, Richard L., 'Imprisonable Offenses', *Journal of Moral Philosophy* 3(3) (2006), pp. 265–87.
* Reprinted in Thom Brooks (ed.), *Law and Legal Theory*. Leiden: Brill, 2014.
Lippke, Richard L., 'Punishing the Guilty, Not Punishing the Innocent', *Journal of Moral Philosophy* 7(4) (2010), pp. 462–88.
* Reprinted in Thom Brooks (ed.), *Law and Legal Theory*. Leiden: Brill, 2014.
Ludwig, Bernd, 'Kant, Garve, and the Motives of Moral Action', *Journal of Moral Philosophy* 4(2) (2007), pp. 183–93.
Lynch, Sterling, 'The Fact of Diversity and Reasonable Pluralism', *Journal of Moral Philosophy* 6(1) (2009), pp. 70–93.
Mahoney, Jon, 'Public Reason and the Moral Foundation of Liberalism', *Journal of Moral Philosophy* 1(3) (2004), pp. 311–31.
* Reprinted in Thom Brooks and Fabian Freyenhagen (eds), *The Legacy of John Rawls*. New York: Continuum, 2005.
March, Andrew F., 'Is There a Right to Polygamy? Marriage, Equality and Subsidizing Families in Liberal Public Justification', *Journal of Moral Philosophy* 8(2) (2011), pp. 246–72.
* Reprinted in Thom Brooks (ed.), *Law and Legal Theory*. Leiden: Brill, 2014.
Marino, Patricia, 'Expressivism, Deflationism and Correspondence', *Journal of Moral Philosophy* 2(2) (2005), pp. 171–91.
Marino, Patricia, 'Moral Rationalism and the Normative Status of Desiderative Coherence', *Journal of Moral Philosophy* 7(2) (2010), pp. 227–52.
Martin, Rex, 'Two Concepts of Rule Utilitarianism', *Journal of Moral Philosophy* 5(2) (2008), pp. 227–55.
Martin, Wayne, 'Hegel and the Philosophy of Food', *Journal of Moral Philosophy* 7(2) (2009), pp. 279–90.
Matravers, Matt, '"Who's Still Standing?" A Comment on Antony Duff's Preconditions of Criminal Liability', *Journal of Moral Philosophy* 3(3) (2006), pp. 320–30.
* Reprinted in Thom Brooks (ed.), *Law and Legal Theory*. Leiden: Brill, 2014.
McKeever, Sean and Michael Ridge, 'Turning on Default Reasons', *Journal of Moral Philosophy* 4(1) (2007), pp. 55–76.
Merritt, Maria W., 'Aristotelian Virtue and the Interpersonal Aspect of Ethical Character', *Journal of Moral Philosophy* 6(1) (2009), pp. 23–49.
* Reprinted in Thom Brooks (ed.), *Ethics and Moral Philosophy*. Leiden: Brill, 2011.
Mookherjee, Monica, 'Feminism and Multiculturalism—Putting Okin and Shachar in Question', *Journal of Moral Philosophy* 2(2) (2005), pp. 237–41.
Moyar, Dean, 'Unstable Autonomy: Conscience and Judgment in Kant's Moral Philosophy', *Journal of Moral Philosophy* 5(3) (2008), pp. 327–60.
Mulnix, M.J., 'Harm, Rights, and Liberty: Towards a Non-Normative Reading of Mill's Liberty Principle', *Journal of Moral Philosophy* 6(2) (2009), pp. 196–217.
Naticchia, Chris, 'The Law of Peoples: The Old and the New', *Journal of Moral Philosophy* 2(3) (2005), pp. 353–69.
* Reprinted in Thom Brooks and Fabian Freyenhagen (eds), *The Legacy of John Rawls*. New York: Continuum, 2005.
Nolan, Daniel, 'Consequentialism and Side Constraints', *Journal of Moral Philosophy* 6(1) (2009), pp. 5–22.
Norman, Richard, 'Particularism and Reasons: A Reply to Kirchin', *Journal of Moral Philosophy* 4(1) (2007), pp. 33–39.

Nussbaum, Martha C., 'Radical Evil in the Lockean State: The Neglect of the Political Emotions', *Journal of Moral Philosophy* 3(2) (2006), pp. 159–78.
O'Neill, Martin, 'The Facts of Inequality', *Journal of Moral Philosophy* 7(2) (2009), pp. 397–409.
O'Neill, Onora, 'Experts, Practitioners, and Practical Judgement', *Journal of Moral Philosophy* 4(2) (2007), pp. 154–66.
O'Neill, Onora, 'Normativity and Practical Judgement', *Journal of Moral Philosophy* 4(3) (2007), pp. 393–405.
* Reprinted in Thom Brooks (ed.), *Ethics and Moral Philosophy*. Leiden: Brill, 2011.
Øverland, Gerhard, 'Self-defence among Innocent People', *Journal of Moral Philosophy* 2(2) (2005), pp. 127–46.
* Reprinted in Thom Brooks (ed.), *Just War Theory*. Leiden: Brill, 2013.
Øverland, Gerhard, 'Poverty and the Moral Significance of Contribution', *Journal of Moral Philosophy* 2(3) (2005), pp. 299–315.
* Reprinted in Thom Brooks (ed.), *Global Justice and International Affairs*. Leiden: Brill, 2012.
Øverland, Gerhard, 'Conditional Threats', *Journal of Moral Philosophy* 7(2) (2010), pp. 334–45.
* Reprinted in Thom Brooks (ed.), *Global Justice and International Affairs*. Leiden: Brill, 2012.
* Reprinted in Thom Brooks (ed.), *Just War Theory*. Leiden: Brill, 2013.
Øverland, Gerhard, 'Dividing Harm', *Journal of Moral Philosophy* 8(4) (2011), pp. 547–66.
* Reprinted in Thom Brooks (ed.), *Just War Theory*. Leiden: Brill, 2013.
Papdaki, Lina, 'What is Objectification?' *Journal of Moral Philosophy* 7(1) (2010), pp. 16–36.
Peterson, Martin, 'The Mixed Solution to the Number Problem', *Journal of Moral Philosophy* 6(2) (2009), pp. 166–77.
* Reprinted in Thom Brooks (ed.), *Ethics and Moral Philosophy*. Leiden: Brill, 2011.
Pink, Thomas, 'Normativity and Reason', *Journal of Moral Philosophy* 4(3) (2007), pp. 406–31.
Pogge, Thomas, 'Allowing the Poor to Share the Earth', *Journal of Moral Philosophy* 8(3) (2011), pp. 335–52.
Preda, Adina, 'Group Rights and Group Agency', *Journal of Moral Philosophy* 9(2) (2012), pp. 229–54.
* Reprinted in Thom Brooks (ed.), *Law and Legal Theory*. Leiden: Brill, 2014.
Primoratz, Igor, 'Patriotism and Morality: Mapping the Terrain', *Journal of Moral Philosophy* 5(2) (2008), pp. 204–26.
* Reprinted in Thom Brooks (ed.), *Global Justice and International Affairs*. Leiden: Brill, 2012.
Redondo, María Cristina, 'Legal Reasons: Between Universalism and Particularism', *Journal of Moral Philosophy* 2(1) (2005), pp. 47–68.
* Reprinted in Thom Brooks (ed.), *Law and Legal Theory*. Leiden: Brill, 2014.
Reitan, Eric, 'Defining Terrorism for Public Policy Purposes: The Group-Target Definition', *Journal of Moral Philosophy* 7(2) (2010), pp. 253–78.
* Reprinted in Thom Brooks (ed.), *Global Justice and International Affairs*. Leiden: Brill, 2012.
* Reprinted in Thom Brooks (ed.), *Just War Theory*. Leiden: Brill, 2013.
Richardson, Henry S., 'Our Call: The Constitutive Importance of the People's Judgment', *Journal of Moral Philosophy* 5(1) (2008), pp. 3–29.
Ridge, Michael, 'Anti-Reductionism and Supervenience', *Journal of Moral Philosophy* 4(3) (2007), pp. 330–48.
* Reprinted in Thom Brooks (ed.), *Ethics and Moral Philosophy*. Leiden: Brill, 2011.
Riley, Evan, 'Libertarian Self-Defeat', *Journal of Moral Philosophy* 7(2) (2010), pp. 200–26.
Riley, Patrick, 'Kant against Hobbes in *Theory and Practice*', *Journal of Moral Philosophy* 4(2) (2007), pp. 194–206.

Riley, Jonathan, 'Ethical Pluralism and Common Decency', *Journal of Moral Philosophy* 1(2) (2004), pp. 211–21.
Rivera, Lisa, 'Harmful Beneficence', *Journal of Moral Philosophy* 8(2) (2011), pp. 197–222.
Ronzoni, Miriam, 'Constructivism and Practical Reason: On Intersubjectivity, Abstraction, and Judgment', *Journal of Moral Philosophy* 7(1) (2010), pp. 74–104.
Rosebury, Brian, 'Reply to Silcox on Moral Luck', *Journal of Moral Philosophy* 6(1) (2009), pp. 109–13.
Sable, Andrew, 'Virtue for Pluralists', *Journal of Moral Philosophy* 2(2) (2005), pp. 207–35.
Scarre, Geoffrey, 'Corrective Justice and Reputation', *Journal of Moral Philosophy* 3(3) (2006), pp. 305–19.
Scarre, Geoffrey, 'The "Banality of Good"?' *Journal of Moral Philosophy* 6(4) (2009), pp. 499–519.
Segall, Shlomi, 'How Devolution Upsets Distributive Justice', *Journal of Moral Philosophy* 4(2) (2007), pp. 257–72.
Segall, Shlomi, 'Should the Best Qualified Be Appointed?' *Journal of Moral Philosophy* 9(1) (2012), pp. 31–54.
Seglow, Jonathan, 'Associative Duties and Global Justice', *Journal of Moral Philosophy* 7(1) (2010), pp. 54–73.
* Reprinted in Thom Brooks (ed.), *Global Justice and International Affairs*. Leiden: Brill, 2012.
Shafer-Landau, Russ, 'Moral and Theological Realism: The Explanatory Argument', *Journal of Moral Philosophy* 4(3) (2007), pp. 311–29.
* Reprinted in Thom Brooks (ed.), *Ethics and Moral Philosophy*. Leiden: Brill, 2011.
Shalom, Stephen R., 'Killing in War and Moral Equality', *Journal of Moral Philosophy* 8(4) (2011), pp. 495–512.
* Reprinted in Thom Brooks (ed.), *Just War Theory*. Leiden: Brill, 2013.
Sheinman, Hanoch, 'Raz on the Social Dependence of Values', *Journal of Moral Philosophy* 3(1) (2006), pp. 77–87.
* Reprinted in Thom Brooks (ed.), *Law and Legal Theory*. Leiden: Brill, 2014.
Silcox, Mark, 'Virtue Epistemology and Moral Luck', *Journal of Moral Philosophy* 3(2) (2006), pp. 179–92.
Silcox, Mark, 'Reply to Rosebury', *Journal of Moral Philosophy* 6(2) (2009), pp. 245–48.
Simpson, Matthew, 'A Paradox of Sovereignty in Rousseau's *Social Contract*', *Journal of Moral Philosophy* 3(1) (2006), pp. 45–56.
Sin, William, 'Trivial Sacrifices, Great Demands', *Journal of Moral Philosophy* 7(1) (2010), pp. 3–15.
* Reprinted in Thom Brooks (ed.), *Ethics and Moral Philosophy*. Leiden: Brill, 2011.
Sinclair, Neil, 'Expressivist Explanations', *Journal of Moral Philosophy* 9(2) (2012), pp. 147–77.
Singleton, Jane, 'Neither Generalism nor Particularism: Ethical Correctness is Located in General Ethical Theories', *Journal of Moral Philosophy* 1(2) (2004), pp. 155–75.
Slomp, Gabriella, 'Kant against Hobbes: Reasoning and Rhetoric', *Journal of Moral Philosophy* 4(2) (2007), pp. 207–22.
Smith, M.B.E., 'Does Humanity Share a Common Moral Faculty?' *Journal of Moral Philosophy* 7(1) (2010), pp. 37–53.
Smith, Stephen R., 'Keeping Our Distance in Compassion-Based Social Relations', *Journal of Moral Philosophy* 2(1) (2005), pp. 69–87.
Sobel, David, 'The Limits of the Explanatory Power of Developmentalism', *Journal of Moral Philosophy* 7(4) (2010), pp. 517–27.
Spector, Jessica, 'The Grounds of Moral Agency: Locke's Account of Personal Identity', *Journal of Moral Philosophy* 5(2) (2008), pp. 256–81.
Stark, Susan, 'A Change of Heart: Moral Emotions, Transformation, and Moral Virtue', *Journal of Moral Philosophy* 1(1) (2004), pp. 31–50.
Statman, Daniel, 'Can Wars Be Fought Justly? The Necessity Condition Put to the Test', *Journal of Moral Philosophy* 8(3) (2011), pp. 435–51.

* Reprinted in Thom Brooks (ed.), *Just War Theory*. Leiden: Brill, 2013.

Steiner, Hillel, 'The *Global Fund*: A Reply to Casal', *Journal of Moral Philosophy* 8(3) (2011), pp. 328–34.

Stern, Robert, 'The Autonomy of Morality and the Morality of Autonomy', *Journal of Moral Philosophy* 6(3) (2009), pp. 395–415.

Stohr, Karen, 'Kantian Beneficence and the Problem of Obligatory Aid', *Journal of Moral Philosophy* 8(1) (2011), pp. 45–67.

Stone, Alison, 'Essentialism and Anti-Essentialism in Feminist Philosophy', *Journal of Moral Philosophy* 1(2) (2004), pp. 135–53.

* Reprinted in Thom Brooks (ed.), *Ethics and Moral Philosophy*. Leiden: Brill, 2011.

Stuchlik, Joshua, 'A Critique of Scanlon on Double Effect', *Journal of Moral Philosophy* 9(2) (2012), pp. 178–99.

Talbert, Matthew, 'Unwitting Behaviour and Responsibility', *Journal of Moral Philosophy* 8(1) (2011), pp. 139–52.

Talisse, Robert B., 'Does Value Pluralism Entail Liberalism?' *Journal of Moral Philosophy* 7(2) (2010), pp. 303–20.

Taylor, Robert S., 'Self-Realization and the Priority of Fair Equality of Opportunity', *Journal of Moral Philosophy* 1(3) (2004), pp. 333–47.

* Reprinted in Thom Brooks and Fabian Freyenhagen (eds), *The Legacy of John Rawls*. New York: Continuum, 2005.

Telfer, Elizabeth, '"Animals Do It Too!": The Franklin Defence of Meat-Eating', *Journal of Moral Philosophy* 1(1) (2004), pp. 51–67.

Teroni, Fabrice and Otto Bruun, 'Shame, Guilt, and Morality', *Journal of Moral Philosophy* 8(2) (2011), pp. 223–45.

Thomas, Alan, 'Practical Reasoning and Normative Relevance: A Reply to McKeever and Ridge', *Journal of Moral Philosophy* 4(1) (2007), pp. 77–84.

Tideman, Nicolaus, 'Secession as a Human Right', *Journal of Moral Philosophy* 1(1) (2004), pp. 9–19.

* Reprinted in Thom Brooks (ed.), *Global Justice and International Affairs*. Leiden: Brill, 2012.

Timmermann, Jens, 'Good but Not Required?–Assessing the Demands of Kantian Ethics', *Journal of Moral Philosophy* 2(1) (2005), pp. 9–27.

* Reprinted in Thom Brooks (ed.), *Ethics and Moral Philosophy*. Leiden: Brill, 2011.

Timmermann, Jens, 'Simplicity and Authority: Reflections on Theory and Practice in Kant's Moral Philosophy', *Journal of Moral Philosophy* 4(2) (2007), pp. 167–82.

Toner, Christopher, 'The Virtues (and a Few Vices) of Daniel Russell's *Practical Intelligence and the Virtues*', *Journal of Moral Philosophy* 8(3) (2011), pp. 453–68.

Tropman, Elizabeth, 'Renewing Moral Intuitionism', *Journal of Moral Philosophy* 6(4) (2009), pp. 440–63.

Tyler, Colin, 'Brian Barry and Writings on Social Justice from the Left', *Journal of Moral Philosophy* 5(2) (2008), pp. 301–12.

Upton, Candace, 'Virtue Ethics, Character, and Normative Receptivity', *Journal of Moral Philosophy* 8(1) (2008), pp. 77–95.

Valdman, Mikhail, 'Autonomy, History, and the Origins of Our Desires', *Journal of Moral Philosophy* 8(3) (2011), pp. 415–34.

Vallier, Kevin, 'Against Public Reason Liberalism's Accessibility Requirement', *Journal of Moral Philosophy* 8(3) (2011), pp. 366–89.

van Zyl, Liezl, 'Agent-based Virtue Ethics and the Problem of Action Guidance', *Journal of Moral Philosophy* 6(1) (2009), pp. 50–69.

Vargas, Manuel, 'Taking the Highway on Skepticism, Luck, and the Value of Responsibility', *Journal of Moral Philosophy* 6(2) (2009), pp. 249–65.

Wall, Edmund, 'The Real Direction of Dancy's Moral Particularism', *Journal of Moral Philosophy* 8(4) (2011), pp. 587–612.

Ward, Lee, 'Locke on Punishment, Property and Moral Knowledge', *Journal of Moral Philosophy* 6(2) (2009), pp. 218–44.
Warmke, Brandon, 'Is Forgiveness the Deliberate Refusal to Punish?' *Journal of Moral Philosophy* 8(4) (2011), pp. 613–20.
Webber, Jonathan, 'Virtue, Character and Situation', *Journal of Moral Philosophy* 3(2) (2006), pp. 193–213.
* Reprinted in Thom Brooks (ed.), *Ethics and Moral Philosophy*. Leiden: Brill, 2011.
Weirich, Paul, 'Utility Maximization Generalized', *Journal of Moral Philosophy* 5(2) (2008), pp. 282–99.
Wenar, Leif, 'The Unity of Rawls's Work', *Journal of Moral Philosophy* 1(3) (2004), pp. 265–75.
* Reprinted in Thom Brooks and Fabian Freyenhagen (eds), *The Legacy of John Rawls*. New York: Continuum, 2005.
Westphal, Kenneth R., 'From "Convention" to "Ethical Life": Hume's Theory of Justice in Post-Kantian Perspective', *Journal of Moral Philosophy* 7(1) (2010), pp. 105–32.
White, Heath, 'Fitting Attitudes, Wrong Kinds of Reasons, and Mind-Independent Goodness', *Journal of Moral Philosophy* 6(3) (2009), pp. 339–64.
Wiland, Eric, 'On Indirectly Self-defeating Moral Theories', *Journal of Moral Philosophy* 5(3) (2008), pp. 384–93.
Wilkinson, Dominic, 'Should We Replace Disabled Newborn Infants?' *Journal of Moral Philosophy* 8(3) (2011), pp. 390–414.
Williams, Reginald, 'Morality and Privilege', *Journal of Moral Philosophy* 5(1) (2008), pp. 118–35.
Wolff, Jonathan, 'Equality: The Recent History of an Idea', *Journal of Moral Philosophy* 4(1) (2007), pp. 125–36.
Zaibert, Leo, 'The Fitting, the Deserving, and the Beautiful', *Journal of Moral Philosophy* 3(3) (2006), pp. 331–50.
Zaibert, Leo, 'The Paradox of Forgiveness', *Journal of Moral Philosophy* 6(3) (2009), pp. 365–93.
* Reprinted in Thom Brooks (ed.), *Law and Legal Theory*. Leiden: Brill, 2014.
Zaibert, Leo, 'On Forgiveness and the Deliberate Refusal to Punish: Reiterating the Differences', *Journal of Moral Philosophy* 9(1) (2012), pp. 103–13.
Ziegler, Rafael, 'Tracing Global Inequality in Eco-space: A Comment on Tim Hayward's Proposal', *Journal of Moral Philosophy* 4(1) (2007), pp. 117–24.

INDEX

www.ingramcontent.com/pod-product-compliance
Lightning Source LLC
LaVergne TN
LVHW020651300926
849161LV00004B/892
9789004247741